MEDIEVAL EUROPE

A SHORT SOURCEBOOK

FOURTH EDITION

C. Warren Hollister
Late of the University of California, Santa Barbara

Joe W. Leedom
Hollins University

Marc A. Meyer
Columbia University

David S. Spear
Furman University

Boston   Burr Ridge, IL   Dubuque, IA   Madison, WI   New York
San Francisco   St. Louis   Bangkok   Bogotá   Caracas   Kuala Lumpur
Lisbon   London   Madrid   Mexico City   Milan   Montreal   New Delhi
Santiago   Seoul   Singapore   Sydney   Taipei   Toronto

McGraw-Hill Higher Education

*A Division of The **McGraw-Hill** Companies*

MEDIEVAL EUROPE: A SHORT SOURCEBOOK
Published by McGraw-Hill, an imprint of The McGraw-Hill Companies, Inc. 1221 Avenue of the Americas, New York, NY, 10020. Copyright © 2002, 1997, 1992, 1982 by The McGraw-Hill Companies, Inc. All rights reserved. No part of this publication may be reproduced or distributed in any form or by any means, or stored in a database or retrieval system, without the prior written consent of The McGraw-Hill Companies, Inc., including, but not limited to, in any network or other electronic storage or transmission, or broadcast for distance learning. Some ancillaries, including electronic and print components, may not be available to customers outside the United States.

This book is printed on acid-free paper.

1 2 3 4 5 6 7 8 9 0 DOC/DOC 0 9 8 7 6 5 4 3 2 1

ISBN 0-07-241738-2

Publisher: *Lyn Uhl*
Developmental editor: *Anne Sachs*
Marketing manager: *Janise Fry*
Project manager: *Anna M. Chan*
Production supervisor: *Michael McCormick*
Cover design: *Matthew Baldwin*
Cover image: *Luttrell Psalter, fol. 62v, British Library, London*
Photo research coordinator: *David A. Tietz*
Photo researcher: *Mary Reeg*
Typeface: *10/12 Times Roman*
Compositor: *Shepherd Incorporated*
Printer: *R. R. Donnelley & Sons Company*

Library of Congress Cataloging-in-Publication Data

Medieval Europe : a short sourcebook / C. Warren Hollister . . . [et al.].—4th ed.
    p. cm.
  ISBN 0-07-241738-2 (alk. paper)
    1. Middle Ages—History—Sources. I. Hollister, C. Warren (Charles Warren), 1930–

D113 .M4 2002
940.1—dc21
                                                              2001044831

www.mhhe.com

ABOUT THE EDITORS

C. WARREN HOLLISTER was professor emeritus at the University of California, Santa Barbara. Author of numerous books and articles, he also served as president of the Medieval Association of the Pacific, the Pacific Coast Branch of the American Historical Association, the Charles Homer Haskins Society, and the North American Conference on British Studies. Professor Hollister died in September 1997.

JOE W. LEEDOM is professor of History at Hollins University in Virginia. He has published articles in such journals as *History* and *The American Journal of Legal History,* and is co-editor of *Laws, Gods and Heroes: Thematic Readings in Western Civilization.*

MARC A. MEYER is Director of Research and Content Development at the Columbia University Center for New Media Teaching and Learning, School of General Studies, Columbia University. He also served as the headmaster of the Ross School in East Hampton, New York, and as professor of history at Berry College in Rome, Georgia. He has taught at the University of Hawaii in Hilo, Colgate Rochester Divinity School, and the University of Rochester. His published works include *The Search for Order: Landmarks of World Civilizations, The Culture of Christendom,* and *A Documentary History of Western Civilization,* as well as many articles and papers.

DAVID S. SPEAR is the William E. Leverette, Jr., Professor of History at Furman University in South Carolina. He is the former editor of the Haskins Society newsletter and former chair of the Furman History Department. He has published articles in such journals as the *Annales de Normandie,* the *Journal of British Studies,* and *Anglo-Norman Studies.* He won Furman's meritorious teaching award in 1995.

CONTENTS

PREFACE

C. Warren Hollister died shortly after the completion of the third edition of *Medieval Europe: A Short Sourcebook.* For four decades Warren had been one of the mainstays of the medieval history profession, no less for his textbooks than for his scholarly books, articles, and papers.

The secret to Warren's success wasn't difficult to find: he was prodigiously bright, and he worked very hard.

Of all Warren's gifts, none was as central to his profession as his amazing facility with words. His abilities as an editor remain legendary: he could repair a weak argument by changing a single phrase, often just a single word. His great talent as a writer of textbooks—evident in the companion to this book, *Medieval Europe: A Short History,* newly revised by Judith Bennett of the University of North Carolina, Chapel Hill—was his skill at reducing complex arguments to their essentials, and communicating those essentials clearly and economically. Warren's prose, like that of other great writers, sounds effortless—which is a testimony to how hard he worked on it. Good writing will always have a place in the creation of good history, and Warren Hollister was a gifted historian and writer. In keeping with that legacy, we have sought to retain as much of Warren's writing as possible in this book.

Still, there are major revisions in this fourth edition. In particular we have sought to expand the geographical focus of the work, both because more source material is available to medievalists, and also because our understanding of the dynamic world of the Middle Ages has changed. Instead of treating Islamic civilization as a single unchanging culture—a view appropriately condemned as "orientalism"—we have tried to place significant developments in a context more appropriate to their times. Women are found in more places in this edition as, in fact, they were found in more places in the Middle Ages than may previously have been acknowledged. The selections on Late Antiquity have been refined and strengthened, mirroring the emergence of a new field of study that scarcely existed when this book was first published, and medieval social history has been incorporated into almost every chapter of the fourth edition.

No book can completely cover the more than 1,000 years of the Middle Ages, now studied in a variety of fields and subdisciplines around the world. Owing to limitations in length, and to our decision to stress certain major themes, many well-known sources are absent. We have also tried to include some lesser known sources not often found in anthologies, knowing that these add interest, detail, and texture, welcome both to the professor and the student.

And we have added some tools to help make more sense of the sources. Each of our three major sections, in addition to a general introduction, now includes a map that indicates the site of the main authors and events the documents cover. It can be terribly frustrating to read about Laon or Constantinople or Reichenau without knowing where these are; and while we cannot plot every location, we are confident that the maps will provide some useful grounding in the geography of the Middle Ages. We have introduced a set of on-line resources for students and teachers who wish to pursue the Middle Ages electronically. Finally, we have included sets of questions at the end of each chapter. It is our hope that these questions will help guide the bewildered while not stifling the venturesome: the questions we offer help tie readings together and point out some obvious directions for study, but in no way limit the richness and variety of information that a careful reading of medieval texts can yield up to the attentive reader.

We are grateful to Philip Daileader, The College of William and Mary; Matthew S. Gordon, Miami University; Lois L. Huneycutt, University of Missouri; Stephen Morillo, Wabash College; Valerie Ramseyer, Wellesley College; Harry Rosenberg, Colorado State University; David R. Smith, California State Polytechnic University—Pomona; and William H. TeBrake, University of Maine for their insightful comments, which we have used to direct this new edition. We are indebted, too, to many hundreds of undergraduate students from around the country for their helpful and encouraging evaluations. Finally, we need to acknowledge the help of Aaron Waldkoetter, Columbia University Center for New Media Teaching and Learning, in tracking down Internet resources.

Joe W. Leedom

Marc A. Meyer

David S. Spear

INTRODUCTION

Many students dislike reading historical sources, yet many professors assign them nonetheless. In our own view, a history course that does not require the reading of original documents is a contradiction in terms. Contemporary sources are the foundations on which historical scholarship is built—the raw materials with which all historians work. Source materials are often difficult to absorb because they lack the tidiness and clarity that one finds in a good work of historical interpretation, or in a good textbook. But one cannot hope to understand the historical edifice without examining its foundations.

The sources will not always speak clearly; the human past is more complex and ambiguous than most textbooks make it out to be. But it is our hope that many readers will appreciate the challenge of being led beyond the generalizations of textbooks and lectures into the underlying human reality. In this book, as in others like it, the reader is led very gently. The documents that follow are a minute sampling of the historical records of the Middle Ages, carefully chosen and edited to illustrate historical trends and events that we regard as significant. In place of the documentary jungle through which the historical scholar must grope, we have provided a small, well-tended garden. In this respect, our book of readings offers only a foretaste of the historian's craft.

Reading an historical source is rather like reading a newspaper: both should be approached with a healthy touch of skepticism. When an event is reported, the careful reader will ask a series of questions about the accuracy and objectivity of the report: did the reporter witness the event? If not, how reliable were the sources used? Is the reporter caught up in some personal hostility or enthusiasm that might affect the tone of the report or the selection of certain facts to the exclusion of others? Is the reporter reputable or reckless, shrewd or gullible?

Reports of past events are known to historians as *narrative sources,* and they must always be evaluated by the criteria suggested above. Whenever possible, relevant information about the narrators quoted in this sourcebook will be provided in an editorial headnote, just as a good newspaper provides the names and affiliations of the writers of its major articles and columns. If your own newspaper does not provide such information, beware of it. Likewise, in reading a work of nonfiction or in viewing a documentary film, you should always ask who produced it and for what purpose.

Many of our documents are not narrative documents but official edicts, laws, charters, creeds, and letters. Known generally as *record sources,* these documents bring us face to face with the past, without the distorting lens of the biased, careless, or misinformed reporter. They are like the verbatim accounts that newspapers sometimes provide of speeches, diplomatic agreements, and court decisions. But here again, they must be read with discrimination and with certain questions in mind. First and most obviously, is the document absolutely authentic, or has it been forged or tampered with? (The speeches of members of Congress often appear in the *Congressional Record* in much improved form, and some were never delivered at all.) If authentic, does the source tell us what was occurring or what its framer(s) hoped might occur? Does a religious creed reflect general belief or is it a response to a growing number of people who believed otherwise? Does a law providing severe penalties for arson suggest that arson was being reduced or that it was increasing to dangerous proportions? Was a particular law, edict, or creed strictly enforced or largely ignored? Is a particular charter typical or atypical? Does a particular law code create new legal conditions or simply perpetuate old ones? What portions of the document are merely conventional formulas (like "Sincerely yours," or "I believe in a new beginning for this great country of ours, where Americans, regardless of creed or race, can live together in peace and prosperity," etc.), and what parts contain the meat of the message? Above all, what were the cultural attitudes and historical circumstances underlying the creation of the record source, and how does the source reflect them? Again, our editorial headnotes will provide some guidance in answering these questions. Of course, not all documents are written ones. We have, accordingly, provided a chapter of *visual source.* These vary considerably, from photographs of huge cathedrals to engravings of tiny gold brooches, but in general the viewer must approach these materials with the same critical eye as for the written sources.

In short, we hope that students who use this book will not simply read the sources but think critically about them as well. The development of a discriminating, sophisticated approach to historical documents can sharpen one's ability to evaluate evidence of all sorts, from campaign oratory, sales pitches, college catalogues, and dot-com investments to the evening television news and the morning paper.

C. Warren Hollister (†)

Joe W. Leedom

Marc A. Meyer

David S. Spear

MEDIEVAL EUROPE

A SHORT SOURCEBOOK

MAJOR LOCATIONS MENTIONED IN PART ONE

THE EARLY MIDDLE AGES

Between about A.D. 300 and 1050, Western Europe underwent wave after wave of incursions and invasions. As a result of the first wave, Roman imperial government disintegrated in the West, giving way by A.D. 500 to a group of loosely organized Germanic kingdoms. Most of these kingdoms were themselves destroyed or transformed by subsequent invasions. East Roman armies reconquered Italy in the mid-sixth century but quickly lost much of it to the assaults of the Germanic Lombards. In the early eighth century, Muslim armies overwhelmed the Visigothic kingdom of Spain and struck deep into France. Between these major invasions, Europe was afflicted by warfare between and within its kingdoms. The population declined, cities shriveled into villages, and commerce ebbed. Europe became a land of isolated agricultural settlements surrounded by forests and wastelands.

During the course of this troubled era, the cultural traditions of the Classical, Christian, and Germanic past gradually fused into a new, Western European civilization. Its great unifying force was the Christian Church, which had spread through the Roman Empire and eventually converted it. When Rome collapsed in the West, the Church remained to preserve its memory and perpetuate its culture. Christian missionaries labored to convert and civilize pagan tribes. Benedictine monasteries, planted in Germanic forests, became oases of devotion, learning, and agrarian enterprise, while in Rome, where emperors had once ruled the West, popes now claimed the allegiance of all Christians and directed the efforts of far-flung missionaries.

In the decades around A.D. 800, the emerging culture of Western Christendom experienced a period of political unification and expansion under a Frankish dynasty known as the Carolingians. The most celebrated of the Carolingian kings, Charlemagne, worked closely with the Roman popes and Benedictine monks to conquer and convert pagan tribes, to reform the Church, and to encourage learning.

Following Charlemagne's death in 814, his empire broke into pieces as a result of internal instability and attacks from without. Europe was struck by new waves of non-Christian invaders: Hungarian horsemen from the east, Muslim pirate bands from the south, and Viking seafarers from the north. These were to be the last invasions that Europe would suffer. Out of the chaos that they brought, strong Christian monarchies emerged in England and Germany. The kingdom of France—the western part of Charlemagne's former empire—remained decentralized, with a weak monarchy and increasingly strong regional principalities: Anjou, Poitou, Champagne, Normandy, and others. Italy survived the invasions to become a land of increasingly vigorous commercial cities.

By A.D. 1050, Europe was once again expanding. Hungary, Scandinavia, and Poland has been Christianized and brought under the loose jurisdiction of the Roman popes. Commerce was reviving, towns were growing along Europe's river valleys, and the population was increasing once again. The old civilization of Rome had evolved, through centuries of turmoil and struggle, into the civilization of Western Europe.

CHAPTER 1

▓ THE TRANSFORMATION OF THE ROMAN WORLD

The documents in this chapter illustrate three major themes: the Christianization of the Roman Empire, the administrative and military problems leading to the Empire's collapse in the West, and the emerging "sub-Roman" culture of the West.

The process of Christianization progressed during the fourth century A.D. from the abolition of imperial persecutions of Christians to the establishment of imperial persecutions of non-Christians. The conversion of Constantine (Reading 1) and the edict granting Christians the same toleration that other religions enjoyed (Reading 2) were followed by imperial efforts to resolve theological disputes within the Christian community (Reading 3). Such involvement forced the emperors to take sides in the debate between two contending Christian groups: the Trinitarians (who believed that God was a Trinity of three equal Persons: Father, Son, and Holy Spirit) and the Arians (who believed that the Son was subordinate to the Father). By the end of the fourth century, it had become imperial policy to tolerate only the Trinitarian Christians and to ban the religious activities of Arians and all non-Christian sects (Reading 4). Of course, Christianization was much more than a political fact: it had (and continues to have) obvious cultural corollaries as well (Reading 5). Perhaps the keenest Christian theologian of the age, St. Augustine, interpreted Christianity in the intellectual context of Classical Antiquity and shaped Christian thought across the Middle Ages and beyond (Reading 6).

During the fourth and fifth centuries, the Roman Empire suffered from internal stresses (Reading 7) and barbarian invasions. Imperial taxes were becoming increasingly severe and inequitable. Civic officials, who had abandoned their cities to avoid financial ruin, were ordered to resume their municipal duties (Reading 8). Others responded to the tax burden by fleeing the Empire to live among the barbarians (Reading 9). Germanic peoples overwhelmed most of the Western Empire, from North Africa (Reading 10) to remote Britain. And while life could go on much as usual for a provincial Roman (Reading 11), the final result of this Germanic inundation of Europe was the removal of the last Western Roman emperor, Romulus Augustulus, in A.D. 476 (Reading 12). The Roman Empire endured in the East for another thousand years, centered on its great capital of Constantinople; the Western provinces passed into the hand of Germanic kings but, as is illustrated by the example of Clovis, king of the Franks, these kings and their people themselves adopted Christianity and thus drew closer in culture and faith to the citizens of the late Empire (Reading 13).

READING 1

Lactantius, Constantine's Victory and Conversion[1]

The conversion of Constantine, the first Christian emperor, was of decisive importance to Roman and Christian history. Lactantius (c. 240–320), a Christian rhetorician and historian who was alive at the time of Constantine's victory at the Milvian Bridge in A.D. 312, provides a firsthand account of his rise to the Western imperial office. Another contemporary, Eusebius of Caesarea, reports, perhaps with some credulity, that Constantine's motivation to provide his troops with Christian insignia was a dream in which he saw a fiery cross in the sky and the words "by this, conquer!" Constantine clearly saw in the Christian God a bringer of victory, and he was not disappointed.

And now a civil war broke out between Constantine and Maxentius. Although Maxentius kept himself within Rome, because the soothsayers had foretold that if he went out of it he should perish, yet he conducted the military operations through able generals. In forces he exceeded his adversary; for he had not only his father's army, but also his own, which he had lately drawn together out of Mauritania and Italy. They fought, and the troops of Maxentius prevailed. At length Constantine, with steady courage and a mind prepared for every event, led his whole force to the neighborhood of Rome, and encamped them opposite to the Milvian Bridge.

Constantine was directed in a dream to cause the heavenly sign to be delineated on the shields of his soldiers, and so to proceed to battle. He did as he had been commanded, and he marked on their shields the letter X, with a perpendicular line drawn through it and turned round thus at the top, being the cipher of Christ. Having this sign, his troops stood to arms. The enemies advanced, but without their emperor, and they crossed the bridge. The armies met, and fought with the utmost exertions of valor, and firmly maintained their ground. In the meantime a sedition arose at Rome, and Maxentius was reviled as one who had abandoned all concern for the safety of the commonweal; and suddenly the people cried with one voice, "Constantine cannot be overcome!" Dismayed at this, Maxentius burst from the assembly, and having called some senators together, ordered the Sibylline books to be searched. In them it was found that "on the same day the enemy of the Romans should perish."

[1]From *Of the Manner in which the Persecutors Died*, tr. A. Roberts and J. Donaldson, in *The Ante-Nicene Fathers of the Christian Church*, vol. VII; New York, Charles Scribner's Sons, 1886, pp. 301–303.

Led by this response to the hopes of victory, he went to the field—The bridge in his rear was broken down. At sight of that the battle grew hotter. The hand of the Lord prevailed, and the forces of Maxentius were routed. He fled towards the broken bridge; but the multitude pressing on him, he was driven headlong into the Tiber.

This destructive war being ended, Constantine was acknowledged as emperor, with great rejoicing, by the senate and people of Rome. The senate, in reward of the valor of Constantine, decreed to him the title of Maximus.

READING 2
The Edict of Milan[2]

The first imperial edict to prohibit the persecution of Christians was issued in 311 by the pagan emperor Galerius, as a deathbed response to the clear failure of the last imperial persecution. Galerius permitted Christians to practice their religion so long as they did so without offending public order. In 313 a much more sweeping edict of toleration was issued by Constantine and his co-emperor, Licinius. Although not actually issued from Milan, the edict promulgates an agreement that the two emperors had previously concluded there.

When we, Constantine Augustus and Licinius Augustus, had happily met at Milan, and were conferring about all things which concern the advantage and security of the state, we thought that amongst other things which seemed likely to profit men generally, the reverence paid to the Divinity merited our first and chief attention. Our purpose is to grant both to the Christians and to all others full authority to follow whatever worship each man has desired; whereby whatsoever Divinity dwells in heaven may be benevolent and propitious to us, and to all who are placed under our authority.

Therefore we thought it salutary and most proper to establish our purpose that no man whatever should be refused complete toleration, who has given up his mind either to the cult of the Christians, or to the religion which he personally

[2]From *A New Eusebius: Documents Illustrative of the History of the Church to A.D. 337,* ed. J. Stevenson; London, Society for Promoting Christian Knowledge, 1957, pp. 300–302. By permission of the Society for Promoting Christian Knowledge.

feels best suited to himself; to the end that the supreme Divinity, to whose worship we devote ourselves under no compulsion, may continue in all things to grant us his wonted favour and beneficence. Wherefore your Dignity should know that it is our pleasure to abolish all conditions whatever which were embodied in former orders directed to your office about the Christians, that what appeared utterly inauspicious and foreign to our Clemency should be done away and that every one of those who have a common wish to follow the religion of the Christians may from this moment freely and unconditionally proceed to observe the same without any annoyance or disquiet. These things we thought good to signify in the fullest manner to your Carefulness, that you might know that we have given freely and unreservedly to the said Christians toleration to practice their cult. And when you perceive that we have granted this favour to the said Christians, your Devotion understands that to others also freedom for their own worship and cult is likewise left open and freely granted, as befits the quiet of our times, that every man may have complete toleration in the practice of whatever worship he has chosen. This has been done by us that no diminution be made from the honour of any religion. Moreover in regard to the legal position of the Christians we have thought fit to ordain this also, that if any appear to have bought, whether from our exchequer or from any others, the places at which they were used formerly to assemble, concerning which definite orders have been given before now, and that, by a letter issued to your office, that the same be restored to the Christians, setting aside all delay and doubtfulness, without any payment or demand of price.

All these things must be delivered over at once and without delay by your intervention to the corporation of the Christians. And since the said Christians are known to have possessed, not those places only whereto they were used to assemble, but others also belonging to their corporation, namely to their churches, and not to individuals, we comprise them all under the above law, so that you will order them to be restored without any doubtfulness or dispute to the said Christians, that is to their corporation and assemblies; provided always as aforesaid, that those who restore them without price, as we said, shall expect a compensation from our benevolence. In all these things you must give the aforesaid Christians your most effective intervention, that our command may be fulfilled as soon as may be, and that in this matter, as well as others, order may be taken by our Clemency for the public quiet. So far we will ensure that, as has been already stated, the Divine favor toward us which we have already experienced in so many affairs shall continue for all time to give us prosperity and successes, together with happiness for the State. But that the tenor of our gracious ordinance may be brought to the knowledge of all men, it will be your duty by a proclamation of your own to publish everywhere and bring to the notice of all men this present document, that the command of this our benevolence may not be hidden.

READING 3

The Nicene Creed[3]

The Nicene Creed is a product of the Trinitarians' victory over the Arians at the Council of Nicea, summoned by Constantine in 325. The outcome of this first universal council of the Church was strongly influenced by Constantine, who had himself been persuaded by important churchmen to support the Trinitarian position. The Nicene Creed expresses what would become the orthodox Christian position of the Trinity and the incarnation of Christ. It rejects explicitly the doctrine of the Alexandrian churchman Arius, who taught that only God the Father was eternal and that God the Son was His creation.

We believe in one God, the Father Almighty, maker of all things visible and invisible; and in one Lord Jesus Christ, the Son of God, the only-begotten of his Father, of the substance of the Father, God of God, Light of Light, true God of true God, begotten not made, being of one substance with the Father; by whom all things were made, both in heaven and in earth. Who for us men and for our salvation came down from heaven and was incarnate and was made man, He suffered and the third day he rose again, and ascended into heaven. And he shall come again to judge both the living and the dead. And we believe in the Holy Spirit. And whosoever shall say that there was a time when the Son of God was not, or that before he was begotten he was not, or that he was made of things that were not, or that he is of a different substance or essence from the Father, or that he is a creature, or subject to change or conversion—all that say so, the Catholic and Apostolic Church anathematizes[4] them.

READING 4

The Theodosian Code: Edicts on Religion[5]

Around the year 438, Emperor Theodosius II (408–450) published a law code intended as a convenient reference to all imperial edicts since the time of Constantine that still remained valid. The excerpts here are edicts

---

[3]From *The Seven Ecumenical Councils,* tr. A. C. McGiffert and E. C. Richardson, in *A Select Library of Nicene and Post-Nicene Fathers of the Christian Church,* 2nd series, vol. XIV; New York, Charles Scribner's Sons, 1900, p. 3.

[4]"Anathema" is a curse, carrying the full authority of the Church, that banishes the recipient from the Christian community.

[5]From *The Theodosian Code and Novels and the Sirmondian Constitutions,* tr. C. Pharr; Princeton, N.J., Princeton University Press, 1952, pp. 450–451, 473. (See also p. 23)

of Emperor Theodosius (378–395), issued in his name and in those of his several co-emperors. Notice the marked shift in imperial religious policy since the Edict of Milan.

A. EMPERORS GRATIAN, VALENTINIAN, AND THEODOSIUS AUGUSTUSES: AN EDICT TO EUTROPIUS, PRAETORIAN PREFECT [A.D. 380]

Crowds shall be kept away from the unlawful congregations of all the heretics. The name of the One and Supreme God shall be celebrated everywhere; the observance, destined to remain forever, of the Nicene faith, as transmitted long ago by Our ancestors and confirmed by the declaration and testimony of divine religion, shall be maintained.

On the other hand, that man shall be accepted as a defender of the Nicene faith and as a true adherent of the Catholic religion who confesses that Almighty God and Christ the son of God are One in name, God of God, Light of Light; who does not violate by denial the Holy Spirit which we hope for and receive from the Supreme Author of things; that man who esteems, with the perception of inviolate faith, the undivided substance of the incorrupt Trinity. The latter beliefs are surely more acceptable to Us and must be venerated.

Those persons, however, who are not devoted to the aforesaid doctrines shall cease to assume, with studied deceit, the alien name of "true religion," and they shall be branded upon the disclosure of their crimes. They shall be removed and completely barred from the threshold of all churches, since We forbid all heretics to hold unlawful assemblies within the towns. If factions should attempt to do anything, We order that their madness shall be banished and that they shall be driven away from the very walls of the cities, in order that Catholic churches throughout the whole world may be restored to all orthodox bishops who hold the Nicene faith.

B. EMPERORS THEODOSIUS, ARCADIUS, AND HONORIUS, TO RUFINUS, PRAETORIAN PREFECT [A.D. 391]

If any man should dare to immolate a victim for the purposes of sacrifice, or to consult the quivering entrails, he shall be reported by an accusation that anyone may levy, and according to the example of a person guilty of high treason he shall receive the appropriate sentence, even though he has inquired nothing contrary to, or with reference to, the welfare of the Emperors. For it is sufficient to constitute an enormous crime that any person should wish to break down the very laws of nature, to investigate forbidden matters, to disclose hidden secrets, to attempt interdicted practices, to seek to know the end of another's life, to promise the hope of another person's death.

If any person should venerate, by placing incense before them, images made by the work of mortals, or should bind a tree with fillets, or should erect an altar of turf he has dug up, or should attempt to honor vain images with the offering of a gift, such a person, as one guilty of the violation of religion, shall be punished by the forfeiture of that house in which it is proved that he served a pagan superstition. For we decree that all places shall be annexed to Our fisc,[6] if it is proved that they have reeked with the vapor of incense, provided, however, that such places are proved to have belonged to such incense burners.

If any person should attempt to perform any such kind of sacrifice in public temples or shrines, or in the buildings or fields of others, and if it is proved that such places were usurped without the knowledge of the owner, the offender shall be compelled to pay twenty-five pounds of gold as a fine. If any person should connive at such a crime, he shall be held subject to the same penalty as that of the person who performed the sacrifice.

It is Our will that this regulation shall be so enforced by the judges, as well as by the defenders and decurions of the several cities, that the information learned by the defenders and decurions shall be immediately reported to the courts, and the crimes so reported shall be punished by the judges. Moreover, if the defenders and the decurions should suppose that any such crime should be concealed through favoritism or overlooked through carelessness, they shall be subjected to judicial indignation. If the judges should be advised of such crimes and should defer punishment through connivance, they shall be fined.

READING 5

St. Jerome, Letter to Laeta[7]

Christianization was more than just a series of edicts and legal transactions: it also involved the grafting of Christian values onto pagan stock and the imposition of Christian values on older social and intellectual traditions. Both influences can be seen at work here.

The Christian Roman matron Laeta prayed to have a baby and promised God that she would make the child a monk or nun if she conceived. Her prayer was answered and her promise kept: she gave birth to Paula and dedicated her to the life of the convent. Laeta asked the celebrated Christian leader St. Jerome (340–420) for advice, and he replied with this letter of A.D. 403. Jerome's views on the body, especially on virginity, were

---

[6]The "fisc" was the collection of lands belonging to the emperors and directly administered by them.

[7]From *The Principal Works of St. Jerome,* tr. W. H. Freemantle, in *A Select Library of Nicene and Post-Nicene Fathers of the Christian Church,* vol. VI; New York, Charles Scribner's Sons, 1890, pp. 189–195.

deeply influential in both the East and the West. His unquestioning acceptance of Laeta's plans for her child's future life, which did not include
asking Paula's opinion on the matter, may well seem strange and unfair to
people of today. But the procedure accorded with the Greco-Roman
tradition of deciding on a child's career and eventual marriage partner
during the child's infancy or even before birth. The forging or tightening
of family alliances through arranged marriage was commonplace in most
traditional societies, and young boys were ordinarily expected to follow
in their fathers' careers. Similarly, the dedication of infant children to the
religious life was by no means unusual. Indeed, before Christianity had
spread through the Empire, infants were commonly consigned to pagan
priesthoods. The letter contains valuable information on the social customs
of the late imperial nobility, customs with which Jerome is perfectly
comfortable and whose obvious inequities he does not question. One of
Jerome's instructions indicates that a properly educated Roman aristocratic
child continued to be instructed in both Latin and Greek, and he expresses
the interesting opinion (his own) that women dedicated to virginity and the
cloister ought not to take baths.

In answer to your prayers and those of the saintly Marcella, I wish to address
you as a mother and to instruct you how to bring up our dear Paula, who has
been consecrated to Christ before her birth and vowed to His service before her
conception. I am confident that having given to the Lord your firstborn you will
be the mother of sons. As then Paula has been born in answer to a promise, her
parents should give her a training suitable to her birth.

Thus must a soul be educated which is to be a temple of God. It must learn to
hear nothing and to say nothing but what belongs to the fear of God. It must
have no understanding of unclean words, and no knowledge of the world's
songs. Its tongue must be steeped while still tender in the sweetness of the
psalms. Boys with their wanton thoughts must be kept from Paula: even her
maids and female attendants must be separated from worldly associates, for if
they have learned some mischief they may teach more. Get for her a set of letters made of boxwood or of ivory and called each by its proper name. Let her
play with these, so that even her play may teach her something. And not only
make her grasp the right order of the letters and see that she forms their names
into a rhyme, but constantly disarrange their order and put the last letters in the
middle and the middle ones at the beginning that she may know them all by
sight as well as by sound. Moreover, so soon as she begins to use the style upon
the wax, and her hand is still faltering, either guide her soft fingers by laying
your hand upon hers, or else have simple copies cut upon a tablet; so that her efforts, confined within these limits, may keep to the lines traced out for her and
not stray outside of these. Offer prizes for good spelling and draw her onwards

with little gifts such as children of her age delight in. And let her have companions in her lessons to excite emulation in her, that she may be stimulated when she sees them praised. You must not scold her if she is slow to learn but must employ praise to excite her mind, so that she may be glad when she excels others and sorry when she is excelled by them. Above all you must take care not to make her lessons distasteful to her lest a dislike for them conceived in childhood may continue into her maturer years. The very words which she tries bit by bit to put together and to pronounce ought not to be chance ones, but names specially fixed upon and heaped together for the purpose, those for example of the prophets or the apostles or the list of patriarchs from Adam downwards as it is given by Matthew and Luke. In this way while her tongue will be well trained, her memory will be likewise developed.

You must see that the child is not led away by the silly coaxing of women to form a habit of shortening long words or of decking herself with gold and purple. Of these habits one will spoil her conversation and the other her character. She must not therefore learn as a child what afterwards she will have to unlearn. When once wool has been dyed purple who can restore it to its previous whiteness? An unused jar long retains the taste and smell of that with which it is first filled. We are always ready to imitate what is evil; and faults are quickly copied where virtues appear unattainable. Paula's nurse must not be intemperate, or loose, or given to gossip.

Let her very dress and garb remind her to Whom she is promised. Do not pierce her ears or paint her face with white lead or rouge. Do not hang gold or pearls about her neck or load her head with jewels, or by reddening her hair make it suggest the fires of gehenna.[8] Let her pearls be of another kind and such that she may sell them hereafter and buy in their place the pearl that is "of great price." Whether you would offer your child or not lay within your choice, but now that you have offered her, you neglect her at your peril. I speak generally for in your case you have no discretion, having offered your child even before her conception. He who offers a victim that is lame or maimed or marked with any blemish is held guilty of sacrileges. How much more then shall she be punished who makes ready for the embraces of the king a portion of her own body and the purity of a stainless soul and then proves negligent of this her offering?

Let her not take her food with others, that is, at her parents' table, lest she sees dishes she may long for. Some, I know, hold it a greater virtue to disdain a pleasure which is actually before them, but I think it a safer self-restraint to shun what must needs attract you. Let her learn even now not to drink wine "wherein is excess." But since, before children come to a robust age, abstinence is dangerous and trying to their tender frames, let her have baths if she require them, and let her take a little wine for her stomach's sake. Let her also be supported on a flesh diet, lest her feet fail her before they commence to run their course. But I

---

[8] Gehenna is literally the "trash heap," but in Christian thinking it had become equated with hell.

say this by way of concession, not by way of command; Paula has been born in response to a vow. Let her life be as the lives of those who were born under the same conditions. If the grace accorded is in both cases the same, the pains bestowed ought to be so too. Let her be deaf to the sound of the organ, and not know even the uses of the pipe, the lyre, and the cithern.

And let it be her task daily to bring to you the flowers which she has culled from scripture. Let her learn by heart so many verses in the Greek, but let her be instructed in the Latin also. For, if the tender lips are not from the first shaped to this, the tongue is spoiled by a foreign accent and its native speech debased by alien elements. You must yourself be her mistress, a model on which she may form her childish conduct. Never either in you nor in her father let her see what she cannot imitate without sin.

Remember both of you that you are the parents of a consecrated virgin, and that your example will teach her more than your precepts. Let her never appear in public unless accompanied by you. Let her never visit a church or a martyr's shrine unless with her mother. Let no young man greet her with smiles; no dandy with curled hair pay compliments to her. If our little virgin goes to keep solemn eves and all-night vigils, let her not stir a hair's breadth from her mother's side. Let her choose for a companion not a handsome well-dressed girl, but one pale and serious, somberly attired and with the hue of melancholy. Let her take as her model some aged virgin of approved faith, character, and chastity, apt to instruct her by word and by example. She ought to rise at night to recite prayers and psalms; to sing hymns in the morning; at the third, sixth, and ninth hours, to take her place in the line to do battle for Christ, and, lastly, to kindle her lamp and to offer her evening sacrifice. In these occupations let her pass the day, and when night comes let it find her still engaged in them. Let reading follow prayer with her, and prayer again succeed to reading. Time will seem short when employed on tasks so many and so varied.

Let her learn too how to spin wool, to hold the distaff, to put the basket in her lap, to turn the spinning wheel and to shape the yarn with her thumb. Let her put away with disdain silken fabrics, Chinese fleeces, and gold brocades: the clothing which she makes for herself should keep out the cold and not expose the body which it professes to cover. Let her food be herbs and wheaten bread with now and then one or two small fishes. And that I may not waste more time in giving precepts for the regulation of appetite, let her meals always leave her hungry and able on the moment to begin reading or chanting. I strongly disapprove—especially for those of tender years—of long and immoderate fasts in which week is added to week and even oil and apples are forbidden as food. I have learned by experience that the ass toiling along the highway makes for an inn when it is weary.

When you go a short way into the country, do not leave your daughter behind you. Leave her no power or capacity of living without you, and let her feel frightened when she is left to herself. Let her not converse with people of the world or associate with virgins indifferent to their vows. Let her not be present at the weddings of your slaves and let her take no part in the noisy games of the household. As regards the use of the bath, I know that some are content with saying that a Christian virgin should not bathe along with eunuchs or with married women, with the former because they are still men at all events in mind, and with the latter because women with child offer a revolting spectacle. For myself, however, I wholly disapprove of baths for a virgin of full age. Such a one should blush and feel overcome at the idea of seeing herself undressed. By vigils and fasts she mortifies her body and brings it into subjection. By a cold chastity she seeks to put out the flame of lust and to quench the hot desires of youth. And by a deliberate squalor she makes haste to spoil her natural good looks. Why, then, should she add fuel to a sleeping fire by taking baths?

Let her treasures be not silks or gems but manuscripts of the holy scriptures; and in these let her think less of gilding, and Babylonian parchment, and arabesque patterns, than of correctness and accurate punctuation. Let her begin by learning the psalter[9] and then let her gather rules of life out of the proverbs of Solomon. From the Preacher let her gain the habit of despising the world and its vanities. Let her follow the example set in Job of virtue and patience. Then let her pass on to the gospels never to be laid aside when once they have been taken in hand. Let her also drink in with a willing heart the Acts of the Apostles and the Epistles. As soon as she has enriched the storehouse of her mind with these treasures, let her commit to memory the prophets, the heptateuch, the books of Kings and of Chronicles, the rolls also of Ezra and Esther. When she has done all these she may safely read the Song of Songs but not before: for, were she to read it at the beginning, she would fail to perceive that, though it is written in fleshly words, it is a marriage song of a spiritual bridal. And not understanding this she would suffer hurt from it. Let her avoid all apocryphal writings, and if she is led to read such not by the truth of the doctrines which they contain but out of respect for the miracles contained in them, let her understand that they are not really written by those to whom they are ascribed, that many faulty elements have been introduced into them, and that it requires infinite discretion to look for gold in the midst of dirt. Let her take pleasure in the works and wits of all in whose books a due regard for the faith is not neglected. But if she reads the works of others let it be rather to judge them than to follow them.

You will answer, "How shall I, a woman of the world, living at Rome, surrounded by a crowd, be able to observe all these injunctions?" In that case do not undertake a burthen to which you are not equal. When you have weaned Paula, send her to her grandmother and aunt; give up this most precious of gems, to be placed in Mary's chamber and to rest in the cradle where the infant Jesus cried. Let her be brought up in a monastery, let her be one amid companies of virgins, let her learn to avoid swearing, let her regard lying as sacrilege, let her

---

[9]The standard "hymnal" based on the Psalms.

be ignorant of the world, let her live the angelic life, while in the flesh let her be without the flesh, and let her suppose that all human beings are like herself. O happy virgin! happy Paula, daughter of Toxotius, who through the virtues of her grandmother and aunt is nobler in holiness than she is in lineage! Yes, Laeta: were it possible for you with your own eyes to see your mother-in-law and your sister you would count as nothing your desire for other offspring and would offer up yourself to the service of God. But because "there is time to embrace, and a time to refrain from embracing," I counsel you to pay back to the full in your offspring what meantime you defer paying in your own person. Moreover, if you will only send Paula, I promise to be myself both a tutor and a foster-father to her. Old as I am I will carry her on my shoulders and train her stammering lips; and my charge will be a far grander one than that of the worldly philosopher, for while he only taught a King of Macedon who was one day to die of Babylonian poison, I shall instruct the handmaid and spouse of Christ who must one day be offered to her Lord in heaven.

READING 6

St. Augustine, City of God[10]

St. Augustine (354–430), as the opening paragraph shows, is responding to the trauma of the sack of Rome by the Visigothic leader Alaric. His *City of God,* of which only a few bare excerpts are provided here, is one of the great intellectual endeavors of Western civilization. Rather than lament the decline of Rome, Augustine set about to redefine the relationship between Christianity—the city of God—and earthly states—the city of man. This relationship between believers and unbelievers underlies all of human history.

Rome had been invaded by the Goths under King Alaric and was staggered by the impact of this great disaster; and the worshippers of false gods, whom we customarily call pagans, working to turn this invasion into an accusation against the Christian religion, began to curse the true God more sharply and more bitterly than ever. Upon which I, burning with the zeal of the house of God, decided to confute their blasphemies and errors in these books on the city of God.

[10]From St. Augustine, *The City of God,* tr. J. W. Leedom.

The first five books of The City of God rebut those who think that the safety of mankind depends on the cult of the gods whom the pagans worshipped, and who contend that these disasters happened, and were as bad as they were, because of the prohibition of that worship. The next five books answer those who, while saying that mortals never have and never will be spared evils—some greater, some lesser, varying with time and place and person—still argue that the cult of many gods, in which sacrifices are made to them, is useful because of the life to be after death. In these ten books, then, are refuted those two false notions that are contrary to the Christian religion.

Of the twelve books following, the first four contain the beginning of the two cities, of which the one is of God, the other of man; the second four, their course or progress; the third, which is the last four, their ends. And all twenty-two books, whether they are about one city or the other, took their title from the better of the two, with the result that they were called by preference The City of God.

I place humanity into two groups, one that lives following man, the other that lives according to God, and about which I might call two cities, that is, two societies, of which one is predestined to reign eternally with God and the other to undergo eternal punishment with the devil. But this is their end, which is to be spoken of later. Now I must detail the paths of the two cities from the time when two people first reproduced to the time when reproduction will come to an end. For the history of the two cities consists of the whole era or age in which the dying give way to the born.

Cain was born first among these two parents of mankind [Adam and Eve], a member of the city of men; Abel afterwards, of the city of God. It is known by experience that in every individual, as the Apostle has said, "it is not the spiritual which is first but the physical, and then the spiritual" (I Corinthians 15:46)—and this is true in the whole of humanity as well. When the two cities began their history through birth and death, first was born the citizen of this world, and after him the alien in this world who belongs to the city of God, predestined by grace, made elect by grace, a pilgrim below by grace, a citizen above by grace. So in himself a person first is reprobate, which by necessity is the beginning—but where we must not remain—and later becomes virtuous, to which we come as we progress and in which we may remain when we arrive. Consequently, not each bad person will be good, but no one will be good who was not first bad.

So it is written that Cain established a city, but Abel, being a foreigner, did not establish one. For in heaven is the city of the saints, although it produces its citizens here, in whom it waits until its kingdom shall come.

The earthly city has its good here, and its society delights in it with such delight as it can. But this kind of good is not the sort that causes no difficulties for those who admire it, so the earthly city is generally divided against itself by lawsuits; or by fights and battles; or by victories that are deadly or temporary. And when one part has risen up in war against the other, it seeks to be victorious over other peoples while itself a captive of vices. And it cannot dominate forever those it may overcome by conquest.

But it is not correct to say that the good things that this earthly city desires are not good, for it is made better, in a human fashion, by these. It desires an earthly peace for these lowest of things, a peace it hopes to come by through war; and if it wins and no one may resist it, there will be peace. This is a peace that requires hard fighting, this is a peace that "glorious" war can win. But if, neglecting the better things that pertain to the supernatural city (where there will be eternal victory and secure perpetual peace), while other things are desired because they are either believed the only good things or are loved more than better ones, it follows by necessity that new misery will augment the old.

Now the household of a person who does not live by faith seeks an earthly peace through the things of this earth; while a household of people who live by faith expects those blessings that are promised in eternity, and they use earthly and temporal things like a wanderer, not being captured by them, or diverted by them from those things that tend towards God. On that account, the things necessary for mortal life are used by both types of people and households; but the purpose of using such differs with each. So the earthly city, which does not live by faith, desires only an earthly peace, securing civil obedience and authority so that there may be a consensus about things useful in this mortal life. But the heavenly city, or that bit of it that sojourns in this mortal life and lives by faith, needs to use such peace only until this weak necessity shall pass. And so, while in the earthly city it leads its life as if in captivity, it does not balk at complying with the laws of the earthly city in the administration of those things that sustain and accommodate this mortal life, since life is common to both.

While this heavenly city is traveling on earth it finds citizens among all peoples and collects a pilgrim society of all tongues and in all tongues, not caring anything about differing customs, laws, institutions, not rescinding or destroying them, but serving and following them (because it allows diversity in different peoples) to the same earthly peace as they tend—as long as the religion which advises the following of the most true high God is not impeded. So the heavenly city uses the earthly peace for itself during its pilgrimage; it makes this earthly peace work for that peace of heaven which alone is truly peace, namely the most orderly and harmonious society in the enjoyment of God and of one another in God. And when we come there, there will be life, certainly, but not mortal life; no animal body corrupting the soul; but a spiritual one, one without wants and one subject in all parts to the will. While on earth the heavenly city has this peace through faith; and by this faith it lives justly, and makes the winning of this peace the goal of every good action, in which it is done for the sake of God and neighbors; for the life of every city is certainly a social life.

READING 7

Socrates Scholasticus, The Murder of Hypatia[11]

Socrates Scholasticus (c. 380–450), a native of Constantinople, was both a lawyer and a historian. He is best known for his continuation of Eusebius' renowned Ecclesiastical History, written at the time of Constantine. The passage from Socrates' continuation excerpted here demonstrates that Constantine's conversion to Christianity, celebrated by Eusebius, brought social consequences to the East Roman Empire that were decidedly mixed.

In the conflict that Socrates describes, the leader of the Christians is the disputatious and short-tempered patriarch of Alexandria, St. Cyril (370–444), backed by the Egyptian clergy. The disputes recorded here are political as much as religious. Cyril wants the imperial prefect, a pagan named Orestes, to treat him as a councilor and is willing to use clerics as his muscle. The first to suffer are the Jews, who are driven out after one of Cyril's followers has provoked a riot. The next victim is Hypatia (d. 415), killed by Egyptian monks both as retribution for the judicial torture of one of their own and as a grim warning to Orestes.

The passage illustrates several crucial points. First, as Christianity became increasingly popular (it was by this time the majority religion in Alexandria), non-Christians became more and more isolated and had to depend on the imperial government for protection from grassroots Christian violence. But by this time, a century after Constantine, the government's only reason to offer protection was to maintain public order, and it did that poorly: both groups of selections from the Theodosian Code (see Reading 4 and Reading 8) find echoes here. Second, the passage shows how disorderly Eastern monasticism could be. It helps account for subsequent major efforts to restrain and regulate monastic life, culminating in the reformed monasticism of St. Basil in the East and, in the West, the Rule of St. Benedict (see pp. 56–63). Third, Hypatia herself is a significant figure—an important pagan philosopher who became the recognized head of the Neoplatonic school of Alexandria and a gifted scientist who has been acclaimed as the first major woman mathematician. Her dazzling intellectual gifts, along with her eloquence, beauty, and pleasing disposition, attracted many students, both pagan and Christian. But as a symbol of "pagan" learning, she became a focus of controversy in the struggle between Christians and non-Christians, and eventually lost her life to a fanatical mob of Christian monks and lay followers of St. Cyril. In the aftermath of Hypatia's savage murder, many scholars abandoned Alexandria, launching the city's decline as an important center of Classical learning.

[11]From Socrates Scholasticus, *Ecclesiastical History*, tr. A. C. Zenos, in *A Select Library of Nicene and Post-Nicene Fathers of the Christian Church*, 2nd series, vol. XI; New York, Charles Scribner's Sons, 1900, pp. 159–160.

About this same time it happened that the Jewish inhabitants were driven out of Alexandria by Cyril the bishop on the following account. A disturbance arose among the populace, not from a cause of any serious importance, but out of an evil that has become very popular in almost all cities, viz. a fondness for dancing exhibitions. In consequence of the Jews being disengaged from business on the Sabbath, and spending their time, not in hearing the Law, but in theatrical amusements, dancers usually collect great crowds on that day, and disorder is almost invariably produced. When therefore Orestes the prefect was publishing an edict—for so they are accustomed to call public notices—in the theater for the regulation of the shows, some of the bishop Cyril's party were present to learn the nature of the orders about to be issued.

There was among them a certain Hierax, a teacher of the rudimental branches of literature, and one who was a very enthusiastic listener of the bishop Cyril's sermons, and made himself conspicuous by his forwardness in applauding. When the Jews observed this person in the theater, they immediately cried out that he had come there for no other purpose than to excite sedition among the people. Now Orestes had long regarded with jealousy the growing power of the bishops, because they encroached on the jurisdiction of the authorities appointed by the emperor, especially as Cyril wished to set spies over his proceedings; he therefore ordered Hierax to be seized, and publicly subjected him to the torture in the theater. Cyril, on being informed of this, sent for the principal Jews, and threatened them with the utmost severities unless they desisted from their molestation of the Christians. The Jewish populace on hearing these menaces, instead of suppressing their violence, only became more furious, and were led to form conspiracies for the destruction of the Christians; one of these was of so desperate a character as to cause their entire expulsion from Alexandria; this I shall now describe. Having agreed that each one of them should wear a ring on his finger made of the bark of a palm branch, for the sake of mutual recognition, they determined to make a nightly attack on the Christians. They therefore sent persons into the streets to raise an outcry that the church named after Alexander was on fire. Thus many Christians on hearing this ran out, some from one direction and some from another, in great anxiety to save their church. The Jews immediately fell upon and slew them, readily distinguishing each other by their rings. At daybreak the authors of this atrocity could not be concealed; and Cyril, accompanied by an immense crowd of people, going to their synagogues—for so they call their house of prayer—took them away from them, and drove the Jews out of the city, permitting the multitude to plunder their goods. Thus the Jews who had inhabited the city from the time of Alexander the Macedonian were expelled from it, stripped of all they possessed, and dispersed some in one direction and some in another.

But Orestes, the governor of Alexandria, was filled with great indignation at these transactions, and was excessively grieved that a city of such magnitude should have been suddenly bereft of so large a portion of its population; he therefore at once communicated the whole affair to the emperor. Cyril so wrote to him, describing the outrageous conduct of the Jews: and in the meanwhile sent persons to Orestes who should mediate concerning a reconciliation: for this the people had urged him to do. And when Orestes refused to listen to friendly advances, Cyril extended toward him the book of gospels, believing that respect for religion would induce him to lay aside his resentment. When, however, even this had no pacific effect on the prefect, but he persisted in implacable hostility against the bishop, the following event afterwards occurred.

Some of the monks inhabiting the mountains of Nitria, of a very fiery disposition, being again transported with an ardent zeal, resolved to fight on behalf of Cyril. About five hundred of them therefore quitting their monasteries, came into the city; and meeting the prefect in his chariot, they called him a pagan idolator, and applied to him many other abusive epithets. Orestes, supposing this to be a snare laid for him by Cyril, exclaimed that he was a Christian, and had been baptized by Atticus the bishop at Constantinople. The monks gave but little heed to his protestations, and a certain one of them named Ammonius threw a stone at Orestes which struck him on the head, and covered him with the blood that flowed from the wound; and all the guards with a few exceptions fled, plunging into the crowd, some in one direction and some in another, fearing to be stoned to death. Meanwhile the populace of Alexandria ran to the rescue of the governor, and put the rest of the monks to flight; but having secured Ammonius they delivered him up to the prefect. But the animosity between Cyril and Orestes did not by any means subside at this point, but was kindled afresh by an occurrence similar to the preceding.

There was a woman at Alexandria named Hypatia, daughter of the philosopher Theon, who made such attainments in literature and science, as to far surpass all the philosophers of her own time. Having succeeded to the school of Plato and Plotinus, she explained the principles of philosophy to her auditors, many of whom came from a distance to receive her instructions. On account of the self-possession and ease of manner that she has acquired in consequence of the cultivation of her mind, she not infrequently appeared in public in presence of the magistrates. Neither did she feel abashed in coming to an assembly of men. For all men on account of her extraordinary dignity and virtue admired her the more. Yet even she fell a victim to the political jealousy which at that time prevailed. For as she had frequent interviews with Orestes, it was calumniously reported among the Christian populace that it was she who prevented Orestes from being reconciled to the bishop. Some of them therefore, hurried away by a fierce and bigoted zeal, whose ringleader was a reader named Peter, waylaid her returning home, and dragging her from her carriage, they took her to the church called Cæsareum, where they completely stripped her, and then murdered her with tiles. After tearing her body in pieces, they took her mangled limbs to a place called Cinaron, and there burnt them. This affair brought not the least opprobrium, not only upon Cyril, but also upon the whole Alexandrian church.

And surely nothing can be farther from the spirit of Christianity than the allowance of massacres, fights, and transactions of that sort. This happened in the month of March during Lent, in the fourth year of Cyril's episcopate, under the tenth consulate of Honorius, and the sixth of Theodosius [A.D. 415].

READING 8

The Theodosian Code: Edicts on Defense[12]

These passages, dating from the early to the mid-fifth century A.D., serve as a chronicle of the declining military fortunes and increasingly desperate attempts to defend the Western Roman Empire.

A. EMPERORS ARCADIUS, HONORIUS, AND THEODOSIUS II AUGUSTUSES TO THE PROVINCIALS [A.D. 406]

In the matter of defense against hostile attacks, We order that consideration be given not only to the legal status of soldiers, but also to their physical strength. Although We believe the freeborn persons are aroused by love of country, We exhort slaves also, by the authority of the edict, that as soon as possible they shall offer themselves for the labors of war, and if they receive their arms as men fit for military service, they shall obtain the reward of freedom, and they shall also receive two solidi each for travel money. Especially, of course, do We urge this service upon the slaves of those persons who are retained in the armed imperial service, and likewise upon the slaves of federated allies and of conquered peoples, since it is evident that they are making war also along with their masters.

B. EMPERORS THEODOSIUS II AND VALENTINIAN III AUGUSTUSES TO THE ROMAN PEOPLE [A.D. 440]

As often as the public welfare demands, We consider that the solicitude of all of you must be summoned as an aid, in order that the provisions which will profit all may be fulfilled by all, and We do not believe that it is burdensome to Our provincials that the regulation is made for the safety of all so that they shall undertake the responsibility of resisting brigands:

---

[12]From *The Theodosian Code and Novels and the Sirmondian Constitutions,* tr. C. Pharr; Princeton, N.J., Princeton University Press, 1952, pp. 170, 172, 387, 544. (See p. 10)

Genseric,[13] the enemy of Our Empire, is reported to have led forth from the port of Carthage a large fleet, whose sudden excursion and fortuitous depredation must be feared by all shores.

Although the solicitude of Our Clemency is stationing garrisons throughout various places and the army of the most invincible Emperor Theodosius, Our Father, will soon approach, and although We trust that the Most Excellent Patrician, Our Aëtius,[14] will soon be here with a large band and the Most Illustrious Master of Soldiers, Sigisvult,[15] does not cease to organize the guards of soldiers and federated allies for the cities and shores, nevertheless, because it is not sufficiently certain, under summertime opportunities for navigation, to what shore the ships of the enemy can come, We admonish each and all by this edict that, with the confidence in the Roman strength and the courage with which they ought to defend their own, with their own men against the enemy, if the occasion should so demand, they shall use those arms which they can, but they shall preserve the public discipline and the moderation of free birth unimpaired. Thus they shall guard Our provinces and their own fortunes with faithful harmony and with joined shields. Of course this hope for each man's exertions is published, namely, that whatever a victor takes away from an enemy shall undoubtedly be his own.

C. THE EMPERORS THEODOSIUS II AND VALENTINIAN III AUGUSTUSES TO MAXIMUS [A.D. 440]

Justice must be preserved both publicly and privately in all matters and transactions, and We must adhere to it especially in those matters that sustain the sinews of the public revenue, since such measures come to the aid of the diminished resources of Our loyal taxpayers with useful equity. Very many persons reject this idea, since they serve only their domestic profits and deprive the common good wherein is contained their true and substantial welfare, although such welfare clearly comes better to each person when it profits all persons, especially since this necessity for tribute so demands, and without such tribute nothing can be provided in peace or in war. Nor can the continuity of such tax payments remain any further if there should be imposed on a few exhausted persons the burden which the more powerful man declines, which the richer man refuses, and which, since the stronger reject it, only the weaker man assumes.

---

[13]"Gaiseric" in most sources: he was the leader of the Vandals who had by then occupied North Africa.

[14]Master of the Troops of the Western Empire.

[15]A Frank, and Aëtius's lieutenant.

D.   THEODOSIUS II, ETC., TO THE PREFECT OF THE EAST [A.D. 441]

Valerianus, a curialis of Emesa, assumed for himself unjustly and surreptitiously the insignia of high office when, accompanied by a great horde of barbarians, he rushed into the private council chamber of the governor of the province and seated himself on the right of the man to whom We have committed the laws. When he had put to flight all the office staff of the governor, he left everything devastated and deserted. He placed a garrison of slaves in opposition to the tax collectors, contrary to public discipline, and thereby Our treasury suffered a great loss through his madness.

E.   VALENTINIAN III, AUGUSTUS, ETC., TO THE PROVINCIALS [A.D. 445]

It shall also be the responsibility of the duke of the province that no one shall be allowed to have armed men, thus creating an opportunity of harassing others, except perhaps those persons who at their own risk with praiseworthy animosity against the enemy have promised their own bands of soldiers and their own forces for the common welfare.

READING 9

Priscus, An Embassy to the Huns[16]

Priscus, Greek inhabitant of the fifth-century Roman Empire, served on an imperial ambassadorial mission to the court of Attila the Hun in 449. He tells here of his encounter with a Greek-speaking man who was living among the "Scythians," a name applied loosely at the time to barbarian tribes coming from southern Russia. Priscus' Scythians were a tributary tribe to the Huns and were settled in present-day Hungary. The Greek whom Priscus meets had once been a prosperous merchant of the Eastern Empire but had been taken prisoner in a barbarian raid. Having been granted his freedom, he chose not to return.

He considered his new life among the Scythians better than his old life among the Romans, and the reasons he urged were as follows: "After war the Scythians live at leisure, enjoying what they have got, and not at all, or very

---

[16]From Priscus of Panium, An Embassy to the Huns, in *Readings in European History,* vol. 1, ed. and tr. James H. Robinson; Boston, Ginn & Company, 1904, pp. 30–33.

little, disturbed. The Romans, on the other hand, are in the first place very liable to be killed, if there are any hostilities, since they have to rest their hopes of protection on others, and are not allowed, by their tyrants, to use arms. And those who do use them are injured by the cowardice of their generals, who cannot properly conduct war.

"But the condition of Roman subjects in time of peace is far more grievous than the evils of war, for the exaction of the taxes is very severe, and unprincipled men inflict injuries on others because the laws are practically not valid against all classes. A transgressor who belongs to the wealthy classes is not punished for his injustice, while a poor man, who does not understand business, undergoes the legal penalty—that is, if he does not depart this life before the trial, so long is the course of lawsuits protracted, and so much money is expended on them. The climax of misery is to have to pay in order to obtain justice. For no one will give a hearing to the injured man except he pay a sum of money to the judge and the judge's clerks."

In reply to this attack on the Empire, I asked him to be good enough to listen with patience to the other side of the question. "The creators of the Roman Republic," I said, "who were wise and good men, in order to prevent things from being done haphazardly, made one class of men guardians of the laws, and appointed another class to the profession of arms, who were to have no other object than to be always ready for battle, and to go forth to war without dread, as though to their ordinary exercise, having by practice exhausted all their fear beforehand. Others again were assigned to attend to the cultivation of the ground, to support themselves and those who fight in their defense by contributing the military corn supply. To those who protect the interests of the litigants a sum of money is paid by the latter, just as a payment is made by the farmers to the soldiers. Is it not fair to support him who assists and requite him for his kindness?

"Those who spend money on a suit and lose it in the end cannot fairly put it down to anything but the injustice of their case. And as to the long time spent on lawsuits, that is due to anxiety for justice, that judges may not fail in passing accurate judgments by having to give sentence offhand; it is better that they should reflect, and conclude the case more tardily, than that by judging in a hurry they should both injure man and transgress against the Deity, the institutor of justice.

"The Romans treat their slaves better than the king of the Scythians treats his subjects. They deal with them as fathers or teachers, admonishing them to abstain from evil and follow the lines of conduct which they have esteemed honorable; they reprove them for their errors like their own children. They are not allowed, like the Scythians, to inflict death on their slaves. They have numerous ways of conferring freedom; they can manumit not only during life, but also by their wills, and the testamentary wishes of a Roman in regard to his property are law."

My interlocutor shed tears, and confessed that the laws and constitution of the Romans were fair, but deplored that the officials, not possessing the spirit of former generations, were ruining the state.

READING 10

Victor of Vita, The Vandal Persecution[17]

Although historians have disagreed as to the identity of Victor of Vita, he was clearly a Catholic Christian, doubtless a churchman, and very likely a bishop of Vita, a city in western Sicily no great distance from Vandal North Africa, about which he writes. His life probably spanned the later decades of the fifth century and extended into the early sixth. (King Gaiseric, about whom he writes, died in 477.)

The Vandals entered North Africa from Spain in the 420s, seized St. Augustine's episcopal city of Hippo in 430 (the year of Augustine's death), and raided Rome in 455. They were both Arians and persecutors; indeed, they were the only consistently active persecutors of Catholic Christians among the Arian Germanic peoples, although other tribes—Burgundians, Ostrogoths, and Visigoths—indulged now and then. And as Victor of Vita shows, the Vandal persecutions cut across lines of class and gender. Notice, too, that the Christian God, here as elsewhere, not only protects His persecuted followers but avenges them as well, by causing the persecutors to suffer or die.

In Vandal North Africa, as in most other Germanic successor states in the post-Roman world, society was radically split between Romans and Germans, Catholics and Arians, soldiers and civilians. Not until Clovis (see Reading 13) did the chasms dividing the post-Roman West begin to close.

There were, at that time, some slaves who belonged to a certain Vandal: Martinianus, Saturianus and their two brothers, as well as a fellow slave, a noteworthy handmaid of Christ called Maxima, who was beautiful in both body and heart. And because Martinianus was the one who made his weapons and always held in high regard by his lord, while Maxima was mistress over the entire household, the Vandal thought that he would unite Martinianus and Maxima in marriage, in order to make these members of his household more faithful to himself.

Martinianus, in the way of young men of this world, wanted to be married, but Maxima, who was already dedicated to God, had no desire for a human marriage. When they came to approach the quiet privacy of their bedroom and Martinianus, ignorant of what God had decreed for him, desired, with the boldness of a husband, to lie with her as with a wife, the abovementioned handmaid of

[17]From *Victor of Vita, A History of the Vandal Persecution,* tr. John Moorhead; Liverpool, England, Liverpool University Press, 1992, pp. 14–16, 21–23.

Christ replied to him in a lively voice: "O brother Martinianus, I have dedicated the limbs of my body to Christ, and as there is a heavenly and true being to whom I am already betrothed, I cannot enter into a human marriage. But I shall give you some advice. If you want to, you as well will be able to gain him, while it is allowed, so that you too may have the delight of serving the one whom I have longed to marry."

So by the Lord's doing it came to pass that the young man was obedient to the virgin, and he too profited his soul. While the Vandal remained ignorant of the spiritual secret they shared, Martinianus, feeling compunction and now a changed man, persuaded his brothers that, inasmuch as they were brothers, they should possess in common the treasure which he had found. And so, after his conversion, he and his three brothers, accompanied by the maiden of God, secretly went forth by night to join the monastery of Tabraca (Tabarka), over which that noble shepherd Andreas then presided. She went to live in a convent of maidens not far away.

The barbarian began to carry out an investigation. He made enquiries and distributed numerous gifts, and what had happened could not be hidden. So it was that, discovering them to be not his slaves but those of Christ, he threw the servants of God into chains and inflicted various torments on them, his purpose being not so much to make them have intercourse but, something worse, to make them defile the ornaments of their faith through the filth of rebaptism. This came to the notice of Gaiseric. The king decreed that the implacable master was to keep afflicting his slaves for as long as it took for them to yield to his will. He ordered that strong cudgels were to be made which had jagged edges like palm branches, in the manner of saws: as these beat upon their backs they would not only break their bones but, as the spikes bored through them, would remain inside them.

As their flesh was torn in pieces the blood poured out and their inner parts were exposed to view, but on each occasion, as Christ healed them, they were restored unharmed on the next day. This happened quite often, over a long period, and no traces of their wounds were to be seen, the Holy Spirit curing them immediately. After this a harsh imprisonment was imposed on Maxima and she was cruelly stretched out on a "spear." The throng of the servants of God who had been visiting her was still there and, as everyone looked on, the putrefaction caused by the enormous pieces of wood vanished. The voices of all made this miracle known, and the man responsible for her custody testified to me on oath that this is what happened.

But when the Vandal refused to recognize divine power, avenging grace began to operate in his house. He and his children died at the same time, and the best from among his household and his animals perished as well. The lady of the house was therefore left a widow, bereft of her husband, children and fortune, and she offered the servants of Christ as a gift to a relative of the king, Sersao. The latter received the people offered to him with joy, but a demon began to trouble his children and the members of his household severely with various disturbances on account of the holy ones. In turn, his relative reported to the king what had happened. Immediately the king decreed that they were to be sent to a king of the Moors, a pagan who bore the name Capsur; so it was that they were banished. But he freed Maxima, the handmaid of Christ who had put him to shame and overcome him, to do as she wished. She lives on, a virgin and the mother of many virgins of God, and is by no means unknown to me.

We know of another man of that time, whose name was Saturus. A shining member of the church of Christ, with catholic freedom he often reproved the Arians for their perversity; he was the superintendent of the household of Huniric. Saturus was cited on the complaint of one Marivadus, a deacon whom the wretched Huniric held in signal honour, and it was decided that he was to become an Arian. Honours and wealth in abundance were promised if he did this; dire punishments were to be prepared if he refused. This was the choice placed before him: if he did not obey the king's commands, an examination was to be conducted. First of all he would lose his house and wealth and all his slaves and children would be sold; then while he was present, his wife would be given in marriage to a camel driver.

But he, filled with God, provoked those wicked people so that things would be set in train more quickly. For this reason his wife, without the knowledge of her husband, thought that she would seek some delay from those who were acting in the matter. Another Eve, directed by the counsel of the serpent, she came to her husband. But he was no Adam who would touch the alluring fruit of the forbidden tree, because his name was not "Needy" but Saturus, having been saturated by the riches of the household of God and having drunk from the torrent of his delights (cf. Ps. 35:9). The wife came to a place where her husband was praying by himself. She had rent her garments and let down her hair; their children were with her and she carried in her hands a little girl who was still at the breast. She placed her at the feet of her unknowing husband, while she herself embraced his knees with her arms and hissed with the voice of a snake: "Take pity on me, sweetest, and on yourself as well; take pity on the children we share, whom you see here. Those whom descent from our stock has made renowned should not be allowed to become slaves. And I should not be subjected to an unworthy and shameful marriage while my husband is alive, I who have always thought myself fortunate among those of my age because of my Saturus. God knows that you will have done against your will something which others may well have done voluntarily."

Then Saturus answered her with the voice of a saint: "'You are speaking just as one of the foolish women' (Job 2:10). I would be afraid, woman, if the bitter sweetness of this life were the only thing. You are the servant, wife, of the cunning of the Devil. If you loved your spouse, you would never entice your own husband to a second death. Let them sell the children, let them take my wife from me, let them carry away all my wealth; trusting in his promises, I shall hold fast to the words of my Lord: 'If anyone does not give up his wife, children, fields or house, he cannot be my disciple'" (cf. Luke 14:26). Why say more? His wife, rebutted, went away with the children, and Saturus was strengthened to receive his crown. He was examined, lost his property, was wearied by punishments and sent away a beggar, forbidden to appear in public. They took everything from him, but they were not able to carry off the stole of baptism.

READING 11

Sidonius Apollinaris, Letters[18]

There is no doubt that the late Empire experienced more than its share of crisis and turmoil (Readings 7–9), but it would be wrong to think that civilized life was impossible, as the letters of Sidonius Apollinaris (c. 432– c. 485) demonstrate. Sidonius was a rich landholder who later in life became bishop of Clermont-Ferrand in south-central Gaul. He was also a writer, poet, and prolific correspondent, many of whose letters have survived. Those letters provide us with illuminating and often vivid depictions of life in late fifth-century Gaul. Sidonius describes it as, on the whole, a good life despite the fact that the Western Roman Empire was disintegrating around him.

As a person of power and wealth, Sidonius was often called upon to exercise his influence on behalf of friends and clients (free people dependent on a superior). So important was the ability to intercede with the powerful for the sake of the humble that it eventually became a religious concept: the "patron saint" who intervened with Christ in order to help sinners. The three letters excerpted here show Sidonius as friend and patron; and the variations in style and tone provide eloquent evidence of the nuances of status and gradation that characterize late Roman society.

A.   LETTER TO PUDENS:

The son of your nurse has run off with the daughter of mine—a scandalous thing, which would have estranged you and me had I not known that you knew nothing of the deed being done. But after some words disclaiming complicity you think fit to beg that this flagrant offence go unpunished. I consent on one condition—that you release the ravisher from his hereditary position of inqui-

[18]From *Sidonius Apollinaris, Poems and Letters,* vol. 11, tr. W. B. Anderson; Cambridge, Mass., Harvard University Press, 1936, pp. 239, 241, 253, 255, 275.

linus,[19] becoming his patron instead of his master. The woman is already free. The only things that will cause her to be regarded as taken in lawful marriage, not made over as a plaything, will be that our culprit, on whose behalf you plead, should promptly be made a client instead of a tribute-payer, and so begin to have the standing of a plebian rather than of a colonus. For nothing short of this agreement or amends can in any degree set right this insult to me: and I am content to make this concession to your prayers and to our friendship—that, if the conferring of freedom releases the husband, no punishment shall fetter the ravisher. Farewell.

B.   SIDONIUS TO THE LORD BISHOP PRAGMATIUS, GREETING

The venerable matron Eutropia[20] is a lady whom I for my part regard as a shining example. She is one in whom abstemiousness and kindliness are equally matched; she feeds herself with fastings no less than she feeds the poor with food; she is unslumbering in Christ's service; sin is the only thing in her that is forced to sleep. Now the burden of a lawsuit has been added to the sorrows of widowhood, and she is hurrying to seek the supreme benefit of your comfort as a cure for her double affliction; she will be highly gratified whether you reckon her business as likely to involve merely a brief absence from home or a prolonged waiting on your pleasure. Well, the aforesaid lady is being worried by sharp practices—I don't want to be abusive and call them villainies—on the part of my reverend brother Agrippinus,[21] now a presbyter. Taking advantage of her unprotected weakness, he never ceases from troubling the serenity of that spiritual soul with blasts of worldly subtleties, although by the loss of her son—and a little later of her grandson—a double blow has recently been added to the wound of her long widowhood. I tried to mediate between the two, as I was specially entitled to do, seeing that my profession gave me a new, and my friendship an old, claim upon them; I expressed opinions on this and that and gave various advice together with many entreaties. You will be surprised, but it was the woman who showed the greater readiness to accede to every basis of agreement; and although the girl's father claimed that his privileged position would enable him to benefit his daughter more effectively, she preferred the liberal offer made by her mother-in-law. This quarrel, half allayed for the time being, is now being confided to your care. Appease the disputants, and by the authority of your episcopal judgment enjoin conciliation on the two parties that now view each other with distrust, and declare the truth. For the saintly Eutropia (if you put any trust in my assurance) will count it a victory if she is saved from litigation even at the

---

[19]A "colonus" or bound laborer.
[20]Otherwise unknown.
[21]Eutropia's son had married Agrippinus' daughter. The son died; and the daughter chose to live with Eutropia, not Agrippinus. These arrangements are the basis of the suit Sidonius describes.

expense of financial loss. This being so, I suspect you will pronounce only one of the two families to be disputatious, although you find both of them disputing. Deign to hold me in remembrance, my Lord Bishop.

C.   LETTER TO CENSORIUS, BISHOP OF AUXERRE

The bearer of this letter holds the honourable office of deacon. He with his family, seeking an escape from the whirlwind of Gothic depredation, was carried into your territory by the very impetus of his flight, so to speak. There on some farm land, belonging to a church over which your holiness is set, this starving newcomer made a small sowing of seed on some half-tilled soil; and he earnestly pleads to be allowed to garner the whole crop. If you cherish him with the kindness due to "them who are of the household of the faith," I mean by waiving the rent due from the land, then he, a stranger whose outlook is as limited as his means, will consider that little acquisition as good as the profits of farming his native soil. Should you, as is your custom, let him off the statutory payment due for his exceedingly small bit of land, he will regard himself as liberally equipped with traveling expenses and will return with words of gratitude on his lips. If by his hand you make me the happy recipient of a characteristically gracious message your letter will be regarded here by the brethren one and all as a blessing dropped straight from heaven. Deign to hold me in remembrance, my lord bishop.

READING 12
Jordanes, The History of the Goths[22]

Jordanes (sixth century), a Christian writer of partly Germanic ancestry, is using earlier sources to describe events that occurred between 60 and 75 years before he wrote. Jordanes exhibits a distinct pro-Gothic bias, and his sympathies have prompted him to exclude certain details from his account. We know from other sources, for example, that Emperor Zeno invited Theodoric to Constantinople and honored him there in order to halt a five-year plundering expedition that Theodoric had been conducting against the Eastern Empire. The Ostrogothic invasion of Italy resulted from a pact between Theodoric and Zeno to get rid of Odoacer. And Theodoric persuaded Odoacer to stop fighting by promising to spare his life and share power with him. A few days later Theodoric had Odoacer murdered along with all his soldiers and their families. In short, this passage teaches us not

[22]From *The Gothic History of Jordanes*, tr. Charles C. Mierow; Princeton, N.J., Princeton University Press, 1915, pp. 119–120, 134–139.

only about the later fifth century but also about the problem of dealing with sources that are at once informative and biased.

The passage begins with the appointment of the young Romulus Augustulus, the last of the Western emperors.

Now when Augustulus had been appointed Emperor by his father Orestes in Ravenna, it was not long before Odoacer, king of the Torcilingi, invaded Italy, as leader of the Sciri, the Heruli and allies of various races. He put Orestes to death, drove his son [Romulus] Augustulus from the throne and condemned him to the punishment of exile in the Castle of Lucullus in Campania [A.D. 476]. Thus the Western Empire of the Roman race, which Octavianus Augustus, the first of the Augusti, began to govern in the seven hundred and ninth year from the founding of the city, perished with this Augustulus in the five hundred and twenty-second year from the beginning of the rule of his predecessors and those before them, and from this time onward kings of the Goths held Rome and Italy. Meanwhile Odoacer, king of nations, subdued all Italy and then at the very outset of his reign slew Count Bracila at Ravenna that he might inspire a fear of himself among the Romans. He strengthened his kingdom and held it for almost thirteen years, until the appearance of Theodoric, of whom we shall speak hereafter.

When the [Eastern] Emperor Zeno heard that Theodoric had been appointed king over his own people [the Ostrogoths], he received the news with pleasure and invited him to come and visit him in Constantinople, sending an escort of honor. Receiving Theodoric with all due respect, he placed him among the princes of his palace. After some time Zeno increased his dignity by adopting him as his son-at-arms and gave him a triumph in the city at his expense. Theodoric was made Consul Ordinary also, which is well known to be the supreme good and highest honor in the world. Nor was this all, for Zeno set up before the royal palace an equestrian statue to the glory of this great man.

Now while Theodoric was in alliance by treaty with the Empire of Zeno and was himself enjoying every comfort in the city, he heard that his tribe, dwelling as we have said in Illyricum, was not altogether satisfied or content. So he chose to seek a living by his own exertions, after the manner customary to his race, rather than to enjoy the advantages of the Roman Empire in luxurious ease while his tribe lived apart.

Therefore Theodoric departed from the royal city and returned to his own people. In company with the whole tribe of the Goths, who gave him their unanimous consent, he set out for Hesperia. He went in straight march through Sirmium to the places bordering on Pannonia and, advancing into the territory of Venice as far as the bridge of the Sontius, encamped there. When he had halted there for some time to rest the bodies of his men and pack animals, Odoacer sent an armed force against him, which he met on the plains of Verona and destroyed with great slaughter. Then he broke camp and advanced through Italy with greater boldness. Crossing the River Po, he pitched camp near the royal city of Ravenna, about the third milestone from the city in the place called Pineta. When Odoacer saw this, he fortified himself within the city. He frequently harassed the army of the Goths at night, sallying forth stealthily with his men, and this not once or twice, but often; and thus he struggled for almost three whole years. But he labored in vain, for all Italy at last called Theodoric its lord and the Empire obeyed his nod. But Odoacer, with his few adherents and the Romans who were present, suffered daily from war and famine in Ravenna. Since he accomplished nothing, he sent an embassy and begged for mercy. Theodoric first granted it and afterwards deprived him of his life.

It was in the third year after his entrance into Italy, as we have said, that Theodoric, by advice of the Emperor Zeno, laid aside the garb of a private citizen and the dress of his race and assumed a costume with a royal mantle, as he had now become the ruler over both Goths and Romans.

READING 13

Gregory of Tours, The History of the Franks[23]

Again we must contend with an account written several generations after the events it describes. Gregory, bishop of Tours (573–594), is, on the whole, a good historian although a bad Latinist. His discussions of the character of Clovis and his conversion to Catholic Christianity ring true. To Clovis, even more than to Constantine, the Christian God was a bringer of military victory. Clovis's conversion was of inestimable importance to the future history of Western Europe in that it eventually brought Classical-Christian culture, at least in attenuated form, to the Franks.

At that time many churches were despoiled by Clovis's army, since he was as yet involved in heathen error. Now the army had taken from a certain church a vase of wonderful size and beauty, along with the remainder of the utensils for the service of the church. And the bishop of the church sent messengers to the king asking that the vase at least be returned, if he could not get back any more of the sacred dishes. On hearing this the king said to the messengers: "Follow us as far as Soissons, because all that has been taken is to be divided there and when the lot assigns me that dish I will do what the bishop asks." Then when he

[23]From *Gregory of Tours, The History of the Franks*, tr. E. Brehaut; New York, Columbia University Press, 1916, pp. 36–38, 45–50.

came to Soissons and all the booty was set in their midst, the king said: "I ask of you, brave warriors, not to refuse to grant me in addition to my share, yonder dish," that is, he was speaking of the vase just mentioned. In answer to the speech of the king, those of more sense replied: "Glorious king, all that we see is yours, and we ourselves are subject to your rule. Now do what seems well-pleasing to you; for no one is able to resist your power." When they said this a foolish, envious and excitable fellow lifted his battle-axe and struck the vase, and cried in a loud voice: "You shall get nothing here except what the lot fairly bestows on you." At this all were stupefied, but the king endured the insult with gentleness of patience, and taking the vase he handed it over to the messenger of the church, nursing the wound deep in his heart. And at the end of the year he ordered the whole army to come with their equipment of armor, to show the brightness of their arms on the field of Mars. And when he was reviewing them all carefully, he came to the man who struck the vase, and said to him: "No one has brought armor so carelessly kept as you; for neither your spear nor sword nor axe is in serviceable condition." And seizing the man's axe he cast it to the earth, and when the other had bent over somewhat to pick it up, the king raised his hands and drove his own axe into the man's head. "This," he said, "is what you did at Soissons to the vase."

Upon the death of this man, he ordered the rest to depart, raising great dread of himself by this action.

It came about that as the armies of the Franks and the Alemanni were fighting fiercely, there was great slaughter, and Clovis's army was in danger of being destroyed. So with remorse in his heart he burst into tears and cried, "Jesus Christ, whom Clotilda [Clovis's wife] asserts to be the son of the living God, and who is said to give aid to those in distress and victory to those who hope in you, I beg the glory of your aid, with the vow that if you grant me the victory over these enemies, I will believe in you and be baptized in your name." And when he said this the Alemanni turned their backs and fled; and their king was killed, and they submitted to the domination of Clovis. And he stopped the fighting, and after encouraging his men, retired in peace and told the queen how he had merit to win the victory by calling on the name of Christ. This happened in the fifteenth year of his reign [500 if Gregory is right, but more likely 496].

Then Clovis the king said to his people, "I take it very hard that these Arians[24] hold part of Gaul. Let us go with God's help and conquer them and bring the land under our control." Then Clovis met with Alaric II, king of the Visigoths, in the plain of Voillé, at the tenth milestone from Poitiers. And when the Goths had fled, as was their custom, King Clovis had the victory by God's aid. At that time there perished a very great number of the people of Auvergne, who had come with Apollinaris and the leading senators. Clovis sent his son to Clermont by way of Albi and Rodez. He went, and brought under his father's

---

[24]Christians who denied the orthodox belief in the Trinity—the equality of the Father, Son, and Holy Spirit. The Visigoths, like many other Germanic peoples, were Arians.

dominion the cities from the boundaries of the Goth [i.e., the Visigoths of Spain] to the limit of the Burgundians. When Clovis had spent the winter at Bordeaux and taken all the treasures of Alaric at Toulouse, he went to Angoulême. And the Lord gave him such grace that the walls fell down of their own accord when he gazed at them. Then he drove the Visigoths out and brought the city under his own dominion. Clovis received an appointment to the consulship from the emperor Anastasius, and in the church of the blessed St. Martin of Tours he clad himself in the purple tunic, and from that day he was called consul or Augustus. Leaving Tours he went to Paris, and there he established the seat of his kingdom.

STUDY QUESTIONS

A What is meant by "Christianization"? Can you trace some of the steps by which the Roman Empire was Christianized? Who took the initiative in this process?
B How did the political authority of the Western Roman Empire collapse? What emphasis would you place on internal forces and what emphasis on external forces?
C What were conditions like in the late Empire? How did the collapse of Rome affect people's lives?

Reading 1: Lactantius, Constantine's Victory and Conversion, 312

What was Constantine looking for in a god? Was Constantine miraculously converted?

Reading 2: The Edict Of Milan, 313

What light does this edict shed on Constantine's conversion? What status does the settlement give to Christianity?

Reading 3: The Nicene Creed, 325

Why was it important to find a uniform statement of Christianity in 325? And given that Constantine called the council and presided, who was now running the church?

Reading 4: The Theodosian Code

What is the purpose of the edict of 480? The edict of 491? Where is the impulse for these decrees originating, and what does that tell you about who leads the church?

Reading 5: St. Jerome, Letter To Laeta

What are the main elements of Jerome's plan of education? In what ways is this plan tailored for girls? How would Jerome argue that boys should be educated? Is there room in Jerome's curriculum for non-Christian ideas and activities?

Reading 6: St. Augustine, The City Of God

Why did Augustine write this book? What is the outline of his argument? What is the role of the state in the life of a Christian? What is the role of the Christian in the state?

Reading 7: Socrates Scholasticus, The Murder of Hypatia

What caused the violence in Alexandria? Was this "popular" violence, or was it inspired by those in authority? What made Hypatia a target of this violence?

Reading 8: The Theodosian Code

What is the significance of the edict of 406? There are two edicts for 440, one anticipating a Vandal attack, and one complaining about taxes: how are these related? What do the last two edicts demonstrate about the effectiveness of the late Roman government?

Reading 9: Priscus, An Embassy to the Huns

What are the chief arguments the ex-slave gives for preferring life among the Huns? How does Priscus attempt to counter these?

Reading 10: Victor of Vita, The Vandal Persecution

What separates the Roman and Vandal populations of North Africa? How does Maxima win fame in this episode? The wife of Saturus argues with her husband's decision to stick to his Trinitarian faith: what reasons does she give? How does Saturus respond?

Reading 11: Sidonius Apollinaris, Letters

How had the decline of Roman power affected Sidonius? What changes have Christianity and barbarian invasions made in the life of a Roman aristocrat?

Reading 12: Jordanes, The History of the Goths

What is Theodoric's relationship with Rome? From whom does he derive his authority?

Reading 13: Gregory of Tours, The History of the Franks

Clovis—still a pagan at the time of the first episode related here—tries to help the local bishop. Why? Does this help explain his conversion later? What is Clovis' relationship with Rome? From whom does he derive his authority?

CHAPTER **2**

🏵 THE HEIRS OF CLASSICAL CIVILIZATION

With the collapse of the Western imperial regime in A.D. 476 and the establishment of Christian-Germanic kingdoms in its place, the cultures of the Eastern Empire and Western Europe began to drift apart. The vast lands that Rome had once ruled split into two distinct civilizations: Byzantium (East Rome) and Western Christendom. A third civilization emerged when the Arab conquests of the seventh and eighth centuries spread the religion and culture of Islam through much of the Middle East and westward across the formerly Roman lands of North Africa and Spain.

The three civilizations of medieval Western Eurasia—Byzantine, Western Christian, and Islamic—were all influenced by the earlier Greco-Roman culture. All were, to some degree, heirs of Classical civilization. And all were committed to monotheistic religions that drew inspiration from ancient Judaism. Muhammad taught that Jesus, Moses, and the Old Testament prophets were, like himself, servants and spokesmen of the one God.

The sources in this chapter deal first with Byzantine civilization (Readings 1–4), then with early Western Christendom through the seventh century (Readings 5–11), and finally with Islam (Readings 12–14). The Byzantine sources begin with an account of one of the holy men who functioned as spiritual heroes and foci of community devotion in early Byzantine society (Reading 1).

38

There follows a description of Emperor Justinian (527–565) and his equally formidable consort, the Empress Theodora (Reading 2). Though Justinian was a conqueror, builder, and theologian, his most enduring achievement was the *Corpus Juris Civilis* (Body of Civil Law), which was to exert a commanding influence on medieval jurisprudence (Reading 3). We continue with an edict that demonstrates Byzantine imperial concern for the peasantry (Reading 4), which is in part responsible for the amazing durability of the Byzantine Empire.

The sources for the early medieval West all emphasize, in one way or another, the creative role of Christianity in preserving and expanding Classical-Christian culture in the Germanic kingdoms, beginning with one of the earliest assertions of papal supremacy (Reading 5) and one of the basic political theories of the Middle Ages (Reading 6). Gifted individuals kept alive the traditions of classical learning, though often in an attenuated form (Reading 7); but perhaps most important of all were the Benedictine monasteries (Reading 8). Of fundamental importance was the conversion of Germanic kings and kingdoms to Christianity, for it enabled them to share in the classical legacy of Rome (Readings 9–11).

Our Islamic documents begin with an excerpt from the Koran (Reading 12), the holy book in which the Islamic faith is rooted. They continue with Muhammad's Constitution of Medina, the political-religious community that foreshadowed the future governance of the Islamic Empire (Reading 13). Playing on internal dissension in the post-Roman world, Muslim armies, galvanized by their religion, created a new empire in the Mediterranean world (Reading 14).

READING 1

The Life of St. Daniel the Stylite[1]

A disciple of the pillar saint Simeon Stylites, St. Daniel was born in Syria in 409 and died near Constantinople in 493. He was a shrewd, uncomplicated man who gave practical advice to people of the neighborhood and travelers from afar. And he served as a living example of heroic Christian sanctity. Daniel's biographer was a younger contemporary, perhaps a disciple and certainly an eyewitness to many of Daniel's activities. Like those of other saints' lives throughout the Middle Ages, Daniel's biographer writes with the purpose of inspiring others to admire and emulate his spiritual hero. If Daniel had faults, we will not discover them here.

Daniel's career was paralleled by those of numerous Byzantine saints who, to a far greater extent than in the West, played intimate, unifying roles in their urban communities.

Before all things it is right that we should give glory to Jesus Christ our God, Who for us was made man and for our salvation endured all things according to the Dispensation; for His sake, too, prophets were killed, and just men crucified themselves because of this faith in Him and by His grace, after having kept patience under their sufferings unswervingly unto the end, they received a crown of glory. These men our Master and Savior Christ gave us as an example that we might know that it is possible for a man by the patient endurance of his sufferings to please God and be called His faithful servant.

The servant of God [St. Daniel] fell into an ecstasy, as it were, and saw a huge pillar of cloud standing opposite him and the holy and blessed Simeon [another famous pillar saint] standing above the head of the column and two men of goodly appearance, clad in white, standing near him in the heights. And he heard the voice of the holy and blessed Simeon saying to him, "Come here to me, Daniel." And he said, "Father, father, and how can I get up to that height?" Then the saint said to the young men standing near him, "Go down and bring him up to me." So the men came down and brought Daniel up to him and he stood there. Then Simeon took him in his arms and kissed him with a holy kiss, and then others called him away, and escorted by them he was borne up to heaven leaving Daniel on the column with the two men. When holy Daniel saw him being carried up to heaven he heard the voice of St. Simeon, "Stand firm and play the man." But he was confused by fear and by that fearful voice, for it was like thunder in his ears. When he came to himself again he declared the vision to

---

[1]From *Three Byzantine Saints,* ed. and tr. E. Dawes and N. H. Baynes; Crestwood, N.J., St. Vladimir's Seminary Press, 1948, pp. 7, 18–19, 29, 36, 43–44, 70–71.

those around him. Then they said to the holy man, "You must mount on to a pillar and take up St. Simeon's mode of life and be supported by the angels." . . .

Now the blessed Emperor Leo [457–474] of pious memory had heard from many of these things and desired for a long time to see the man. Therefore he sent for the pious Sergius, who carried the saint's messages, and through him he asked that the saint would pray and beseech God to grant him a son. And Daniel prayed, and through God's good pleasure the emperor's wife, the Empress Verina, thereafter conceived and begot a son, whereupon the emperor immediately sent and had the foundations laid of a third column. . . .

It happened about the same time that Gubazius, the king of the Lazi, arrived at the court of the Emperor Leo, who took him up to visit the holy man. When he saw this strange sight Gubazius threw himself on his face and said "I thank You, heavenly King, that by means of an earthly king You have deemed me worthy to behold great mysteries; for never before in this world have I seen anything of this kind." And these kings had a point in dispute touching the Roman policy; and they laid the whole matter open to the servant of God and through the mediation of the holy man they agreed upon a treaty which satisfied the claims of each. After this the emperor returned to the city and dismissed Gubazius to his native land, and when the latter reached his own country he related to all his folk what he had seen. Consequently the men who later on came up from Lazica to the city [of Constantinople] invariably went up to Daniel. Gubazius himself, too, wrote to the holy man and besought his prayers and never ceased doing so to the end of his life. . . .

At about that time the blessed Emperor Leo heard from many about a certain Titus, a man of vigor who dwelt in Gaul and had in his service a number of men well trained for battle; so he sent for him and honored him with the rank of count that he might have him to fight on his behalf if he were forced to go to war. This Titus he sent to the holy man for his blessing; on his arrival the saint watered him with many and diverse counsels from the holy writing and proved him to be an ever-blooming fruit-bearing tree; and Titus, beholding the holy man, marveled at the strangeness of his appearance and his endurance and just as good earth when it has received the rain brings forth much fruit, so this admirable man Titus was illuminated in mind by the teaching of the holy and just man and no longer wished to leave the enclosure, for he said, "The whole labor of man is spent on growing rich and acquiring possession in this world and pleasing men; yet the single hour of his death robs him of all his belongings; therefore it is better for us to serve God rather than men." With these words he threw himself down before the holy man begging him to receive him and let him be enrolled in the brotherhood. And Daniel, the servant of the Lord, willingly accepted his good resolve. Thereupon that noble man Titus sent for all his men and said to his soldiers, "From now on I am the soldier of the heavenly King; aforetime my rank among men made me your captain and yet I was unable to benefit either you or myself, for I only urged you on to slaughter and bloodshed.

From today, however, and henceforth I bid farewell to all such things; therefore those of you who wish it, remain here with me, but I do not compel any one of you, for what is done under compulsion is not acceptable. See, here is the money, take some, each of you, and go to your homes." Then he brought much gold and he took and placed it in front of the column and gave to each according to his rank. Two of them, however, did not choose to take any, but remained with him. All the rest embraced Titus and went their ways.

When the emperor heard this he was very angry and sent a messenger up to the holy man to say to Titus, "I brought you up from your country because I wanted to have you quite near me and I sent you to the holy man to pray and receive a blessing, but not that you should separate yourself from me." Titus replied to the messenger, "From now on, since I have listened to the teaching of this holy man, I am dead to the world and to all the things of the world. Whatever the just man says about me to you, tell to the emperor, for Titus your servant is dead." Then the messengers went outside into the enclosure to the holy man and told him everything. And the holy man sent a letter of counsel by them to the emperor, beseeching him and saying, "You yourself need no human aid; for owing to your perfect faith in God you have God as your everlasting defender; do not therefore covet a man who today is and tomorrow is not; for the Lord does all things in accordance with His will. Therefore dedicate your servant to God Who is able to send your Piety in his stead another still braver and more useful; without your approval I never wished to do anything."

And the emperor was satisfied and sent and thanked the holy man and said, "To crown all your good deeds there yet remained this good thing for you to do. Let the man, then, remain under your authority, and may God accept his good purpose." Not long afterwards they were deemed worthy of the holy robe, and both made progress in the good way of life; but more especially was this true of Titus, the former count. . . .

Let us now in a short summary review his whole life down to the end of his time on earth.

Our all-praiseworthy father Daniel said good-bye to his parents when he was twelve years old, then for twenty-five years he lived in a monastery; after that during five years he visited the fathers and from each learned what might serve his purpose, making his anthology from their teachings. At the time when the crown of his endurance began to be woven the saint had completed his forty-second year, and at that age became by divine guidance, as we have explained above, to this our imperial city. He dwelt in the church for nine years, standing on the capital of a column, thus training himself beforehand in the practice of that discipline which he was destined to bring to perfection. For he had learned from many divine revelations that his duty was to enter upon the way of life practiced by the blessed and sainted Simeon.

For three and thirty years and three months he stood for varying periods on the three columns, as he changed from one to another, so that the whole span of his life was a little more than eighty-four years.

During these he was deemed worthy to receive "the prize of his high calling"; he blessed all men, he prayed on behalf of all, he counseled all not to be covetous, he instructed all in the things necessary to salvation, he showed hospitality to all, yet he possessed nothing on earth beyond the confines of the spot on which the enclosure and religious houses had been built. And though many, amongst whom were sovereigns and very distinguished officials occupying the highest posts, wished to present him with splendid possessions he never consented, but he listened to each one's offer and then prayed that he might be recompensed by God for his pious intention.

READING 2
Procopius, Justinian and Theodora[2]

Procopius of Caesarea (c. 500–565?) was a minor official attached to the staff of Belisarius, one of Justinian's chief generals. His great work is the *History of the Wars,* which recounts Justinian's campaigns both in the east and the west; but Procopius also wrote a *History of Justinian's Buildings* (at the emperor's request) and the scurrilous and polemical *The Secret History*. The following selection from *The Secret History* deals with the Nika riots of 532, an attempt by a coalition of popular and aristocratic factions to limit the power of the emperor.

At this time [1 January 532] an insurrection broke out unexpectedly in Byzantium among the populace, and, contrary to expectation, it proved to be a very serious affair, and ended in great harm to the people and to the senate, as the following account will show.

In every city the population has been divided for a long time past into the Blues and the Greens factions; but within comparatively recent times it has come about that, for the sake of these names and the seats which the rival factions occupy in watching the games, they spend their money and abandon their bodies to the most cruel tortures, and even do not think it unworthy to die a most shameful death. And they fight against their opponents knowing not for what end they imperil themselves, but knowing well that, even if they overcome their enemy the fight, the conclusion of the matter for them will be to be carried off straight away to the prison, and finally, after suffering extreme torture, to be

[2]Procopius, *The Secret History,* tr. Richard Atwater, [Chicago: P. Covici, 1927; New York: Covici Friede, 1927], reprinted, Ann Arbor, Mich.: University of Michigan Press, 1961, Book I, chapter 7.

destroyed. So there grows up in them against their fellow men a hostility which has no cause, and at no time does it cease or disappear, for it gives place neither to the ties of marriage nor of relationship nor of friendship, and the case is the same even though those who differ with respect to these colors be brothers or any other kin. I, for my part, am unable to call this anything except a disease of the soul.

At this time the officers of the city administration in Byzantium were leading away to death some of the rioters. But the members of the two factions conspiring together and declaring a truce with each other, seized the prisoners and then straightway entered the prison and released all those who were in confinement there. Fire was applied to the city as if it had fallen under the hand of an enemy. The emperor and his consort, with a few members of the senate shut themselves up in the palace and remained quietly there. Now the watch-word which the populace passed to one another was Nike [meaning "Conquer"].

On the fifth day of the insurrection in the late afternoon the Emperor Justinian gave orders to Hypatius and Pompeius, nephews of the late emperor, Anastasius, to go home as quickly as possible, either because he suspected that some plot was being matured by them against his own person, or, it may be, because destiny brought them to this. But they feared that the people would force them to the throne (as in fact fell out), and they said that they would be doing wrong if they should abandon their sovereign when he found himself in such danger. When the Emperor Justinian heard this, he inclined still more to his suspicion, and he bade them quit the palace instantly.

On the following day at sunrise it became known to the people that both men had quit the palace where they had been staying. So the whole population ran to them, and they declared Hypatius emperor and prepared to lead him to the market place to assume the power. But the wife of Hypatius, Mary, a discreet woman, who had the greatest reputation for prudence, laid hold of her husband and would not let go, but cried out with loud lamentation and with entreaties to all her kinsmen that the people were leading him on the road to death. But since the throng overpowered her, she unwillingly released her husband, and he by no will of his own came to the Forum of Constantine, where they summoned him to the throne.

The emperor and his court were deliberating as to whether it would be better for them if they remained or if they took to flight in the ships. And many opinions were expressed favoring either course. And the Empress Theodora also spoke to the following effect: "My opinion then is that the present time, above all others, is inopportune for flight, even though it bring safety. For one who has been an emperor it is unendurable to be a fugitive. May I never be separated from this purple, and may I not live that day on which those who meet me shall not address me as mistress. If, now, it is your wish to save yourself, O Emperor, there is no difficulty. For we have much money, and there is the sea, here the boats. However consider whether it will not come about after you have been saved that you would gladly exchange that safety for death. For as for myself, I approve a certain ancient saying that royalty is a good burial-shroud." When the queen had spoken thus, all were filled with boldness, and, turning their thoughts towards resistance, they began to consider how they might be able to defend themselves if any hostile force should come against them. All the hopes of the emperor were centered upon Belisarius and Mundus, of whom the former, Belisarius, had recently returned from the Persian war bringing with him a following which was both powerful and imposing, and in particular he had a great number of spearmen and guards who had received their training in battles and the perils of warfare.

When Hypatius reached the hippodrome, he went up immediately to where the emperor is accustomed to take his place and seated himself on the royal throne from which the emperor was always accustomed to view the equestrian and athletic contests. And from the palace Mundus went out through the gate which, from the circling descent, has been given the name of the Snail. Belisarius, with difficulty and not without danger and great exertion, made his way over ground covered by ruins and half-burned buildings, and ascended to the stadium. Concluding that he must go against the populace who had taken their stand in the hippodrome—a vast multitude crowding each other in great disorder—he drew his sword from its sheath and, commanding the others to do likewise, with a shout he advanced upon them at a run. But the populace, who were standing in a mass and not in order, at the sight of armored soldiers who had a great reputation for bravery and experience in war, and seeing that they struck out with their swords unsparingly, beat a hasty retreat. [Mundus] straightway made a sally into the hippodrome through the entrance which they call the Gate of Death. Then indeed from both sides the partisans of Hypatius were assailed with might and main and destroyed. There perished among the populace on that day more than thirty thousand. The soldiers killed both [Hypatius and Pompeius] on the following day and threw bodies into the sea. This was the end of the insurrection in Byzantium.

READING 3
Justinian, The Institutes[3]

During the early years of the reign (527–565) of the Byzantine emperor Justinian, a commission of imperial lawyers headed by Tribonian carried out the emperor's order to systematize and produce official texts of the whole of Roman law still in effect. The result of this immense effort, the

[3]From *Corpus Juris Civilis,* vol. 1, ed. Paul Krueger; Berlin, Weidmann, 1882, pp. 2–4; tr. Marc Anthony Meyer.

Corpus Juris Civilis, included all valid imperial statutes since the time of Hadrian (the *Codex*) along with a synthesis of the authoritative writings of Roman legal officials (the *Digest*) and an introductory textbook on the fundamental principles of Roman law (the *Institutes*). It is from the *Institutes,* completed in 533, that the following passages are drawn.

A. PROLOGUE

In the name of our Lord Jesus Christ. The emperor Caesar Flavius Justinian, conqueror of the Alamanni, Goths, Franks, Germans, Antes, Alani, Vandals and Africans, rightly fortunate and renowned, victorious and triumphant, ever Augustus, to the young [scholars] desirous of legal knowledge.

The imperial majesty should not only be embellished with arms but also strengthened by laws, so that the times of both war and peace can be ordered correctly and that the Roman emperor [*princeps*] may emerge not only victorious in battle with enemies but also, eliminating the iniquities of villains through legal means, may be as solicitous of the law as he is triumphant over conquered foes.

1. We have reached each of these objectives through the greatest vigilance and foresight, and by the will of God. And the barbarian nations brought under our subjection know of our military achievements, and Africa as well and many other provinces have been restored after a very long time to Roman domination through our victories, and with divine guidance we have achieved and proclaimed our empire. Truly, all of the people are now also governed by laws that have been promulgated or compiled by us.

2. And after bringing the revered constitutions, previously in a confused state, into lucid harmony, we turned our attention to the great mass of venerable jurisprudence and, as if crossing the open sea, we completed—by the favor of heaven—a nearly hopeless task.

3. And when, with God's help, this had been done, we called together Tribonian, a great man and teacher and ex-quaestor of our sacred palace, and Theophilus and Dorotheus, both illustrious men—all of whose ingenuity and legal expertise and tried obedience to our orders we have had ample proof. We issued a special mandate that by our authority and with our encouragement they should compose the *Institutes* so that you might acquire your first knowledge of the law not from old stories but through the splendor of the emperor [and] that your ears and minds might receive nothing useless or false but that which is deemed proper in these matters. And whereas in the past at least four years would go by before the imperial constitutions were read, you can now do this from the beginning, meriting such honor and discovering with such happiness that the beginning and the end of your legal studies proceed from the mouth of the emperor.

4. Therefore, with all endeavor and eager study, receive these our laws and show yourselves so learned that you may cherish the marvelous hope that, at the end of your legal studies, you may even be able to order our state [*res publica*] in that part given over to you.

B.   ON JUSTICE AND LAW

Justice is the constant and perpetual desire to give to each person his own due right [*ius*].

1. Jurisprudence [*iurisprudentia*] is the acquaintance with both human and divine things, the knowledge of what is just and unjust.
2. These are the precepts of law [*ius*]: to live honestly, not to injure another, and to render to each his own.
3. The two aspects of this study are public and private: public law is that which pertains to the Roman state, private is that which concerns the benefit of the individual. This is to say, therefore, that private law has three parts, indeed, it consists of natural precepts or either those of nations or of states.

C.   ON NATURAL LAW, THE LAW OF NATIONS AND CIVIL LAW

Natural law [*ius naturale*] is that which nature has instilled in all animals, because this law is not characteristic of humankind but of all animals which are born on land and in the air and in the sea. From this derives the association of man and woman which we call marriage, as well as procreation and the rearing of off-spring because we see that animals are imbued with the experience of this law.

1. Civil law [*ius civile*] and the law of nations [*ius gentium*], however, are divided in this way: all peoples who are governed by laws [*leges*] and customs [*mores*] use law which is in part particular to themselves and in part common to all men. The law that each people has established for itself is particular to that state and is called civil law as being specifically of that state. Yet, what natural reason has established among all men is kept equally by all peoples and is called the law of nations, as it were, the law common to all peoples. And hence, the Roman people observe partly their own particular law [and] partly that which is common to all peoples. . . .
3. Our law is derived from written or unwritten [sources], just as among the Greeks: some laws are written, others unwritten. . . .
4. A 'law' [*lex*] is that which the Roman people commanded on a question submitted by a senatorial magistrate, like a consul. A 'plebiscite' [*plebiscitum*] is that which the plebs ordered put by a plebian magistrate, like a tribune. The plebs, however, differ from the people as a 'species' is distinguished from a 'genus' because the term 'people' means all the citizens, including as well

patricians and senators, while the name 'plebeians' signifies the other citizens, excluding the patricians and the senators. Yet, with the passing of the lex *Hortensia*[4] the plebiscites came to be no less valid than the laws.

5. A *'senatus consultum'* is that which the senate orders and directs, for when the Roman people had increased in its number, it became difficult to call it together in one place for the enactment of a law, [and thus] it seemed best instead to invoke the senate in place of the people.

6. The emperor's voice has the force of law as well since, by the "law of kings" [*lex regia*] which regulated his authority [*imperium*], the people conceded to him and placed in him all their power and authority. Thus, whatever the emperor directed by letter or decreed in a hearing or ordered by edict is to be conceived as law: these are what are called "constitutions." Some of these, of course, are special cases which are not to be used as precedents, for the emperor did not intend this to go beyond the individual because he views one person favorably because of merits or inflicts a penalty on another or offers relief to another. Others, however, when general in intent, undoubtedly apply to everyone.

7. Furthermore, praetorian[5] edicts have no ordinary authority as law. We normally call this the law of honor because those who bear honor, that is a magistrate, have given their authority to this law. And *curule aediles*[6] as well issued edicts concerning certain cases and that kind of edict is part of honorary law.

8. The responses of the learned [jurists] are sentences and opinions of those to whom it was permitted to lay down the law; for in ancient times it was instituted that there were those who publicly interpreted the law—who are called jurisconsult—to whom the right of responding [in legal matters] was given by the Caesar. All of their sentences and opinions [when unanimous] held such authority that judges were not permitted to differ from their responses, so that it is a constitution.

9. Unwritten law is that which usage has approved, for long-observed customs take on the effect of law by consent of those who observe them. . . .

10. And natural laws, which are followed by all nations alike, deriving from divine providence, remain always firm and unchangeable: truly, those which each state constitutes for itself often subject to alteration whether by the tacit approval of the people or else by subsequent legislation.

---

[4]In 287 B.C. the "struggle of the orders" culminated in the promulgation of the *lex Hortensia*, which decreed that plebiscites were to be as fully valid as laws [*leges*] proper.

[5]The praetor was responsible for the administration of justice in both the Republic and Empire periods, but the authority of this high office was restricted by the superior authority of the consul. When Roman authority was established outside the boundaries of Italy, the praetors acted as provincial governors of the Senate; but with the dictatorship of Sulla in the first century B.C., these officers were required to remain in the capital to preside over criminal courts.

[6]In their capacity as market officers the *curule aediles* were responsible for important features of the Roman law of sale.

READING 4

Basil II, On the Protection of Peasants' Lands[7]

Basil II (957–1025) was a great Byzantine emperor known affectionately as the Bulgar Slayer. Like their counterparts in the medieval West, Byzantine rulers faced a problem when great landholders encroached on the lands of poor, for the great landlords were better able to evade taxes and imperial dues than were lesser landholders. Basil II attempted to address the problem in this law. But the emperor is not necessarily the friend of the poor that this passage might suggest: on one occasion he had 14,000 war captives blinded (though, charitably, he left one out of every hundred with one eye intact to lead the others home).

1. Whereas our imperial majesty, by the grace of God from whom we have received the imperial authority, has undertaken to scrutinize the legal cases initiated by both rich and poor, we have found that those powerful *dynatoi*[8] who desire to aggrandize [their lands] have a legitimate excuse for their personal covetousness, that is, the prescription of up to forty years [a kind of statute of limitations], and that they anxiously await to pass through this period either by means of bribes and gifts or through the power they possess and then to enjoy in full ownership whatever they have wrongly appropriated at the expense of the poor. Therefore we have promulgated the present legislation, which on the one hand rectifies what has previously occurred but, on the other hand, also curbs the present-day *dynatoi* and forbids those in the future from undertaking such things [to attack the poor], since they now have the knowledge that they will get no assistance from this quarter. Not only will they themselves be stripped of the property belonging to others, but so also will their children and whomever else they leave it to as heirs. From this we wish it to be clear that our imperial majesty does not without purpose or investigation overturn ownership [based upon] prescription of long-standing, but takes pity on the poor and watches out for the common welfare and conditions and embraces justice and provides a remedy against this fearful passion of desire for aggrandizement. Because of this circumstance we have been very disturbed on behalf of the poor, and we have observed with our own eyes (when we traversed the themes[9] of our empire and set out on campaigns) the avarice and injustices every day perpetrated against

[7]From D. J. Geanakoplos, *Byzantium, Church Society and Civilization as Seen through Contemporary Eyes;* Chicago, University of Chicago Press, 1984, pp. 245–247.
[8]Member of the landed nobility.
[9]Administrative and military districts.

the poor. Indeed how can time be of any assistance at all since, as has happened, the *dynatoi,* who is powerful and prosperous and aggrandizes himself at the expense of the poor man, will profit from the passage of time and will bequeath to his heirs his power and wealth?

Therefore, we decree by our present enactment, that those properties which have been acquired by the *dynatoi* in communities of peasant villages up to the initial law of our great-grandfather Emperor Romanus the Elder and which derive their validity from written documents or supporting witnesses, be preserved and kept in their owner's hands, as has been declared in earlier laws. For this reason we seek written privileges and supporting witnesses to be adduced, so that the *dynatoi* might not by means of subterfuge allege that the lands recently acquired by them carry over to them by written documents from a long time ago. But from that time when the written prescription was issued through the law published by our great-grandfather Emperor Romanus the Elder, until the present (which is the first of January, of the year 996 and also into the future), [we declare] that in no way at all can time [elapsed] have [legal] validity or be made use of against the poor, when they have dealings with the *dynatoi,* but their possessions should be given back to the poor, nor [should anything be brought up] concerning the return of any costs [paid] or necessary improvements made by the *dynatoi,* because they have been discovered to transgress the aforementioned law and are indeed liable to be called to account. For when the aforesaid emperor, our great-grandfather Emperor Romanus the Elder, wrote and said: "From now I forbid the *dynatoi* to acquire property among lands in peasant villages," he meant that he forbade them forever and for eternity, and he did not give them [a prescription of] time as a method of assistance. . . .

2. Since we have found many [of our] subjects listed in [imperial] surveys recorded in chrysobulls,[10] and many such cases have been brought before our tribunal, we decree that those surveys which are adduced [as evidence] have no validity, nor shall those utilizing them derive any legal benefit from the ambiguity which may exist in these documents. For the surveys are not issued with imperial knowledge or assent but for the benefit of those receiving them. Moreover, the chief secretaries who draw up the chrysobulls are neither present nor do they observe when the [actual] measuring [of the property] or the notification [of the results] occurs. For this reason, as has been made clear, we wish that those surveys in which ambiguity exists be considered invalid and have no effect. But if such surveys happen to be among the archives of the imperial treasury or in some other [legally] substantiating documents, we command that they be heeded and obeyed.

---

[10]Manuscripts written in gold ink.

READING 5

Pope Leo I, On the Authority of St. Peter[11]

Pope Leo the Great (440–461), who won fame by facing down Attila the Hun and persuading him to turn back from Rome, was one of the earliest proponents of papal supremacy over the Church. He here uses the argument, to be advanced countless times by future popes, that St. Peter was singled out by Jesus Christ as his chief apostle. Originally named Simon, the apostle was renamed Peter (in Aramaic, "rock") by Jesus, who said, "Upon this rock I will build my Church." Peter was believed to be the first bishop of Rome—the first pope—and his bones are believed, to this day, to lie beneath the great papal basilica in Rome that bears his name. In this passage, Leo places the papacy in the tradition of the superiority of Peter over the other apostles.

Although we be found both weak and slothful in fulfilling the duties of our office, because we are hindered by the very frailty of our condition; yet worthily and piously rejoice over His dispensation, whereby, though He has delegated the care of His sheep to many shepherds, yet He has not abandoned the guardianship of His flock. And the strength of the foundation, on which the whole superstructure of the Church is raised, is not weakened by the weight of the temple that rests upon it.

The dispensation of Truth therefore abides, and the blessed Peter has not abandoned the helm of the Church. For he was ordained before the rest in a special way that, from his being called the "rock" (i.e., "Peter"), from his being pronounced the foundation, from his being constituted the doorkeeper of the kingdom of heaven, from his being set as the judge to bind and loose, from all these mystical titles we might know the nature of his association with Christ. And still today he performs what is entrusted to him, and carries out every part of his duty and charge in Him and with Him, through whom he has been glorified. And so if anything is won from the mercy of God by our daily prayers, it is of His work and merits whose power lives and whose authority prevails in His see.

[11]From *The Sermons of Leo the Great*, tr. C. L. Feltoe, in *A Select Library of Nicene and Post-Nicene Fathers of the Christian Church*, vol. XII; New York, Charles Scribner's Sons, 1895, p. 117.

READING 6

Pope Gelasius I, On Priestly and Royal Power[12]

In 494 Pope Gelasius I (492–496) set forth, in this letter to the East Roman emperor, the classic papal argument on the superiority of priestly to royal power—the so-called doctrine of the two swords. Gelasius's words would be repeated by popes and other churchmen throughout the Middle Ages.

Two there are, august emperor, by which this world is chiefly ruled, the sacred authority [*auctoritas*] of the priesthood and the royal power [*potestas*]. Of these the responsibility of the priests is more weighty in so far as they will answer for the kings of men themselves at the divine judgment. You know, most clement son, that, although you take precedence over all mankind in dignity, nevertheless you piously bow the neck to those who have charge of divine affairs and seek from them the means of your salvation, and hence you realize that, in the order of religion, in matters concerning the reception and right administration of the heavenly sacraments, you ought to submit yourself rather than rule, and that in these matters you should depend on their judgment rather than seek to bend them to your will. For if the bishops themselves, recognizing that the imperial office was conferred on you by divine disposition, obey your laws so far as the sphere of public order is concerned lest they seem to obstruct your decrees in mundane matters, with what zeal, I ask you, ought you obey those who have been charged with administering the sacred mysteries? Moreover, just as no light risk attends pontiffs who keep silent in matters concerning the service of God, so too no little danger threatens those who show scorn—which God forbid—when they ought to obey. And if the hearts of the faithful should be submitted to all priests in general who rightly administer divine things, how much more should assent be given to the bishop of that see which the Most High wished to be pre-eminent over all priests, and which the devotion of the whole church has honored ever since. As your piety is certainly well aware, no one can ever raise himself by purely human means to the privilege and place of him whom the voice of Christ has set before all, whom the Church has always venerated and held in devotion as its primate. The things which are established by divine judgment can be assailed by human presumption; they cannot be overthrown by anyone's power.

---

[12]From Pope Gelasius' letter to Emperor Anastasius, in *The Crisis of Church and State, 1050–1300*, ed. Brian Tierney; Englewood Cliffs, N.J., Prentice Hall, 1964, pp. 13–14. Reprinted by permission.

READING 7

Boethius, The Consolation of Philosophy[13]

Anicius Manlius Severinus Boethius (c. 480–525) was a Roman statesman, a Neo-Platonic philosopher, and perhaps a Christian martyr. Boethius was well versed in Greek and the philosophy of Plato and Aristotle and attempted to translate and comment on their works. Late in Theodoric's reign, Boethius, who had become a secretary to the king, was accused of treason, imprisoned in Pavia, sentenced without trial, and executed (c. 525). However much ambiguity surrounds the charge, it is clear that his imprisonment and impending death caused Boethius to seek answers to the most pressing philosophical and theological questions of the time. This search resulted in a dialogue between himself and Lady Philosophy as revealed in his masterwork, *The Consolation of Philosophy*. Alternating between verse and prose, the *Consolation* is a Platonic argument for the existence of a highest "Good," which is synonymous with both happiness and divinity. Boethius also allows humanity free will, but in a way that is congruous with divine order and prescience. Boethius' Platonism and classical style caused *The Consolation of Philosophy* to be one of the most widely read works of the Middle Ages.

The night was put to flight the darkness Bed,
And to my eyes their former strength returned:
Like when the wild west wind accumulates
Black clouds and stormy darkness fills the sky:
The sun lies hid before the hour the stars
Should shine, and night envelops all the earth:
But should the North wind forth from his Thracian cave
Lash at the darkness and loose the prisoner day,
Out shines the sun with sudden fight suffused
And dazzles with its rays the blinking eye.

In the same way, the clouds of my grief dissolved and I drank in the light. With my thoughts recollected I turned to examine the face of my physician. I turned my eyes and fixed my gaze upon her, and I saw that it was my nurse in whose house I had been cared for since my youth—Philosophy. I asked her why she had come down from the heights of heaven to my lonely place of banishment.

---

[13]Boethius, *The Consolation of Philosophy*, tr. W. V. Cooper; London, J. M. Dent, 1902. The Temple Classics.

"Is it to suffer false accusation along with me?" I asked.

"Why, my child," she replied, "should I desert you? Why should I not share your labor and the burden you have been saddled with because of the hatred of my name? Should I be frightened by being accused? Or cower in fear as if it were something unprecedented? This is hardly the first time wisdom has been threatened with danger by the forces of evil."

"You say you are eager to hear more. You would be more than eager if you knew the destination I am trying to bring you to."

I asked what it was and she told me that it was true happiness.

"Your mind dreams of it," She said, "but your sight is clouded by shadows of happiness and cannot see reality."

I begged her to lead on and show me the nature of true happiness without delay.

She stood gazing at the ground for a while, as if she had retreated into the recesses of thought, and then began to speak again.

"In all the care with which they toil at countless enterprises, mortal men travel by different paths, though all are striving to reach one and the same goal, namely, happiness, which is a good which once obtained leaves nothing more to be desired. It is the perfection of all good things and contains in itself all that is good; and if anything were missing from it, it couldn't be perfect, because something would remain outside it, which could still be wished for. It is clear, therefore, that happiness is a state made perfect by the presence of everything that is good, a state, which, as we said, all mortal men are striving to reach though by different paths. For the desire for true good is planted by nature in the minds of men, only error leads them astray towards false good."

[Lady Philosophy then said,] "As to where it is to be found, then, you should think as follows. It is the universal understanding of the human mind that God, the author of all things, is good. Since nothing can be conceived better than God, everyone agrees that that which has no superior is good. Reason shows that God is so good that we are convinced that His goodness is perfect. Otherwise, He couldn't be the author of creation. There would have to be something else possessing perfect goodness over and above God, which would seem to be superior to Him and of greater antiquity. For all perfect things are obviously superior to those that are imperfect. Therefore, to avoid an unending argument, it must be admitted that the supreme God is to the highest degree filled with supreme and perfect goodness. But we have agreed that perfect good is true happiness; so that it follows that true happiness is to be found in the supreme God." Then, as if she were starting a fresh argument, she spoke as follows.

"The generation of all things, the whole progress of things subject to change and whatever moves in any way, receive their causes, their due order and their form from the unchanging mind of God. In the high citadel of its oneness, the mind of God has set up a plan for the multitude of events. When this plan is thought of as in the purity of God's understanding, it is called Providence, and when it is thought of with reference to all things, whose motion and order it controls, it is called by the name the ancients gave it, Fate. If anyone will examine their meaning, it will soon be clear to him that these two aspects are different. Providence is the divine reason itself. It is set at the head of all things and disposes all things. Fate, on the other hand, is the planned order inherent in things subject to change through the medium of which Providence binds everything in its own allotted place. Providence includes all things at the same time, however diverse or infinite, while Fate controls the motion of different individual things in different places and in different times. So this unfolding of the plan in time when brought together as a unified whole in the foresight of God's mind is Providence; and the same unified whole when dissolved and unfolded in the course of time is Fate."

"They are different, but the one depends on the other. The order of Fate is derived from the simplicity of Providence. A craftsman anticipates in his mind the plan of the thing he is going to make, and then sets in motion the execution of the work and carries out in time the construction of what he has seen all at one moment present to his mind's eye. In the same way God in his Providence constructs a single fixed plan of all that is to happen, while it is by means of Fate that all that He has planned is realized in its many individual details in the course of time. So, whether the work of Fate is done with the help of divine spirits of Providence, or whether the chain of Fate is woven by the soul of the universe, or by the obedience of all nature, by the celestial motions of the stars, or by the power of the angels, by the various skills of other spirits, or by some of these, or by all of them, one thing is certainly clear: the simple and unchanging plan of events is Providence, and Fate is the ever-changing web, the disposition in and through time of all the events which God has planned in His simplicity."

"Everything, therefore, which comes under Fate, is also subject to Providence, to which Fate itself is subject, but certain things which come under Providence are above the chain of Fate. These are things which rise above the order of change ruled over by Fate in virtue of the stability of their position close to the supreme Godhead. Imagine a set of revolving concentric circles. The inmost one comes closest to the simplicity of the center, while forming itself a kind of center for those set outside it to revolve round. The circle furthest out rotates through a wider orbit and the greater its distance from the indivisible center point, the greater the space it spreads through. Anything that joins itself to the middle circle is brought close to simplicity, and no longer spreads out widely. In the same way whatever moves any distance from the primary intelligence becomes enmeshed in ever stronger chains of Fate, and everything is the freer from Fate the closer it seeks the center of things. And if it cleaves to the steadfast mind of God, it is free from movement and so escapes the necessity imposed by Fate. The relationship between the ever-changing course of Fate and the stable simplicity of Providence is like that between reasoning and understanding, between that which is coming into being and that which is, between time and eternity, or between the moving circle and the still point in the middle."

"The course of Fate moves the sky and the stars, governs the relationship between the elements and transforms them through reciprocal variations; it renews
all things as they come to birth and die away by like generations of offspring
and seed. It holds sway, too, over the acts and fortunes of men through the indis-
soluble chain of causes; and since it takes its origins from unchanging Providence, it follows that these causes, too, are unchanging. For the best way of con-
trolling the universe is if the simplicity immanent in the divine mind produces
an unchanging order of causes to govern by its own incommutability everything
that is subject to change, and which will otherwise fluctuate at random."

"It is because you men are in no position to contemplate this order that
everything seems confused and upset. But it is no less true that everything has
its own position which directs it towards the good and so governs it. There is
nothing that can happen because of evil or because engineered by the wicked
themselves, and they, as we have most amply demonstrated, are deflected from
their search for the good by mistake and error, while the order which issues
from the supreme good at the center of the universe cannot deflect anyone from
his beginning."

READING 8

St. Benedict, The Rule[14]

The Rule of St. Benedict (c. 480–544), based in part on earlier models,
spread throughout Western Christendom to govern the lives of countless
monks and nuns of the Middle Ages and beyond. The excerpts that follow
stress two fundamental elements in Benedictine monasticism: humility and
poverty. This is one of the key texts in the cultural and intellectual history
of the West.

PROLOGUE

Hear, my son, the precept of your master, and incline the ear of your heart, willingly receive and faithfully fulfill the admonition of your loving Father, that you
may return by the labor of obedience to Him from Whom you had departed
through the sloth of disobedience. Therefore, my little speech is now addressed
to you—whoever you are—that, renouncing your own will, you take up the
strong and bright weapons of obedience to fight for the Lord Christ, our true

---

[14]From *Patrologiae Cursis Completus,* series Latina, vol. 66, ed. J. P. Migne; Paris, 1844,
columns 215–218, 371–376, 551–552, 839–840; tr. Marc Anthony Meyer.

King. In the first place, whatever good work you begin to do, beg Him with most earnest prayer to perfect it; that He Who has now vouchsafed to count us in the number of His sons may not be grieved at any time by our evil deeds. For we must always serve Him with the good things He has given us, that not only may He never, as an angry father, disinherit His children, but may never, as an irate lord, incensed by our sins, deliver us to everlasting punishment, as most wicked servants who would not follow Him to glory.

Therefore, we are founding a school of the Lord's service, in which institution we hope will be ordered nothing harsh or nothing rigorous. But if anything is somewhat strictly laid down, according to the dictates of equity, for the amendment of vices or the preservation of charity, do not on account of this flee in dismay from the road of salvation, whose beginning cannot but be straight. But as we go forward in our life and faith, we will, with hearts enlarged and with unspeakable sweetness of love, run in the way of God's commandments; so that never departing from His guidance, but persevering in His teaching in the monastery until death, we may by patience share in the sufferings of Christ, that we may deserve to be consorts of His kingdom.

CHAPTER 4: INSTRUMENTS OF GOOD WORKS

1. In the first place, to love the Lord God with the whole heart, the whole soul, the whole strength.
2. Then, one's neighbor as one's self.
3. Then, not to kill.
4. Not to commit adultery.
5. Not to steal.
6. Not to covet.
7. Not to bear false witness.
8. To honor all men.
9. And what one would not have done to himself, not to do to another.
10. To deny one's self in order to follow Christ.
11. To chastise the body.
12. Not to seek after pleasures.
13. To love fasting.
14. To relieve the poor.
15. To clothe the naked.
16. To visit the sick.
17. To bury the dead.
18. To help in trouble.
19. To console the sorrowing.
20. To hold one's self separate from worldly ways.
21. To prefer nothing to the love of Christ.
22. Not to give way to anger.

23. Not to foster a desire for revenge.
24. Not to entertain deceit in the heart.
25. Not to make a false peace.
26. Not to forsake charity.
27. Not to swear, lest perchance one swear falsely.
28. To speak the truth with heart and tongue.
29. Not to return evil for evil.
30. To do no injury, yea, even patiently to bear the injury done us.
31. To love one's enemies.
32. Not to curse them that curse us, but rather to bless them.
33. To bear persecution for justice sake.
34. Not to be proud.
35. Not to be given to wine.
36. Not to be a great eater.
37. Not to be drowsy.
38. Not to be slothful.
39. Not to be a mutterer.
40. Not to be a detractor.
41. To put one's trust in God.
42. To attribute what good one sees in himself, not to self, but to God.
43. But as to any evil in himself, let him be convinced that it is his own and charge it to himself.
44. To fear the day of judgment.
45. To be in dread of hell.
46. To desire eternal life with all spiritual longing.
47. To keep death before one's eyes daily.
48. To keep a constant watch over the actions of our life.
49. To hold as certain that God sees us everywhere.
50. To dash at once against Christ the evil thoughts that rise in one's heart.
51. And to disclose them to our spiritual father.
52. To guard one's tongue against bad and wicked speech.
53. Not to love much speaking.
54. Not to speak useless words and such as provoke laughter.
55. Not to love much or boisterous laughter.
56. To listen willingly to holy reading.
57. To apply one's self often to prayer.
58. To confess one's past sins to God daily in prayer with sighs and tears, and to amend them for the future.
59. Not to fulfill the desires of the flesh.
60. To hate one's own will.
61. To obey the commands of the abbot in all things, even though he himself which Heaven forbid, act otherwise, mindful of that precept of the Lord: "What they say, do ye; what they do, do ye not".

62. Not to desire to be called holy before one is; but to be holy first, that one may be truly so called.

63. To fulfill daily the commandments of God by works.

64. To love chastity.

65. To hate no one.

66. Not to be jealous; not to entertain envy.

67. Not to love strife.

68. Not to love pride.

69. To honor the aged.

70. To love the younger.

71. To pray for one's enemies in the love of Christ.

72. To make peace with an adversary before the setting of the sun.

73. And never to despair of God's mercy.

Behold, these are the instruments of the spiritual art, which, if they have been applied without ceasing day and night and approved on judgment day, will merit for us from the Lord that reward which He hath promised.

CHAPTER 5: OF OBEDIENCE

The first degree of humility is obedience without delay. This becomes those who, on account of the holy subjection that they have promised, or of the fear of hell, or the glory of life everlasting, hold nothing dearer than Christ. As soon as anything has been commanded by the superior they permit no delay in the execution, as if the matter had been commanded by God Himself.

Such as these, therefore, instantly quitting their own work and giving up their own will, with hands disengaged, and leaving unfinished what they were doing, follow up, with the ready step of obedience, the work of command with deeds; and thus, as if in the same moment, both matters—the master's command and the disciple's finished work—are, in the swiftness of the fear of God, speedily finished together, whereunto the desire of advancing to eternal life urge them.

This obedience, however, will be acceptable to God and agreeable to men then only, if what is commanded is done without hesitation, delay, half-heartedness, grumbling or complaint, because the obedience which is rendered to superiors is rendered to God.

CHAPTER 6: OF SILENCE

Let us do what the Prophet says: "I said, I will take heed of my ways, that I sin not with my tongue: I have set a guard to my mouth, I was dumb, and was humbled, and kept silence even from good things" [Psalms 38(39):2–3]. Here the prophet shows that, if at times we ought to refrain from useful speech for the sake of silence, how much more ought we to abstain from evil words on account of the punishment due to sin.

Therefore, because of the importance of silence, let permission to speak be seldom given to perfect disciples even for good and holy and edifying discourse. For it belongs to the master to speak and teach; it becomes the disciple to be silent and to listen. If, therefore, anything must be asked of the superior, let it be asked with all humility and respectful submission. But coarse jests, and idle words or speech provoking laughter, we condemn everywhere to eternal exclusion; and for such speech we do not permit the disciple to open his lips.

CHAPTER 7: OF HUMILITY

The Holy Scripture cries out to us, brothers, saying: "Everyone who exalts himself will be humbled, and he who humbles himself shall be exalted." Hence, brothers, if we wish to arrive at the highest point of humility and quickly reach the heavenly exaltation to which we can only ascend by the humility of this present life, we must by our ever-ascending actions erect such a ladder as that which Jacob beheld in his dream, by which the angels appeared to him descending and ascending [Genesis 28]. This descent and ascent signify nothing else but that we descend by exaltation and ascend by humility. And the ladder thus erected is our life in the world which, if the heart is humble, is lifted up by the Lord to heaven. The sides of the same ladder we understand to be our body and soul, in which the call of God has placed various degrees of humility or discipline, which we must ascend.

The first degree of humility, then, is that a man must always keep the fear of God before his eyes [and] avoid all forgetfulness; and that he must remember all that God has commanded and that those who despise God will be consumed in hell for their sins; and that he must consider that life everlasting is prepared for those who fear Him. And keeping himself at all times from sin and vice, whether of the thoughts, the tongue, the eyes, the hands, the feet, of his own will, let him quickly hasten to cut off the desires of the flesh. Let him consider that he is always seen from heaven by God, and that his actions are everywhere seen by the eye of the Divine Majesty and are "every hour reported to Him by His angels."

The second degree of humility is that a man should not love his own will, nor delight in gratifying his own desires; but should carry out in his own deeds that saying of the Lord: "I came not to do my own will, but the will of Him who sent me."

The third degree of humility is that for the love of God a man should surrender himself in all obedience to his superior.

The fourth degree of humility is that if in this very obedience hard and contrary things, or even injuries, are done to him, he should embrace them patiently with silent consciousness, and not grow weary or submit.

The fifth degree of humility is to hide from one's abbot none of the evil thoughts that beset one's heart, nor the sins committed in secret, but humbly confess them.

The sixth degree of humility is for a monk to be contented with the vilest and worst of everything and in all that is enjoined him to esteem himself a bad and worthless laborer.

The seventh degree of humility is that he should not only call himself with his tongue lower and viler than all else, but also believe himself with intimate affection of the heart to be so, humbling himself.

The eighth degree of humility is for a monk to do nothing except what is authorized by the common rule of the monastery or by the example of his seniors.

The ninth degree of humility is that a monk should refrain his tongue from speaking, keeping silence until a question is asked him.

The tenth degree of humility is that he should not be easily or quickly moved to laughter, because it is written: "The fool lifts up his voice in laughter."

The eleventh degree of humility is that when a monk speaks he should do so gently and without laughter, humbly and with gravity, or with few words and reasonable speech.

The twelfth degree of humility is that a monk, not only in his heart but also in his very body, should always show his humility to all who see him, that is, in work, in the oratory, in the monastery, in the garden, on the road, in the field, or wherever he may be, whether sitting, walking or standing, with head always bent down, and eyes fixed on the earth; that he always thinks of the guilt of his sins and imagines himself already present before the terrible judgment of God.

Therefore, having ascended all these degrees of humility, the monk will presently arrive at the love of God which, being perfect, casts out fear; whereby he will begin to keep, without labor, and as it were naturally and by custom, all those precepts which he had once observed only out of fear; no longer through dread of hell, but for the love of Christ, and of a good habit and a delight in virtue, which God will deem to make manifest by the Holy Spirit in His laborer, now cleansed from sin and vice.

CHAPTER 33: IF MONKS SHOULD HAVE ANYTHING OF THEIR OWN

Above all let the vice of private ownership be cut off from the monastery by the roots. Let no one presume to give or receive anything without leave of the abbot, or to keep anything as their own—either book or writing tablet or pen or anything whatsoever—since they are permitted to have neither body nor will in their own power. But let them hope to receive all necessities from the abbot of the monastery; nor let them keep anything which the abbot has not given or permitted. Let all things be common to all, as it is written; nor let anyone say or assume that anything is his own. But if anyone shall be found to indulge in this most horrible vice, and after one or two admonitions he does not make amends, let him be subjected to correction.

CHAPTER 48: OF DAILY WORK

Idleness is the enemy of the soul; and therefore the brothers ought to be employed in manual labor at certain times, at others, in devout reading. Hence, we believe that the time for each will be properly ordered by the following arrangement; namely, that from Easter till the calends of October, they go out in the morning from the first till about the fourth hour, to do the necessary work, but that from the fourth till about the sixth hour they devote to reading. After the sixth hour, however, when they have risen from table, let them rest in their beds in complete silence; or if, perhaps, anyone desires to read for himself, let him so read that he doth not disturb others. Let Nones be said somewhat earlier, about the middle of the eighth hour; and then let them work again at what is necessary until Vespers. If, however, the needs of the place, or poverty should require that they do the work of gathering the harvest themselves, let them not be downcast, for then are they monks in truth, if they live by the work of their hands, as did also our forefathers and the Apostles. However, on account of the faint-hearted let all things be done with moderation.

From the calends of October till the beginning of Lent,[15] let them apply themselves to reading until the second hour complete. At the second hour let Tierce be said, and then let all be employed in the work that has been assigned to them till the ninth hour. When, however, the first signal for the hour of None hath been given, let each one leave off from work and be ready when the second signal shall strike. But after their repast let them devote themselves to reading or the psalms.

During the Lenten season let them be employed in reading from morning until the third hour, and till the tenth hour let them do the work that is imposed on them. During these days of Lent let all receive books from the library, and let them read them through in order. These books are to be given out at the beginning of the Lenten season.

Above all, let one or two of the seniors be appointed to go about the monastery during the time that the brethren devote to reading and take notice, lest perhaps a slothful brother be found who gives himself up to idleness or vain talk, and doth not attend to his reading, and is unprofitable, not only to himself, but disturbs also others. If such a one be found which God forbid, let him be punished once and again. If he doth not amend, let him come under the correction of the Rule in such a way that others may fear. And let not brother join brother at undue times.

On Sunday also let all devote themselves to reading, except those who are appointed to the various functions. But if anyone should be so careless and slothful that he will not or cannot meditate or read, let some work be given him to do, that he may not be idle.

---

[15]Roughly, mid-fall to mid-spring.

Let such work or charge be given to the weak and the sickly brothers, that they are neither idle, nor so wearied with the strain of work that they are driven away. Their weakness must be taken into account by the abbot.

CHAPTER 73: THE WHOLE OBSERVANCE OF RIGHTEOUSNESS IS NOT LAID DOWN IN THIS RULE

Now, we have written this Rule that, observing it in monasteries, we may show that we have acquired at least some moral righteousness, or a beginning of the monastic life.

Conversely, he that hastens on to the perfection of the religious life, hath at hand the teachings of the holy Fathers, the observance of which leads a man to the height of perfection. For what page or what utterance of the divinely inspired books of the Old and the New Testament is not a most exact rule of human life? Or, what book of the holy Catholic Fathers doth not loudly proclaim how we may go straight to our Creator? So, too, the collations of the Fathers, and their institutes and lives, and the rule of our holy Father, Basil—what are they but the monuments of the virtues of exemplary and obedient monks? But for us slothful, unedifying, and negligent monks they are a source for shame and confusion.

You, therefore, who hastens to the heavenly home, with the help of Christ fulfill this least rule written for a beginning; and then you shall with God's help attain at last to the greater heights of knowledge and virtue which we have mentioned above.

READING 9

Letters of Pope Gregory the Great[16]

St. Gregory I (called Gregory the Great) (590–604) was one of the most learned popes of the early Middle Ages and perhaps the ablest. His letter to John, bishop of Ravenna (letter A), better known as *The Book of Pastoral Care,* was written shortly after his accession to the papacy. A wise and authoritative guide to the responsibilities of bishops, it achieved tremendous popularity across Western Christendom. Gregory's letter to Emperor Maurice (letter B), echoing Pope Gelasius' two-swords doctrine, discloses the precarious semi-independent position of the papacy in central Italy. Rome and the lands around it were under Byzantine rule in Gregory's time as a result of Justinian's reconquest (535–555), but imperial authority

[16]From *Letters of Pope Gregory the Great,* tr. James Barmby, in *A Select Library of Nicene and Post-Nicene Fathers of the Christian Church,* vol. XII; New York, Charles Scribner's Sons, 1895, pp. 1, 7, 24–25, 71,175–177, 202–203, 205–206.

was being undermined by the attacks of Lombard warriors. Despite the unsettled conditions in Rome, Gregory worked effectively toward the reform and expansion of Western Christendom. The monks he sent to pagan England in 596 (letters C–D) succeeded in converting the southern kingdom of Kent, thereby launching a missionary process that would eventually bring all of England into the Christian fold.

A.   THE BOOK OF PASTORAL CARE

With kind and humble intent you reprove me, dearest brother, for having wished by hiding myself to flee from the burdens of pastoral care; as to which, lest to some they should appear light, I express with my pen in the book before you all my own estimate of their heaviness, in order both that he who is free from them may not unwarily seek them, and that he who has freely sought them may tremble for having gotten them.

What manner of man ought to come to rule? A man ought by all means be drawn to be an example of good living who already lives spiritually, dying to all passions of the flesh; who disregards worldly prosperity; who is afraid of no adversity; who desires only inward wealth; whose intention the body, in good accord with it, thwarts not at all by its frailness, nor the spirit greatly by its disdain—one who is not led to covet the things of others but gives freely of his own; who through the bowels of compassion is quickly moved to pardon, yet is never bent down from the fortress of rectitude by pardoning more than is necessary; who perpetrates no unlawful deeds, yet deplores those perpetrated by others as though they were his own; who out of affection of the heart sympathizes with another's infirmity and so rejoices in the good of his neighbor as though it were his own advantage; who so insinuates himself as an example to others in all he does that among them he has nothing, at any rate of his own past deeds, to blush for; who studies so to live that he may be able to water even dry hearts with the streams of sacred learning; who has already by the use and trial of prayer that he can obtain what he has requested from the Lord, having already been told, as it were, through the voice of experience, "While you are still speaking, I will say, here am I." For if by chance anyone should come to us asking us to intercede for him with some great man, who was incensed against him, but unknown to us, we should at once reply, we cannot go to intercede for you since we have no familiar acquaintance with that man. If, then, a man blushes to become an intercessor with another man on whom he has no claim, with what idea can anyone grasp the duty of intercession with God for the people, who does not know himself to be in favor with Him through the merit of His own life? And how can he ask pardon of Him for others while ignorant whether towards himself He is appeased? And in this matter there is still another thing to be more anxiously feared; namely, lest one who is supposed to be competent to appease wrath should himself provoke it on account of guilt of his own. For we all know well that when one who is in disfavor is sent to intercede with an incensed person the mind of the latter is provoked to greater severity. Wherefore, let one who is still tied and bound with earthly desires beware lest by more grievously incensing the strict Judge, while he delights himself in his place of honor, he becomes the cause of ruin to his subordinates.

How the ruler, while living well, ought to teach and admonish those who are placed under him: Since, then, we have shown what manner of man the pastor ought to be, let us now set forth after what manner he should teach. For as long before us Gregory Nazianzen[17] of reverend memory has taught, one and the same exhortation does not suit all, since all people are not bound together by similarity of character. For the things that profit some often hurt others; seeing that also for the most part herbs which nourish some animals are fatal to others; and the gentle hissing that quiets horses incites puppies; and the medicine which abates one disease aggravates another; and the bread which invigorates the life of the strong kills little children. Therefore, according to the quality of the listeners the discourse ought to be fashioned by teachers to suit all and each for their different needs, and yet never deviate from the art of common edification. For what are the intent minds of listeners but, so to speak, a kind of tight tension of strings in a harp, which the skillful player strikes variously that he may produce a tune not at variance with itself? And for this reason the strings render back a consonant modulation, that they are struck indeed with one quill, but not with one kind of stroke. Whence every teacher also, that he may edify all in the one virtue of charity, ought to touch the hearts of his listeners out of one doctrine, but not with one and the same exhortation. . . . Differently, then, men and women are to be admonished because on the former heavier injunctions and on the latter lighter ones are to be laid so that [men] may be exercised by great things, but women overwhelmingly converted by light ones. Differently to be admonished are young and old men because for the most part severity of admonition directs the former to improvement, while kind remonstrance disposes the latter to better deeds.

How the preacher, when he has accomplished his task, should return to himself lest either his life or his preaching puff him up. But since often, when preaching is abundantly poured forth in fitting ways, the mind of the preacher is elevated in itself by a hidden delight in self-display, great care is necessary that he may gnaw himself with the laceration of fear, lest he who recalls the diseases of others to health by remedies should himself swell through neglect of his own;

---

[17]Gregory of Nazianzus (d. 389) is one of the four great Greek doctors of the Church and is associated with the final defeat of the Arian heresy in the East. Gregory was made bishop of Constantinople in 380, but the difficulties he encountered forced him to resign within a few weeks and he ended his life in contemplation near Arianzus in Iona.

lest in helping others he deserts himself, lest in lifting up others he falls. For some the greatness of their virtue has often been the occasion of their perdition, causing them, while inordinately secure in confidence of strength, to die unexpectantly through negligence. For virtue strives with vice—the mind flatters itself with a certain delight in it—and it comes to pass that the soul of a well-intentioned man casts aside the fear of its circumspection and rests secure in self-confidence; and to it, now torpid, the cunning seducer enumerates all things that it has done well, and exalts it in swelling thoughts as though super-excellent beyond all beside it. Whence it is brought about that before the eyes of the just Judge the memory of virtue is a pitfall of the soul; because, in calling to mind what it has done well, while it lifts itself up in its own eyes, it falls before the Author of humility.

B.   TO THE EMPEROR MAURICE, c. 591–592

The piety of my lords in their most serene commands, while set on refuting me on certain matters, in sparing me have by no means spared me. For by the use therein of the word "simplicity" they politely call me silly. It is true indeed that in Holy Scripture, when simplicity is used in a good sense, it is often carefully associated with prudence and uprightness. . . .

Indeed if the captivity of my land were not increasing day by day, I would gladly pass over in silence contempt and ridicule of myself. But this does afflict me exceedingly, that from my bearing the charge of falsehood it ensues also that Italy is daily led captive under the yoke of the Lombards. And, while my representations are not believed, the strength of the enemy is increasing. This, however, I suggest to my most pious lord, that he would think anything that is bad of me, but with regards to the advantage of the Republic and the cause of the rescue of Italy, not easily lend his pious ears to anyone, but believe facts rather than words. Moreover, let our lord, in virtue of his earthly power, not too hastily disdain priests, but with excellent consideration, on account of Him Whose servants they are, so rule over them as also to pay the reverence that is due to them. For in Holy Scripture priests are sometimes called gods and sometimes angels, and even Moses said of him who is to be put upon his oath, "Bring him unto the gods"—that is "unto the priests." Why, then, should it be strange if your piety were to condescend to honor those to whom even God Himself in His word gives honor, calling them angels or gods? Ecclesiastical history also testifies that when accusations in writing against bishops have been given to the emperor Constantine of pious memory, he received the written accusations; but calling together the bishops who had been accused, he burnt before their eyes the documents he had received, saying, "You are gods, constituted by the true God. Go and settle your causes among yourselves, for it is not fit that we should judge gods." Yet in this sentence, my pious lord, he conferred more on himself by his humility than on them by the reverence paid to them. For before him there were pagan princes in the Republic who knew not the true God but worshipped gods of wood and stone; and yet they paid the greatest honor to their priests. What wonder then if a Christian emperor should condescend to honor the priests of the true God, when pagan princes, as we have already said, knew how to bestow honor on priests who served gods of wood and stone?

These things, then, I suggest to the piety of my lords, not in my behalf but in behalf of all priests. For I am a man who is a sinner. And since I offend against Almighty God incessantly every day, I surmise that there will be some amends for this at the tremendous judgment, that I am stricken incessantly every day by blows. And I believe that you appease the same Almighty God all more as you more severely afflict me who serve Him badly. For I had already received many blows, and when the commands of my lords came in addition, I found consolations that I was not hoping for. For if I can, I will briefly enumerate these blows.

First, the peace which, without any cost to the Republic, I had made with the Lombards who were in Tuscany was withdrawn from me. Then, the peace having been broken, the [imperial] soldiers were removed from the Roman city. And indeed some were slain by the enemy, but others were placed at Nami and Perugia, and Rome was left that Perugia might be held. But a still heavier blow was the arrival of Agilulph,[18] so that I saw with my own eyes Romans tied by the neck with ropes like dogs to be taken to Gaul sale. And, because we who were in the city under the protection of God caped his hand, a reason was then sought for making us look culpable particularly because corn ran short, which cannot by any means be kept long in large quantities in this city, as I have written more fully in another chapter. On my own account, I was in no way disturbed since I declare, my conscience bearing witness, that I was prepared to suffer any adversity whatever so long as I came out of all these things with the safety of my soul. But the glorious men, Gregory the prefect and Castorius the military commander, I have been distressed to a great degree, seeing that they did not neglect to do all that could be done and endured most severe toil in watching and guarding the city during the siege; and after all this were smitten by the indignation of my lord. As to them, I clearly understand that it is not the conduct but my person that goes against them. For having along with me I bored in trouble, they are alike troubled after labor.

Now as to the piety of my lord holding over me the formidable and terrible judgment of Almighty God, I ask you by the same Almighty God to this no more. . . . [And] this I say briefly, that, unworthy sinner as I am, I rely more on the mercy of Jesus when He comes than on the justice of your piety. And there are many things that men are ignorant of with regards to this judgment; for

---

[18]Agilulph of Turin succeeded the great Lombard king Authari c. 591 and also took the dead king's Catholic wife, Theodolinda of Bavaria, as his queen. Many of Gregory's letters are addressed to the powerful Theodolinda, who was herself partly responsible for the conversion of the Lombards to Catholicism.

perhaps He will blame what you praise and praise what you blame. Therefore, among all these uncertainties I return to tears only, praying that the same Almighty God may both direct our most pious lord with His hand and in that terrible judgment find him free of all defaults. And may He make so to please men, if need be, as not to offend His eternal grace.

C.   TO THE MISSIONARIES GOING TO ENGLAND, AUGUST 596

Gregory, servant of the servants of God, to the servants of our Lord Jesus Christ.

Since it had been better not to have begun what is good than to return from it when begun, you must, most beloved sons, fulfill the good work which you have started with the help of the Lord. Let, then, neither the toil of the journey nor the tongues of evil-speaking men deter you; but with all constancy and fervor go on with what under God's guidance you have begun, knowing that great toil is followed by the glory of an eternal reward. Humbly obey all things your leader Augustine who is returning to you [and] whom we have appointed your abbot, knowing that whatever may be fulfilled in you through his admonition will in all ways profit your souls. May Almighty God protect you with his grace, and grant to me to see the fruit of your work in the eternal country, that I may be found together with you in the joy of the reward, for in truth I desire to labor. God keep you safe, most beloved sons.

D.   TO QUEEN BRUNECHILD, 596

Gregory to Brunechild, etc.

The Christianity of your excellence had long been so truly known to us that we do not in the least doubt your goodness but rather hold it to be in all ways certain that you will devoutly and zealously concur with us in the case of faith and supply most abundantly the succor of your religious sincerity. Being for this reason well assured and greeting you with paternal charity, we inform you that it has come to your knowledge how the nation of the English, by God's authority, is anxious to become Christian, but that the priests who are in their neighborhood have no pastoral solicitude with regards to them. And lest their souls should by chance perish in eternal damnation, it has been our care to send to them the bearer of these presents, Augustine, the servant of God, whose zeal and earnestness are well known to us, with other servants of God, that through them we might be able to learn their wishes, and as far as possible, you also striving with us, to take thought to their conversion. We have also charged them that for carrying out this design they should take with them preachers from the neighboring regions. Therefore, your excellency, habitually prone to good works [and] on account of our request as well as with regards to the fear of God, deign to hold him in all ways as commended to you and earnestly bestow on him the favor of your protection, and lend the aid of your patronage to his labor, and, that he may have the fullest fruit thereof, provide for his going secure under your protection to the above-mentioned nation of the English to the end that our God, who has adorned you in this world with good qualities well pleasing to Him, may cause you to give thanks here and in eternal rest with his saints.

READING 10

Eddius, The Synod of Whitby[19]

As Pope Gregory's monks and their successors spread Roman Christianity through England, they encountered rival missionaries from the Celtic monasteries of Ireland and southern Scotland. Celtic Christians, isolated from Rome and the Continent by the barbarian invasions, had developed distinctive customs and modes of organization: they used a different formula for calculating the date of Easter, they employed a different tonsure, and their church was organized around monasteries rather than bishoprics. Celtic and Roman-Benedictine missionaries had both been active in the conversion of the kingdom of Northumbria (northern England and southeastern Scotland). In 664, King Oswiu (or Oswy) of Northumbria summoned a council to meet at the Benedictine nunnery of Whitby to decide between the two forms of Christian practice. Although much of the argument at Whitby turned on the seemingly minor issue of the Easter date, far more was actually at stake. Northumbria had become the most powerful kingdom in England, and the decision at Whitby brought Northumbria out of the Celtic backwater into the papal-Benedictine mainstream. The champion of the papal cause at Whitby was the celebrated Benedictine missionary, Wilfrid of Hexham, better known as Wilfrid of Ripon. The account below was written by Eddius, one of his disciples and perhaps an eyewitness, shortly after Wilfrid's death.

On a certain occasion while Colman was bishop of York and metropolitan archbishop, during the reign of Oswiu and Alhfrith,[20] abbots, priests, and clerics of every rank gathered at Whitby Abbey in the presence of the most holy

---

[19]From Eddius, "The Life of St. Wilfrid of Hexham," in *Lives of the Saints,* tr. J. F. Webb; New York, Penguin Books, 1965, pp. 141–143.

[20]King Oswy and his son, King Alhfrith, ruled jointly for a time. Oswy controlled the entire kingdom of Northumbria, of which Deira, Alhfrith's area of jurisdiction, was a part. The young king died shortly after the synod of Whitby and his father survived another six years, dying in 670.

abbess Hilda, the two kings, and bishops Colman and Agilberht [of the West Saxons], to discuss the proper time for celebrating Easter: whether the practice of the British, Irish and the northern province of keeping it on the Sunday between the fourteenth and twenty-second day of the moon was correct or whether they ought to give way to the Roman plan for fixing it for the Sunday between the fifteenth and twenty-first days of the moon. Bishop Colman, as was proper, was given the first chance to state his case. He spoke with complete confidence, as follows: "Our fathers and theirs before them, clearly inspired by the Holy Spirit, as was Columba, stipulated that Easter Sunday should be celebrated on the fourteenth day of the moon if that day were a Sunday, following the example of St. John the Evangelist 'who leaned on the Lord's breast at supper,' the disciple whom Jesus loved. He celebrated Easter on the fourteenth day of the moon, as did his disciples, and Polycarp and his disciples, and as we do on their authority. Out of respect to our fathers we dare not change, nor do we have the least desire to do so. I have spoken for our party. Now let us hear your side of the question."

Agilberht, the foreign prelate, and his priest Agatho bade St. Wilfrid, priest and abbot [of Hexham], use his winning eloquence to express in his own words the case of the Roman Church and Apostolic See. His speech was, as usual, humble. "This question has already been admirably treated by a gathering of our most holy and learned fathers, three hundred and eighteen strong, at Nicaea, a city in Bithynia. Among other things they decided upon a lunar cycle recurring every nineteen years. This cycle gives no room for celebrating Easter on the fourteenth day of the moon. This is the rule followed by the Apostolic See and by nearly the whole world. At the end of the decrees of the fathers of Nicaea come these words: 'Let him who condemns any one of these decrees be anathema.'"

At the end of Wilfrid's speech Oswiu asked them, with a smile on his face, "Tell me, which is greater in the Kingdom of Heaven, Columba or the apostle Peter?"

Then the whole synod with one voice and one accord cried: "The Lord Himself settled this question when He declared, 'Thou art Peter and upon this rock I will build my Church and the gates of hell shall not prevail against it. And I will give you the keys of the Kingdom of Heaven; and whatsoever thou shalt bind on earth shall be bound in Heaven and whatsoever thou shalt loose on earth shall be loosed in Heaven.'" To this the king added, showing his wisdom: "He is the keeper of the door and the keys. I will neither enter into strife and controversy with him, nor will I condone any who do. As long as I live shall abide by his every decision."

Bishop Colman was told that if, out of respect for his own country's customs, he should reject the Roman tonsure and method of calculating Easter he was to resign his see in favor of another and better candidate. This he did.

READING 11

Bede, Saint Hilda of Whitby[21]

Bede (c. 672–735) was an Anglo-Saxon Benedictine monk, esteemed primarily for his scriptural commentaries as well as his histories and saint's lives. Little is known of Bede's life, but what is known is found in the *Ecclesiastical History of the English People.* Bede entered the monastery Wearmouth and at Jarrow, Northumbria, England, when he was seven years old. He was made a priest at the canonical age of thirty. He spent his entire life in the vicinity of his monastery. *Bede's Ecclesiastical History* records the history of Britain from prehistoric times to the early eighth century. Bede's standards were set extremely high, and though there are miraculous and mystical events included, the sources he used were only those he considered the most venerable and reliable. One of the most memorable stories in the *Ecclesiastical History* relates the story of the powerful Abbess Hilda of Whitby and Caedmon, a simple shepherd who miraculously learned how to recite Old English poetry.

In the year of the incarnation of our Lord 680, the most religious servant of Christ, Hilda, abbess of the monastery called Whitby, after having performed many heavenly works on earth, passed from it to receive the rewards of the heavenly life, on the 17th of November, at the age of sixty six years; the first thirty three of which she spent living most nobly in the secular habit; and more nobly dedicated the remaining half to our Lord in a monastic life. For she was nobly born, being the daughter of Hereric, nephew to King Edwin, with which king she also embraced the faith and mysteries of Christ, at the preaching of Paulinus, the first bishop of the Northumbrians, of blessed memory, and preserved the same undefiled till she attained to the sight of him in heaven.

Resolving to quit her secular life, and to serve Him alone, Hilda withdrew into the province of the East Angles, for she was allied to the king; being desirous to pass over from thence into France, to forsake her native country and all she had, and so live a stranger for our Lord in the monastery of Cale, that she might with more ease attain to the eternal kingdom in heaven; because her sister Hereswitha, mother to Aldwulf, king of the East Angles, at that time living in the same monastery, under regular discipline, was waiting for her eternal reward. Being led by her example, she continued a whole year in the aforesaid province, with the design of going abroad; afterwards, Bishop Aidan being

[21]Source: L. C. Jane, *Bede's Ecclesiastical History of the English Nation,* vol. IV; London, J. M. Dent, 1910, pp. 23–24.

recalled home, he gave her the land of one family on the north side of the River Wear; where for a year she also led a monastic life, with very few companions.

After this she was made abbess in the monastery called Hartlepool, which monastery had been founded, not long before, by the religious servant of Christ, Heiu, who is said to have been the first woman that in the province of the Northumbrians took upon her the habit and life of a nun, being consecrated by Bishop Aidan; but she, soon after she had founded that monastery, went away to the city of Colchester, and there fixed her dwelling. Hilda, the servant of Christ, being set over that monastery, began immediately to reduce all things to a regular system, according as she had been instructed by learned men; for Bishop Aidan, and other religious men that knew her and loved her, frequently visited and diligently instructed her, because of her innate wisdom and inclination to the service of God.

When she had for some years governed this monastery, wholly intent upon establishing a regular life, it happened that she also undertook either to build or to arrange a monastery in the place called Whitby, which work she industriously performed; for she put this monastery under the same regular discipline as she had done the former; and taught there the strict observance of justice, piety, chastity, and other virtues, and particularly of peace and charity; so that, after the example of the primitive church, no person was there rich, and none poor, all being in common to all, and none having any property. Her prudence was so great, that not only indifferent persons, but even kings and princes, as occasion offered, asked and received her advice; she obliged those who were under her direction to attend so much to reading of the Holy Scriptures, and to exercise themselves so much in works of justice, that many might be there found fit for ecclesiastical duties, and to serve at the altar.

When she had governed this monastery many years, it pleased Him who has made such merciful provision for our salvation, to give her holy soul the trial of a long sickness, to the end that, according to the apostle's example, her virtue might be perfected in infirmity. Falling into a fever, she fell into a violent heat, and was afflicted with the same for six years continually; during all which time she never failed either to return thanks to her Maker, or publicly and privately to instruct the flock committed to her charge; for by her own example she admonished all persons to serve God dutifully in perfect health, and always to return thanks to Him in adversity, or bodily infirmity. In the seventh year of her sickness, the distemper turning inwards, she approached her last day, and about cock-crowing, having received the holy communion to further her on her way, and called together the servants of Christ that were within the same monastery, she admonished them to preserve evangelical peace among themselves, and with all others; and as she was making her speech, she joyfully saw death approaching, or if I may speak in the words of our Lord, passed from death to life.

That same night it pleased Almighty God, by a manifest vision, to make known her death in another monastery, at a distance from hers, which she had built that same year, and is called Hackness. There was in that monastery, a certain nun called Begu, who, having dedicated her virginity to God, had served Him upwards of thirty years in monastic conversation. This nun, being then in the dormitory of the sisters, on a sudden heard the well-known sound of a bell in the air, which used to awake and call them to prayers, when any one of them was taken out of this world, and opening her eyes, as she thought, she saw the top of the house open, and a strong light pour in from above; looking earnestly upon that light, she saw the soul of the aforesaid servant of God in that same light, attended and conducted to heaven by angels. Then awaking, and seeing the other sisters lying round about her, she perceived that what she had seen was either in a dream or a vision; and rising immediately in a great fright, she ran to the virgin who then presided in the monastery instead of the abbess, and whose name was Frigyth, and, with many tears and sighs, told her that the Abbess Hilda, mother of them all, had departed this life, and had in her sight ascended to eternal bliss, and to the company of the inhabitants of heaven, with a great light, and with angels conducting her. Frigyth having heard it, awoke all the sisters, and calling them to the church, admonished them to pray and sing psalms for her soul; which they did during the remainder of the night; and at break of day, the brothers came with news of her death, from the place where she had died. They answered that they knew it before, and then related how and when they had heard it, by which it appeared that her death had been revealed to them in a vision the very same hour that the others said she had died. Thus it was by Heaven happily ordained, that when some saw her departure out of this world, the others should be acquainted with her admittance into the spiritual life which is eternal. These monasteries are about thirteen miles distant from each other.

There was in this abbess's monastery a certain brother [Caedmon], particularly remarkable for the grace of God, who was wont to make pious and religious verses, so that whatever was interpreted to him out of Scripture, he soon after put the same into poetical expressions of much sweetness and humility, in English, which was his native language. By his verses the minds of many were often excited to despise the world, and to aspire to heaven. Others after him attempted, in the English nation, to compose religious poems, but none could ever compare with him, for he did not learn the art of poetry from men, but from God; for which reason he never could compose any trivial or vain poem, but only those which relate to religion suited his religious tongue; for having lived in a secular habit till he was well advanced in years, he had never learned anything of versifying; for which reason being sometimes at entertainments, when it was agreed for the sake of mirth that all present should sing in their turns, when he saw the instrument come towards him, he rose up from table and returned home.

Having done so at a certain time, and gone out of the house where the entertainment was, to the stable, where he had to take care of the horses that night, he there composed himself to rest at the proper time; a person appeared to him in his sleep, and saluting him by his name, said, "Caedmon, sing some song to me." He answered, "I cannot sing; for that was the reason why I left the entertainment, and retired to this place because I could not sing." The other who talked to him, replied, "However, you shall sing." "What shall I sing?" rejoined he. "Sing the beginning of created beings," said the other. Thereupon he presently began to sing verses to the praise of God, which he had never heard, the purport whereof was thus:

We are now to praise the Maker of the heavenly kingdom, the power of the Creator and his counsel, the deeds of the Father of glory. How He, being the eternal God, became the author of all miracles, who first, as almighty preserver of the human race, created heaven for the sons of men as the roof of the house, and next the earth.

This is the sense, but not the words in order as he sang them in his sleep; for verses, though never so well composed, cannot be literally translated out of one language [Old English] into another [Latin], without losing much of their beauty and loftiness. Awaking from his sleep, he remembered all that he had sung in his dream, and soon added much more to the same effect in verse worthy of the Deity.

In the morning he came to the steward, his superior, and having acquainted him with the gift he had received, was conducted to the abbess, by whom he was ordered, in the presence of many learned men, to tell his dream, and repeat the verses, that they might all give their judgment what it was, and whence his verse proceeded. They all concluded, that heavenly grace had been conferred on him by our Lord. They expounded to him a passage in holy writ, either historical, or doctrinal, ordering him, if he could, to put the same into verse. Having undertaken it, he went away, and returning the next morning, gave it to them composed in most excellent verse; whereupon the abbess, embracing the grace of God in the man, instructed him to quit the secular habit, and take upon him the monastic life; which being accordingly done, she associated him to the rest of the brethren in her monastery, and ordered that he should be taught the whole series of sacred history. Thus Caedmon keeping in mind all he heard, and as it were chewing the cud, converted the same into most harmonious verse; and sweetly repeating the same, made his masters in their turn his hearers. He sang the creation of the world, the origin of man, and all the history of Genesis, and made many verses on the departure of the children of Israel out of Egypt, and their entering into the land of promise, with many other histories from holy writ; the incarnation, passion, resurrection of our Lord, and his ascension into heaven; the coming of the Holy Ghost, and the preaching of the apostles, also the terror of future judgment, the horror of the pains of hell, and the delights of heaven; besides many more about the Divine benefits and judgments, by which he endeavored to turn away all men from the love of vice, and to excite in them the love of, and application to, good actions; for he was a very religious man, humbly submissive to regular discipline, but full of zeal against those who behaved themselves otherwise; for which reason he ended his life happily.

READING 12

The Qu'ran[22]

Islam was yet another of the world's great religions born in the deserts of southwest Eurasia. Muhammad (c. 571–632), the founder of Islam, preached the relatively simple message that devotees must submit to the will of Allah, the one and only Creator and merciful and benevolent god of Islam, and also recognize that Muhammad was a prophet of God. The Qu'ran, the central text of the Moslem religious canon, records the Prophet's utterances as they were dictated to him by the angel Gabriel. The text is divided into 114 chapters, varying in length and complexity; but regardless of the subject matter of a sura, or chapter, each one has essentially the same message—every person should submit to the will of Allah. Muhammad also makes plain that Allah is the God of Abraham, of the Old and New Testaments. He respects Jews and Christians as "People of the Book," but chides those among them who have rejected the teachings of God's last prophet.

NIGHT (SURA 92): IN THE NAME OF ALLAH, THE COMPASSIONATE, THE MERCIFUL

By the night, when it covers all things with darkness; by the day, when it shines forth; by him who has created the male and the female: verily your endeavor is different. Know whosoever is obedient, and fears God, and professes the truth of that faith which is most excellent; unto him will we facilitate the way to happiness: but whosoever shall be covetous, and shall be wholly taken up with this world, and shall deny the truth of that which is most excellent; unto him will we facilitate the way to misery; and his riches shall not profit him, when he shall fall headlong into hell. Verily unto us appertains the direction of mankind: and ours is the life to come and the present life. Wherefore I threaten you with fire which burns fiercely, which none shall enter to be burned except the most wretched; who shall have disbelieved, and turned back. But he who strictly bewares idolatry and rebellion, shall be removed far from the same; who gives his substance in alms, and by whom no benefit is bestowed on any, that it may be recompensed, but who bestows the same for the sake of his Lord, the most High: and hereafter he shall be well satisfied with his reward.

[22]*The Koran,* tr. G. Sale; London, Frederick Warne and Co., 1900. The translation has been slightly modernized.

THE PROOF (SURA 98): IN THE NAME OF ALLAH, THE COMPASSIONATE, THE MERCIFUL

The unbelievers among those to whom the scriptures were given, and among the idolaters, did not stagger, until the clear evidence had come unto them: an apostle from God, rehearsing unto them pure books or revelations; wherein are contained right discourses. Neither were they unto whom the scriptures were given divided among themselves, until after the clear evidence had come unto them. And they were commanded no other in the scriptures than to worship God, exhibiting unto him the pure religion, and being orthodox; and to be constant at prayer, and to give alms: and this is the right religion. Verily those who believe not, among those who have received the scriptures, and among the idolaters, shall be cast into the fire of hell, to remain therein for ever. These are the worst of creatures. But they who believe, and do good works; these are the best of creatures: their reward with their Lord shall be gardens of perpetual abode, through which rivers flow; they shall remain therein for ever. God will be well pleased in them; and they shall be well pleased in him. This is prepared for him who shall fear his Lord.

THE COW (SURA 2): IN THE NAME OF ALLAH, THE COMPASSIONATE, THE MERCIFUL

This book is not to be doubted; it is a direction to the pious who believe in the mysteries of faith, who observe the appointed times of prayer, and distribute alms out of what we have bestowed on them; and who believe in that revelation, which has been sent down unto you and unto the prophets before you, and have firm assurance in the life to come: these are directed by their Lord, and they shall prosper.

Surely those who believe, and those who Judaize, and the Christians, and Sabians, whoever believes in God, and the last day, and does that which is right, they shall have their reward with the Lord; there shall come no fear on them, neither shall they be grieved.

We formerly delivered the book of the law unto Moses, and caused apostles to succeed him, and gave evident miracles to Jesus the son of Mary, and strengthened him with the holy spirit. Do you therefore, whenever an apostle comes unto you with that which your souls desire not, proudly reject him, and accuse some of imposture, and slay others? The Jews say, Our hearts are uncircumcised: but God has cursed them with their infidelity, therefore few shall believe. And when a book came unto them from God, confirming the scriptures which were with them, although they had before prayed for assistance against those who believed not, yet when that came unto them which they knew to be from God, they would not believe therein: therefore the curse of God shall be on the infidels.

It is not the desire of the unbelievers, either among those unto whom the scriptures have been given, or among the idolaters, that any good should be sent down unto you from your Lord: but God will appropriate his mercy unto whom he pleases; for God is exceeding beneficent. Whatever verse we shall abrogate, or cause you to forget, we will bring a better than it, or one like unto it. Do you not know that God is almighty? Do you not know that unto God belongs the kingdom of heaven and earth? Neither have you any protector or helper except God.

Who will be adverse to the religion of Abraham, but he whose mind is infatuated? Surely we have chosen him in this world, and in that which is to come he shall be one of the righteous. When his Lord said unto him, Resign yourself unto me; he answered, I have resigned myself unto the Lord of all creatures. And Abraham bequeathed this religion to his children, and Jacob did the same, saying, My children, verily God has chosen this religion for you, therefore die not, unless you also be resigned.

They say, become Jews or Christians that you may be directed. Say, No, we follow the religion of Abraham the orthodox, who was no idolater. Say, we believe in God, and that which has been sent down unto us, and that which has been sent down unto Abraham, and Ismael, and Isaac, and Jacob, and the tribes, and that which was delivered unto Moses, and Jesus, and that which was delivered unto the prophets from their Lord: We make no distinction between any of them, and to God we are resigned. . . .

As we have sent unto you an apostle from among you, to rehearse our signs unto you, and to purify you, and to teach you the book of the Koran and wisdom, and to teach you the that which you knew not: therefore remember me, and I will remember you, and give thanks unto me, and be not believers. O true believers, beg assistance with patience and prayer, for God is with the patient. And say not of those who are slain in fight for the religion of God, that they are dead; yea, they are living.

It is not righteousness that you turn your faces in prayer towards the east and the west, but righteousness is of him who believes in God and the last day, and the angels and the scriptures, and the prophets; who gives money for God's sake unto his kindred, and unto orphans and the needy and the stranger, and to those who ask and for redemption of captives; who is constant at prayer, and gives alms; and of those who perform their covenant, when they have covenanted, and who behaved themselves patiently in adversity and hardships and in time of violence: these are they who are true, and these are they who fear God.

O true believers, a fast is ordained you, as it was ordained unto those before you, that you may fear God. A certain number of days shall you fast: but he among you who shall be sick, or on a journey, shall fast an equal number of other days. And those who can keep it, and do not, must redeem their neglect by maintaining of a poor man. And he who voluntarily deals better with the poor man than is obligated, this shall be better for him. But if you fast it will be better for you, if you knew it. The month of Ramadan shall you fast, in which the *Koran* was sent down from heaven, a direction unto men, and declarations of direction, and the distinction between good and evil. Therefore let those among you who shall be present in this month, fast the same month. . . .

And fight for the religion of God against those who fight against you, but transgress not by attacking them first, for God loves not the transgressor. And kill them wherever you find them, and turn them out of that whereof they have dispossessed you; for temptation to idolatry is more grievous than slaughter: yet fight not against them in the holy temple, until they attack you therein; but if they attack you, slay them there. This shall be the reward of the infidels. But if they desist, God is gracious and merciful. Fight therefore against them, until there be no temptation to idolatry, and the religion be God's: but if they desist, then let there be no hostility, except against the ungodly. . . .

Contribute out of your substance towards the defense of the religion of God, and throw not yourselves with your own hands into perdition; and do good, for God loves those who do good. Perform the pilgrimage of Mecca, and the visitation of God; and if you be besieged, send that offering which shall be the easiest; and shave not your heads, until your offering reaches the place of sacrifice. But whoever among you is sick, or is troubled with any distemper of the head, must redeem the shaving of his head by fasting, or alms, or some offering. . . .

Carefully observe the appointed prayers, and the middle prayer, and be assiduous of therein, with devotion towards God. But if you fear any danger, pray on foot or on horseback; and when you are safe, remember God, how he has taught you what as yet you knew not. . . .

God! there is no God but he; the living, the self-subsisting: neither slumber nor sleep seizes him; to him belongs whatsoever is in heaven, and on earth. Who is he that can intercede with him, but through his good pleasure? He knows that which is past, and that which is to come unto them, and they shall not comprehend anything of his knowledge, but so far as he pleases. His *Corsi* [throne] is extended over heaven and earth, and the preservation of both is no burden unto him. He is the high, the mighty.

Let there be no violence in religion. Now is right direction manifestly distinguished from deceit: whoever therefore shall deny *Tagut* [idols], and believe in God, he shall surely take hold on a strong handle, which shall not be broken; God is he who hears and sees. God is the patron of those who believe; he shall lead them out of darkness into light; but as to those who believe not, their patrons are Tagut; they shall lead them from the light into darkness; they shall be the companions of hell fire, and they shall thus remain therein forever. . . .

Whatever is in heaven and on earth is God's; and whether you manifest that which is in your minds, or conceal it, God will call you to account for it, and will forgive whom he pleases, and will punish whom he pleases; for God is almighty. The apostle believes in that which has been sent down unto him from his Lord, and the faithful also. Every one of them believes in God, and his angels, and his scriptures, and his apostles: we make no distinction at all between his apostles. And they say, we have heard, and do obey: we implore your mercy, O Lord, for unto you we must return. God will not force any soul beyond its capacity: it shall have the good which it gains, and it shall suffer the evil which it gains. O Lord, punish us not, if we forget, or act sinfully: O Lord, lay not on us a burden like that which you have laid on those who have been before us; neither make us, O Lord, to bear what we have not strength to bear, but be favorable unto us, and spare us, and be merciful unto us. You are our patron, help us therefore against the unbelieving nations.

WOMEN (SURA 4): IN THE NAME OF ALLAH, THE COMPASSIONATE, THE MERCIFUL

O men, fear your Lord, who has created you out of one man, and out of him created his wife, and from the two has multiplied many men and women: and fear God by whom you beseech one another; and respect women, who have borne you, for God is watching over you. And give the orphans when they come to age their substance; and render them not in exchange bad for good: and devour not their substance, by adding it to your substance; for this is a great sin. And if you fear that you shall not act with equity towards orphans of the female sex, take in marriage of such other women as please you, two, or three, or four, and not more. But if you fear that you cannot act equitably towards so many, marry one only, or the slaves that you shall have acquired. This will be easier, that you swerve not from righteousness. And give women their dowry freely; but if they voluntarily remit unto you any part of it, enjoy it with satisfaction and advantage.

If any of your women be guilty of whoredom, produce four witnesses from among you against them, and if they bear witness against them, imprison them in separate apartments until death release them, or God affords them a way to escape.

O true believers, it is not lawful for you to be heirs of women against their will, nor to hinder them from marrying others, that you may take away part of what you have given them in dowry; unless they have been guilty of a manifest crime: but converse kindly with them. And if you hate them, it may happen that you may hate a thing wherein God has placed much good. You are also forbidden to take to wife free women who are married, except those women whom your right hands shall possess as slaves. This is ordained you from God. Whatever is beside this, is allowed you; that you may with your substance provide wives for yourselves, acting that which is right, and avoiding whoredom. And for the advantage which you receive from them, give them their reward, according to what is ordained: but it shall be no crime in you to make any other agreement among yourselves, after the ordinance shall be complied with; for God is knowing and wise.

Men shall have the preeminence above women, because of those advantages wherein God has caused the one of them to excel the other, and for that which they expend of their substance in maintaining their wives. The honest women are obedient, careful in the absence of their husbands, for that God preserves them, by committing them to the care and protection of the men. But those, whose perverseness you shall be apprehensive of, rebuke; and remove them into separate apartments, and chastise them. But if they shall be obedient unto you, seek not an occasion of quarrel against them; for God is high and great. Who is better in point of religion than he who resigns himself unto God, and is a worker of righteousness, and follows the law of Abraham the orthodox? Since God took Abraham for his friend: and to God belongs whatsoever is in heaven and on earth; God comprehends all things. They will consult you concerning women; Answer, God instructs you concerning them, and that which is read unto you in the book of the *Koran* concerning female orphans, to whom you give not that which is ordained them, neither will you marry them, and concerning weak infants, and that you observe justice towards orphans: whatever good you do, God knows it. If a woman fear ill usage, or aversion, from her husband, it shall be no crime in them if they agree the matter amicably between themselves; for a reconciliation is better than a separation. Men's souls are naturally inclined to covetousness: but if you be kind towards women, and fear to wrong them, God is well acquainted with what you do. You can by no means carry yourselves equally between women in all respects, although you study to do it; therefore turn not from a wife with all manner of aversion, nor leave her like one in suspense: if you agree, and fear to abuse your wives, God is gracious and merciful; but if they separate, God will satisfy them both of his abundance; for God is extensive and wise, and unto God belongs whatsoever is in heaven and on earth. . . .

God is witness of that revelation which he has sent down unto you; he sent it down with his special knowledge; the angels were also witnesses thereof; but God is a sufficient witness. They who believe not, and turn aside others from the way of God, have erred in a wide mistake. Verily those who believe not, and act unjustly, God will by no means forgive, neither will he direct them into any other way than the way of hell; they shall remain therein forever: and this is easy with God. O men, now is the apostle come unto you, with truth from your Lord; believe therefore, it will be better for you. But if you disbelieve, verily unto God belongs whatsoever is in heaven and on earth; and God is knowing and wise. O you who have received the scriptures, exceed not the just bounds in your religion, neither say of God any other than the truth. Verily Christ Jesus the son of Mary is the apostle of God, and his Word, which he conveyed into Mary, and a spirit proceeding from him. Believe therefore in God, and his apostles, and say not, There are three Gods; forbear this; it will be better for you. God is but one God. Far be it from him that he should have a son! Unto him belongs whatsoever is in heaven and on earth; and God is a sufficient protector. Christ does not proudly disdain to be a servant unto God; neither the angels who approach near to his presence; and whoso disdains his service, and is puffed up with pride, God will gather them all to himself, on the last day. Unto those who believe, and do that which is right, he shall give their rewards, and shall superabundantly add unto them of his liberality: but those who are disdainful and proud, he will punish with a grievous punishment; and they shall not find any to protect or to help them, besides God.

READING 13

The Constitution of Medina[23]

In 622, Muhammad left his home city of Mecca, where he had won only a small following, to become the civil and religious leader of the city of Yathrib, later renamed Medina, "the Prophet's City." From Medina, Muhammad's followers made war on Mecca—raiding its caravans, blockading its commerce, and eventually accepting its submission. The sacred community that Muhammad forged in Medina, at once a state and a church, foreshadowed the later organization of the Islamic Empire under the caliphs. The Constitution of Medina, the first official document of the Islamic political community, also foreshadowed the relatively tolerant policy of the Islamic Empire toward its Jewish inhabitants.

The Prophet wrote a document concerning the emigrants and the helpers in which he made a friendly agreement with the Jews and established them in their religion and their property, and stated the reciprocal obligations, as follows:

In the name of God the Compassionate, the Merciful. This is a document from Muhammad the prophet [governing the relations] between the believers and Muslims of Quraysh and Yathrib [Medina], and those who followed them and joined them and labored with them. They are one community [umma] to the exclusion of all other men. The Quraysh emigrants according to their present custom shall pay the blood-price within the company and shall redeem their prisoners with the kindness and justice common among believers. . . . Believers shall not leave anyone destitute among them by not paying his redemption money or blood-price in kindness.

---

[23]From Ibn Ishaq, "Life of the Prophet," in *The Life of Mohammad: a Translation of Ishaqs Sirat Rasul Allah,* ed. and tr. A. Guillaume; New York, Oxford University Press, 1955, pp. 231–233. By permission of Oxford University Press.

A believer shall not take as an ally the freedman of another Muslim against him. The God-fearing believers shall be against the rebellious or him who seeks to spread injustice, or sin or enmity, or corruption between believers; the hand of every man shall be against him even if he be a son of one of them. A believer shall not slay a believer for the sake of a believer nor shall he aid an unbeliever against a believer. God's protection is one, the least of them may give protection to a stranger on their behalf. Believers are friends one to the other to the exclusion of outsiders. To the Jew who follows us belong help and equality. He shall not be wronged nor shall his enemies be aided. The peace of the believers is indivisible. No separate peace shall be made when believers are fighting in the way of God. Conditions must be fair and equitable to all. In every foray a rider must take another behind him. The believers must avenge the blood of one another shed in the way of God. The God-fearing believers enjoy the best and most upright guidance. No polytheist [the heathen Arabs of Medina] shall take the property or person of Quraysh under his protection nor shall he intervene against a believer. Whosoever is convicted of killing a believer without good reason shall be subject to retaliation unless the next of kin is satisfied [with blood-money], and the believers shall be against him as one man, and they are bound to take action against him.

It shall not be lawful to a believer who holds by what is in this document and believes in God and the last day to help an evil-doer [*muhdith*] or to shelter him. The curse of God and His anger on the day of resurrection will be upon him if he does, and neither repentance nor ransom will be upon him if he does, and neither repentance nor ransom will be received from him. Whenever you differ about a matter it must be referred to God and to Muhammad.

The Jews shall contribute to the cost of war so long as they are fighting alongside the believers. The Jews of the Bani Auf are one community with the believers [the Jews have their religion and the Muslims have theirs], their freedmen and their persons except those who behave unjustly and sinfully, for they hurt but themselves and their families. . . . Loyalty is a protection against treachery. The freedmen of Tha'laba are as themselves. The close friends of the Jews are as themselves. None of them shall go out to war save with the permission of Muhammad, but he shall not be prevented from taking revenge for a wound. He who slays a man without warning slays himself and his household, unless it be one who has wronged him, for God will accept that. The Jews must bear their expenses and the Muslims their expenses. Each must help the other against anyone who attacks the people of this document. They must seek mutual advice and consultation, and loyalty is a protection against treachery. A man is not liable for his ally's misdeeds. The wronged must be helped. The Jews must pay with the believers so long as war lasts. Yathrib shall be a sanctuary for the people of this document. A stranger under protection shall be as his host doing no harm and committing no crime. A woman shall only be given protection with the consent of her family. If any dispute or controversy likely to cause trouble should arise it must be referred to God and to Muhammad the prophet of God. God accepts what is nearest to piety and goodness in this document. Quraysh and their helpers shall not be given protection. The contracting parties are bound to help one another against any attack on Yathrib. If they are called to make peace and maintain it they must do so; and if they make a similar demand on the Muslims it must be carried out except in the case of a holy war. Every one shall have his portion from the side to which he belongs; the Jews of al-Aus, their freedmen and themselves have the same standing with the people of this document in pure loyalty from the people of this document.

Loyalty is a protection against treachery: He who acquires it ought to acquire it for himself. God approves of this document. This deed will not protect the unjust and the sinner. The man who goes forth to fight and the man who stays at home in the city is safe unless he has been unjust and sinned. God is the protector of the good and God-fearing man and Muhammad is the prophet of God.

READING 14

Dionysius of Tel-Mahre, The Arab Conquest of the Middle East[24]

Dionysius of Tel-Mahre (c. 770–845) (also referred to as Dionysius Telmaharensis) was one of the most important figures in the Syrian church. First a monk, he was elected patriarch in 815 and then in 818 ordained a priest in the Jacobite church. During his reign, though being continually tested by a rival schismatic sect, Dionysius was able to maintain peaceful relations between the Syrian Christians and their Muslim rulers. Dionysius composed a long chronicle, parts of which survive, on the history of the Syrian Christian church; and it is one of the best sources on Middle Eastern history in this turbulent period.

After the death of Muhammad, Abu Bakr became king and sent an army of 30,000 Arabs to conquer Syria in the first year of his reign. On inspecting these forces outside the city Abu Bakr gave them the following exhortation:

"In the land you will invade kill neither the aged, nor the little child, nor the woman. Do not force the stylite from his high perch and do not harass the solitary. They have devoted themselves to the service of God. Do not cut down any

[24]Andrew Palmer, *The Seventh Century in West-Syrian Chronicles;* Liverpool, England, Liverpool University Press, 1993, pp. 144–149.

fruit-tree, neither damage any crop, neither maim any domestic animal, large or small. Wherever you are welcomed by a city or a people, make a solemn pact with them and give them reliable guarantees that they will be ruled according to their laws and according to the practices which obtained among them before our time. They will contract with you to pay in tribute whatever sum shall be settled between you, then they will be left alone in their confession and in their country. But as for those who do not welcome you, make war on them. Be careful to abide by all the just laws and commandments which have been given to you by God through our prophet, lest you excite the wrath of God."

The forces sent out by Abu-Bakr approached [Syria] by the desert route to the south of Damascus. When Heraclius [the emperor] was informed that they had invaded Moab, he summoned the forces of the Romans and the Christian Arabs to join him in Damascus and after impressing on them the imperative of guarding the cities, he sent them to meet the Arabs in battle and to expel them from the country. He himself marched with a large army to Antioch. Of the four generals sent by Abu Bakr one came, as we have said, to the land of Moab *en route* for Palestine; the second went to Egypt and Alexandria; the third set out against the Persians; and the last attacked the Christian Arabs who were subject to the Romans.

The opposite number of the general sent to Palestine was the Patrikios Sergius, to whom Heraclius had committed Palestinian Caesarea and its region. When he learned of the Arab army's approach he assembled his own forces and sent for 5,000 Samaritan foot soldiers to strengthen his army in the coming encounter with the Arabs. When the Arabs heard about these preparations they concentrated their forces and laid an ambush by which to surprise and destroy the Romans.

Already the Romans were on the march. They had reached the place where the ambush had been laid. Unaware, as yet, of the presence of the Arabs, they requested permission from Sergius to rest a little and to lay down their burdens, for most of them were foot soldiers. The Patrikios refused. He knew by this time that the enemy were close at hand. He ordered the trumpets to be sounded, the drums to be beaten. The Romans were just preparing to charge, when the Arabs, mightily armed, sprang out of their hiding places and advanced on them with deafening, angry shouts. The first ranks to meet their onslaught were those of the Samaritans, for these had marched at the head of the column. Under the attack they collapsed and every one of them perished by the sword. The Patrikios saw this and began to flee headlong to save his skin. The Arabs pursued the Romans, like harvesters scything a ripe field of corn. Sergius fell from his horse, but his attendants came to his aid and set him back on again. He stayed briefly in the saddle, then fell again. Again his companions held ranks and set him back on his mount. A few steps further on he fell to the ground for the third time. They were making as if to put him back in the saddle, when he said: "Leave me! Save yourselves! Otherwise you and I shall drink the cup of death together."

So they left him behind; and indeed they had not gone far before the pursuers swooped in on him and killed him on the spot. They continued their pursuit and slaughter of the Romans until darkness fell. A few got away by hiding in trees, behind stone walls and in vineyards. And so the Arabs entered Caesarea.

When Heraclius heard of the death of the Patríkios Sergius and of the defeat of the combined forces of the Romans and the Samaritans, he gave his brother Theodoric orders to muster all the Romans who were with him in northern Mesopotamia and all those on the west side of the Euphrates. With all present and ready and the army at full strength, they marched off, swaggering with unbounded arrogance and conceit, confident in their greater numbers and their superior arms. [At evening] every tent in the camp became a place of dancing, rejoicing, drinking and song. And they shot out their lips, and they wagged their heads, and they said: "We will not give those Arabs a second thought. They are dead dogs, no more, no less."

When they reached the village of al Jusiya in the region of Emesa, Theodoric approached a stylite standing on his pillar; the man was a Chalcedonian. At the end of the long conversation which ensued between them, the stylite said to Theodoric, "If you will only promise that on your safe and victorious return from the war you will wipe out the followers of Severus [the Syrian Patriarch, head of a "heretical" group of Christians] and crush them with excruciating punishments . . . "; to which the Patrikios Theodoric replied, "I had already decided to persecute the Severans without having heard your advice." These words were overheard by an Orthodox soldier standing near by; though he smarted with indignation, respect for superior rank prevented him from speaking. So the Romans, still puffed up with conceit, left that place and approached the Arab positions. They pitched camp near the tents of the Arabs, and from May until October the two armies were encamped side by side, menacing one another. Then, suddenly, they were ranged in opposing battle-lines. For one hour at the start it seemed that the Romans would be stronger. But then the Arabs turned on them—and they trembled. In that moment the spirit went out of them and they lost their nerve, turned tail and took to flight. Even so they could not escape alive, because divine Providence had abandoned them. They were trampled underfoot by their enemies, who put them all to the sword. No one was able to defend himself except for Theodoric, who escaped with a handful of men. That soldier who was a believer saw Theodoric on the point of losing consciousness—his eyes staring out into impenetrable darkness—and he found the courage to say to him, "Well, Theodoric? What has become of your stylite and his promises? This is a fine achievement to add to your successes. Will you bring the news of the victory to the King?" The Patrikios took this in but did not even answer back. So the whole Roman army was destroyed, while Theodoric himself got away to the King. The Arabs switched their attention to the fortified camp of the Romans and secured for themselves more gold, silver, expensive clothing, slaves and slave-girls than they could count. Rich men they became that day and much wealth they acquired.

STUDY QUESTIONS

A What makes Byzantium one of the "heirs of classical civilization"? What makes Islam one of the "heirs of classical civilization"? What makes the early medieval West one of the "heirs of classical civilization"?

B Do all three civilizations have anything in common? How do they differ?

C Why does religion play a central role in all three civilizations? Is its role the same in all three?

Reading 1: Life of St. Daniel the Stylite

How did Daniel acquire his influence? What kinds of influence did Daniel have? In what ways did Daniel's political influence rest on his spiritual authority?

Reading 2: Procopius, Justinian and Theodora

In what ways do the Nike revolt and circus factions illustrate the "Byzantine" nature of Byzantine politics? Theodora is often given credit for saving the government: does she deserve it?

Reading 3: Justinian, The Institutes

How do Justinian's *Institutes* establish the primacy of the principle of right (*ius*) in relation to a law (*lex*)? How do the *Institutes* differ from the customary law practiced by the Germanic peoples of Western Europe?

Reading 4: Basil II, On the Protection of Peasants' Lands, 996

What is the purpose of this law? How does it help peasants? How does it help the emperor extend his authority?

Reading 5: Leo I, On the Authority of St. Peter

What is Leo claiming? Why is this doctrine so important in church-state relations throughout the Middle Ages?

Reading 6: Pope Gelasius I, On Priestly and Royal Power

What does Gelasius see as the proper relationship between church and state? How does Pope Gelasius justify the value he puts on the church and the value he puts on the state?

Reading 7: Boethius, The Consolation of Philosophy

What cultural, philosophical, and religious influences can be discerned in the *Consolation of Philosophy,* and how do they affect the direction of Boethius' quest for truth and wisdom?

Reading 8: St. Benedict, The Rule

The Rule is often praised for its "flexibility:" how is this evident? Why would the monastic life appeal to men and women of the early Middle Ages? In what way is Benedict's Roman sense of order evident?

Reading 9: Letters of Pope Gregory the Great

What characteristics does Gregory think are necessary for a bishop? What kinds of activities occupy Gregory himself? What is Pope Gregory the Great's vision of "Christendom"?

Reading 10: Eddius, The Synod of Whitby, 664

Why was the outcome of the Synod of Whitby so important to the spread of Christianity in the Early Middle Ages? What argument swayed King Oswiu?

Reading 11: Bede, Saint Hilda of Whitby

What spiritual values does the Venerable Bede seem to be promoting in his story of Hilda of Whitby and Caedmon the poet?

Reading 12: The Qu'ran

What is the status of Jews and Christians? What is the status of women? What are the requirements of the Islamic faith?

Reading 13: The Constitution of Medina

What is the relationship between those of Muslim faith and the "people of the book" established in the *Constitution of Medina?* How does this put into practice some of the teachings of the Qu'ran?

Reading 14: Dionysius of Tel-Mahre, The Arab Conquest of the Middle East

Why were the Romans—the troops of the Byzantine empire—so easily overcome? What were their weaknesses? What were the Arabs' strengths?

CHAPTER 3

❈ CAROLINGIAN EUROPE

The eighth century witnessed a revival of Classical-Christian culture among the papal missionaries and in the kingdom of the Franks under a powerful new dynasty, the Carolingians. The papacy broke more and more from its ties with the Byzantine Empire (Reading 1) and drew closer to English Benedictine missionary scholars such as St. Boniface, who labored to convert pagan Germanic tribes to the northeast of Christian Francia and to reform the Frankish Church itself. Like the monks whom Pope Gregory the Great had sent to England more than a century before, St. Boniface worked under the supervision of the papacy (Readings 2–3).

It was Boniface, acting as a representative of Pope Zacharias, who anointed the first Carolingian king, Pepin the Short, bringing to an end the rule of the Merovingian dynasty (Reading 4). King Pepin reciprocated by leading an army into Italy, at the papacy's urging, to rescue Rome from the Lombard menace. Defeating the Lombards in battle, Pepin granted the papacy authority over extensive territories in central Italy known thereafter as the Papal States, or the Patrimony of St. Peter. The papacy justified its claim to these lands by asserting that they had been given originally to Pope Sylvester I by Emperor Constantine back in the early fourth century. Happily, an imperial letter known as the Donation of Constantine conveniently materialized in just the nick of time to provide documentary authority for the papal position (Reading 5).

Charlemagne, Pepin's son and successor, extended the boundaries of the Carolingian realm by military conquests (Reading 6). He appointed loyal dukes and counts as regional governors throughout his dominions, established close relations with the papacy (Reading 7), and was crowned Roman emperor by Pope Leo III on Christmas Day, A.D. 800, under circumstances that are disputed to this day (Reading 8). Elements of his administrative machinery are seen in his agents called *missi dominici,* or "envoys of the lord" (Reading 8).

Charlemagne's patronage and encouragement gave rise to an intellectual and cultural revival centering on major bishoprics and Benedictine abbeys (Readings 10–12) and on the royal court (Reading 13), where Charlemagne assembled a group of scholars from the length and breadth of Western Christendom. This Carolingian Renaissance, which continued through the reigns of Charlemagne's successors, contributed much to solidifying Europe's Classical-Christian foundations.

READING 1
Pope Gregory II, Letter to Emperor Leo III[1]

The papacy grew up in the Roman world and long maintained its allegiance to the Roman—that is, Byzantine—Empire. By the mid-eighth century, the papacy broke with Byzantium and allied with the Carolingian Franks. Even a generation earlier, as this letter from the feisty Pope Gregory II (715–731) makes clear, relations between the papacy and the Byzantine Empire were not warm.

You know that the dogmas of the holy Church are not the concern of emperors but of pontiffs, who ought to teach securely. The pontiffs who preside over the Church do not meddle in affairs of state, and likewise the emperors ought not to meddle in ecclesiastical affairs, but to administer the things committed to them.

The Lombards and Sarmatians and others who live in the north have attacked the wretched Decapolis and occupied Ravenna itself. They have deposed your governors and appointed governors of their own, and they have determined to do the same at other imperial cities in this neighborhood and even at Rome itself, since you are unable to defend us.

All this is the result of your imprudence and stupidity. But you wish to strike terror into them, and you say, "I will send to Rome and destroy the image of St. Peter, and having overcome Pope Gregory, will carry him off." You ought rather to know and to hold for certain that the pontiffs who have ruled at Rome preside there in order to maintain peace, like a wall joining east and west, occupying the middle ground between them, and that they are arbitrators and promoters of peace. If you insolently threaten and insult us there is no need for us to descend to fighting with you. The Roman pontiff will withdraw for a few miles into Campania; then you may go and chase the wind.

Would that I might, by God's gift, tread the same path as Pope Martin [who died in exile during the reign of Constantine (d. 337)]. And yet I wish to survive and to live for the sake of the people, since the whole western world has turned its eyes upon our humility and the people greatly trust in us and in him whose statue you threaten to cast down and destroy, namely St. Peter, whom all the kingdoms of the west regard as an earthly god.

[1]From *The Crisis of Church and State*, ed. Brian Tierney; Englewood Cliffs, N.J., Prentice-Hall, 1964, pp. 19–20.

READING 2

Letters of St. Boniface[2]

These three documents show Boniface (680–754) first as a servant of the pope and of Catholic orthodoxy (Reading A), next as a missionary among Germanic pagans (Reading B), and finally as a pastoral adviser (Reading C). They reveal something of the communications network connecting the churches of Rome, England, Francia, and pagan Germany—and, in the letter to Abbess Bugga, the hazards of travel within Christendom. The letter of Bishop Daniel of Winchester (723–724), with its deep-set confidence in the intellectual plausibility of Christianity as against the idol worship of rival religions, will help explain the eventual success of Christian missions to central and eastern Europe.

A.   OATH OF BONIFACE TO POPE GREGORY II, 722

In the name of the Lord God and of our Savior Jesus Christ. In the sixth year of Leo, by the grace of God emperor, in the sixth year of his consulship and in the fourth year of his son, the Emperor Constantine, in the sixth indiction:

I, Boniface, by the grace of God bishop, promise to you, blessed Peter, chief of the Apostles, and to your vicar, the blessed Pope Gregory [II] and to his successors, in the name of the Father, the Son, and the Holy Spirit, the indivisible Trinity, and of this, thy most sacred body, that I will show entire faith and sincerity toward the holy catholic doctrine and will persist in the unity of the same, so God help me—that faith in which, beyond a doubt, the whole salvation of Christians consists. I will in no wise agree to anything which is opposed to the unity of the Church Universal, no matter who shall try to persuade me; but I will, as I have said, show in all things a perfect loyalty to you and to the welfare of your Church, to which the power to bind and loose is given by God, and to your vicar and his successors.

But, if I shall discover any bishops who are opponents of the ancient institutions of the holy Fathers, I will have no part nor lot with them, but so far as I can, will restrain them or, if that is impossible, will make a true report to my apostolic master. But if (which God forbid!) I should be tempted into any action contrary to this my promise, in any way or by any device or pretext whatsoever, may I be found guilty at the last judgment who dared to defraud you by making a false declaration of their property.

[2]From *The Letters of St. Boniface*, tr. E. Emerton; New York, Columbia University Press, 1940, nos. viii, xv, xix.

This text of my oath, I, Boniface, a humble bishop, have written with my own hand and laid above thy most sacred body. I have taken this oath, as is prescribed, in the presence of God, my witness and my judge, and I pledge myself to observe it.

B.   LETTER OF BISHOP DANIEL OF WINCHESTER, ENGLAND, TO BONIFACE

To the venerable and beloved prelate Boniface, Daniel, servant of the people of God.

I rejoice, beloved brother and fellow priest, that you are deserving of the highest prize of virtue. You have approached the hitherto stony and barren hearts of the pagans, trusting in the plenitude of your faith, and have labored untiringly with the plowshare of Gospel preaching, striving by your daily toil to change them into fertile fields. To you may well be applied the Gospel saying: "The voice of one crying in the wilderness," etc. Yet a part of the second prize shall be given, not unfittingly, to those who support so pious and useful a work with what help they can give and supplement the poverty of those laborers with means sufficient to carry on zealously the work of preaching which has already been begun and to raise up new sons to Christ.

And so I have with affectionate good will taken pains to suggest to Your Prudence a few things that may show you how, according to my ideas, you may most readily overcome the resistance of those uncivilized people. Do not begin by arguing with them about the origin of their gods, false as those are, but let them affirm that some of them were begotten by others through the intercourse of male with female, so that you may at least prove that gods and goddesses born after the manner of men are men and not gods and, since they did not exist before, must have had a beginning.

Then, when they have been compelled to learn that their gods had a beginning since some were begotten by others, they must be asked in the same way whether they believe that the world had a beginning or was always in existence without beginning. If it had a beginning, who created it? Certainly they can find no place where begotten gods could dwell before the universe was made. I mean by "universe" not merely this visible earth and sky, but the whole vast extent of space, and this the heathen too can imagine in their thoughts. But if they argue that the world always existed without beginning, you should strive to refute this and to convince them by many documents and arguments. Ask your opponents who governed the world before the gods were born, who was the ruler? How could they bring under their dominion or subject to their law a universe that had always existed before them? And whence, or from whom or when, was the first god or goddess set up or begotten? Now, do they imagine that gods and goddesses still go on begetting others? Or, if they are no longer begetting, when and why did they cease from intercourse and births? And if they are still producing offspring, then the number of gods must already be infinite. Among so many and different gods, mortal men cannot know which is the most powerful, and one should be extremely careful not to offend that most powerful one.

Do they think the gods are to be worshipped for the sake of temporal and immediate good or for future eternal blessedness? If for temporal things, let them tell in what respect the heathen are better off than Christians. What gain do the heathen suppose accrues to their gods from their sacrifices, since the gods already possess everything? Or why do the gods leave it in the power of their subjects to say what kind of tribute shall be paid? If they are lacking in such things, why do they not themselves choose more valuable ones? If they have plenty, then there is no need to suppose that the gods can be pleased with such offerings of victims.

These and many similar things which it would take long to enumerate you ought to put before them, not offensively or so as to anger them, but calmly and with great moderation. At intervals you should compare their superstitions with our Christian doctrines, touching upon them from the flank, as it were, so that the pagans, thrown into confusion rather than angered, may be ashamed of their absurd ideas and may understand that their infamous ceremonies and fables are well known to us.

This point is also to be made: if the gods are all-powerful, beneficient, and just, they not only reward their worshipers but punish those who reject them. If, then, they do this in temporal matters, how is it that they spare us Christians who are turning almost the whole earth away from their worship and overthrowing their idols? And while these, that is, the Christians, possess lands rich in oil and wine and abounding in other resources, they have left to those, that is, the pagans, lands stiff with cold where their gods, driven out of the world, are falsely supposed to rule. They are also frequently to be reminded of the supremacy of the Christian world, in comparison with which they themselves, very few in number, are still involved in their ancient errors.

If they boast that the rule of the gods over those peoples has been, as it were, lawful from the beginning, show them that the whole world was once given over to idol-worship, until by the grace of Christ and through the knowledge of one God, its Almighty Founder and Ruler, it was enlightened, brought to life, and reconciled to God. For what is the daily baptism of the children of believing Christians but purification of each one from the uncleanness and guilt in which the whole world was once involved?

I have been glad to call these manners to your attention, my brother, out of my affection for you, though I suffer from bodily infirmities so that I may well say with the Psalmist: "I know, Oh Lord, that thy judgments are right and that thou in faithfulness hast afflicted me." Wherefore I earnestly pray Your Reverence and all those who serve Christ in spirit to make supplication for me that the Lord Who gave me to drink of the wine of remorse, may be swift in mercy, that He who was just in condemnation may graciously pardon, and by His mercy enable me to sing in gratitude the words of the Prophet: "In the multitude of my thoughts within me thy comforts delight my soul."

I pray for your welfare in Christ, my very dear colleague, and beg you to bear me in mind.

C.   LETTER OF BONIFACE TO ABBESS BUGGA, PRE-738

To the beloved lady, Abbess Bugga, sister and dearest of all women in Christ, Boniface, a humble and unworthy bishop, wishes eternal salvation in Christ.

I desire you to know, dearest sister, that in the matter about which you wrote asking advice of me, unworthy though I am, I dare neither forbid your pilgrimage on my own responsibility nor rashly persuade you to it. I will only say how the matter appears to me. If, for the sake of rest and divine contemplation, you have laid aside the care for the servants and maids of God and for the monastic life which you once had, how could you now subject yourself with labor and wearing anxiety to the words and wishes of men of this world? It would seem to me better, if you can in no way have freedom and a quiet mind at home on account of worldly men, that you should obtain freedom of contemplation by means of a pilgrimage, if you so desire and are able, as our sister Wiethburga did. She has written me that she has found at the shrine of St. Peter the kind of quiet life which she had long sought in vain. With regard to your wishes, she sent me word, since I had written to her about you, that you would do better to wait until the rebellious assaults and threats of the Saracens who have recently appeared about Rome should have subsided. God willing, she will then send you an invitation. To me also this seems the best plan. Make ready what you will need for the journey, wait for word from her, and then act as God's grace shall command.

In regard to the writings which you have requested of me, you must excuse my remissness, for I have been prevented by pressure of work and by my continual travels from completing the book you ask for. When I have finished it, I shall see that it is sent to you.

In return for the gifts and garments you have sent me, I offer my grateful prayers to God that he may give you a reward with the angels and the archangels in the highest heavens. I exhort you, then, in God's name, my very dear sister— nay mother and most sweet lady—to pray earnestly for me, since for my sins I am wearied with many sorrows and am far more disturbed by anxiety of mind than by the labor of my body. May you rest assured that the long-tried friendship between us shall never be found wanting.

Farewell in Christ.

READING 3

Willibald, Life of Boniface[3]

Willibald (c. 700/05–786), West Saxon bishop and missionary, was a kinsman of Saint Boniface, whose life he wrote. Willibald made a pilgrimage to Palestine and recorded his experiences in the *Hodoeporicon,* the earliest known English travelogue. From Palestine he returned to Italy, where he entered the St. Benedict's monastery at Monte Casino until Pope Gregory II ordered him to assist Boniface's efforts to convert the German Saxons—pagan tribes related to the Anglo-Saxons of England. In this selection from the Life of Saint Boniface, Willibald relates the story of the end of Boniface's life.

During the rule of Carloman all the bishops, priests, deacons, and clerics and everyone of ecclesiastical rank gathered together at the ruler's instance and held four synodal councils. At these Archbishop Boniface presided, with the consent and support of Carloman and of the metropolitan of the see and city of Mainz. And being a legate of the Roman Church and the Apostolic See, sent as he was by the saintly and venerable Gregory II and later by Gregory III, he urged that the numerous canons and ordinances decreed by these four important and early councils should be preserved in order to ensure the healthy development of Christian doctrine.

After he had set before all ranks of society the accepted norm of the Christian life and made known to them the way of truth, Boniface, now weak and decrepit, showed great foresight both as regards himself and his people by appointing a successor to his see, as ecclesiastical law demands. . . . He promoted two men of good repute to the episcopate, Willibald[4] and Burchard, dividing between them the churches that were under his jurisdiction in the land of eastern Franks and on

---

[3]C. H. Talbot, *The Anglo-Saxon Missionaries in Germany, Being the Lives of SS. Willibrord, Boniface, Leoba and Lebuin together with the Hodoepericon of St. Willibald and a selection from the correspondence of St. Boniface;* London and New York, Sheed & Ward, 1954.
[4]The author of this selection.

the Bavarian frontier. To Willibald he entrusted the diocese of Eichstatt, to Burchard that of Würzburg, putting under his care all the churches within the borders of the Franks, Saxons, and Slavs. Nevertheless, even to the day of his death he did not fail to instruct the people in the way of life.

Then Pepin, with the help of the Lord, took over the rule of the kingdom of the Franks as the happy successor to his above-mentioned brother [Carloman]. When disorders among the people had subsided, he was elevated to the kingship. From the outset he conscientiously carried out the vows he had sworn to the Lord, to put into effect without delay the synodal decrees, and he renewed the canonical institutions which his brother, following the advice of the holy archbishop Boniface, had so dutifully set on foot.

When the Lord willed to deliver his servant from the trials of this world and to set him free from the vicissitudes of this mortal life, it was decided, under God's providence, that he should travel in the company of his disciples to Frisia, from which he had departed in body though not in spirit. And this was done so that in dying there he might receive the divine recompense in the place where he had begun his preaching.

When, as we have already said, the faith had been planted strongly in Frisia and the glorious end of the saint's life drew near, he took with him a picked number of his personal followers and pitched a camp on the banks of the river Bordne, which flows through the territories called Ostor and Westeraeche and divides them. Here he fixed a day on which he would confirm by the laying-on of hands all the neophytes and those who had recently been baptized.

But events turned out otherwise than expected. When the appointed day arrived and the morning light was breaking through the clouds after sunrise, enemies came instead of friends, new executioners in place of new worshipers of the faith. A vast number of foes armed with spears and shields rushed into the camp brandishing their weapons. In the twinkling of an eye the attendants sprang from the camp to meet them and snatched up arms here and there to defend the holy band of martyrs (for that is what they were to be) against the insensate fury of the mob. But the man of God, hearing the shouts and the onrush of the rabble, straightway called the clergy to his side, and, collecting together the relics of the saints, which he always carried with him, came out of his tent. At once he reproved the attendants and forbade them to continue the conflict, saying: "Sons, cease fighting. Lay down your arms, for we are told in Scripture not to render evil for good but to overcome evil by good. The hour to which we have long looked forward is near and the day of our release is at hand. Take comfort in the Lord and endure with gladness the suffering He has mercifully ordained. Put your trust in Him and He will grant deliverance to your souls."

Whilst with these words he was encouraging his disciples to accept the crown of martyrdom, the frenzied mob of pagans rushed suddenly upon them with swords and every kind of warlike weapon, staining their bodies with their precious blood.

Suddenly, after the mortal remains of the just had been mutilated, the pagan mob seized with exultation upon the spoils of their victory (in reality the cause of their damnation) and, after laying waste the camp, carried off and shared the booty; they stole the chests in which the books and relics were preserved and, thinking that they had acquired a hoard of gold and silver, carried them off, still locked, to the ships. Now the ships were stocked with provisions for the feeding of the clerics and attendants and a great deal of wine still remained. Finding this goodly liquor, the pagans immediately began to slake their sottish appetites and to get drunk. After some time, by the wonderful dispensation of God, they began to argue among themselves about the booty they had taken and discussed how they were to share the gold and silver they had not even seen. . . . It was not long before the weapons that had earlier murdered the holy martyrs were turned against each other in bitter strife. After the greater part of the mad freebooters had been slain, the survivors, surrounded by the corpses of their rivals for the booty, swooped down upon the treasure that had been obtained by so much loss of life. They broke open the chests containing the books and found, to their dismay, that they held manuscripts instead of gold vessels, pages of sacred texts instead of silver plate. Disappointed in their hope of gold and silver, they littered the fields with the books they found, throwing some of them into reedy marshes, hiding away others in widely different places. But by the grace of God and through the prayers of the archbishop and martyr Saint Boniface the manuscripts were discovered, a long time afterward, unharmed and intact, and they were returned by those who found them to the monastery, in which they are used with great advantage to the salvation of souls even at the present day.

READING 4

The Coronation of Pepin the Short[5]

The abbey of Lorsch in southern Germany, like many other abbeys across Christendom, compiled brief, year-by-year records of events that seemed particularly important. These records, known as annals, reflect the perspectives and biases of their respective monasteries. The events they include might range from eclipses, storms, and the births of two-headed cows to matters of major political importance such as the one recorded here.

By 751 the Merovingian dynasty of Frankish kings had become impoverished and politically impotent. Actual power was exercised by the chief official of the royal household, the *Major Domus*. This office was in the hereditary control of a great Frankish aristocratic family known later as

---

[5]From *The Lesser Annals of Lorsch,* in *A Sourcebook of Medieval History,* ed. F. A. Ogg; New York, American Book Company, 1907, pp. 106–107. Reprinted by permission.

the Carolingians. Pepin the Short (741–768), the Carolingian *Major Domus* in 751, hungered for the crown. But the Merovingians, even though powerless, were an ancient and revered royal dynasty, and Pepin therefore needed potent spiritual backing for his coup d'état. Pope Zacharias was harassed by hostile Byzantines and rampaging Lombards and viewed Pepin as a potential military supporter who might rescue the papacy from its predicament. Pepin and Zacharias were thus well placed to help each other, as these documents describe.

In the year [751] of the Lord's incarnation Pepin sent ambassadors to Rome to Pope Zacharias [r. 741–752], to inquire concerning the kings of the Franks who, though they were of the royal line and were called kings, had no power in the kingdom, except that charters and privileges were drawn up in their names. They had absolutely no kingly authority, but did whatever the *Major Domus* of the Franks desired. But on the first day of March in the Campus Martius, according to ancient custom, gifts were offered to these kings by the people, and the king himself sat in the royal seat with the army standing round him and the *Major Domus* in his presence, and he commanded on that day whatever was decreed by the Franks; but on all other days thenceforth he remained quietly at home. Pope Zacharias, therefore, in the exercise of his apostolic authority, replied to their inquiry that it seemed to him better and more expedient that the man who held power in the kingdom should be called king and be king, rather than he who falsely bore the name. Therefore the aforesaid pope commanded the king and people of the Franks that Pepin, who was exercising royal power, should be called king, and should be established on the throne. This was therefore done by the anointing of the holy archbishop Boniface in the city of Soissons. Pepin was proclaimed king, and Childeric, who was falsely called king, was shaved[6] and sent into a monastery.

READING 5

The Donation of Constantine[7]

King Pepin expressed his gratitude by defeating the Lombards and granting the papacy large portions of central Italy. Since the Lombards had only recently seized this territory from the Byzantine Empire, the Byzantines

---

[6]Ie., his head was shaved. Uncut hair was a mark of royalty among male members of the Merovingian dynasty.

[7]From *The Medieval World, 300–1300*, 2nd ed., ed. Norman Cantor; New York, Macmillan Publishing Co., 1968, pp. 132–139. Reprinted with permission of Macmillan Publishing Co., Inc.

regarded Pepin's grant as a usurpation of imperial lands. The papacy responded by pointing to the legend, current in Rome, that Constantine I had long ago granted the papacy perpetual dominion over Italy and all the West. The papal court evidently accepted this tale as historically accurate but the documentary proof was lacking. Accordingly, the Donation of Constantine was forged, with the intent not of rewriting history but of supplying the missing documentation. Such was the intent of a great number of forged grants throughout the Middle Ages. The Donation of Constantine was exposed as a forgery first around A.D. 1000 by court scholars of Emperor Otto III, and then, more decisively, by the fifteenth-century Italian humanist, Lorenzo Valla. Notice the logical inconsistency in the two references to Constantinople.

In the name of the Holy and Undivided Trinity. The emperor Caesar Flavius Constantinus in Christ to the most holy and blessed Father of fathers, Sylvester, Bishop of the city of Rome and Pope, and to all his successors, who shall forever sit on the throne of Saint Peter until the end of time.

On the first day, then, after receiving the mystery of holy Baptism and after the cure of my body from the filth of leprosy,[8] I recognized that there was no other God except the Father and the Son and the Holy Spirit, whom the most blessed Pope Sylvester preaches, Trinity in Unity, Unity in Trinity. For all the gods of the heathen which up to now I have worshipped, have been proved to be demons, the hand-made work of men. That same venerable father told very plainly to us the great power in heaven and earth which our Saviour had committed to the blessed Apostle Peter when, finding him faithful under questioning, he said: "Thou art Peter and upon this rock I will build my Church and the gates of hell shall not prevail against it." Take note, Oh mighty sovereigns, and incline the attention of your heart to what the good Master and Lord gave in addition to His disciple when He said: "And I will give unto you the keys of the kingdom of heaven; whatsoever thou shall bind on earth shall be bound also in heaven and whatsoever thou shall loose on earth shall be loosed also in heaven." It is a very wonderful and glorious thing to bind and loose on earth and to have that sentence of binding and loosing carried out in heaven.

While the blessed Sylvester was preaching these things I understood them and found that I was restored to full health by the beneficence of the same blessed Peter. So, we together with all our satraps and the whole Senate and all the nobles and the whole Roman people which is subject to the glory of our Empire, judged it in the public interest that, because St. Peter was made Vicar of the

[8]The "Donation" begins with an elaborate statement concerning Constantine's conversion to Christianity and a theological part explaining the Christian Creed. Constantine was believed (incorrectly) to have been miraculously cured of leprosy by Pope Sylvester I.

Son of God on earth, the Pontiffs also, who are the successors of the same Prince of the Apostles, may obtain from us and our Empire greater governmental power than the earthly clemency of our Imperial serenity has so far conceded to them; thus we chose the same Prince of the Apostles and his Vicar to be our powerful patrons with God. And because our Imperial power is earthly, we have decided to honor reverently his most holy Roman Church, and to exalt the most holy See of blessed Peter in glory above our own Empire and earthly throne, ascribing to it power and glorious majesty and strength and Imperial honor.

And we command and decree that he should have primacy over the four principal Sees of Antioch, Alexandria, Constantinople and Jerusalem, as well as over all the Churches of God throughout the whole world; and the Pontiff who occupies at any given moment the See of that same most holy Roman Church shall rank as the highest and chief among all the priests of the whole world and by his decision all things are to be arranged concerning the worship of God or the security of the faith of Christians. For it is just that the holy law should have its center of government at the place where the institutor of the holy laws, our Saviour, commanded blessed Peter to set up the chair of his apostolate.

Let every people and the nations of the Gentiles in all the world rejoice therefore with us; we exhort you all that you return thanks abundantly to our God and Saviour Jesus Christ, because he is God in Heaven above and on earth beneath, Who, visiting us through His holy Apostles made us worthy to receive the holy Sacrament of Baptism and bodily health. In recompense for this we concede to those same holy Apostles, my lords the most blessed Peter and Paul and through them also to blessed Sylvester our father, Supreme Pontiff and Universal Pope of the City of Rome, and to all his successors, the Pontiffs who will preside over the See of blessed Peter until the end of the world, and by this present document we confer, our Imperial palace of the Lateran, which surpasses and excels all palaces in the whole world, then a diadem which is the crown of our head, and at the same time the tiara; also the shoulder covering, that is the strap which is wont to surround our Imperial neck; also the purple cloak and the crimson tunic and all our Imperial garments. They shall also receive the rank of those who preside over the Imperial cavalry. We confer on them also the Imperial scepters and at the same time the spears and standards, also the banners and various Imperial decorations and all the prerogatives of our supreme Imperial position and the glory of our authority.

We decree that those very reverend men, the clerics who serve the most holy Roman Church in various orders, shall have the same dignity, distinction, power and preeminence, by the glory of which our Senate is decorated; and we decree that the clergy of the most holy Roman Church shall be adorned as are the soldiers of the Empire. Above all, in addition, we grant to the same our most holy father Sylvester, Bishop of the City of Rome and Pope, and to all the most blessed Pontiffs who shall come after him in succession for ever, for the honor and glory of Christ our God, to add to the numbers in that same great Catholic and Apostolic Church of God any one from our court who shall wish of his own free choice to become a cleric, and to add any to the number of monastic clergy. Let no one presume to act arrogantly in all these matters.

To correspond to our own Empire and so that the supreme Pontifical authority may not be dishonored, but may rather be adorned with glorious power greater than the dignity of any earthly empire, behold, we give to the often-mentioned most holy Pontiff, our father Sylvester, the Universal Pope, not only the above-mentioned palace, but also the city of Rome and all the provinces, districts and cities of Italy and the Western regions, relinquishing them to the authority of himself and his successors as Pontiffs by a definite Imperial grant. We have decided that this should be laid down by this our divine, holy and lawfully framed decree and we grant it on a permanent legal basis to the holy Roman Church.

Therefore we have seen it to be fitting that our Empire and the power of the kingdom should be transferred and translated to the Eastern regions and that in the province of Byzantium in the most suitable place a city should be built in our name and our Empire established there; because it is not just that an earthly Emperor should exercise authority where the government of priests and the Head of the Christian religion have been installed by the heavenly Emperor.

We decree also that all the things, which we have established and approved by this our holy Imperial edict and by other divine decrees shall remain uninjured and unbroken until the end of the world; so, in the presence of the living God, Who ordered us to reign, and in the presence of His terrible judgment, we solemnly warn, by this our Imperial enactment, all our successors as Emperors and all our nobles, the satraps, the most honorable Senate and all people throughout the world, now and in the future and in all times previously subject to our Empire, that none of them will be permitted in any way to oppose or destroy or to take away any of these privileges, which have been conceded by our Imperial decree to the most holy Roman Church and to its Pontiffs.

READING 6
Einhard, The Life of Charlemagne[9]

Einhard (c. 770–840) was reared in the monastery of Fulda, founded by St. Boniface, and joined Charlemagne's court in the early 790s. He served Charlemagne as an administrative official and knew him well. Einhard wrote his biography a few years after Charlemagne's death (814). As secretary to Charlemagne's son and heir, Louis the Pious, Einhard had

---

[9]From *Early Lives of Charlemagne,* ed. and tr. A. J. Grant; London, Chatto & Windus, Ltd., 1922, part 1, chaps. 7, 8, 9, 11.

easy access to court annals and official records. He also drew on his own intimate knowledge of the great emperor. Modeling his work on *The Lives of the Caesars* by the ancient Roman historian Suetonius, Einhard borrowed a number of descriptive passages from Suetonius's life of Augustus. Later medieval biographers, using a similar methodology, borrowed heavily from Einhard. But Einhard borrowed cautiously and intelligently, and his work, despite its Suetonian echoes and admiring tone, brings us closer to the historical Charlemagne than does any other source. Later biographies portray Charlemagne as a legendary hero performing impossible deeds. The Gascon attack on Charlemagne's rearguard as his army withdrew from Spain was expanded and embroidered in later centuries into the great epic poem *The Song of Roland.*

When [the war in Aquitaine] was ended the Saxon war, which seemed dropped for a time, was taken up again. Never was there a war more prolonged nor more cruel than this, nor one that required greater efforts on the part of the Frankish peoples. For the Saxons, like most of the races that inhabit Germany, are by nature fierce, devoted to the worship of demons and hostile to our religion, and they think it no dishonor to confound and transgress the laws of God and man. There were reasons, too, which might at any time cause a disturbance of the peace. For our boundaries and theirs touch almost everywhere on the open plain, except where in a few places large forests or ranges of mountains are interposed to separate the territories of the two nations by a definite frontier; so that on both sides murder, robbery, and arson were of constant occurrence. The Franks were so irritated by these things that they thought it was time no longer to be satisfied with retaliation but to declare open war against them.

So war was declared, and was fought for thirty years[10] continuously with the greatest fierceness on both sides, but with heavier loss to the Saxons than the Franks. The end might have been reached sooner had it not been for the perfidy of the Saxons. It is hard to say how often they admitted themselves beaten and surrendered as suppliants to King Charles; how often they promised to obey his orders, gave without delay the required hostages, and received the ambassadors that were sent to them. Sometimes they were so cowed and broken that they promised to abandon the worship of devils and willingly to submit themselves to the Christian religion. But though sometimes ready to bow to his commands they were always eager to break their promise, so that it is impossible to say which course seemed to come more natural to them, for from the beginning of the war there was scarcely a year in which they did not both promise and fail to perform.

[10]The Saxon wars lasted from 772 until 804.

But the high courage of the King and the constancy of his mind, which remained unshaken by prosperity and adversity, could not be conquered by their changes nor forced by weariness to desist from his undertakings. He never allowed those who offended in this way to go unpunished, but either led an army himself, or sent one under the command of his counts, to chastise their perfidy and inflict a suitable penalty. So that at last, when all who had resisted had been defeated and brought under his power, he took ten thousand of the inhabitants of both banks of the Elbe, with their wives and children, and planted them in many groups in various parts of Germany and Gaul. And at last the war, protracted through so many years, was finished on conditions proposed by the King and accepted by them; they were to abandon the worship of devils, to turn from their national ceremonies, to receive the sacraments of the Christian faith and religion, and then, joined to the Franks, to make one people with them.

In this war, despite its prolongation through so many years, he did not himself meet the enemy in battle more than twice,[11] once near the mountain called Osning, in the district of Detmold, and again at the river Haase, and both these battles were fought in one month, with an interval of only a few days.[12] In these two battles the enemy were so beaten and cowed that they never again ventured to challenge the King nor to resist his attack unless they were protected by some advantage of ground.

In this war many men of noble birth and high office fell on the side both of the Franks and Saxons. But at last it came to an end in the thirty-third year, though in the meanwhile so many and such serious wars broke out against the Franks in all parts of the world, and were carried on with such skill by the King, that an observer may reasonably doubt whether his endurance of toil or his good fortune deserves the greater admiration. For the war in Italy began two years before the Saxon war [in 770], and though it was prosecuted without intermission no enterprise in any part of the world was dropped, nor was there anywhere a truce in any struggle, however difficult. For this King, the wisest and most high-minded of all who in that age ruled over the nations of the world, never refused to undertake or prosecute any enterprise because of the labor involved, nor withdrew from it through fear of its danger. He understood the true character of each task that he undertook or carried through, and thus was neither broken by adversity nor misled by the false flatteries of good fortune.

While the war with the Saxons was being prosecuted constantly and almost continuously he placed garrisons at suitable places on the frontier, and attacked Spain with the largest military expedition that he could collect. He crossed the Pyrenees, received the surrender of all the towns and fortresses that he attacked, and returned with his army safe and sound, except for a reverse which he

---

[11]In addition to the two battles mentioned by Einhard, Charlemagne also met the Saxons at a battle near Lübeck in 775 and one at Bochult in 779, both sites in northern Germany.

[12]These engagements were fought in 783.

experienced through the treason of the Gascons on his return through the passes of the Pyrenees. For while his army was marching in a long line, suiting their formation to the character of the ground and the defiles, the Gascons placed an ambuscade on the top of the mountain—where the density and extent of the woods in the neighborhood rendered it highly suitable for such a purpose—and then rushing down into the valley beneath threw into disorder the last part of the baggage train and also the rear-guard which acted as a protection to those in advance. In the battle which followed the Gascons slew their opponents to the last man.[13] Then they seized upon the baggage, and under cover of the night, which was already falling, they scattered with the utmost rapidity in different directions. The Gascons were assisted in this feat by the lightness of their armor and the character of the ground where the affair took place. In this battle Eggihard, who was in charge of the King's table, Anselm, the count of the Palace, and Roland, lord of the Breton frontier, were killed along with very many others. Nor could this assault be punished at once, for when the deed had been done the enemy so completely disappeared that they left behind them not so much as a rumor of their whereabouts. . . .

Then the Bavarian war broke out suddenly, and was swiftly ended. It was caused by the pride and folly of Tassilo, Duke of Bavaria.[14] For upon the instigation of his wife—who thought that she might revenge through her husband the banishment of her father Desiderius, King of the Lombards—Tassilo made an alliance with the Huns,[15] the eastern neighbors of the Bavarians, and not only refused obedience to King Charles but even dared to challenge him in war. The high courage of the King could not bear his overweening insolence, and he forthwith called a general levy for an attack on Bavaria, and came in person with a great army to the river Lech, which separates Bavaria from Germany. He pitched his camp upon the banks of the river, and determined to make trial of the mind of the Duke before he entered the province. But Duke Tassilo saw no profit either for himself or his people in stubbornness, and threw himself upon the King's mercy. He gave the hostages who were demanded, his own son Theodo among the number, and further promised upon oath that no one should ever persuade him again to fall away from his allegiance to the King. And thus a war which seemed likely to grow into a very great one came to a most swift ending. But Tassilo was subsequently summoned into the King's presence, and was not allowed to return,[16] and the province that he ruled was for the future committed to the administration not of dukes but of counts.

---

[13]It was Basques, not Gascons, who engaged the rear-guard on August 15, 778, in the Battle of Roncevaux, so called since the composition of the "Song of Roland" in the late eleventh century.

[14]This war took place in 787–788.

[15]More properly the Avars, yet Einhard continually refers to them as the "Huns."

[16]Duke Tassilo was forcibly placed in the monastery at Jumièges.

READING 7

Charlemagne, Letter to Pope Leo III[17]

This letter, written about four years before Pope Leo III (795–816) crowned Charlemagne (768–814) Roman emperor, shows not only Charlemagne's policy toward the papacy but also his ideas about the proper functions of spiritual and secular power. The idea persists, from the conversion of Constantine and of Clovis, that the Christian God is the god of military victory.

As I have done with your predecessors, I desire to establish with your blessedness an inviolable covenant of faith and charity so that divine mercy obtained by the prayers of your apostolic holiness and your apostolic blessing may follow me everywhere while, God willing, the most holy See of the Roman Church will always be defended by our devotion. Indeed, it is our task with divine help to shield everywhere with our arms the Holy Church of Christ from all her enemies abroad, from the incursions of the heathen and the devastations of the infidel, and to fortify her from within by the profession of the Catholic faith. It is your part, holy father, to assist the success of our arms with your hands raised in prayer to God, as Moses did, so that by your intervention, God willing and granting, the Christian people will forever achieve victory over the enemies of His name, and the name of our Lord Jesus Christ will be glorified throughout the world.

READING 8

Documents Relating to the Imperial Coronation of Charlemagne[18]

All historians are agreed that Pope Leo III crowned Charlemagne Roman emperor on Christmas Day, A.D. 800, thereby reviving the Western Empire after a hiatus of nearly 325 years. They are not agreed, however, on whether the initiative was Leo's or Charlemagne's. These sources bear on the issue, but they do not resolve it.

[17]From S. Ehler and J. B. Morral, *Church and State through the Centuries;* New York, Bilbo and Tannen, Inc., 1967, p. 12.

[18] From S. C. Easton and H. Wieruszowski, *The Era of Charlemagne;* Princeton, N. J., Van Nostrand, Inc., 1961, pp. 126–129.

A.   ALCUIN, LETTER TO CHARLEMAGNE, JUNE 799

To this day three persons have held the highest positions in this world: The apostolic sublimity who as the vicar of the blessed Peter, prince of the apostles, occupies his See. Thanks to your care I have been informed of the fate of the last incumbent [i.e., Leo III] of this See.[19] The second is the imperial dignity and the secular power of the Second Rome. The rumor of the impious fashion in which the present head of the empire was deposed not by foreigners but by relatives and fellow citizens has spread everywhere. The third person is the royal dignity to the peak of which you have been exalted as the ruler of the Christian people: it excels the two others in power, renowned for wisdom, and sublime royal dignity. The welfare of the Church is now in danger and rests on you alone: you are the avenger of evil deeds, the guide of those who go astray, the comforter of those who mourn, the glory of the good.

B.   THE ANNALS OF LORSCH, C. 800

And as the title of an emperor had then come to an end among the Greeks, since they had a woman [Irene] on the imperial throne, it seemed to Pope Leo[20] and the holy fathers assembled at the council as well as to the rest of the Christian people that they should give the title of emperor to Charles, King of the Franks, since he held not only Rome itself, where the Caesars used to reside, but the other seats in Italy, Gaul, and Germany as well. Since the almighty God had given into his possession all these places, they deemed it right that with the assistance of God and according to the request of the whole Christian people he should bear the title also. King Charles was not able to refuse this demand: in all humility he submitted to God and to the request of the whole Christian people and on the day of the nativity of our Lord Jesus Christ he assumed the title of an emperor and was consecrated by Pope Leo.

C.   THE LIFE OF POPE LEO III, 812

After this [the purgation oath of Leo taken in the Basilica of St. Peter] all convened again on the day of the nativity in the abovementioned Basilica of the blessed apostle Peter. And then the venerable and peaceful pontiff crowned him with his own hands with that most precious crown. Then all the faithful Romans who saw how he was eager to defend and how he loved the Holy Roman Church and its vicar, cried out with one voice—and this was the will of God and of the blessed Peter, the key-holder to the kingdom of heaven: To Charles, the most pious Augustus, crowned by God, the great and peaceful emperor, life and vic-

---

[19]Leo III was accused of wrongdoing by hostile Roman townspeople and in 799 was forced to flee Rome and take refuge at Charlemagne's court.
[20]Leo cleared himself of the charges against him by publicly swearing his innocence.

tory! This was announced three times before the holy confession of the Blessed Apostle Peter while they were invoking various saints; and he was established by all as Emperor of the Romans.

Thereupon the most holy prelate and pontiff anointed King Charles, his most excellent son, with the holy oil on that very day of the nativity of our Lord Jesus Christ.

D. EINHARD, LIFE OF CHARLEMAGNE, 814

Although [Charlemagne] held [the Roman Church] in great respect, he only traveled to Rome to fulfill his vows and make his supplications four times during the forty-seven years of his reign.

But for his last journey there was still another reason. The Romans had inflicted many injuries upon Pope Leo, tearing out his eyes and cutting out his tongue so that he felt compelled to implore the help of the king. Therefore he went to Rome to restore order in the much disturbed affairs of the Church, and stayed there for the whole winter. At this time he received the titles of Emperor and Augustus. But at first he disliked this act so much that he declared that, had he anticipated the intention of the pontiff, he would not have entered the church on that day when it happened, although it was a great feast day. But he endured very patiently the jealousy of the emperors who were indignant about his assuming these titles. By sending them frequent embassies and letters in which he addressed them as brothers, he overcame their contempt with his magnanimity, in which he was undoubtedly their superior.

READING 9

The General Capitulary for the Missi[21]

This imperial ordinance (capitulary), issued shortly after Charlemagne's coronation as Roman emperor, provides valuable evidence regarding the administration of the Carolingian realm. It discloses, among other things, the way in which the *missi dominici* were employed, the importance of oaths of loyalty (to the emperor as distinct from the empire), the workings of the Germanic-based legal system, the intimate connection between empire and church, and—by implication—the high incidence of crime and violence within Charlemagne's dominions. What the document does not reveal is the degree to which Charlemagne's commands were actually carried out.

[21]From *The Reign of Charlemagne*, ed. H. R. Loyn and J. Percival; London, Edward Arnold, Ltd., 1975, pp. 74–79. Reprinted by permission of Edward Arnold, Ltd.

1. Concerning the commission dispatched by our lord the emperor. Our most serene and most Christian lord and emperor, Charles, has selected the most prudent and wise from among his leading men, archbishops and bishops, together with venerable abbots and devout laymen, and has sent them out into all his kingdom, and bestowed through them on all his subjects the right to live in accordance with a right rule of law. Wherever there is any provision in the law that is other than right or just he has ordered them to inquire most diligently into it and bring it to his notice, it being his desire, with God's help, to rectify it. And let no one dare or be allowed to use his wit and cunning, as many do, to subvert the law as it is laid down or the emperor's justice, whether it concerns God's churches, or poor people and widows and orphans, or any Christian person. Rather should all men live a good and just life in accordance with God's commands, and should with one mind remain and abide each in his appointed place or profession: the clergy should live a life in full accord with the canons without concern for base gain, the monastic orders should keep their life under diligent control, the laity and secular people should make proper use of their laws, refraining from ill-will and deceit, and all should live together in perfect love and peace. And the missi[22] themselves, as they wish to have the favor of Almighty God and to preserve it through the loyalty they have promised, are to make diligent inquiry wherever a man claims that someone has done him an injustice; so everywhere, and amongst all men, in God's holy churches, among poor people, orphans and widows, and throughout the whole people they may administer law and justice in full accordance with the will and the fear of God. And if there be anything which they themselves, together with the counts of the provinces, cannot correct or bring to a just settlement, they should refer it without any hesitation to the emperor's judgment along with their reports. And in no way, whether by some man's flattery or bribery, or by the excuse of blood relationship with someone, or through fear of someone more powerful, should anyone hinder the right and proper course of justice.

2. Concerning the promise of fealty to our lord the emperor. He has given instructions that in all his kingdom all men, both clergy and laity, and each according to his vows and way of life, who before have promised fealty to him as king, should now make the same promise to him as Caesar; and those who until now have not made the promise are all to do so from twelve years old and upwards. And that all should be publicly informed, so that each man may understand how many important matters are contained in that oath—not only, as many have thought until now, the profession of loyalty to our lord the emperor throughout his life, and the undertaking not to bring any enemy into his kingdom for hostile reasons, nor to consent to or be silent about anyone's infidelity towards him, but also that all men may know that the oath has in addition the following meaning within it.

---

[22]The closest modern equivalent of "missus" or "missi" is "commissioner," but neither it nor "envoy" conveys its full meaning.

3. First, that everyone on his own behalf should strive to maintain himself in God's holy service, in accordance with God's command and his own pledge, to the best of his ability and intelligence, since our lord the emperor himself is unable to provide the necessary care and discipline to all men individually.

4. Second, that no man, through perjury or any other craft or deceit, or through anyone's flattery or bribery, should in any way withhold or take away or conceal our lord the emperor's serf, or his landmark, or his land, or anything that is his by right of possession; and that no one should conceal the men of his fisc[23] who run away and unlawfully and deceitfully claim to be free men, nor take them away by perjury or any other craft.

5. That no one should presume to commit fraud or theft or any other criminal act against God's holy churches or against widows or orphans or pilgrims; for the lord emperor himself, after God and his saints, has been appointed their protector and defender.

6. That no one should dare neglect a benefice [land granted on condition of service] held of our lord the emperor, and build up his own property from it.

7. That no one should presume to ignore a summons to the host from our lord the emperor, and that no count should be so presumptuous as to dare to excuse any of those who ought to go with the host, either on the pretext of kinship or through the enticement of any gift.

8. That no one should presume to subvert in any way any edict or any order of our lord the emperor, nor trifle with his affairs nor hinder nor weaken them, nor act in any other way contrary to his will and his instructions. And that no one should dare to be obstructive about any debt or payment that he owes.

9. That no one in court should make a practice of defending another man in an unlawful manner, by arguing the case weakly through a desire for gain, by hampering a lawful judgment by showing off his skill in pleading, or by presenting a weak case in an attempt to do his client harm. Rather should each man plead for himself, be it a question of tax or debt or some other case, unless he is infirm or unacquainted with pleading; for such men the missi or the chief men who are in the court or a judge who knows the case can plead it before the court, or if necessary a man can be provided to plead, who is approved by all parties and has a good knowledge of the case at issue; this, however, should only be done at the convenience of the chief men or missi who are present. At all events, it must be done in accordance with justice and the law; and no one should be allowed to impede the course of justice by offering a reward or fee, by skillful and ill-intentioned flattery, or by the excuse of kinship. And let no one make an unlawful agreement with anyone, but let all men be seriously and willingly prepared to see that justice is done. . . .

---

[23]The "fisc" is an administrative unit of the royal estates that can be translated "crown lands" or "crown estate," though at times it means, as in this case, the "royal purse."

25. That the counts and *centenarii*[24] should strive to see that justice is done and should have as assistants in their duties men in whom they can have full confidence, who will faithfully observe justice and the law, will in no wise oppress the poor, and will not dare, for flattery or a bribe, to conceal in any manner of concealment any thieves, robbers or murderers, adulterers, evil-doers and performers of incantations and auguries, and all other sacriligious people, but rather will bring them to light, that they may receive correction and punishment according to the law, and that with God's indulgence all these evils may be removed from among our Christian people.

26. That the justices should give right judgment according to the written law, and not according to private opinions.

27. We ordain that no one in all our kingdom, whether rich or poor, should dare to deny hospitality to pilgrims; that is, no one should refuse a roof, a hearth and water to any pilgrims who are traveling the country in the service of God, or to anyone who is journeying for love of God or for the salvation of his soul. And if a man should be willing to offer any further benefit to such people, let him know that God will give him the best reward, as he himself said: "Whoever shall receive one such little child in my name receiveth me"; and in another place, "I was a stranger, and ye took me in" [Matthew 18:5; 25:35].

28. Concerning the commissions coming from our lord the emperor: The counts and the *centenarii* should, as they are desirous of the favor of our lord the emperor, provide for the missi who are sent upon them with all possible attention, that they may go about their duties without any delay; and he has given instructions to all men that it is their duty to make such provision, that they suffer no delay to occur anywhere, and that they help men to go upon their way with all haste, and make such provision for this as our missi may require.

29. Concerning those poor men who owe payment of the royal fine and to whom the lord emperor in his mercy has given remission: the counts or the missi are not to have the right for their part to bring constraint upon people so excused.

30. Concerning those whom the lord emperor wishes, with Christ's blessing, to have peace and protection in his kingdom, that is, those who have thrown themselves upon his mercy, those who, whether Christians or pagans, have desired to offer any information, or who from poverty or hunger have sought his intervention: let no one dare to bind them in servitude or take possession of them or dispose of them or sell them, but rather let them stay where they themselves choose, and live there under the lord emperor's protection and in his mercy. If anyone should presume to transgress this instruction, let him know that a man so presumptuous as to despise the lord emperor's orders must pay for it with the loss of his life.

---

[24]*Centenarii* were subordinates of a count with administrative and judicial functions within the territorial divisions of a county.

31. For those who administer the justice of our lord the emperor let no one dare to devise harm or injury, nor bring any hostility to bear upon them. Anyone who presumes to do so must pay the royal fine; and if he is guilty of a greater offence, the orders are that he be brought to the king's presence.

32. Murder, by which a great multitude of our Christian people perish, we ordain should be shunned and avoided by every possible means; Our Lord himself forbade hatred and enmity among his faithful, and murder even more. How can a man feel confident that he will be at peace with God, when he has killed the son most close to himself? Or who can believe that Christ Our Lord is on his side, when he has murdered his brother? It is, moreover, a great and unacceptable risk with God the Father and Christ the ruler of heaven and earth to arouse the hostility of men. With men, we can escape for a time by hiding, but even so by some chance of fortune we fall into our enemy's hands; but where can a man escape from God, from whom no secrets are hid? What rashness to think to escape his anger! For this reason we have sought, by every kind of precept, to prevent the people entrusted to us for ruling from perishing as a result of this evil; for he who feels no dread at the anger of God should not receive mild and benevolent treatment from us; rather would we wish a man who had dared to commit the evil act of murder to receive the severest of punishments. Nevertheless, in order that the crime should not increase further, and in order that serious enmity should not arise among Christians when they resort to murders at the persuasion of the devil, the guilty person should immediately set about making amends, and should with all possible speed pay the appropriate recompense to the relatives of the dead men for the evil he has done to them. And this we firmly forbid, that the parents of the dead man should dare in any way to increase the enmity arising from the crime committed, or refuse to allow peace when the request is made; rather, they should accept the word given to them and the compensation offered, and allow perpetual peace, so long as the guilty man does not delay payment of the compensation. And when a man sinks to such a depth of crime as to kill his brother or a relative, he must betake himself immediately to the penance devised for him, and do so as his bishop instructs him and without any compromising. He should strive with God's help to make full amends, and should pay compensation for the dead man according to the law and make his peace in full with his kinsmen; and once the parties have given their word let no one dare to arouse further enmity on the matter. And anyone who scorns to pay the appropriate compensation is to be deprived of his inheritance pending our judgment.

33. We forbid absolutely the crime of incest. If anyone is stained by wicked fornication he must in no circumstances be let off without severe penalty, but rather should be punished for it in such a way that others will be deterred from committing the same offence, that filthiness may be utterly removed from our Christian people, and that the guilty person himself may be fully freed from it through the penance that is prescribed for him by his bishop. The woman

concerned should be kept under her parents' supervision subject to our judgment. And if such people are unwilling to agree to the bishop's judgment concerning their improvement they are to be brought to our presence, mindful of that exemplary punishment for incest imposed by Fricco upon a certain nun.

34. That all should be fully and well prepared for whenever our order or announcement may come. And if anyone then maintains that he is not ready and disregards our instructions he is to be brought to the palace—and not he alone, but all those who presume to go against our edict or our orders.

35. That all bishops and their priests should be accorded all honor and respect in their service to God's will. They should not dare to stain themselves or others with incestuous unions. They should not presume to solemnize marriages until the bishops and priests, together with the elders of the people, have carefully inquired to see if there be any blood relationship between the parties, and should only then give their blessing to the marriage. They should avoid drunkenness, shun greediness, and not commit theft; disputes and quarrels and blasphemies, whether in normal company or in a legal sense, should be entirely avoided; rather, they should live in love and unity.

36. That all men should contribute to the full administration of justice by giving their agreement to our missi. They should not in any way give their approval to the practice of perjury, which is a most evil crime and must be removed from among our Christian people. And if anyone after this is convicted of perjury he should know that he will lose his right hand; but he is also to be deprived of his inheritance subject to our judgment.

37. That those who commit patricide or fratricide, or who kill an uncle or a father-in-law or any of their kinsmen, and who refuse to obey and consent to the judgment of bishops, priests, and other justices, are for the salvation of their souls and for the carrying out of the lawful judgment to be confined by our missi and counts in such custody that they will be safe, and will not pollute the rest of the people, until such time as they are brought to our presence. And in the meantime they are not to have any of their property.

38. The same is to be done with those who are arraigned and punished for unlawful and incestuous unions, and who refuse to mend their ways or submit to their bishops and priests, and who presume to disregard our edict.

39. That no one should dare to steal our beasts in our forests; this we have forbidden already on many occasions, and we now firmly ban it again, that no one should do it any more and should take care to keep the faith which everyone has promised to us and desires to keep. And if any count or *centenarius* or vassal of ours or any of our officials should steal our game he must at all costs be brought to our presence to account for it. As for the rest of the people, anyone who steals the game in this way should in every case pay the appropriate penalty, and under no circumstances should anyone be let off in this matter. And if anyone knows that it has been done by someone else, in accordance with the faith he has promised to us to keep and has now to promise again he should not dare to conceal this.

40. Finally, therefore, from all our decrees we desire it to be known in all our kingdom through our missi now sent out: among the clergy, the bishops, abbots, priests, deacons, clerks, and all monks and nuns, that each one in his ministry or profession should keep our edict or decree, and when it is right should of his good will offer thanks to the people, give them help, or if need be correct them in some way. Similarly for the laity, in all places everywhere, if a plea is entered concerning the protection of the holy churches, or of widows or orphans or less powerful people, or concerning the host [army], and is argued on these cases, we wish them to know that they should be obedient to our order and our will, that they maintain observance of our edict, and that in all these matters each man strive to keep himself in God's holy service. This in order that everything should be good and well-ordered for the praise of Almighty God, and that we should give thanks where it is due; that where we believe anything to have gone unpunished we should so strive with all earnestness and willingness to correct it that with God's help we may bring it to correction, to the eternal reward both of ourselves and of all our faithful people. Similarly concerning the counts and *centenarii,* our officers [*ministerialibus*], we wish all the things above mentioned in our deliberations to be known. So be it.

READING 10

Charlemagne, Letter to Abbot Baugulf, Late 700s[25]

Although undated, this letter must have been written before Charlemagne's imperial coronation in 800 because he titles himself "patrician" rather than "emperor of the Romans." The letter reflects Charlemagne's policy of using the church to advance literacy and learning. It also reflects, by implication, the state of learning at the time. Although addressed to Abbot Baugulf of Fulda, the letter was intended for all bishops and abbots—as its conclusion attests. One can only hope that they possessed sufficient learning and patience to decipher the tangled sentence that follows the address clause.

Charles, by the grace of God, king of the Franks and Lombards and patrician of the Romans, to Abbot Baugulf and to all the congregation, also to the faithful committed to you, we have directed a loving greeting by our ambassadors in the name of omnipotent God.

[25]From *Translations and Reprints from Original Sources of European History,* vol. VI, no. 5, ed. and tr. D. C. Munro; Philadelphia, University of Pennsylvania Press, 1897, pp. 12–14.

Be it known, therefore, to your devotion pleasing to God, that we, together with our faithful, have considered it useful that the bishoprics and monasteries entrusted by the favor of Christ to our control, in addition to the order of monastic life and the intercourse of holy religion, in the culture of letters also ought to be zealous in teaching those who by the gift of God are able to learn, according to the capacity of each individual, so that just as the observance of the rule imparts order and grace to honesty of morals, so also zeal in teaching and learning may do the same for sentences, so that those who desire to please God by living rightly should not neglect to please him also by speaking correctly. For it is written: "Either from thy words thou shalt be justified or from thy words thou shalt be condemned." For although correct conduct may be better than knowledge, nevertheless knowledge precedes conduct. Therefore, each one ought to study what he desires to accomplish, so that so much the more fully the mind may know what ought to be done, as the tongue hastens in the praises of omnipotent God without the hindrances of errors. For since errors should be shunned by all men, so much the more ought they to be avoided as far as possible by those who are chosen for this very purpose alone, so that they ought to be the especial servants of truth. For when in the years just passed, letters were often written to us from several monasteries in which it was stated that the brethren who dwelt there offered up in our behalf sacred and pious prayers, we have recognized in most of these letters both correct thoughts and uncouth expressions; because what pious devotion dictated faithfully to the mind, the tongue, uneducated on account of the neglect of study, was not able to express in the letter without error. Whence it happened that we began to fear lest perchance, as the skill in writing was less, so also the wisdom for understanding the Holy Scriptures might be much less than it rightly ought to be. And we all know well that, although errors of speech are dangerous, far more dangerous are errors of the understanding. Therefore, we exhort you not only not to neglect the study of letters, but also with most humble mind, pleasing to God, to study earnestly in order that you may be able more easily and more correctly to penetrate the mysteries of the divine Scriptures. Since, moreover, images, tropes and similar figures are found in the sacred pages, no one doubts that each one in reading these will understand the spiritual sense more quickly if previously he shall have been fully instructed in the mastery of letters. Such men truly are to be chosen for this work as have both the will and the ability to learn and a desire to instruct others. And may this be done with a zeal as great as the earnestness with which we command it. For we desire you to be, as it is fitting that soldiers of the church should be, devout in mind, learned in discourse, chaste in conduct and eloquent in speech, so that whosoever shall seek to see you out of reverence for God, or on account of your reputation for holy conduct, just as he is edified by your appearance, may also be instructed by your wisdom, which he has learned from your reading or singing, and may go away joyfully giving thanks to omnipotent God. Do not neglect, therefore, if you wish to have our favor, to send copies of this letter to all your suffragans and fellow bishops and to all the monasteries.

READING 11

Letters of Alcuin of York to Charlemagne[26]

We have already encountered a brief letter of Alcuin's commenting on the papal, imperial, and royal dignities shortly before Charlemagne's coronation as Roman emperor (see Reading 8A). The two letters that follow are concerned with books and learning at the court of Charlemagne, at Alcuin's monastery of St. Martin of Tours, and throughout Francia.

As one of the chief architects of the Carolingian Renaissance, the Northumbrian scholar Alcuin of York (c. 732–804) has left more than 300 letters written to individuals and religious communities. Many of them involve the spiritual and intellectual activities surrounding the royal court of Charlemagne and its palace school, which Alcuin directed between 782 and 796, when he became abbot of St.-Martin, Tours. The king gathered a distinguished assemblage of scholar-churchmen from all over Europe to help revitalize learning and the arts throughout his extensive realm. In Alcuin's correspondence with Charlemagne, the two men habitually referred to each other as Flaccus (Horace) and David, respectfully, thus rendering playful homage to both the Augustan age of Rome and the Biblical kingdom of Israel.

A. LETTER TO CHARLEMAGNE, 796 OR 797

I, your Flaccus, according to your exhortation and encouragement, am occupied in supplying to some under the roof of St. Martin the honey of the sacred Scriptures; am eager to inebriate others with the old wine of ancient learning; begin to nourish others on the fruits of grammatical subtlety; long to illumine some with the order of the stars, like the painted ceiling of a great man's house; becoming many things to many men [I Corinthians 9:22], that I may instruct many to the profit of the Holy Church of God and to the adornment of your imperial kingdom, that the grace of the Almighty be not void in me [I Corinthians 15:101], nor the bestowal of your bounty in vain.

But I, your servant, miss to some extent the rarer books of scholastic learning which I had in my own country through the excellent and devoted zeal of my master [Æthelbert, afterwards archbishop of York] and also through some toil of my own. I tell these things to your Excellency, in case it may perchance be agreeable to your counsel, which is most eager for the whole of knowledge, that I send some of our pupils to choose there what we need, and to bring into France the flowers of Britain; that not in York only there may be a 'garden enclosed,' but in

---

[26]From *English Historical Documents, c. 500–1042,* ed. and tr. Dorothy Whitelock; New York, Oxford University Press, 1968, p. 786; and Stewart C. Easton and Helene Wieruszowski, *The Era of Charlemagne;* New York, Van Nostrand Company, 1961, pp. 174–176.

Tours the 'plants of Paradise with the fruit of the orchard,' that the south wind may come and blow through the gardens by the River Loire, and the aromatical spices thereof may flow; and finally, that there may come to pass what flows in the Canticle from which I have taken this metaphor: 'Let my beloved come into his garden and eat the fruit of his apple trees'; and he may say to his young men: "Eat, friends, and drink and be inebriated, my dearly beloved." I sleep, and my heart watcheth [Song of Songs, 4:16; 5:1 ff]; or that admonitory utterance of the prophet Isaiah on the teaching of wisdom: 'All you that thirst, come to the waters. And you that have no money, make haste, buy and eat. Come ye: buy wine and milk without money and without any price' [Isaiah 55: 1].

B.   LETTER TO CHARLEMAGNE, 799

Most venerable and devout king, we thank you for allowing our book, which you commanded us to write and send, to be read out to you; we also thank you for drawing attention to our mistakes and returning the book for correction, although you would have been much better qualified to correct these mistakes; it very often happens that the judgment of an outsider is more valuable than that of the author himself.

I have not seen the *Disputation between Felix and the Saracen,* nor can I find it in our library; indeed, I had not even heard of his name. Then I made further careful inquiry whether any member of our household had any information about this book and I was told I might find it in the possession of Leidrad, bishop of Lyons. I speedily sent my messenger to the bishop and told him to dispatch the book, if it were found, as quickly as possible.

When as a young man I went to Rome and was staying for a few days in the royal city of Pavia there was a Jew called Lullus who disputed with Master Peter [of Pisa]: I have heard that there exists in that city a written account of this disputation. He is the same Peter who has now become famous as a teacher of grammar at your palace. Perhaps your 'Homer' [Angilbert] has heard the above-named master speak about this.

I have sent your Excellency some specimens of style, which are backed by the authority of examples or verses of the venerable father [Master Peter]; for your enjoyment I have added some subtle formulae of arithmetic on the tablet which was blank when you sent it; it was bare when I first saw it and now I have clothed it and return it to you. Indeed, I think it is fit that this tablet which came to us ennobled by your seal should thus be further honored by our literary composition. And in case I have left out any type of style among the examples which I have selected, Beselel [Einhard],[27] our mutual friend and partner in work could

---

[27]The author of *The Life of Charlemagne* (Reading 6, p. 101).

add some verse written by the same father. Moreover, he can also give his opinion on the calculations contained in my book on arithmetic.

Clauses and sub-clauses correctly punctuated give an extremely fine polish to
a sentence; but authors are no longer familiar with them on account of their lack
of erudition. But your noble efforts have now brought about a rebirth of civilized
standards in every kind of knowledge and of useful erudition. Therefore it seems
to me highly desirable that writers should again learn to phrase their sentences
correctly.

As far as I am concerned I am engaged in a daily struggle against the illiter-
acy which prevails at Tours—although progress is rather slow. I can only wish
that your authority may stimulate the education of the children at the palace;
they should reproduce in their best style the lucid words by which you convey
your thought so that, wherever the king's writ runs, it should display the noble-
ness of the king's wisdom.

READING 12

John Scotus Erigena, On The Division of Nature[28]

John Scotus Erigena (c. 800–877), though a singular and enigmatic figure
who stood outside the mainstream, is now widely accepted as the most
original philosopher of the early Middle Ages. Born in Ireland in about
800, he later moved to France, where he became master of the palace
school at the invitation of Charles the Bald. Owing to his proficiency in
Greek Erigena was one of the first theologians to introduce the ideas of
Neo-Platonism into the Western European intellectual tradition. His
greatest work, *Periphyseon* (or *On The Division of Nature*), was composed
865 to 870. Tradition records that toward the end of his life he became
Abbot of Malmesbury in southern England and was stabbed to death by
some monks with their pens for "trying to get them to think." His works
were condemned as heretical at the Council of Sens in 1225, and later by
Pope Gregory XIII in 1585. The work is presented as a dialogue between
teacher (*nutritor,* literally, nurse) and student (*alumnus,* literally, nursling).
The first half of this argument anticipates the writing of Aquinas several
centuries later (see p. 262); the second half shows the odd, ultimately
heretical, directions his thought took him.

[28]From John Scotus Erigena, *Periphyseon (The Division of Nature),* tr. I. P. Sheldon-Williams,
revised by John O'Meara; Washington, D.C. and Montreal: Dumbarton Oaks and Editions
Bellarmin, 1987, Chapter 1, pp. 1–7, 11–12, 13–14.

Nutritor: As I frequently ponder and, so far as my talents allow, ever more carefully investigate the fact that the first and fundamental division of all things which either can be grasped by the mind or lie beyond its grasp is into those that are and those that are not, there comes to mind as a general term for them all what in Greek is called *Physis* and in Latin *Natura.* Or do you think otherwise?

Alumnus: No, I agree. For I too, when I enter upon the path of reasoning, find that this is so.

Nutritor: Nature, then, is the general name, as we said, for all things, for those that are and those that are not.

Alumnus: It is. For nothing at all can come into our thought that would not fall under this term.

Nutritor: Then since we agree to use this term for the genus, I should like you to suggest a method for its division by differentiations into species; or, if you wish, I shall first attempt a division, and your part will be to offer sound criticism.

It is my opinion that the division of Nature by means of four differences results in four species, [being divided] first into that which creates and is not created, secondly into that which is created and also creates, thirdly into that which is created and does not create, while the fourth neither creates nor is created. But within these four there are two pairs of opposites. For the third is the opposite of the first, the fourth of the second; but the fourth is classed among the impossibles, for it is of its essence that it cannot be.

I am sure you see the opposition of the third species to the first—for the first creates and is not created; it therefore has as its contrary that [which is created and does not create—and of the second to the fourth, for the second both is created and creates; it therefore has as its contrary in all respects the fourth,] which neither creates nor is created.

Alumnus: I see [that] clearly. But I am much perplexed by the fourth species that you have introduced. For about the other three I should not presume to raise any question at all, because, as I think, the first is understood to be the Cause of all things that are and that are not, Who is God; the second to be the primordial causes; and the third those things that become manifest through coming into being in times and places. For this reason a more detailed discussion which shall take each species individually is required, as I think.

Nutritor: Well, then: of the aforesaid divisions of Nature the first difference, as has seemed to us, is that which creates and is not created. And rightly so: for such a species of Nature is correctly predicated only of God, Who, since He alone creates all things, is understood to be [*anarxos*], that is, without beginning, because He alone is the principal Cause of all things which are made from Him and through Him, and therefore He is also the End of all things that are from Him, for it is He towards Whom all things strive.

Alumnus: I most firmly believe and, as far as I may, understand that only of the Divine Cause of all things is this rightly predicated; for it alone creates all things that are from it, and is not itself created by any cause which is superior [to itself] or precedes it.

Nutritor: Just so. But, as I think, in what has already been said considerable headway has been made towards the solution of this question. For we agreed that the motion of the Divine Nature is to be understood as nothing else but the purpose of the Divine Will to establish the things that are to be made. Therefore it is said that in all things the Divine Nature is being made, which is nothing else than the Divine Will. For in that Nature being is not different from willing, but willing and being are one and the same in the establishment of all things that are to be made. For example, one might say: this is the end to which the motion of the Divine Will is directed: that the things that are may be. Therefore, it creates all things which it leads forth out of nothing so that they may be, from not-being into being; but it is (also) created because nothing except itself exists as an essence since itself is the essence of all things. For as there is nothing that is good by its nature, except (the divine nature) itself, but everything which is said to be good is so by participation in the One Supreme Good, so everything which is said to exist exists not in itself but by participation in the Nature which truly exists. For our intellect also, before it enters upon thought and memory, is not unreasonably said not to be. For in itself it is invisible and known only to God and ourselves; but when it enters upon thoughts and takes shape in certain fantasies it is not inappropriately said to come into being. For it does so in the memory when it receives certain forms of things and sounds and colors and [other] sensibles—for it had no form before it entered into the memory—; then it receives, as it were, a second formation when it takes the form of certain signs of forms and sounds—I mean the letters which are the signs of sounds, and the figures which are the signs of mathematical forms—or other perceptible indicators by which it can be communicated to the senses of sentient beings. By this analogy, far removed as it is from the Divine Nature, I think it can be shown all the same how that Nature, although it creates all things and cannot be created by anything, is in an admirable manner created in all things which take their being from it; . . . so the Divine Essence which when it subsists by itself surpasses every intellect is correctly said to be created in those things which are made by itself and through itself and in itself [and for itself], so that in them either by the intellect, if they are only intelligible, or by the sense, if they are sensible, it comes to be known by those who investigate it in the right spirit.

I should like you to tell me whether you understand that anything opposed to God or conceived alongside of Him exists. By "opposed" I mean either deprived of Him or contrary to Him or related to Him or absent from Him; while by "conceived alongside of Him" I mean something that is understood to exist eternally with Him without being of the same essence with him.

Alumnus: I see clearly what you mean. And therefore I should not dare to say that there is either anything that is opposed to Him or anything understood in association with Him which is [*heterousion*], that is, which is of another essence than what He is. For opposites by relation are always so opposed to one another that they both begin to be at the same time and cease to be at the same time, whether they are of the same nature. For the same reason I do not know of anyone who would be so bold as to affirm that anything is co-eternal with God which is not co-essential with Him. For if such a thing can be conceived or discovered it necessarily follows that there is not one Principle of all things, but two [or more], widely differing from each other—which right reason invariably rejects without any hesitation: for from the One all things take their being; from two [or more], nothing.

Nutritor: You judge correctly, as I think. If therefore the Divine Names are confronted by other names directly opposed to them, the things which are properly signified by them must also of necessity be understood to have contraries opposite to them; and therefore they cannot properly be predicated of God, to Whom nothing is opposed, and with Whom nothing is found to be co-eternal which differs from Him by nature. For right reason cannot find a single one of the names already mentioned or others like them to which another name, disagreeing with it, being opposed or differing from it within the same genus, is not found; and what we know to be the case with the names we must necessarily know to be so with the [things] which are signified by them. But since the expressions of divine significance which are predicated of God in Holy Scripture by transference from the creature to the Creator—if, indeed, it is right to say that anything can be predicated of Him, which must be considered in another place—are innumerable and cannot be found or gathered together within the small compass of our reasoning, only a few of the Divine Names can be set forth for the sake of example. Thus, [God] is called Essence, but strictly speaking He is not essence: for to being is opposed not-being. Therefore He is [*hyperousios*], that is, superessential. Again, He is called Goodness, but strictly speaking He is not goodness: for to goodness wickedness is opposed. Therefore [He is] [*hyperagathos*] that is, more-than-good, and [*hyperagathotas*], that is, more-than-goodness. He is called God, but He is not strictly speaking God: for to vision is opposed blindness, and to him who sees he who does not see. Therefore He is [*hypertheos*] that is, more-than-God-for [*theos*] is interpreted "He Who sees." But if you have recourse to the alternative origin of this name, so that you understand [*theos*], that is, God, to be derived not from the verb [*theoro*], that is, "I see," but from the verb [*theo*], that is, "I run," the same reason confronts you. For to him who runs he who does not run is opposed, as slowness to speed. Therefore He will be [*hypertheos*], that is, more-than-running, as it is written: "His Word runneth swiftly": for we understand this to refer to God the Word, Who in an ineffable way runs through all things that are, in order that they may be. For the present, as I think, enough has been said [concerning these matters].

READING 13

Dhuoda, Handbook for William[29]

Dhuoda was a Frankish noblewoman living during the ninth century. Not much is known about her life except that she married Bernard, Duke of Septimania, in 824, and that they had two sons, William and Bernard. Her husband imprisoned Dhuoda—for unknown reasons—in a castle at Uzes. He was away at court and supposedly had an affair with Judith, wife of King Louis the Pious. To restore his position and as an act of loyalty he gave his eldest son William to Louis's son Charles the Bald as a prisoner. Dhuoda's younger son, Bernard, was also taken away from her (before he was even baptized). Confined at Uzes and without her children she wrote the *Liber Manualis,* or Handbook for William, which was intended to instruct William (and Bernard) about how he should conduct his life. The Handbook displays Dhuoda's breadth of knowledge in theology, philosophy, philology, and mathematics. She finished her manual in 843 and is believed to have died shortly thereafter. And perhaps the Handbook served its purpose, for Bernard was the father of Duke William of Aquitaine, the founder of the monastery of Cluny (Ch. 4, Reading 5). The following sections of the Handbook are taken from the very end of the work.

ON THE AGE YOU HAVE ATTAINED

You have now reached four times four years.
If my second son too were of this age,
I would have another copy of this little book made for him.
And if in twice as many years and half again
I were to see your image,
I would write to you of more difficult things, and in more words.
But because the time of my parting hastens,
And the suffering of pains everywhere wears my body down,
I have in haste gathered this book for your benefit and your brother's.
Knowing that I cannot reach that time I have mentioned,
I urge you to taste this as if it were the food of your mouth,
Like a sweetened drink mixed with grain.
For the time at which I came to your father,
Or when you were born of us into this earthly world—

---

[29]From Dhuoda, *Handbook for William: A Carolingian Woman's Counsel for Her Son,* tr. Carol Neel; Lincoln and London, University of Nebraska Press, 1991, pp. 95–100.

All this is known to us according to the dates of the months.
From the first line of this little book
To its last syllable, know that
All this is written for your salvation.
All the verses here—above and below, with all the rest—
I have dictated for the good of your spirit and your body.
I never cease directing you to read them aloud and keep them in your heart.
On the verses I have begun with the letters of your name.
So that you may flourish and be strong, best of children,
Do not hesitate to read the things I have spoken,
Written down, and addressed to you.
 There you will easily find what is pleasing for you.
God's word is living. Seek it out.
Diligently study its sacred learning.
For your mind will be filled with great joy
 Throughout all time.
May that great and strong king, the good, bright Lord,
Deign to nurture your mind through all that befalls you,
My young son. May he protect you and defend you
 In every hour.
May you be humble of mind and chaste
Of body, ready to do good service,
So that you can readily accommodate yourself to all,
 Both great and small.
Foremost, fear and love the Lord God
With all your mind and heart, and all your strength,
And then honor your father
 In every ways
As for that bountiful descendant of a line,
Scion of his race and lineage,
Him who shines in his great deeds—
 Never hesitate to serve him constantly.
Love the great magnates; esteem
Those who are first in the court, and act as the equal of those of low degree.
Join yourself to those of good will, and take care
 Not to yield to the proud and the evil.
Always hold in honor the rightly constituted ministers of the divine rites,
Those who are worthy of the prelate's status.
With simple sincerity, commend yourself always with outstretched hands
 To those who keep the altars.
Help widows and orphans often,
And be generous to pilgrims with food and drink,
Prepare lodgings for them, and extend your hand with

Clothing for the naked.
Be a strong and fair judge in legal matters,
Never take a bribe from anyone,
Nor oppress anyone. For he who has been your benefactor
    Will repay you.
Generous in gift giving, always watchful and prudent,
Agreeable to all, with a winning manner,
Profoundly joyful—such a countenance
    Will always be yours.
There is one who weighs out, who gives out in one direction or another.
He returns for the merits of all what their deeds deserve,
Granting the greatest reward, the stars of heaven,
    For words and works.
And so, my noble son, seek diligently.
Take care to hasten to receive
Such great rewards, and turn away your eyes
    From the fires of blackened wood.
Although you count to your flourishing youth
Only four times four years, growth,
Your tender limbs grow older
    As you travel your course.
It seems very far from me,
Wishing as I do to see the shape of your face—
If strength were given me, still my merits
    Are not enough to win it.
May you live for him who made you
With a clear mind, and join the worthy company of his servants,
So that you may rise again in joy
    After your course is ended.
Although my mind is wrapped in shadows,
Nevertheless I urge this, that you constantly read
The pages of this little book written out above,
    And that you fix them in your mind.
With God's help these verses end,
Now that eight years have twice gone by,
At the beginning of December, feast of St. Andrew,
    The season of the coming of the Word
    The verses end.

A POSTSCRIPT ON PUBLIC LIFE

Here the words of this little book concluded I have dictated them with an eager mind and have had them copied down for your benefit, as a model for you.

"For I wish and urge that, when with God's help you have grown to manhood, you may arrange your household well, in appropriate order. As is written
of another man who lived in this fashion, 'a man like the most tender little worm
of the wood,' perform all the duties of your public life with loyalty, in a well-
ordered fashion.

As for whether I survive to that time when I may see this with my own eyes, I
am uncertain—uncertain in my own merits, uncertain in my strength, battered as
I am among the waves in my frail toil. Although such is what I am, all things are
possible for the Almighty. It is not in man's power to do his own will, rather
whatever men accomplish is according to God's will. In the words of Scripture,
it is not of him that willeth nor of him that runneth, but of God that showeth
mercy. Now, trusting in him, I say nothing else but as it shall be the will of God
in heaven so it be done. Amen.

Returning to myself, I grieve.

The sweetness of my great love for you and my desire for your beauty have
made me all but forget my own situation. I wish now, the doors being shut, to
return to my own self. But because I am not worthy to be numbered among
those who are mentioned above; I still ask that you—among the innumerable
people who may do so—pray without ceasing for the remedy of my soul on account of your special feeling for me, which can be measured.

You know how much, because of my continual illnesses and other circumstances, I have suffered all these things and others like them in my fragile
body—according to the saying of a certain man, in perils from my own nation,
in perils from the Gentiles—because of my pitiful merits. With God's help and
because of your father, Bernard, I have at last confidently escaped these dangers,
but my mind still turns back to that rescue. In the past I have often been lax in
the praise of God, and instead of doing what I should in the seven hours of the
divine office, I have been slothful seven times seven ways. That is why, with a
humble heart and with all my strength, I pray that I may take my pleasure in
continually beseeching God for my sins and my transgressions. May he deign to
raise even me into heaven, shattered and heavy though I am.

And since you see me as I live in the world, strive with watchful heart—not
only in vigils and prayer but also in alms to the poor—that I may be found worthy, once I am liberated from the flesh and from the bonds of my sins, to be
freely received by the good Lord who judges us.

Your frequent prayer and that of others is necessary to me now. It will be
more and more so in time to come if, as I believe, my moment is upon me. In my
great fear and grief about what the future may bring me, my mind casts about in
every direction. And I am unsure how, on the basis of my merits, I may be able to
be set free in the end. Why? Because I have sinned in thought and in speech. Ill
words themselves lead to evil deeds. Nevertheless I will not despair of the mercy
of God. I do not despair now and I will never despair. I leave no other such as

you to survive me, noble boy, to struggle on my behalf as you do and as many may do for me because of you, so that I may finally come to salvation.

I acknowledge that, to defend the interests of my lord and master Bernard, and so that my service to him might not weaken in the March and elsewhere so that he not abandon you and me, as some men do—I know that I have gone greatly into debt. To respond to great necessities, I have frequently borrowed great sums, not only from Christians but also from Jews. To the extent that I have been able, I have repaid them. To the extent that I can in the future, I will always do so. But if there is still something to pay after I die, I ask and I beg you to take care in seeking out my creditors. When you find them, make sure that everything is paid off either from my own resources, if any remain, or from your assets—what you have now or what you eventually acquire through just means, with God's help.

What more shall I say? As for your little brother, I have above directed you time and again concerning what you should do for him. What I ask now is that he too, if he reaches the age of manhood, deign to pray for me. I direct both of you, as if you were together here before me, to have the offering of the sacrifice and the presentation of the host made often on my behalf.

Then, when my redeemer commands that I depart this world, he will see fit to prepare refreshment for me. And if this transpires through your prayers and the worthy prayers of others, he who is called God will bring me into heaven in the company of his saints.

This handbook ends here. Amen. Thanks be to God."

STUDY QUESTIONS

A What were the strengths of the Carolingian Empire? What were its weaknesses?
B What role(s) did the church play in the Carolingian Empire?
C What were the accomplishments of the Carolingians? What problems did they bequeath to future generations?

Reading 1: Pope Gregory II, Letter to Emperor Leo III, 727

What issues underlie the tensions that existed between the Roman church and Byzantine Empire in the early Middle Ages? What is the significance of the estrangement between the papacy and Byzantium (see Readings 5 and 8)?

Reading 2: Letters of Saint Boniface

Why did the pope want an oath of loyalty? What problems might he be attempting to prevent? What kinds of arguments does Daniel suggest Boniface use to convert the pagan Germans? Where is the center of Christianity for Bugga (and Boniface)?

Reading 3: Willibald, Life of Boniface

What is the connection between Boniface and the Frankish aristocracy? Why would the Franks help Boniface? Why would Boniface help the Franks?

Reading 4: The Coronation of Pepin the Short, 751

What was the difficulty the Frankish mayors faced? Who had the authority to make a new king? To what extent does this reveal a new source of political legitimacy? (Compare the coronation of Pepin with the story of another Frankish ruler, Clovis, in Chapter 1, Reading 13.)

Reading 5: The Donation of Constantine

What does the donation of Constantine set forth as the proper relationship between church and state in the West? How does this help set the stage for the coronation of Charlemagne (Reading 8)?

Reading 6: Einhard, The Life of Charlemagne

In what ways does Einhard's portrait of Charlemagne establish the ideal of medieval kingship?

Reading 7: Charlemagne, Letter to Pope Leo III, 796

What does Charlemagne see as the proper relationship between church and state? Does this conflict with the papal view set forth in the donation of Constantine (Reading 5)?

Reading 8: Documents Relating to the Imperial Coronation of Charlemagne

What really seemed to have happened on Christmas Day in 800? Who took the initiative? What did Charlemagne gain by this? What did the pope gain?

Reading 9: The General Capitulary for the Missi, 802

What does the *Capitulary for the Missi* tell us about the nature and workings of Carolingian government in the early ninth century? What is the role of the secular aristocracy? What is the role of the church?

Reading 10: Charlemagne, Letter to Abbot Baugulf, Late 700s

What does Charlemagne want the churches to do for education? In what ways were Charlemagne's "educational" initiatives a means to extend his royal authority?

Reading 11: Letters of Alcuin of York to Charlemagne

How do Alcuin's letters to Charlemagne illustrate the intellectual flavor and level of achievement of the Carolingian Renaissance?

Reading 12: John Scotus Erigena, On the Division of Nature

What is the connection between the natural and the supernatural worlds in Erigena? How does reason lead from one to the other? What elements of Platonic philosophy are evinced in Erigena's *On the Division of Nature*?

Reading 13: Dhuoda, Handbook for William

What advice does Dhuoda give her son? What do you learn about Dhuoda herself? What does this selection tell you about the role and status of noblewomen in the age of Charlemagne?

CHAPTER 4

◼ ORDEAL AND SURVIVAL

The materials in this chapter illustrate how various regions of Western Christendom responded to the breakdown of the Carolingian Empire and the attacks of the Vikings and Hungarians.

When Charlemagne's son and heir, Louis the Pious, died in 840 after a reign marred by internal upheavals and Viking raids, his three sons—Lothar, Louis the German, and Charles the Bald—struggled with one another over the division of the Empire (Reading 1). A truce between Louis and Charles, recorded in the oaths of Strasbourg of A.D. 842 (Reading 2), illustrates the linguistic difference between the Frankish and Germanic parts of the former empire (the Germanic ruler, Louis, gave his oath in Frankish so that his brother's troops could understand it; and Charles the Bald, for the same reason, did the reverse).

The eventual settlement between the three brothers—the Treaty of Verdun of 843—partitioned the former Carolingian Empire into a western kingdom (France), an eastern kingdom (Germany), and an unstable middle kingdom stretching from the Netherlands to Italy. Under continued Viking pressure, the kingdom of France broke up into smaller units as the counts and dukes of Carolingian officialdom converted their former administrative offices into hereditary lordships and acquired increasing numbers of sworn followers (documents 3A–D). These followers—"vassals"—often received lands from their lords in return for their service and loyalty, and sometimes granted portions of these lands to their own oath-bound retainers. The process resulted in a tenurial chain commonly described as feudalism, which was complemented by what historians refer to as manorialism (documents 3E and 3F).

Amid the political confusion and incessant warfare of late Carolingian Europe there gradually emerged a strong movement of resistance against the invaders. In England, after a century of Viking raids and conquests, the kings of the West Saxons managed to reverse the Danish tide (Reading 4) and, eventually, to unite all England under their rule. A movement for Church reform and social order emerged in France, centering on the Burgundian abbey of Cluny and gradually spreading across Christendom (Reading 5). Germany saw a revival of royal power under a new Saxon dynasty whose ablest member, Otto the Great, routed the Hungarians in 955 at the battle of the Lechfeld (Reading 6). Bringing northern Italy under his control, Otto the Great was crowned Roman emperor in 962—the first of a long line of king-emperors who reigned over both Germany and northern Italy (Reading 7). The relative stability that Otto and his successors brought to northern Italy provided an encouraging environment for the development of Italian commerce and urban life (Reading 9). Italy's cities were to play a commanding role in the commercial revolution that would transform Europe in the High Middle Ages. Roswitha of Gandersheim embodies the Ottonian Renaissance (Reading 8).

In the course of the eleventh century, the revival of Europe's commerce and political order brought the invasions to an end. The Vikings, Hungarians, and Slavs were themselves converted to Christianity and were incorporated into European civilization (Reading 10). The final document in this chapter demonstrates that the seafaring Vikings had much to contribute to Europe's land-bound culture; their activities were by no means limited to murder and devastation. With Christopher Columbus so deeply etched in our minds, it is too easy to forget that Europe's first discovery of America occurred not in 1492 but close to the year 992 (Reading 11).

READING 1

Nithard, The History of the Sons of Louis the Pious[1]

Nithard (d. 844) was one of the few lay historians of the early Middle Ages. An illegitimate son of one of Charlemagne's daughters, he was reared and educated at the Carolingian court and subsequently joined the following of King Charles the Bald, the youngest of Louis the Pious's three surviving sons. On Louis's death in 840, Charles and his two royal brothers—Lothar and Louis the German—struggled over the division of the Carolingian Empire. Having fought for Charles the Bald on more than one occasion, Nithard was well placed to report the fraternal struggle but quite unable to mask his own sympathies.

When Lothar [r. 840–855] heard of his father's [Louis the Pious] death, he immediately sent emissaries everywhere, especially all over Francia. They proclaimed that he was coming into the empire which had once been given to him. He promised that he wished to grant everyone the benefices which his father had given and that he would make them even bigger. He gave orders also that oaths of fealty should be exacted from those who were still uncommitted. In addition, he ordered that all should join him as fast as they could; those who were unwilling to appear he threatened with death. He himself advanced slowly since he wanted to find out how the wind was blowing before he crossed the Alps.

Presently, men from everywhere joined him, driven by either greed or fear. When Lothar saw that, his prospects and power made him bold, and he began to scheme about how he might best seize the whole empire. He decided to send an army against Louis [the German] first, since this would not take him out of his way, and to devote himself with all his might to the destruction of Louis' forces. In the meantime he was shrewd enough to send emissaries to Charles [the Bald] in Aquitaine, informing Charles that he was friendly toward him, as their father had demanded and as was proper for one to feel toward a godchild. But he begged him to spare their nephew, Pepin's son [Pepin II of Aquitaine], until he had spoken to him. Having settled this, he turned to the city of Worms.

At that time [June 840] Louis had left part of his army as a garrison in Worms and had gone to meet the Saxons who were in revolt. But after a small skirmish Lothar put the defenders to flight and, crossing the Rhine with his entire army, headed for Frankfort. Here they suddenly came upon each other, Lothar approaching from one side and Louis from the other. After peace had

[1]From *Carolingian Chronicles,* ed. and tr. Bernhard W. Schloz; Ann Arbor, University of Michigan Press, 1970, pp. 141–145, 174. Reprinted by permission of the University of Michigan Press.

been arranged for the night, they pitched their camps, not exactly in brotherly love, Lothar right at the place where they had met and Louis at the point where the Main flows into the Rhine. Since Louis' opposition was vigorous and his brother was not sure that he could make him give in without a fight, Lothar thought it might be easier to get the better of Charles first. He therefore put off battle with the understanding that he would meet Louis again at the same place on November 11. Unless an agreement could be negotiated beforehand, they would settle by force what each of them was going to get. And so, giving up his initial schemes, Lothar set out to subdue Charles.

At this time [July 840] Charles had come to Bourges to the assembly which Pepin was going to attend, as his men had sworn. When Charles had learned what he could from everybody, he selected as ambassadors Nithard and Adalgar[2] and dispatched them as speedily as possible to Lothar, enjoining and entreating him to remember the oaths they had sworn each other and to preserve what their father had arranged between them. He also reminded him that he, Charles, was his brother and godson. Lothar should have what belonged to him; but should also permit Charles to have without a fight what his father had granted him with Lothar's consent. Charles pledged, if Lothar should do this, that he was willing to be loyal and subject to him, as it is proper to behave toward one's first-born brother. Besides, Charles promised that he would whole-heartedly forgive whatever Lothar had done to him up to that time. He implored him to stop stirring up his people and disturbing the kingdom committed to him by God, and send word to Lothar that peace and harmony should rule everywhere. This peace he and his people considered most desirable and were willing to preserve. If Lothar did not believe this, Charles promised to give him whatever assurances he wanted.

Lothar pretended to receive this message kindly, but permitted the emissaries to return with greetings only and the reply that he would answer fully through his own envoys. Moreover, he deprived Charles' emissaries of the benefices which his father had given them because they did not want to break their fealty and join him. In this way he unwittingly betrayed his designs against his brother. Meanwhile, all men living between the Meuse and the Seine sent to Charles, asked him to get there before the land was taken over by Lothar, and promised to wait for his arrival. Charles quickly set out with only a few men and marched from Aquitaine to Quierzy. There he received graciously those who had come from the Charbonnière and the land on this side of it.[3] Beyond the Charbonnière, however, Herefrid, Gislebert, Bovo, and the others duped by Odulf[4] disregarded their sworn fealty and defected.

---

[2]This Nithard is the author of the *Histories,* and Adalgar was a count of Charles the Bald's court party.

[3]This territory constitutes the frontier between Neustria and Austrasia, the central and eastern parts of the Frankish kingdom.

[4]Ordulf was the lay-abbot of St.-Josse in northern France.

At the same time [August 840] a messenger coming from Aquitaine announced that Pepin and his partisans wanted to attack Charles' mother. Charles left the Franks at Quierzy by themselves, but ordered them to move his way if his brother should attempt to subdue them before his return. In addition, he dispatched Hugo, Adalhard, Gerard, and Hegilo to Lothar. Repeating everything that he had said before, he entreated Lothar again for God's sake not to subvert Charles' men and further to whittle away at the kingdom which God and his father had given to Charles with Lothar's consent. After making this appeal to Lothar he rushed into Aquitaine, fell upon Pepin and his men, and put them to flight.

Meanwhile [October 840], Lothar was returning from the confrontation with Louis and being joined by every man on this side of the Charbonnière. He thought it best to cross the Meuse and advance as far as the Seine. On his way there Hilduin, abbot of St. Denis, and Gerard, count of the city of Paris, came and met him. They had broken their fealty and defected from Charles. When Pepin, son of Bernard, king of the Lombards, and others saw this treachery, like slaves they also chose to break their word and disregard their oaths rather than give up their holdings for a little while. That is why these men broke faith, followed the example of those we mentioned already, and submitted to Lothar. Then Lothar became bold and crossed the Seine, sending ahead, as he always did, to the inhabitants between the Seine and the Loire men who were to make them defect by threats and promises. He himself followed slowly, as usual, heading for the city of Chartres. When he learned that Theodoric and Eric were on the way with the rest who had decided to join him, he resolved to proceed as far as the Loire, putting his confidence in his great numbers. Charles returned from the pursuit in which he had dispersed Pepin and his followers, and since he had no place where he could safely leave his mother, they both hastily departed for Francia.

In the meantime Charles heard of all these defections and that Lothar was determined to hound him to the death with an immense army, while Pepin on one side and the Bretons on the other had raised arms against him. So he and his men sat down to think about all these troubles. They easily found a simple solution. Since they had nothing left but their lives and their bodies, they chose to die nobly rather than betray and abandon their king.

They headed [in November 840] in Lothar's direction, and both sides thus approached the city of Orléans. They pitched camps at a distance of barely six Gallic miles from each other, and both parties dispatched emissaries. Charles only asked for peace and justice, but Lothar tried to think of a way he could deceive and get the better of Charles without a fight. This scheme came to nothing because of strong resistance on the other side. Then Lothar hoped that his own forces would continue to grow from day to day, and he thought he might be able to conquer his brother more easily when Charles' following had further dwindled.

But he was disappointed in the hope and refrained from battle. The condition of the truce was that Charles should be granted Aquitaine, Septimania, Provence, and ten counties between the Loire and the Seine, with the stipulation that he should be satisfied with them and remain there for the time being until they met again at Attigny on May 8.[5] Lothar promised that he was indeed willing to talk over and settle the interests of both parties by mutual consent. The leaders of Charles' party also realized that the problems at hand were more than they could handle. They feared, if it came to a battle, that they might be hard put to save the king in view of their small numbers, and all of them set great store by his talents. So they consented to the stipulations if only Lothar from now on would be as loyal a friend to Charles as a brother should be, permit him to hold peacefully the lands he had allotted to him, and in the meantime also refrain from hostilities against Louis. Otherwise, they should be absolved from the oath they had sworn.

By this device they both rescued their king from danger and soon freed themselves from an oath. For those who had sworn this had not yet left the house when Lothar tried to seduce some of them from Charles and by the next day in fact he received a few defectors. He immediately sent into the lands which he had assigned to his brother, to stir up trouble so that they would not submit to Charles. Then he moved on in order to receive homage from those coming to him out of Provence and tried to think of ways to overcome Louis by force or deception.

From this history, everyone may gather how mad it is to neglect the common good and to follow only private and selfish desires, since both sins insult the Creator, so much in fact that He turns even the elements against the madness of the sinner. I shall easily prove this by examples still known to almost everyone. In the times of Charles the Great [d. 814] of good memory, who died almost thirty years ago, peace and concord ruled everywhere because our people were treading the one proper way, the way of the common welfare, and thus the way of God. But now since each goes his separate way, dissension and struggle abound. Once there was abundance and happiness everywhere, now everywhere there is want and sadness. Once even the elements smiled on everything and now they threaten, as scripture testifies: "And the world will wage war against the madness."

READING 2
The Oaths of Strasbourg[6]

The bilingual versions of these oaths, which record an alliance between Louis the German (804–876) and Charles the Bald (823–877) against their older brother Lothar, illustrate the linguistic split between the western and eastern

---

[5]Of the lands assigned to Charles at Worms in 839, one-third, which included Burgundy, were now left out.

[6]From *Monumenta Germania Historica, Scriptores: 'Nithardi Historianum'* Libri IV iii, 5, ed. G. H. Pertz; Hannover, Germany, Weidmann, 1870, pp. 38–39; tr. J. W. Leedom.

halves of the former Carolingian Empire. Not only are these among the earliest documents in French and German, they also show the strong ethnic differences that undermined centralized Carolingian administration.

THE FRENCH VERSION

Pro Deo amur et pro Christian poblo et nostro, commun salvament dist di in avant, in quant Deus savir et podir me dunat, si salvarai eo cist meon fradre Karlo et in adiudha et in cadhuna cosa, si cum om per driet son fradre salvar dist, in o quid il mi altresi fazet; et ab Ludher nul plaid numquam prindrai, qui meon vol cist meon fradre Kario in damno sit.

THE GERMAN VERSION

In Godes minna ind in thes Christianes folches ind unser bedhero gealtnissi, fort thesemo dage frammordes, so fram so mir God gewizci indi madh furgibit, so haldih thesan minan broudher so man mit rehtu sinan broudher scal, in thiu, thaz er mig so sama duo; indi mit Ludheren in nohheiniu thing ne gegango, the minan willon imo ce scadhen werben.

ENGLISH TRANSLATION

For the love of God and for the Christian people and our common salvation, it is decreed from this day forward that, so long as God grants me the knowledge and ability, I will aid my brother just as one should by right aid a brother—so long as he does the same for me—and I will enter into no compact or concord with Lothar through which my brother may be harmed.

READING 3
Select Feudal Documents[7]

The following sources illustrate the evolution of lord-vassal relationships and hereditary tenures from pre-Carolingian to post-Carolingian times. The element of reciprocal rights and obligations between lord and vassal is

[7]From "Frankish Commendation," in *Translations and Reprints of Original Sources of European History,* vol. 4, no. 3, ed. and tr. E. P. Cheyney; Philadelphia, University of Pennsylvania Press, 1897, pp. 3–4; "Capitulary of Mersen," in *ibid,* p. 5; "Capitulary of Quierzy," in *ibid,* p. 14; "Letter of Fulbert of Chartres," in *ibid,* pp. 23–24; "Survey of the Manor of Neuillay," in Georges Duby, *Rural Economy and Country Life in the Medieval West,* Columbia, University of South Carolina Press, 1976, pp. 204–205; and "The Rights and Ranks of People," in *English Historical Documents,* vol. 2, ed. and tr. D. C. Douglas and G. W. Greenaway; Oxford, Oxford University Press, 1953, pp. 813–814.

particularly evident in the letter of Fulbert, bishop of Chartres (1002–1028), a celebrated scholar and schoolmaster. Reciprocity also characterized the relationships between aristocratic benefactors and the religious houses that they founded; monks were normally expected to serve benefactors, with prayers for their souls and, often, with knights who were granted lands on the monastic estates.

A.   A COMMENDATION FORMULA

To that magnificent lord [blank], 1, [blank]. Since it is known familiarly to all how little I have whence to feed and clothe myself, I have therefore petitioned your piety, and your good will has decreed to me that I should hand myself over or commend myself to your guardianship, which I have thereupon done; that is to say in this way, that you should aid and succor me as well with food as with clothing, according as I shall be able to serve you and deserve it.

And so long as I shall live I ought to provide service and honor to you, suitably to my free condition; and I shall not during the time of my life have the ability to withdraw from your power or guardianship; but must remain during the days of my life under your power or defense. Wherefore it is proper that if either of us shall wish to withdraw himself from these agreements, he shall pay [blank] shillings to the other party, and this agreement shall remain unbroken.

B.   THE CAPITULARY OF MERSEN, 847

We [Emperor Lothar and Kings Lewis the German and Charles the Bald] will moreover that each free man in our realms shall choose a lord, from us or our faithful, such a one as he wishes.

We command moreover that no man shall leave his lord without just cause, nor should any one receive him, except in such a way as was customary in the time of our predecessors.

And we wish you to know that we want to grant right to our faithful subjects and we do not wish to do anything to them against reason. Similarly we admonish you and the rest of our faithful subjects that you grant right to your men and do not act against reason toward them.

And we will that the man of each one of us in whosoever kingdom he is, shall go with his lord against the enemy, or in his other needs unless there shall have been (as may there not be) such an invasion of the kingdom as is called a *landwer*, so that the whole people of that kingdom shall go together to repel it.

C.   THE CAPITULARY OF QUIERZY, 877

If a count of this kingdom, whose son is with us, shall die, our son with the rest of our faithful shall appoint some one of the nearest relatives of the same count, who, along with the officials of his province and with the bishop in whose diocese the same province is, shall administer that province until announcement is made to us, so that we may honor his son who is with us with his honors.

If, however, he had a minor son, this same son, along with the officials of that province and with the bishop in whose diocese it is, shall make provision for the same province until the notice of the death of the same count shall come to us, that his son may be honored, by our concession, with his honors.

If, however, he had no son, our son along with the rest of the faithful, shall take charge, who, along with the officials of the same province and with the proper bishop shall make provision for the same province until our order may be made in regard to it. Therefore, let him not be angry who shall provide for the province if we give the same province to another whom it pleases us, rather than to him who has so far provided for it.

Similarly also shall this be done concerning our vassals. And we will and command that as well the bishops as the abbots and the counts, and any others of our faithful also, shall study to preserve this toward their men.

D.   LETTER TO FULBERT OF CHARTRES, 1020

To William most glorious duke of the Aquitanians, Bishop Fulbert the favor of his prayers.

Asked to write something concerning the form of fealty, I have noted briefly for you on the authority of books the things which follow. He who swears fealty to his lord ought always to have these six things in memory; what is harmless, safe, honorable, useful, easy, practicable. Harmless, that is to say that he should not be injurious to his lord in his body; safe, that he should not be injurious to him in his secrets or in the defenses through which he is able to be secure; honorable, that he should not be injurious to him in his justice or in other matters that pertain to his honor—; useful, that he should not be injurious to him in his possessions; easy or practicable, that that good which his lord is able to do easily, he make not difficult, nor that which is practicable he make impossible to him.

However, that the faithful vassal should avoid these injuries is proper, but not for this does he deserve his holding; for it is not sufficient to abstain from evil, unless what is good is done also. It remains, therefore, that in the same six things mentioned above he should faithfully counsel and aid his lord, if he wishes to be looked upon as worthy of his benefice and to be safe concerning the fealty which he has sworn.

The lord also ought to act toward his faithful vassal reciprocally in all these things. And if he does not do this he will be justly considered guilty of bad faith, just as the former, if he should be detected in the avoidance of or the doing of or the consenting to them, would be perfidious and perjured.

E. SURVEY OF THE MANOR OF NEUILLAY, c. 860

There is in Neuillay a seigneurial manor amply equipped with other buildings. There are 10 fields, which can be sown with 200 muids of oats. There are 9 arpents [nearly 3 acres] of meadow, from which 10 loads of hay can be harvested. There is forest there; it is estimated to be 3 leagues long and 1 league wide. In it 800 pigs can find forage.

Electeus a slave and his wife a "colona" [a type of serf], Landina. They are dependents of St. Germain. They live in Neuillay. He holds half a farm, which has in arable land 19 acres, in meadow 1/2 arpent [less than a third of an acre]. He plows in the winter field 4 perches [a small measurement of land] and in the spring field 13. He carts manure to the lord's field, and performs no other service nor pays anything in addition.

Abrahil a slave and his wife, a "lida" [a public slave], by the name of Berthildis. They are dependents of St. Germain. And Ceslinus a lidus and his wife a lida, named Leutberga. And Godalbertus a lidus. These three families live in Neuillay. They hold a farm, which has in arable land 47 1/2 acres and in meadow 4 arpents. They do carting to Anjou, and in the month of May to Paris. They pay for the army tax 2 muttons, 8 chickens, 30 eggs, 100 planks and as many shingles, 12 staves, 6 hoops, and 12 torches. They bring 2 loads of wood to Sutre. They enclose, in the lord's court, 4 perches with a palisade, in the meadow 4 perches with a fence, and at the harvest as much as is necessary. They plow in the winter field 8 perches and in the spring field 26 perches. Along with their corvees [public taxes payable in labor] and labor services, they cart manure into the lord's field. Each pays a poll tax of 4 pennies.

There are in Neuillay 6 and 1/2 inhabited farms, and 1/2 not occupied. They are distributed among 16 families. They pay to the army tax 12 muttons; in poll tax, 5 shillings and 4 pennies; 48 chickens, 160 eggs, 600 planks and as many shingles, 54 staves and as many hoops, and 72 torches. They make two cartings for wine, and during May, 2 and 1/2 cartings, and give 1/2 an ox.

F. THE RIGHTS AND RANKS OF PEOPLE, c. 1050

The Cottar's right is according to the custom of the estate: in some he must work for his lord each Monday throughout the year, or 3 days each week at harvest-time. . . . He does not make land payment. He should have 5 acres: more if it be common on the estate; and it is too little if it ever be less; because his work must be frequent. Let him give his hearth-penny [Peter's pence] on Ascension Day even as each freeman ought to do. Let him also perform services on his lord's demesne-land if he is ordered, by keeping watch on the sea-coast and working at the king's deer fence and such things according to his condition. Let him pay his church dues at Martinmas.

The boor's duties are various, in some places heavy and in others light. On some estates the custom is that he must perform week-work for 2 days in each week of the year as he is directed, and 3 days from the Feast of the Purification to Easter. If he perform carrying service he need not work while his horse is out. At Michaelmas he must pay 10 pence for rent, and at Martinmas 23 sesters of barley, and 2 hens, and at Easter a young sheep or 2 pence. And he must lie from Martinmas to Easter at his lord's fold as often as it falls to his lot; and from the time when ploughing is first done until Martinmas he must each week plough 1 acre, and himself present the seed in the lord's barn. Also [he must plough] 3 acres of boon-work, and 2 for pasturage. If he needs more grass, let him earn it as he may be permitted. Let him plough 3 acres as his tribute land [the lord's demesne strips of the open fields] and sow it from his own barn, and pay his hearth-penny. And every pair of boors must maintain 1 hunting dog, and each boor must give 6 loaves to the herdsman of the lord's swine when he drives his herd to the mast-pasture. On the same land to which the customs apply a farmer ought to be given for his occupation of the land 2 oxen, 1 cow, 6 sheep and 7 acres sown on his rood of land. [During] that year let him perform all the dues that fall to him, and let him be given tools for his work and utensils for his house. When death befalls him let the lord take charge of what he leaves. . . . [The text continues by listing the duties and rights of people and slaves who perform specific functions on the manor.]

About men's provisioning. Every slave ought to have as provisions 12 pounds of good corn and 2 carcasses of sheep and 1 good cow for food and the right of cutting wood according to the custom of the estate.

About women's provisioning. For a female slave 8 pounds of corn for food, 1 sheep or 3 pence for winter food, 1 sester of beans for lenten food, whey in summer or 1 penny.

All slaves belonging to the estate ought to have food at Christmas and Easter, a strip of land for ploughing and a "harvest-handful" besides their dues.

READING 4

The Anglo-Saxon Chronicle[8]

The Anglo-Saxon Chronicle is an unusual and diabolically complex document. Unlike most of our sources, it was written not in Latin but in the Old English vernacular, a distant ancestor of modern English. From the 890s onward, copies of the Anglo-Saxon Chronicle were circulated to a number of English monasteries, at a few of which they were kept up to date

---

[8]From Two of the Anglo-Saxon *Chronicles Parallel*, vol. 1, ed. Charles Plummer and John Earle; Oxford, England, The Clarendon Press, 1899, pp. 54, 62–76; tr. Marc Anthony Meyer.

more or less year by year. Thus, the so-called chronicle is actually a series of interrelated annals varying in content between one manuscript and another. The selections here outline the early Viking attacks on the Anglo-Saxon kingdoms, and the desperate resistance of Alfred of Wessex.

789. In this year . . . three [of the Norsemen's] ships came [to Portland, Dorset] for the first time; and then the reeve rode there and tried to force them to go to the king's manor because he did not know who they were; and they slew him. These ships were the first of the Danes who attacked the English.

836. In this year King Ecgbert fought with thirty-five ships' crews at Carhampton, and great slaughter was made there, and the Danes had possession of the place of slaughter. . . .

838. In this year a large hostile army came into west Wales [Cornwall], and [the Britons] joined forces with them and continued to fight against King Ecgbert of Wessex. When the king heard this, he and his levies fought against them at Hingston Down and there put to flight both the Britons and the Danes.

840. In this year the ealdorman[9] Wulfheard fought against thirty-three ships' crews at Southampton and he made great slaughter there and won a victory. And Wulfheard died that same year. And in the same year, Ealdorman Æthelhelm with the Dorset levies fought against the Danish host at Portland, and for a long time put the host to flight; but the Danes had possession of the place of battle and killed the ealdorman.

851. In this year Ealdorman Ceorl with the Devonshire levies fought against the heathens at Wicga's Hill and great slaughter was made there, and he won the victory. And that same year King Athelstan and Ealdorman Ealhhere annihilated a great army at Sandwich in Kent and seized nine ships and scattered the rest. And for the first time the heathens pitched a winter camp [in England]. And then in the following year [852], three hundred and fifty ships came to the mouth of the River Thames and attacked Canterbury and London, and the heathens put to flight King Beorhtwulf of Mercia and his army. Then they went south, crossing the Thames into Surrey, and King Æthelwulf and his son Ethelbald and the West Saxon army fought against them at *Acleah,* and there the greatest slaughter was made of the heathen army of which we have heard until the present day, and the West Saxons won the battle.

860. In this year King Æthelbald died and his body lies at Sherborne; and then his brother Æthelbert succeeded to the whole kingdom and maintained it in good peace and great tranquility. And in his days a great heathen army landed and attacked Winchester [the capital town of Wessex], and Ealdorman

---

[9]The ealdorman is a leading man of high birth found throughout the Anglo-Saxon kingdoms, and the English equivalent of the continental "count."

Osric and the Hampshire levies and Ealdorman Æthelwulf and the men of Berkshire fought against the enemy host, put them to flight and had possession of the place of slaughter. And King Æthelbert ruled for five years and his body lies at Sherborne.

865. In this year the heathen army camped on the Isle of Thanet and made peace with the men of Kent, and the Kentishmen promised them money in return for that peace. And under the shelter of that peace and promise of money, the heathen army covertly traveled at night and devastated all of eastern Kent. In this year [866], Æthelred, King Ethelbert's brother, succeeded to the West Saxon kingdom. And in that same year, a great hostile army came to the land of the English and set up winter quarters in East Anglia, crossing the mouth of the Humber to York in Northumbria [in 867], where there was great discord among those people. They had rejected their king, Osbert, and had accepted Ella as king, a man without a proper claim to rule. Only late in the year, when they began to make war on the heathens, did they gather a great army and move to attack them at York. They stormed the city [on March 21 or 23, 867] and some of them got inside, but the Northumbrians were very soundly defeated—some inside and some outside—and both kings were killed and the rest of the Northumbrians made peace with the enemy host. . . .

870. In this year the heathen army rode across Mercia into East Anglia and set up winter quarters at Thetford; and that winter King Edmund[10] fought against them, but the Danes were victorious and killed the king and subdued the whole kingdom.

871. In this year the enemy army came to Reading [a royal residence] in Wessex, and after three nights two jarls[11] rode up-country. Then Ealdorman Æthelwulf met them at Englefield and fought against them and won the victory. Then after four nights, King Ethelred and his brother Alfred [the Great] led a great army to Reading and fought against the enemy, and great slaughter was made on both sides, and Ealdorman Æthelwulf was killed and the Danes had possession of the place of slaughter. And after four nights King Ethelred and his brother Alfred fought at Ashdown against the whole heathen army which was in two companies; in one was Bagsecg and Halfdan [son of Ragnar, Lothbrok], and in the other the jarls. And there King Æthelred fought against the company of the heathen kings, whence King Bagsecg was slain. And Alfred, the king's brother, fought against the company of the jarls, and Jarls Sidroc the Elder and Sidroc the Younger, and Jarls Osbearn, Fraena, and Harald were slain. Both companies were put to flight and many thousands were killed and fighting con-

[10]King Edmund is said to have refused to share his Christian kingdom with the heathen Vikings, and they tied him to a tree and shot him with arrows and cut off his head. His cult spread quickly, and his body was enshrined at Bury, where in 1020 a monastery was founded and dedicated to St. Edmund, King and Martyr.

[11]The jarl, or chieftain, was a Scandinavian warrior who had gathered a band of other warriors around himself and united his area of country.

tinued until nightfall. And two weeks later, King Æthelred and his brother Alfred fought against the enemy host at Basing, and there the Danes won a victory. And after two months, King Æthelred and his brother Alfred fought at *Meretun* against the enemy who, again, were in two companies; and the [English] levies put both to flight and until late in the day were victorious. There was much bloodshed on both sides; but afterwards the Danes held the place of slaughter. And Bishop Heahmund was killed there along with many other good men. And after this fight, a great summer host came. And then, after Easter [April 15], King Æthelred died, having ruled for five years; and his body lies at Wimborne.

Then his brother Alfred, son of Æthelwulf, succeeded to the West Saxon kingdom. And one month later, King Alfred, with a small force, fought against the whole heathen army at Wilton, and for a long while during the day fought off the host; but then the Danes had possession of the battlefield. And during this year, nine pitched battles were fought against the enemy army in this kingdom south of the Thames besides the many small encounters that King Alfred, the king's brother, and a single ealdorman and king's thegns[12] rode on which were not counted. And during this year, nine jarls and one king were killed; and in this year the West Saxons made peace with the Viking host.

874. In this year the heathens went from Lindsey to Repton [in Northumbria] and constructed a winter camp there, and they drove King Burgred [of Mercia] across the sea twenty-two years after he succeeded to the kingdom, and they conquered the whole kingdom. And the king traveled to Rome and settled there, and his body lies in the church of Saint Mary in the English school.[13] And in the same year, the heathens gave the kingdom of Mercia to a foolish king's thegn, and he swore oaths and gave hostages to them so that at all times the kingdom would be held ready for them whenever they needed it, and he would hold himself in readiness and, with his followers, would serve the needs of the enemy army in all things.

876. In this year the Viking host stole away inland into Wareham and eluded the West Saxon levies, and the king concluded a peace with the heathen army, and they swore oaths to him on the sacred ring[14] which before they would not do for any nation, that they would immediately depart from the kingdom. And the enemy army stole away from the West Saxon levies by night under shelter of this pact and, provided with horses, the enemy got to Exeter. And in this year Halfdan distributed the land of the Northumbrians [among his followers] and they engaged in ploughing and tilling for themselves.

---

[12]Free warriors of the king to whom he often granted land and other privileges. A thegn is the English equivalent of the continental knight.

[13]The English "school" is not really a school at all, but a quarter of the city: it was located on the Vatican Hill and was frequented by churchmen, nuns and monks, pilgrims, and others who had business in Rome.

[14]The sacred ring was worn by the chief at assemblies and otherwise kept in the inner sanctuary of the heathen temple.

878. In this year the heathen army stole away inland to Chippenham in the middle of winter over Twelfth Night and attacked and occupied the land of the West Saxons and drove a great part of the people overseas and, with the exception of King Alfred, conquered the greater part of those people who remained. And with a small company the king went with extreme difficulty through the woods [of Selwood] and into defensible positions in the swamps [of Somerset]. And during this same winter a brother of Ivar [the Boneless] and Halfdan was in the kingdom of Wessex, in Devonshire, with twenty-three ships and was slain there and eight hundred men with him and forty men of his retinue. And the Easter after this [March 23], King Alfred with a small force built a stronghold at Athelney and with the men of that part of Somerset nearest to it continued fighting against the heathens. Then in the seventh week after Easter he rode to Egbert's stone to the east of Selwood and there met all the men of Somerset, Wiltshire and that part of Hampshire which was on this side of the sea [west of Southampton Water]; and they gladly received him. After one night he journeyed from that camp to Iley Oak and after another to Edington, and there fought against the whole heathen army, and put it to flight and pursued it up to the stronghold [at Chippenham] and laid siege there for fourteen nights. And then the host gave him preliminary hostages and great oaths that they would leave his kingdom and vowed as well that their king would receive baptism; and they fulfilled that promise in this way. After three weeks the king, Guthrum, one of thirty very honorable men in the host, came to him at Allen, which is near Athelney. King Alfred stood sponsor for him there and [some time afterwards] the loosening of the baptismal fillet' was performed at Wedmore, where for twelve days Guthrum stayed with the king, who honored him and his companions with gifts.

READING 5

Foundation Charter for the Abbey of Cluny[15]

Duke William of Aquitaine (909–918), founded the abbey of Cluny in 909 (or possibly 910); He granted it far greater privileges and liberties than were customary at the time, thereby providing the precondition for Cluny's subsequent role as a generator of ecclesiastical reform across Western Christendom.

---

[15]From Ernest F. Henderson, ed. *Select Historical Documents of the Middle Ages.* London: G. Bell and sons, Ltd., 1925, pp. 329–333.

To all right thinkers it is clear that the providence of God has so provided for certain rich men that, by means of their transitory possessions, if they use them well, they may be able to merit everlasting rewards.

I, William, count and duke by the grace of God, diligently pondering this, and desiring to provide for my own safety while I am still able, have considered it advisable that, from the temporal goods which have been conferred upon me, I should give some little portion for the gain of my soul.

Therefore be it known to all that, for the love of God and of our Saviour Jesus Christ, I hand over from my own rule to the holy apostles, Peter and Paul, the possessions over which I hold sway the town of Cluny namely, the court and demesne manor, and the church in honor of St. Mary the mother of God and of St. Peter the prince of the apostles, together with all the things to pertaining to it, the villas, the chapels, the serfs of both sexes, the vines, the fields, the meadows, the woods, the waters and their outlets, the mills, the incomes and revenues, what is cultivated and what is not, all in their entirety. I give these things, moreover, with this understanding, that in Cluny a regular monastery shall be constructed in honor of the holy apostles Peter and Paul, and that there the monks shall congregate and live according to the rule of St. Benedict.

And let the monks themselves, together with the aforesaid possessions, be under the power and dominion of the abbot Berno, who, as long as he shall live, shall preside over them regularly according to his knowledge and ability. But after his death, those same monks shall have power and permission to elect any one of their order whom they please as abbot and rector, following the will of God and the rule promulgated by St. Benedict,—in such wise that neither by the intervention of our own or of any other power may they be impeded from making a purely canonical election.

Every five years, moreover, the aforesaid monks shall pay to the church of the apostles at Rome ten shillings to supply them with lights; and they shall have the protection of those same apostles and the defense of the Roman pontiff; and those monks may, with their whole heart and soul, according to their ability and knowledge, build up the aforesaid place.

We will further, that in our times and in those of our successors, according as the opportunities and possibilities of that place shall allow, there shall daily, with the greatest zeal, be performed there works of mercy towards the poor, the needy, strangers and pilgrims.

It has pleased us also to insert in this document that, from this day, those same monks there congregated shall be subject neither to our yoke, nor to that of our relatives, nor to the sway of the royal might, nor to that of any earthly power. And, through God and all his saints, and by the awful day of judgment, I warn and objure that no one of the secular princes, no count, no bishop whatever, not the pontiff of the aforesaid Roman see, shall invade the property of these servants of God, or alienate it, or diminish it, or exchange it, or give it as a benefice to any one, or constitute any prelate over them against their will.

Done publicly city of Bourges. I, William, commanded this act to be made and drawn up, and confirmed it with my own hand.

READING 6

Widukind of Corvey, The Battle of Lechfeld[16]

Widukind (10th c.), a monk of the Saxon abbey of Corvey, was well trained in the Roman classics. He began writing his "Deeds of the Saxons" during the reign (936–973) of Otto I (called Otto the Great), the second of the Saxon kings of Germany and, after 962, emperor of the Romans. Widukind was thus contemporary or nearly contemporary with the events he described. His outlook was shaped by his own kinship to the Saxon royal family and by the fact that his abbey was a royal foundation. He dedicated his history to Otto I's daughter with the express purpose of intensifying her admiration for the exploits of her family. Otto emerges in the pages of Widukind as an heroic warrior in the ancient tradition of imperial Rome. The excerpt translated here, an account of Otto's decisive victory over the Hungarians, is inflated in tone but trustworthy in detail.

King Otto, returning to Saxony about the first of July, had a meeting there with legates of the Hungarians, who were there to demonstrate their thanks and their ancient fidelity. They stayed for several days, and Otto sent them away in peace, having given them little gifts. But then he heard from agents of his brother Henry, the Duke of the Bavarians: "Watch out! The Hungarians have gone far and wide and invaded your land; they mean to go to war." Hearing this, Otto organized an expedition against the enemy, although only a few of his Saxons were with him because he had been preparing to fight the Slavs. He set up his camp in Augsburg, and an army of Franks and Bavarians came to help him. With them as well came Duke Conrad of Lorraine with many horsemen: his arrival cheered the soldiers, who now wished to hasten to battle, for Conrad was by nature a daring soul and—rare for a brave man—wise in counsel. Whenever he went against the enemy, on horse or on foot, he was unstoppable.

[16]Widukindi monachi Corbeieusis Rerum gestarum Saxonicarum Libri tres, ed. G. Waitz, Hannover, Hahnsche Buchhandlung, 1935, pp. 63–66. Tr. J. W. Leedom.

Scouts from both sides determined that the two armies were not far off from one another. In the camp, all were ordered to fast, and to prepare themselves for battle the next day. At daybreak, they received a blessing from Otto, swore an oath to one another, raised their banners, and marched from the fort—eight legions in all.

The army was led through harsh and difficult places, so that the enemy would not be able to disturb them with the arrows with which they were so well-supplied. The First, Second and Third Legions were the Bavarians, led by the agents of Duke Henry.[17] In the Fourth were Franks, led and defended by Duke Conrad. In the Fifth Legion, which was the largest (known as the Royal Legion), was Otto himself, defended by a thousand chosen young warriors, and by the Archangel Michael, the power of victory, thronged around by marching soldiers. The Sixth and Seventh were made up of Swabians and commanded by Burchard, who married the daughter of the king's brother.[18] In the Eighth—last in line of march, and thought to be in the safest place—were the Bohemians, a thousand picked soldiers, made strong not through good luck but training. They guarded the baggage and supplies and equipment.

It was assumed the Hungarians would hold back; but things happened differently than was supposed. For the Hungarians did not wait to cross the Lech, but went around Otto's army, and began to harass the rearguard—the Eighth Legion—with arrows. Then they charged with a shout: and then they cut and they captured, and they took the army's supplies, and forced the remainder of the legion to flee.

In the same way the Hungarians attacked the Seventh Legion and the Sixth Legion, and many from those units turned in flight. The king, however, understanding that the battle was yet in front, while the after-columns were in new danger, sent back Conrad with his Fourth Legion, who rescued the captives, snatched the plunder, and drove the brigands forward.

The enemy was now surrounded, and, with the tokens of victory, the duke returned to the king. It is curious that veteran soldiers, used to the glory of victories, hesitated; while Conrad triumphed with new recruits ignorant of the ways of war.

The whole weight of battle Otto saw now ahead of him, and so he rallied his comrades in this manner: "My soldiers! The work falls to us, the great-hearted, in this grave necessity, as you yourselves see, not to watch the enemy at a distance, but to get to them face-to-face. Up to now I have used your willing hands and victorious weapons outside my borders and my imperium; and so why, in my own land and my own kingdom, should I turn my back? We are bested by their multitudes; but not by their courage or their arms. We know that almost all

---

[17]Otto's brother, mortally ill because of a previous campaign.

[18]Burchard III, Duke of Swabia (954–973), married Hedwig, daughter of Henry, Duke of Bavaria (947–955), who was a brother of King Otto I.

of them wear no armor; and what is an even greater assurance to us, they do not have the help of God. For help, they have only a wall of daring; we have divine protection. It would shame all the lords of all Europe to falter now. If the end is to come now, my soldiers, better to die gloriously in battle, than to be defeated, dragged into slavery, throttled like animals. I would say more, my soldiers, if with words I might bolster your courage or your spirit. Now, though, it is best that we start this conference with swords, not tongues." And having said this, Otto took his shield, and the Holy Lance[19] and was the first to turn his horse to the enemy: a courageous fighter, and a fine commander.

The more daring of the enemy resisted at first; but then they saw their companions turning back, and, stunned at being surrounded by us, they were wiped out. Others, whose horses were exhausted, entered nearby villages: our soldiers surrounded them, and burned them in their houses. Still others swam the river; but they could not climb the further bank, and so were swallowed up by the flood and perished. That same day the Hungarian camp was sacked, and all the captives released; on the second and third days, the stragglers from the neighboring towns were rounded up, and none—or very few—escaped. Three of their leaders were captured and handed over to Duke Henry: he strung them up, and they died badly, as they deserved.

In triumph King Otto, made great by his army, was dubbed "father of his country," and imperator;[20] and he in turn decreed that honor and the highest praise be offered to God, and to His Holy Mother, in each and every church. With a procession, and with the greatest joy, the conqueror returned to Saxony, received there most lovingly by his people, for there had been no such royal victory in the 200 years before him.

READING 7

Liudprand of Cremona, Otto the Great in Italy[21]

The title of "emperor," conferred on Charlemagne, passed to weaker and weaker descendants until it was extinguished in the early tenth century. It was revived in a new and dramatic form by Otto I (936–973) of Germany. Otto invaded Italy in 961; but it took three years to consolidate his

---

[19]The Holy Lance, which supposedly contained in its shaft one of the nails of the Cross of Christ, became a symbol of rule among the Germans even as late as World War II.

[20]"Imperator" means both victorious field commander and emperor, and in this case the former is meant.

[21]F. A. Wright, *The Works of Liudprand of Cremona,* London: George Routledge & Sons, 1930, pp. 259–270.

position, which was not accomplished until his chief antagonists, including
the pope, were arrested, exiled, or deposed. The description of these
actions is provided by Liudprand of Cremona (c. 920–972), one of Otto's
ministers who was himself a participant in these events.

Berengar and Adalbert were reigning,[22] or rather raging, in Italy, where they
exercised the worst of tyrannies, when John, the supreme pontiff and universal
pope, sent envoys from the holy church of Rome to Otto, at that time the most
serene and pious king and now our august emperor, humbly begging him, for
the love of God and the holy apostles Peter and Paul, to rescue him and the
holy Roman church from their jaws, and restore it to its former prosperity and
freedom.

The most pious king was moved by the tearful complaints, and considered
not himself but the cause of Jesus Christ. Therefore, although it was contrary to
custom, he appointed his young son Otto as king, and leaving him in Saxony,
collected his forces and marched in haste to Italy.[23] There he drove Berengar
and Adalbert from the realm at once, the more quickly inasmuch as it is certain
that the holy apostles Peter and Paul were fighting under his flag. Then he advanced on Rome to do the same again.

He was welcomed with marvelous ceremony and unexampled pomp, and was
anointed as emperor by John the supreme bishop and universal pope.[24] To the
church he not only gave back her possessions but bestowed lavish gifts of jewels, gold and silver. Furthermore Pope John and all the princes of the city swore
solemnly that they would never give help to Berengar and Adalbert. Thereupon
Otto returned to Pavia with all speed.

Then Pope John, forgetful of his oath and the promise he had made to the sacred emperor, sent to Adalbert asking him to return and swearing that he would
assist him against the power of the most sacred emperor.

The emperor for his part could not understand why Pope John was now
showing such affection to the very man whom previously he had attacked in bitter hatred. Accordingly he called together some of his intimates and sent off to
Rome to inquire of this report was true. When the envoys on their return gave
this report to the emperor, he said: "He is only a boy, and will soon alter if good
men set him an example. I hope that honorable reproof and generous persuasion
will quickly cure him of these vices. Perchance if he is forced into good ways,
he will be ashamed to get out of them again."

[22]Berengar II of Ivrea and his son Adalbert were joint kings of Italy, 950–963.
[23]In August, 961.
[24]In February, 962.

So Otto collected his forces and, at the secret invitation of the Romans, drew near to the city. When the emperor pitched his camp in the vicinity, the pope and Adalbert made their escape together from Rome. The citizens welcomed the holy emperor and all his men into their town, promising again to be loyal and adding under a strong oath that they would never elect or ordain a pope except with the consent and approval of the august Caesar Otto the lord emperor and his son King Otto.

At the request of the bishops and people of Rome a synod was held in the church of St Peter, attended by the emperor and the Italian archbishops. When all had taken their seats and complete silence was established, the holy emperor began thus: "How fitting it would have been for the lord Pope John to be present at this glorious holy synod. I ask you, holy fathers, to give your opinion why he has refused to attend, for you live as he does and share in all his interests."

Thereupon the Roman bishops and the cardinal priests and deacons together with the whole populace said: "John is not now even one of those who come in sheep's clothing and within are ravening wolves: his savageness is manifest, he is openly engaged in the devil's business, and he makes no attempt at disguise."

The emperor replied: "It seems to us right that the charges against the pope should be brought forward *seriatim*, and that the whole synod should then consider what course we should adopt."

Thereupon the cardinal priest Peter got up and testified that he had seen the pope celebrate mass without himself communicating. John bishop of Narni and John cardinal deacon then declared that they had seen the pope ordain a deacon in a stable and at an improper season. Benedict cardinal deacon with his fellow deacons and priests said that they knew the pope had been paid for ordaining bishops, and that in the city of Todi he had appointed a bishop for ten years. On the question of his sacrilege, they said, no inquiries were necessary; knowledge of it was a matter of eyesight, not of hearsay. As regards his adultery, though they had no visual information, they knew for certain that he had carnal acquaintance with Rainer's widow, Stephana; his father's concubine, the widow Anna; and his own niece; and that he had turned the holy palace into a brothel and resort for harlots. He had gone hunting publicly; he had blinded his spiritual father, Benedict, who died of his injuries; he had caused the death of cardinal subdeacon John by castrating him; he had set houses on fire and appeared in public equipped with sword, helmet and cuirass. At dice, they said, he asked the aid of Jupiter, Venus, and the other demons; he did not celebrate matins nor observe the canonical hours nor fortify himself with the sign of the cross.

When he had heard this, as the Romans could not understand his native Saxon tongue, the emperor bade Liudprand bishop of Cremona[25] to deliver the follow-

---

[25]The author of this selection.

ing speech in the Latin language to all the Romans. "It often happens that men set in high positions are besmirched by the foul tongue of envy. For this reason we still regard as doubtful the charges against the pope and we are uncertain whether they originated from zeal for righteousness or from impious envy. Therefore cast no foul words against the lord pope nor accuse him of anything that he has not really done and that has not been witnessed by men on whom we can rely."

So the holy synod pronounced: "If it please the holy emperor, let a letter be sent to the lord pope, that he come here and purge himself from all these charges."

Thereupon a letter was sent to him as follows: "To the supreme pontiff and universal pope lord John, Otto, august emperor by the grace of God, sends greeting in the name of the Lord. Know that you are charged, not by a few men but by all the clergy and laity alike, of homicide, perjury, sacrilege and of the sin of unchastity. Therefore we earnestly beg your paternal highness not to refuse under any pretence to come to Rome and clear yourself of all these charges. If perchance you fear the violence of a rash multitude, we declare under oath that no action is contemplated contrary to the sanction of the holy canons."

After reading this letter, the pope sent the following reply: "Bishop John, servant of God's servants, to all the bishops: We hear say that you wish to make another pope. If you do, I excommunicate you by Almighty God, and you have no power, to ordain no one or celebrate mass."

On this occasion the emperor said: "We are now assured that he will not attend. Let the holy synod now declare its decision."

Thereupon the Roman pontiffs and the other clergy and all people replied: "A mischief for which there is no precedent must be cauterized by methods equally novel. We therefore ask your imperial majesty that this monster shall be driven from the holy Roman church, and another be appointed in his place, who may prove himself both ruler and benefactor, living rightly himself and setting us an example of like conduct." Then the emperor said: "I agree with what you say; nothing will please me more than for you to find such a man and to give him control of this holy universal see."

READING 8

Roswitha of Gandersheim, *Abraham*[26]

The Benedictine nun Roswitha of Gandersheim (c. 935–1003), a member of the upper aristocracy of Ottonian Germany, is a figure of importance in

[26]From *The Plays of Roswitha,* tr. Christopher St. John; New York, Cooper Square Publishers, Inc., 1966, pp. 71–91.

the history of literature. She was the first female poet of the Middle Ages and the first medieval playwright of either sex. *Abraham* is one of Roswitha's six plays. Like the others, it exemplifies her procedure of adapting the engaging style of the pagan Roman playwright Terence to less racy, more edifying topics centering on Christian virtue and redemption. Before each of her plays, Roswitha wrote a brief synopsis, or argument, to inform her audience of the spiritual significance of the drama. *Abraham,* she writes, recounts the fall and repentance of Mary, the niece of the hermit Abraham, who, after she has spent twenty years in the religious life as a solitary, abandons it in despair, and, returning to the world, does not shrink from becoming a harlot. But two years later Abraham, in the disguise of a lover, seeks her out and reclaims her. For twenty years she does penance for her sins with many tears, fastings, vigils, and prayers.

SCENE ONE

[In this scene, Abraham expresses to his dear friend Ephrem his concerns about young Mary's future.]

SCENE TWO

Abraham: Mary, my child by adoption, whom I love as my own soul! Listen to my advise as to a father's, and to Brother Ephrem's as that of a very wise man. Strive to imitate the chastity of the holy Virgin whose name you bear.

Ephrem: Child, would it not be a shame if you, who through the mystery of your name are called to mount to the stars where Mary the mother of God reigns, chose instead the low pleasures of the earth?

Mary: I know nothing about the mystery of my name, so how can I tell what you mean?

Eph: My child, "Mary" means "star of the sea"—that star which rules the world and all peoples in the world.

Mary: Why is it called the star of the sea?

Eph: Because it never sets, but shines always in the heavens to show mariners their right course.

Mary: And how can such a poor thing as I am—made out of slime, as my uncle says—shine like my name?

Eph: By keeping your body unspotted, and your mind pure and holy.

Mary: It would be too great an honor for any human being to become like the stars.

Eph: If you choose you can be as the angels of God, and when at last you cast off the burden of this mortal body they will be near you. With them you will pass through the air, and walk on the sky. With them you will sweep round the zodiac, and never slacken your steps until the Virgin's Son takes you in His arms in His mother's dazzling bridal room!

Mary: Who but an ass would think little of such happiness! So I choose to despise the things of earth, and deny myself now that I may enjoy it!

Eph: Out of the mouths of babes and sucklings! A childish heart, but a mature mind!

Abr: God be thanked for it!

Eph: Amen to that.

Abr: But though by God's grace she has been given the light, at her tender age she must be taught how to use it.

Eph: You are right.

Abr: I will build her a little cell with a narrow entrance near my hermitage. I can visit her there often, and through the window instruct her in the psalter and other pages of the divine law.

Eph: That is a good plan.

Mary: I put myself under your direction, Father Ephrem.

Eph: My daughter! May the Heavenly Bridegroom to Whom you have given yourself in the tender bud of your youth shield you from the wiles of the devil!

SCENE THREE

Abr: Brother Ephrem, Brother Ephrem! When anything happens, good or bad, it is to you I turn. It is your counsel I seek. Do not turn your face away, brother—do not be impatient, but help me.

Eph: Abraham, Abraham, what has come to you? What is the cause of this immoderate grief? Ought a hermit to weep and groan after the manner of the world?

Abr: Was any hermit ever so stricken? I cannot bear my sorrow.

Eph: Brother, no more of this. To the point; what has happened?

Abr: Mary! Mary! my adopted child! Mary, whom I cared for so lovingly and taught with all my skill for ten years!

Eph: Well, what is it?

Abr: Oh God! She is lost!

Eph: Lost? What do you mean?

Abr: Most miserably. And afterwards she ran away.

Eph: But by what wiles did the ancient enemy bring about her undoing?

Abr: By the wiles of false love. Dressed in a monk's habit, the hypocrite went to see her often. He succeeded in making the poor ignorant child love him. She leapt from the window of her cell for an evil deed.

Eph: I shudder as I listen to you.

Abr: When the unhappy girl knew that she was ruined, she beat her breast and dug her nails into her face. She tore her garments, pulled out her hair. Her despairing cries were terrible to hear.

Eph: I am not surprised. For such a fall a whole fountain of tears should rise.

Abr: She moaned out that she could never be the same.

Eph: Poor, miserable girl!

Abr: And reproached herself for having forgotten our warning.

Eph: She might well do so.

Abr: She cried that all her vigils, prayers, and fasts had been thrown away.

Eph: If she perseveres in this penitence she will be saved.

Abr: She has not persevered. She has added worse to her evil deed.

Eph: Oh, this moves me to the depths of my heart!

Abr: After all those tears and lamentations she was overcome by remorse, and fell headlong into the abyss of despair.

Eph: A bitter business!

Abr: She despaired of being able to win pardon, and resolved to go back to the world and its vanities.

Eph: I cannot remember when the devil could boast of such a triumph over the hermits.

Abr: Now we are at the mercy of the demons.

Eph: I marvel that she could have escaped without your knowledge.

Abr: If I had not been so blind! I ought to have paid more heed to that terrible vision. Yes, I see now that it was sent to warn me.

Eph: What vision?

Abr: I dreamed I was standing at the door of my cell, and that a huge dragon with a loathsome stench rushed violently towards me. I saw that the creature was attracted by a little white dove at my side. It pounced on the dove, devoured it, and vanished.

Eph: There is no doubt what this vision meant.

Abr: When I woke I turned over in my mind what I had seen, and took it as a sign of some persecution threatening the Church, through which many of the faithful would be drawn into error. I prostrated myself in prayer, and implored Him Who knows the future to enlighten me.

Eph: You did right.

Abr: On the third night after the vision, when for weariness I had fallen asleep, I saw the beast again, but now it was lying dead at my feet, and the dove was flying heavenwards safe and unhurt.

Eph: I am rejoiced to hear this, for to my thinking it means that some day Mary will return to you.

Abr: I was trying to get rid of this uneasiness with which the first vision had filled me by thinking of the second, when my little pupil in her cell came to my mind. I remembered, although at the time I was not alarmed, that for two days I had not heard her chanting the divine praises.

Eph: You were too tardy in noticing this.

Abr: I admit it. I went at once to her cell, and, knocking at the window, I called her again and again, "Mary! My child! Mary!"

Eph: You called in vain?

Abr: "Mary," I said. "Mary, my child, what is wrong? Why are you not saying your office?" It was only when I did not hear the faintest sound that I suspected.

Eph: What did you do then?

Abr: When I could no longer doubt that she had gone, I was struck with fear to my very bowels. I trembled in every limb.

Eph: I do not wonder, since I, hearing of it, find myself trembling all over.

Abr: Then I wept and cried out to the empty air, "What wolf has seized my lamb? What thief has stolen my little daughter?"

Eph: You had good cause to weep! To lose her whom you had cherished so tenderly!

Abr: At last some people came up who knew what had happened. From them I learned that she had gone back to the world.

Eph: Where is she now?

Abr: No one knows.

Eph: What is to be done?

Abr: I have a faithful friend, who is searching all the cities and towns in the country. He says he will never give up until he finds her.

Eph: And if he finds her—what then?

Abr: Then I shall change these clothes, and in the guise of a worldling seek her out. It may be that she will heed what I say, and even after this shipwreck turn again to the harbor of her innocence and peace. . . .

Eph: May He Who is supreme good itself, without Whom no good thing can be done, bless your enterprise and bring it to a happy end!

SCENE FOUR

[Abraham meets a friend who has been looking for Mary for two years. He tells the old hermit that his niece has become a prostitute. Abraham determines to seek her out for the salvation of her soul.]

SCENES FIVE AND SIX

[Abraham finds the inn where Mary works as a prostitute. Not recognizing Abraham, who is in disguise, she invites him to her chambers.]

SCENE SEVEN

Mary: Look! How do you like this room? A handsome bed, isn't it? Those trappings cost a lot of money. Sit down and I will take off your shoes. You seem tired.

Abr: First bolt the door. Someone may come in.

Mary: Have no fear. I have seen to that.

Abr: The time has come for me to show my shaven head, and make myself known! Oh, my daughter! Oh, Mary, you who are part of my soul! Look at me. Do you not know me? Do you now know the old man who cherished you with a father's love, and wedded you to the Son of the King of Heaven?

Mary: God, what shall I do! It is my father and master Abraham!

Abr: What has come to you, daughter?

Mary: Oh, misery!

Abr: Who deceived you? Who led you astray?

Mary: Who deceived our first parents?

Abr: Have you forgotten that once you lived like an angel on earth!

Mary: All that is over.

Abr: What has become of your virginal modesty? Your beautiful purity?

Mary: Lost. Gone!

Abr: Oh, Mary, think what you have thrown away! Think what a reward you had earned by your fasting, and prayers, and vigils. What can they avail you now! You have hurled yourself from heavenly heights into the depths of hell!

Mary: Oh God, I know it!

Abr: Could you not trust me? Why did you desert me? Why did you not tell me of your fall? Then dear brother Ephrem and I could have done a worthy penance.

Mary: Once I had committed that sin, and was defiled, how could I dare to come near you who are so holy?

Abr: Oh, Mary, has anyone ever lived on earth without sin except the Virgin's Son?

Mary: No one, I know.

Abr: It is human to sin, but it is devilish to remain in sin. Who can be justly condemned? Not those who fall suddenly, but those who refuse to rise quickly.

Mary: Wretched, miserable creature that I am!

Abr: Why have you thrown yourself down there? Why do you lie on the ground without moving or speaking? Get up, Mary! Get up, my child, and listen to me!

Mary: No! no! I am afraid. I cannot bear your reproaches.

Abr: Remember how I love you, and you will not be afraid.

Mary: It is useless. I cannot.

Abr: What but love for you could have made me to leave the desert and relax the strict observance of our rule? What but love could have made me, a true hermit, come into the city and mix with the lascivious crowd? It is for your sake that these lips have learned to utter light, foolish words, so that I might not be known! Oh, Mary, why do you turn away your face from me and gaze upon the ground? Why do you scorn to answer and tell me what is in your mind?

Mary: It is the thought of my sins which crushes me. I dare not look at you; I am not fit to speak to you.

Abr: My little one, have no fear. Oh, do not despair! Rise from this abyss of desperation and grapple God to your soul!

Mary: No, no! My sins are too great. They weigh me down.

Abr: The mercy of heaven is greater than you or your sins. Let your sadness be dispersed by its glorious beams. Oh, Mary, do not let apathy prevent your seizing the moment for repentance. It matters not how wickedness has flourished. Divine grace can flourish still more abundantly!

Mary: If there were the smallest hope of forgiveness, surely I should not shrink from doing penance.

Abr: Have you no pity for me? I have sought you out with so much pain and weariness! Oh shake off this despair which we are taught is the most terrible of sins. Despair of God's mercy—for that alone there is not forgiveness. Sin can no more embitter His sweet mercy than a spark from a flint can set the ocean on fire.

Mary: I know that God's mercy is great, but when I think how greatly I have sinned, I cannot believe any penance can make amends.

Abr: I will take your sins on me. Only come back and take up your life again as if you had never left it.

Mary: I do not want to oppose you. What you tell me to do I will with all my heart.

Abr: My daughter lives again! I have found my lost lamb and she is dearer to me than ever.

Mary: I have a few possessions here—a little gold and some clothes. What ought I to do with them?

Abr: What came to you through sin, with sin must be left behind.

Mary: Could it not be given to the poor, or sold for an offering at the holy altar?

Abr: The price of sin is not an acceptable offering to God.

Mary: Then I will not trouble any more about my possessions.

Abr: Look! The dawn! It is growing light. Let us go.

Mary: You go first, dearest father, like the good shepherd leading the lost lamb that has been found. The lamb will follow in your steps.

Abr: Not so! I am going on foot, but you—you shall have a horse so that the stony road shall not hurt your delicate feet.

Mary: Oh, let me never forget this tenderness! Let me try all my life to thank you! I was not worth pity, yet you have shown me no harshness; you have led me to repent not by threats but by gentleness and love.

Abr: I ask only one thing, Mary. Be faithful to God for the rest of your life.

Mary: With all my strength I will persevere, and though my flesh may fail, my spirit never will.

Abr: You must serve God with as much energy as you have served the world.

Mary: If His will is made perfect in me it will be because of your merits.

Abr: Come, let us hasten on our way.

Mary: Yes, let us set out at once. I would not stay here another minute.

SCENE EIGHT

[Abraham tells Mary he must share the good news
of her spiritual rebirth with his friend Ephrem.]

SCENE NINE

Eph: Well, brother! If I am not mistaken, you bring good news.

Abr: The best in the world.

Eph: You have found your lost lamb?

Abr: I have, and, rejoicing, have brought her back to the fold.

Eph: Truly this is the work of divine grace.

Abr: That is certain.

Eph: How is she spending her days? I should like to know how you have ordered her life. What does she do?

Abr: All that I tell her.

Eph: That is well.

Abr: Nothing is too difficult for her—nothing too hard. She is ready to endure anything.

Eph: That is better.

Abr: She wears a hair shirt, and subdues her flesh with continual vigils and fasts. She is making the poor frail body obey the spirit by the most rigorous discipline.

Eph: Only through such a severe penance can the stains left by the pleasures of the flesh be washed away.

Abr: Those who hear her sobs are cut to the heart, and the tale of her repentance has turned many from their sins.

Eph: It is often so.

Abr: She prays continually for the men who through her were tempted to sin, and begs that she who was their ruin may be their salvation.

Eph: It is right that she should do this.

Abr: She strives to make her life as beautiful as for a time it was hideous.

Eph: I rejoice at what you tell me. To the depths of my heart.

Abr: And with us rejoice phalanxes of angels, praising the Lord for the conversion of a sinner.

Eph: Over whom, we are told, there is more joy in heaven than over the just man who needs no penance.

Abr: The more glory to Him, because there seemed no hope on earth that she could be saved.

Eph: Let us sing a song of thanksgiving—let us glorify the only begotten Son of God, Who of His love and mercy will not let them perish whom He redeemed with His holy blood.

Abr: To Him honor, glory, and praise through infinite ages. Amen.

READING 9

An Account of the Lombard Kingdom[27]

In this passage an anonymous Pavian writer of the early eleventh century looks back at the flourishing state of the Lombard kingdom and its capital at Pavia several decades earlier, not long after Otto I had absorbed the kingdom into his empire. Otto and his successors were usually content to rule northern Italy gently and from a distance, but by contributing to its political stability, they encouraged the growing vitality of its commerce. Like Einhard (see pp. 101–104) and many other medieval writers, our anonymous author seems to have modeled his description on another source, the nearly contemporary *Book of the Prefect* relating to Constantinople. Nevertheless, the account of Lombard Italy abounds in factual information that can almost certainly be trusted.

Merchants entering the kingdom used to pay the 10 per cent tax [*decima*] on all merchandise at the customs houses and at the beginning of the roads subject to the king.[28] All persons coming from beyond the mountains into Lombardy are obligated to pay the *decima* on horses, male and female slaves, woolen, linen, and hemp cloth, tin, and swords. On all merchandise they are obligated to give the *decima* to the delegate of the treasurer. But everything that pilgrims bound for Rome take with them for personal expenses is to be passed without payment of the *decima.*

And the nation of the Angles and Saxons, who came and used to come with their merchandise and wares, when they saw their trunks and sacks being emptied at the gates, grew angry and started rows with the employees of the treasury. Abusive words were exchanged and, moreover, very often the parties inflicted wounds upon one another. But in order to cut short such great evils and to

---

[27]From *Instituta regalia et ministeria camere regnum Longobardum,* in *The Tenth Century,* ed. R. S. Lopez; New York, Holt, Rinehart & Winston, 1959, pp. 15–17. By permission.

[28]At this period, the king of Italy and the German emperor were the same person.

remove all danger, the king of the Angles and Saxons and the king of the Lombards agreed together as follows: The nation of the Angles and Saxons is no longer to be subject to the *decima*. And in return for this the king of the Angles and Saxons and their nation are expected and obligated to send to the king's palace in Pavia and to the king's treasury, every third year, fifty pounds of refined silver, two large and handsome greyhounds, hairy or furred, in chains, with collars covered with gilded plates seated or enameled with the arms of the king, two excellent embossed shields, two excellent lances, and two excellent swords wrought and tested. And to the master of the treasury they are obligated to give two large coats of miniver[29] and two pounds of refined silver. And they are to receive a passport from the master of the treasury, that they may not suffer any annoyance as they come and return home.

And the duke of the Venetians, together with his Venetians, is obligated to give every year in the king's palace in Pavia fifty pounds of Venetian deniers. These deniers are of one ounce each, equally good as the Pavian deniers in regard to weight and silver content. And to the master of the treasury the duke is obligated to give one excellent silk cloak on account of the rights belonging to the king of the Lombards. And that nation [of the Venetians] does not plow, sow, or gather vintage. This tribute is called pact, and by it the nation of the Venetians are allowed to buy grain and wine in every marketplace and to make their purchases in Pavia, and they are not to suffer any annoyance.

Many wealthy Venetian merchants used to come to Pavia with their merchandise, and they paid to the monastery of Saint Martin, which is called Outgate, the fortieth shilling on all merchandise. When the prominent Venetians come to Pavia, each of them is obligated to give to the master of the treasury every year one pound of pepper, one pound of cinnamon, one pound of galangal, and one pound of ginger; and to the wife of the master of the treasury, an ivory comb and a mirror and a set of accessories, or twenty shillings of good Pavian deniers.

Likewise the men of Salerno, Gaeta, and Amalfi used to come to Pavia with abundant merchandise. And they used to give to the treasury in the king's palace the fortieth shilling, and to the wife of the treasurer they gave individually spices and accessories just as did the Venetians.

And the great and honorable and very wealthy merchants of Pavia have always received from the hand of the emperor the most honorable credentials, so that they suffer no harm or annoyance in any way, wherever they may be, whether in a market or traveling by water or by land. And whoever acts contrary to this is obligated to pay a thousand gold mancusi into the king's treasury.

And the mystery [guild] of the mint of Pavia is obligated to have nine noble and wealthy masters above all the other moneyers, who are to supervise and to

[29]Miniver was a white fur used mainly for robes of state.

direct all other moneyers jointly with the master of the treasury, so that no deniers be ever struck that be inferior to those they always have struck in regard to weight and silver content, to wit, ten of twelve. And these nine masters are obligated to pay for the rent of the mint twelve pounds of Pavian deniers into the king's treasury every year and four pounds of the same to the count palatine of Pavia. If a mint master discover a forger, they are to act in this way: jointly with the count of Pavia and the master of the treasury, they are under obligation to have the right hand of the forger cut off and to turn over his entire property to the king's treasury. . . .

And there are all the gold washers who send their accounts to the treasury in Pavia, and must never sell gold to anyone else but the sworn moneyers, and are obligated to deliver it to them and to the treasurer. And the latter are obligated to buy all that gold obtained from the rivers.

And there are in Pavia fishermen, who are obligated to have a master from the best members of the whole mystery. And they are obligated to keep sixty boats, and to give for every boat two deniers on the first day of each month. And these two monthly deniers they are obligated to give to their master . . . and to make sure that whenever the king is in Pavia, fish is purchased with those deniers or their own fish is brought to him in the most honorable manner. And they are obligated to give fish every Friday to the master of the treasury.

There also are in Pavia twelve tanners preparing leather, with twelve junior members. And they are obligated to prepare every year twelve excellent oxskins and to give them to the royal treasury, in order that no other man be allowed to prepare leather. And let whoever acts contrary to this pay a hundred Pavian shillings into the royal treasury. And whenever a tanner first enters the mystery to become one of these senior tanners, he is obligated to give four pounds, one half to royal treasury and the other half to the other tanners.

There also are other mysteries. All shipmen and boatmen are obligated to furnish two good men as masters under the authority of the treasurer in Pavia. Whenever the king is in Pavia, these men are obligated to go with the ships. And these two masters are obligated to outfit two large vessels, one for the king and one for the queen, and to build a house with planks, and to cover it well. As for the pilots, let them have one vessel, so that the others may be safe on the water; and they are entitled, together with their juniors, to receive every day their expenses from the king's court.

And there was in Pavia the mystery of the soapmakers, who used to make soap and to give every year on the steelyard a hundred pounds of soap to the royal treasury and ten pounds to the treasurer, in order that no one else be entitled to make soap in Pavia.

And concerning all these mysteries you should know this: that no man is entitled to perform their functions unless he is a member. And should another man perform them, he is obligated to pay the *bannum* [fine] into the king's treasury and to swear that he will no longer do so. Nor ought any merchant to conclude his business in any market, unless he is a Pavian merchant. And let any one acting contrary to this pay the *bannum.*

READING 10

The Russian Primary Chronicle[30]

The Kievan state originated in the ninth century and grew vastly in size and strength during the tenth to become the dominant power in Ukraine and beyond. Its most renowned ruler, Vladimir (956–1015), became prince of Novgorod in 970 and ten years later seized Kiev from his own brother and assumed the title Grand Prince of Kiev, which he held from 980 until his death in 1015. He succeeded in extending his dominions from the Baltic to the Black Sea, and his growing commercial relations with the Byzantine Empire (accompanied by occasional raids on Byzantine ports) culminated in his marriage to the emperor's sister Anna and his conversion to Christianity (988–989), followed by the conversion of his subjects, many of them by force. His baptism by Byzantine churchmen reflected the established imperial strategy of combining Orthodox Christian missionary activity with the advancement of diplomatic goals.

Our best contemporary account of the Kievan state is an anonymous Slavic vernacular history known as the *Russian Primary Chronicle.* Extending from early Slavic times into the second decade of the twelfth century, it remains an invaluable source for the history of medieval Russia.

[In 987] Vladimir summoned together his noblemen and the city-elders, and said to them, "Behold, the Bulgars came before me urging me to accept their religion. Then came the Germans and praised their own faith; and after them came the Jews [from Khazar]. Finally the Greeks appeared, criticizing all other faiths but commending their own, and they spoke at length, telling the history of the whole world from its beginning. Their words were artful, and it was wondrous to listen and pleasant to hear them. They preach the existence of another world. 'Whoever adopts our religion and then dies shall arise and live forever. But whosoever embraces another faith, shall be consumed with fire in the next world.' What is your opinion on this subject, and what do you answer?" The no-

[30]From *The Russian Primary Chronicle, tr.* Samuel Hazard Cross and Olgerd P. Sherbowitz-Wetzor; Cambridge, Mass., Medieval Academy of American, 1953, pp. 110–113.

blemen and the elders replied, "You know, oh Prince, that no man condemns his own possessions, but praises them instead. If you desire to make certain, you have servants at your disposal. Send them to inquire about the ritual of each and how he worships God."

Their counsel pleased the prince and all the people, so that they chose good and wise men to the number of ten, and directed them to go first among the Bulgars and inspect their faith. The emissaries went their way, and when they arrived at their destination they beheld the disgraceful actions of the Bulgars and their worship in the mosque; then they returned to their country. Vladimir then instructed them to go likewise among the Germans, and examine their faith, and finally to visit the Greeks. They thus went into Germany, and after viewing the German ceremonial, they proceeded to [Constantinople], where they appeared before the Emperor. He inquired on what missions they had come, and they reported to him all that had occurred. When the Emperor heard their words, he rejoiced, and did them great honor on that very day.

On the morrow, the Emperor sent a message to the Patriarch [Nicholas II] to inform him that a Russian delegation had arrived to examine the Greek faith, and directed him to prepare the church and the clergy, and to array himself in his sacerdotal robes, so that the Russians might behold the glory of the God of the Greeks. When the Patriarch received these commands, he bade the clergy assemble, and they performed the customary rites. They burned incense, and the choirs sang hymns. The Emperor accompanied the Rus' to the church, and placed them in a wide space, calling their attention to the beauty of the edifice, the chanting, and the pontifical services and the ministry of the deacons, while he explained to them the worship of his God. The Russians were astonished, and in their wonder praised the Greek ceremonial. Then the Emperors Basil [II] and Constantine invited the envoys to their presence, and said, "Go hence to your native country," and dismissed them with valuable presents and great honor.

Thus they returned to their own country, and the prince called together his noblemen and the elders. Vladimir then announced the return of the envoys who had been sent out, and suggested that their report be heard. He thus commanded them to speak out before his retinue. The envoys reported, "When we journeyed among the Bulgars, we beheld how they worship in their temple, called a mosque, while they stand ungirt. The Bulgar bows, sits down, looks hither and thither like one possessed, and there is no happiness among them, but instead only sorrow and a dreadful stench. Their religion is not good. Then we went among the Germans, and saw them performing many ceremonies in their temples; but we beheld no glory there. Then we went to Greece, and the Greeks led us to the edifices where they worship their God, and we know not whether we were in heaven or in earth. For on earth there is no such splendor or such beauty, and we are at a loss how to describe it. We only know that God dwells there among men, and their service is fairer than the ceremonies of other nations. For we cannot forget that beauty. Every man, after tasting something sweet, is afterward unwilling to accept that which is bitter, and therefore we cannot dwell longer here." Then the noblemen spoke and said, "If the Greek faith were evil, it would not have been adopted by your grandmother Olga who was wiser than all other men." Vladimir then inquired where they should all accept baptism, and they replied that the decision rested with him. . . .

[In 988] Vladimir proceeded with an armed force against Kherson, a Greek city [in the Crimea], and the people of Kherson barricaded themselves therein. Vladimir halted at the farther side of the city beside the harbor, a bowshot from the town, and the inhabitants resisted energetically while Vladimir besieged the town. Eventually, however, they became exhausted, and Vladimir warned them that if they did not surrender, he would remain on the spot for three years. When they failed to heed his threat, Vladimir marshaled his troops and ordered the construction of an earthwork in the direction of the city. While this work was under construction, the inhabitants dug a tunnel under the city-wall, stole the heaped-up earth, and carried it into the city, where they piled it up in the center of the town. But the soldiers kept on building, and Vladimir persisted. Then a man of Kherson, Anastasius by name, shot into the Russian camp an arrow on which he had written, "There are springs behind you to the east, from which water flows in pipes. Dig down and cut them off." When Vladimir received this information, he raised his eyes to heaven and vowed that if this hope was realized, he would be baptized. He gave orders straightway to dig down above the pipes, and the water-supply was thus cut off. The inhabitants were accordingly overcome by thirst, and surrendered.

Vladimir and his retinue entered the city, and he sent messages to the Emperors Basil and Constantine, saying, "Behold, I have captured your glorious city. I have also heard that you have an unwedded sister. Unless you give her to me to wife, I shall deal with your own city as I have with Kherson." When the Emperors heard this message they were troubled, and replied, "It is not proper for Christians to give in marriage to pagans. If you are baptized, you shall have her to wife, inherit the kingdom of God, and be our companion in the faith. Unless you do so, however, we cannot give you our sister in marriage." When Vladimir learned their response, he directed the envoys of the Emperors to report to the latter that he was willing to accept baptism, having already given some study to their religion, and that the Greek faith and ritual, as described by the emissaries sent to examine it, had pleased him well. When the Emperors heard this report, they rejoiced, and persuaded their sister Anna to consent to the match. Then they requested Vladimir to submit to baptism before they could send their sister to him, but Vladimir desired that the Princess should herself bring priests to baptize him. The Emperors complied with his request, and sent forth their sister, accompanied by some dignitaries and priests. Anna, however, departed with reluctance. "It is as if I were setting out into captivity," she lamented; "better were it for me to die at home." But her brothers protested,

"Through your agency God turns the land of Russia to repentance, and you will relieve Greece from the danger of grievous war. Do you not see how much harm the Russians have already brought upon the Greeks? If you do not set out, they may bring on us the same misfortunes." It was thus that they overcame her hesitation only with great difficulty. The Princess embarked upon a ship, and after tearfully embracing her kinfolk, set forth across the sea and arrived at Kherson. The natives came forth to greet her, and conducted her into the city, where they settled her in the palace.

By divine agency, Vladimir was suffering at that moment from a disease of the eyes, and could see nothing, being in great distress. The Princess declared to him that if he desired to be relieved of this disease, he should be baptized with all speed, otherwise it could not be cured. When Vladimir heard her message, he said, "If this proves true, then of a surety is the God of the Christians great," and gave order that he should be baptized. The Bishop of Kherson, together with the Princess's priests, after announcing the tidings, baptized Vladimir, and as the Bishop laid his hand upon him, he straightway received his sight. Upon experiencing this miraculous cure, Vladimir glorified God, saying, "I have now perceived the one true God." When his followers beheld this miracle, many of them were also baptized.

Vladimir was baptized in the Church of St. Basil, which stands at Kherson upon a square in the center of the city, where the Khersonians trade. The palace of Vladimir stands beside this church to this day, and the palace of the princess is behind the altar. After his baptism, Vladimir took the princess in marriage. Those who do not know the truth say he was baptized in Kiev, while others assert this event took place in Vasiliev, while still others mention other places.

Hereupon Vladimir took the princess and Anastasius and the priests of Kherson, together with the relics of St. Clement and of Phoebus his disciple, and selected also sacred vessels and images for the service. In Kherson he thus founded a church on the mound which had been heaped up in the midst of the city with the earth removed from his embankment; this church is standing at the present day. Vladimir also found and appropriated two bronze statues and four bronze horses, which now stand behind the Church of the Holy Virgin, and which the ignorant think are made of marble. As a wedding present for the princess, he gave Kherson over to the Greeks again, and then departed for Kiev.

When the prince arrived at his capital, he directed that the idols should be overthrown and that some should be cut to pieces and others burned with fire. He thus ordered that Perun should be bound to a horse's tail and dragged along Borichev to the river. He appointed twelve men to beat the idol with sticks, not because he thought the wood was sensitive, but to affront the demon who had deceived man in this guise, that he might receive chastisement at the hands of men. Great art thou, O Lord, and marvelous are thy works! Yesterday he was honored of men, but today held in derision. While the idol was being dragged along the stream to the Dnepr, the unbelievers wept over it, for they had not yet received holy baptism. After they had thus dragged the idol along, they cast it into the Dnepr. But Vladimir had given this injunction: "If it halts anywhere, then push it out from the bank, until it goes over the falls. Then let it loose." His command was duly obeyed. When the men let the idol go, and it passed through the falls, the wind cast it out on the bank, which since that time has been called Perun's Shore, a name that it bears to this very day.

Thereafter Vladimir sent heralds throughout the whole city to proclaim that if any inhabitant, rich or poor, did not betake himself to the river, he would risk the prince's displeasure. When the people heard these words, they wept for joy, and exclaimed in their enthusiasm, "If this were not good, the prince and his boyars would not have accepted it." On the morrow the prince went forth to the Dnepr with the priests of the princess and those from Kherson, and a countless multitude assembled. They all went into the water: some stood up to their necks, others to their breasts, the younger near the bank, some of them holding children in their arms, while the adults waded farther out. The priests stood by and offered prayers. There was joy in heaven and upon earth to behold so many souls saved. But the devil groaned, lamenting: "Woe is me! How am I driven out hence! For I thought to have my dwelling place here, since the apostolic teachings do not abide in this land. Nor did this people know God, but I rejoiced in the service they rendered unto me. But now I am vanquished by the ignorant, not by apostles and martyrs, and my reign in these regions is at an end."

When the people were baptized, they returned each to his own abode. Vladimir, rejoicing that he and his subjects now knew God himself, looked up to heaven and said: "O God, who hast created heaven and earth, look down, I beseech thee, on this thy new people, and grant them, O Lord, to know thee as the true God, even as the other Christian nations have known thee. Confirm in them the true and unalterable faith, and aid me, O Lord, against the hostile adversary, so that, hoping in thee and in thy might, I may overcome his malice." Having spoken thus, he ordained that churches should be built and established where pagan idols had previously stood. He thus founded the Church of St. Basil on the hill where the idol of Perun and the other images had been set, and where the prince and the people had offered their sacrifices. He began to found churches and to assign priests throughout the cities, and to invite the people to accept baptism in all the cities and towns. He took the children of the best families, and sent them to schools for instruction in book learning. The mothers of these children wept bitterly over them, for they were not yet strong in faith, but mourned as for the dead. When these children were assigned for study, there was thus fulfilled in the Russian land the prophecy which says, "In those days, the deaf shall hear words of Scripture, and the voice of the stammerers shall be made plain" (Isaiah, 29:18). For these persons had not ere this heard words of Scripture, and now heard them only by the act of God, for in his mercy the Lord took pity upon them, even as the Prophet said, "I will be gracious to whom I will be gracious" (Exodus, 33:19).

READING 11

The Greenland Saga[31]

The Icelandic sagas mark the pinnacle of medieval Norse literature. The Greenland Saga, like others of its kind, is based on actual historical events. But as poetic celebrations of heroic deeds, transmitted orally for several generations before being transcribed, the sagas tend to coat historical facts with a crust of legend. The voyage described here took place around A.D. 1000; the saga was probably first committed to writing in the later 1100s. Our oldest surviving text, in the *Flateyjarbok of* the later 1300s, is based on earlier texts that have since perished.

Bjarni Herjolfsson sailed from Greenland to Norway and visited Earl Eirik,[32] who received him well. Bjarni told the earl about his voyage and the lands he had sighted. People thought he had shown great lack of curiosity, since he could tell them nothing about these countries, and he was criticized for this. Bjarni was made a retainer at the earl's court, and went back to Greenland the following summer.

There was now great talk of discovering new countries. Leif, the son of Eirik the Red of Brattahlid, went to see Bjarni Herjolfsson and bought his ship from him, and engaged a crew of thirty-five.

Leif asked his father Eirik to lead this expedition too, but Eirik was rather reluctant: he said he was getting old, and could endure hardships less easily than he used to. Leif replied that Eirik would still command more luck than any of his kinsmen. And in the end, Eirik let Leif have his way.

As soon as they were ready, Eirik rode off to the ship which was only a short distance away. But the horse he was riding stumbled and he was thrown, injuring his leg. "I am not meant to discover more countries than this one we now live in," said Eirik. "This is as far as we go together."

Eirik returned to Brattahlid, but Leif went aboard the ship with his crew of thirty-five. Among them was a Southerner called Tyrkir.[33]

They made their ship ready and put out to sea. The first landfall they made was the country that Bjarni had sighted last. They sailed right up to the shore

[31]From the *Graenlendiga Saga,* in *The Vinland Sagas: The Norse Discovery of America,* ed. and tr. Magnus Magnusson and Hermann Palsson; London, Penguin Classics, 1965, pp. 54–58. Copyright Magnus Magnusson and Hermann Palsson, 1965. Reprinted by permission of Penguin Books, Ltd.
[32]Then ruler of Norway.
[33]"Southerner" refers to someone from central or southern Europe; Tyrkir appears to have been a German.

and cast anchor, then lowered a boat and landed. There was no grass to be seen, and the hinterland was covered with great glaciers, and between glaciers and shore the land was like one great slab of rock. It seemed to them a worthless country.

Then Leif said, "Now we have done better than Bjarni where this country is concerned—we at least have set foot on it. I shall give this country a name and call it *Helluland*."

They returned to their ship and put to sea, and sighted a second land. Once again they sailed right up to it and cast anchor, lowered a boat and went ashore. This country was flat and wooded, with white sandy beaches wherever they went; and the land sloped gently down to the sea. Leif said, "This country shall be named after its natural resources: it shall be called *Markland*."[34]

They hurried back to their ship as quickly as possible and sailed away to sea in a north-east wind for two days until they sighted land again. They sailed towards it and came to an island which lay to the north of it.

They went ashore and looked about them. The weather was fine. There was dew on the grass, and the first thing they did was to get some of it on their hands and put it to their lips, and to them it seemed the sweetest thing they had ever tasted. Then they went back to their ship and sailed into the sound that lay between the island and the headland jutting out to the north.

They steered a westerly course round the headland. There were extensive shallows there and at low tide their ship was left high and dry, with the sea almost out of sight. But they were so impatient to land that they could not bear to wait for the rising tide to float the ship; they ran ashore to a place where a river flowed out of a lake. As soon as the tide had refloated the ship they took a boat and rowed out to it and brought it up the river into the lake, where they anchored it. They carried their hammocks ashore and put up booths. Then they decided to winter there, and built some large houses.

There was no lack of salmon in the river or the lake, bigger salmon than they had ever seen. The country seemed to them so kind that no winter fodder would be needed for livestock: there was never any frost all winter and the grass hardly withered at all.

In this country, night and day were of more even length then in either Greenland or Iceland: on the shortest day of the year, the sun was already up by 9 A.M., and did not set until after 3 P.M.[35]

---

[34]*Markland* was a heavily wooded country between *Helluland* and *Vinland,* named by Leif on his voyage and probably the southeast coast of Labrador or perhaps Newfoundland.

[35]This statement indicates that the location of *Vinland* must have been south of latitude fifty and north of latitude forty—anywhere between the Gulf of St. Lawrence and New Jersey.

When they had finished building their houses, Leif said to his companions, "Now I want to divide our company into two parties and have the country explored; half of the company are to remain here at the houses while the other half go exploring—but they must not go so far that they cannot return the same evening, and they are not to become separated."

They carried out these instructions for a time. Leif himself took turns at going out with the exploring party and staying behind at the base.

Leif was tall and strong and very impressive in appearance. He was a shrewd man and always moderate in his behavior.

One evening news came that someone was missing: it was Tyrkir the Southerner. Leif was very displeased at this, for Tyrkir had been with the family for a long time, and when Leif was a child had been devoted to him. Leif rebuked his men severely, and got ready to make a search with twelve men.

They had gone only a short distance from the houses when Tyrkir came walking towards them, and they gave him a warm welcome. Leif quickly realized that Tyrkir was in excellent humor.

Tyrkir had a prominent forehead and shifty eyes, and not much more of a face besides; he was short and puny-looking but very clever with his hands.

Leif said to him, "Why are you so late, foster-father? How did you get separated from your companions?"

At first Tyrkir spoke for a long time in German, rolling his eyes in all directions and pulling faces, and no one could understand what he was saying. After a while he spoke in Icelandic. "I did not go much farther than you," he said. "I have some news. I found vines and grapes."

"Is that true, foster-father?" asked Leif.

"Of course it is true," he replied. "Where I was born there were plenty of vines and grapes."

They slept for the rest of the night, and next morning Leif said to his men, "Now we have two tasks on our hands. On alternate days we must gather grapes and cut vines, and then fell trees, to make a cargo for my ship."

This was done. It is said that the tow-boat was filled with grapes. They took on a full cargo of timber; and in the spring they made ready to leave and sailed away. Leif named the country after its natural qualities and called it *Vinland*.

STUDY QUESTIONS

A What were the weaknesses of the Carolingian Empire? What were the factors—foreign and domestic—that led to its decline?

B How did Europe respond to the "second invasions"? Which country was most successful, and why?

C What are the signs that European civilization was reviving around the year 1000?

Reading 1: Nithard, The History of the Sons of Louis the Pious

What led to the civil war following the death of Louis the Pious? How does this selection help to explain the breakup of the Carolingian Empire?

Reading 2: The Oaths of Strasbourg

What is the significance of the fact that the Oath of Strasbourg was taken in different languages? What does this suggest about the unity of the Carolingian Empire?

Reading 3: Select Feudal Documents

It became common in the Middle Ages to distinguish between obligations freely accepted—which came to be seen as "noble"—and obligations imposed on an individual—which came to be seen as "servile." Can you distinguish these two types of obligations in these documents? Why were ties between individuals necessary? How did the church come to be involved in feudalism? Can you detect ways in which modern government could grow out of feudal foundations? How do manors and manorialism provide the economic foundations for Europe's elites?

Reading 4: The Anglo-Saxon Chronicle

What was the impact of the Vikings on England? Can you trace the steps by which Danish raids become an attempt to conquer the island? How was Alfred able to defeat them? Why did Alfred require that Guthrum accept Christianity?

Reading 5: Foundation Charter for the Abbey of Cluny

What features of the Cluny foundation charter help account for its success as a monastic institution? Why did this become a model for later monastic reform?

Reading 6: Widukind of Corvey, The Battle of the Lechfeld

Who led the resistance to the invaders? Does this help explain the strength of the German monarchy?

Reading 7: Liudprand of Cremona, The Imperial Coronation of Otto I

How does the coronation of Otto I compare to the coronation of Charlemagne (Chapter 3, Reading 8)? What was Otto's purpose in becoming emperor? How did he treat the church—and does that give some clue to his motives?

Reading 8: Roswitha of Gandersheim, *Abraham*

What were the highest virtues and values for Roswitha? Why did the character of Mary in the play abandon them? What does this suggest is Roswitha's view of female nature? How did Mary atone?

Reading 9: An Account of the Lombard Kingdom

What goods were traded in Pavia? What crafts were practiced there? Does this help explain why kings and nobles wanted to control towns? Does it help explain the German monarch's interest in northern Italy?

Reading 10: The Russian Primary Chronicle

Why did the Kievans accept eastern Orthodox Christianity? How does Vladimir's reasoning compare with Oswiu's at the Synod of Whitby (Chapter 2, Reading 10)?

Reading 11: The Greenland Saga

The Vikings are most often seen through the eyes of their enemies, but in this reading we see how they described themselves. How is this picture different?

MAJOR LOCATIONS MENTIONED IN PART TWO

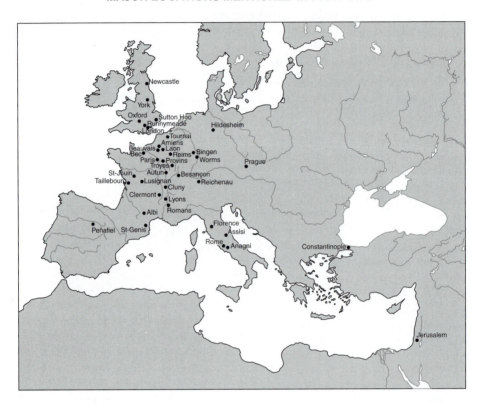

PART **TWO**

THE HIGH MIDDLE AGES

The period from about 1050 to 1300 has been called the High Middle Ages because it represented, in important respects, the zenith of medieval culture. Europe transformed itself during these years from an embattled, agrarian culture to an expanding and increasingly urbanized civilization. The papacy reached the height of its power in the course of its protracted struggle with the Holy Roman Empire. The English and French monarchies evolved toward early-modern states, with bureaucracies, official archives, a growing sense of national identity, and, in England, the beginnings of Parliament. This was the age of Europe's first universities, where students flocked to study the liberal arts and sometimes advanced into graduate-level studies in philosophy, theology, medicine, and law.

Historians have traditionally regarded this period as an age of faith, pointing to the building of the great cathedrals, the power of the papacy, and the proliferation of new religious orders—Cistercians, Dominicans, Franciscans, and many more. But the splendor of this religious culture was made possible by a great commercial revival. The overall balance of trade shifted in Europe's favor, and cities rose and flourished in its river valleys—the Rhine, Rhône, Loire, Seine, Po, Arno, Thames, and countless others. Warriors and crusaders expanded Europe's territorial frontiers in all directions, reconquering most of Spain from the

Muslims, establishing new principalities on the eastern shores of the Mediterranean, pushing northeastward along the Baltic coast, and carving out a prosperous new kingdom in southern Italy and Sicily at the expense of Byzantium and Islam.

Not all these territories would remain in European hands, and in subsequent centuries hostile armies and economic recession led to a series of crises in European culture and civilization. Nevertheless, the changes that Western Christendom experienced during the High Middle Ages proved to be decisive. Western Christendom had become a civilization of cities and commerce, of sophisticated states and flourishing universities—and so it would remain.

CHAPTER 5

🔯 NEW FRONTIERS:
CITIES AND CRUSADES

Emerging from a world of peasants, clerics, and warriors, the townspeople of the High Middle Ages were obliged to secure from their lords or princes the privileges essential to their new vocation (Reading 1). These privileges, won by negotiation or rebellion (Reading 2), mark the birth of a new class, the burghers, or bourgeoisie, whose wealth and power would grow across the centuries. The towns achieved a corporate status—the right to operate their own courts, collect their own taxes, and pay their lords' dues in a lump sum.

Medieval towns, unlike many Roman towns, were not just political and administrative districts, but also centers of economic growth, expansion, and exchange (Reading 3). Urban wealth funded the building of cathedrals, parish churches, and hospitals, as well as the launching of crusades.

The conquests of warriors and crusaders, in turn, opened new markets and drew new cities into Europe's expanding commercial network. The relationship between urban wealth and crusading zeal was nowhere more evident than in the First Crusade, manned by northern European knights (Reading 4).

The same spirituality that launched the crusades around the turn of the twelfth century also launched the Cistercian Order, whose most celebrated member, St. Bernard of Clairvaux, wrote the Rule for the Crusading Order of Knights Templars (Reading 5). The Templars, through their banks, eventually offered badly needed capital to Europe's emerging towns.

In this way, a cycle of faith, fervor, and fortune reinforced medieval piety and strengthened the medieval economy, helping inaugurate Europe's first great age of expansion.

173

READING 1

The Customs of Newcastle-upon-Tyne[1]

This document typifies a great many royal charters granting privileges to towns, but it is not itself a charter. It is a list, compiled during the reign (1154–1189) of Henry II, of the customs that the Newcastle townspeople (burgesses) enjoyed under the reign (1100–1135) of Henry II's grandfather, Henry I. If Henry I conceded these privileges to Newcastle in a charter, it has been lost.

These are the laws and customs which the burgesses of Newcastle-upon-Tyne had in the time of Henry, king of England, and which they still have by right:

The burgesses may distrain foreigners [i.e., seize their goods in pledge for debts or damages] within their markets and without, and within their houses and without, and within their borough and without, and they may do this without the permission of the reeve (royal official), unless the [royal] courts are being held within the borough, or unless they are in the field on army service [for the king], or are doing castle-guard. But a burgess may not distrain on another burgess without the permission of the reeve.

If a burgess shall lend anything in the borough to someone dwelling outside, the debtor shall pay back the debt if he admit it, or otherwise do right in the court of the borough.

Pleas which arise in the borough shall there be held and concluded except those which belong to the king's crown.

If a burgess shall be sued in respect of any plaint he shall not plead outside the borough except for defect of court; nor need he answer, except at a stated time and place, unless he has already made a foolish answer, or unless the case concerns matters pertaining to the crown.

If a ship comes to the Tyne and wishes to unload, it shall be permitted to the burgesses to purchase what they please. And if a dispute arises between a burgess and a merchant, it shall be settled before the third tide.

Whatever merchandise a ship brings by sea must be brought to the land; except salt and herring which must be sold on board ship.

If anyone has held land in burgage for a year and a day justly and without challenge, he need not answer any claimant, unless the claimant is outside the kingdom of England, or unless he be a boy not having the power of pleading.

[1]From *English Historical Documents, Volume II, 1042–1189*, ed. D. C. Douglas and G. W. Greenaway; Oxford, England, Oxford University Press, 1953, pp. 970–971. Reprinted by permission.

If a burgess have a son in his house and at his table, his son shall have the same liberty as his father.

If a villein come to reside in the borough, and shall remain as a burgess in the borough for a year and a day, he shall thereafter always remain there, unless there was a previous agreement between him and his lord for him to remain there for a certain time.

If a burgess sues anyone concerning anything, he cannot force the burgess to trial by battle, but the burgess must defend himself by his oath, except in a charge of treason when the burgess must defend himself by battle. Nor shall a burgess offer battle against a villein unless he has first quitted his burgage.

No merchant except a burgess can buy wool or hides or other merchandise outside the town, nor shall he buy them within the town except from burgesses.

If a burgess incurs forfeiture he shall give 6 oras to the reeve.

In the borough there is no "merchant" nor "heriot" nor "bloodwite" nor "stengesdint."[2]

Any burgess may have his own oven and handmill if he wishes, saving always the rights of the king's oven.

If a woman incur a forfeiture concerning bread or ale, none shall concern himself with it except the reeve. If she offend twice she shall be punished by the forfeiture. If she offend thrice justice shall take its course.

No one except a burgess may buy cloth for dyeing or make or cut it.

A burgess can give or sell his land as he wishes, and go where he will, freely and quietly unless his claim to the land is challenged.

READING 2

Guibert of Nogent, On the Revolt of the Laon Commune[3]

Guibert, abbot of Nogent (d. c. 1125), describes here in vivid, firsthand, and highly opinionated terms a bloody revolt by the commune of the northern French hilltop town of Laon against its bishop. The revolt occurred in 1112, and Guibert recorded it in his autobiographical memoirs in about 1115. City development posed a problem in medieval society, for a city was ordinarily the property of some local lord. In cathedral towns like Laon, the city usually "belonged" to the bishop, who

---

[2]Specific fines relate to marriage, inheritance, and crimes of assault with and without bloodshed.

[3]From *Self and Society in Medieval France: The Memoirs of Abbot Guibert of Nogent (c. 1064–c. 1125)*, ed. and tr. John F. Benton, based on the tr. of C. C. Swinton Bland; New York, Harper-Collins, 1970, pp. 167, 174–176.

had the right to select town officers and to judge urban disputes. But burgesses often had interests quite different from those of the landed aristocracy. When townspeople banded together to form their own, self-governing corporation, it was called a "commune." This obviously posed a threat to the dominion of the lord, who often tried to suppress the commune. The following is a description of a blood-chilling fight for a commune in the French cathedral city of Laon. Note that the author was a churchman: his bias in this case is clear.

Now, "commune" is a new and evil name for an arrangement for them all to pay the customary head tax, which they owe their lords as a servile due, in a lump sum once a year, and if anyone commits a crime, he shall pay a fine set by law, and all other financial exactions which are customarily imposed on serfs are completely abolished. Seizing on this opportunity for commuting their dues, the people gathered huge sums of money to fill the gaping purse of so many greedy men. Pleased with the shower of income poured upon them, those men established their good faith by proffering oaths that they would keep their word in this matter.

After this sworn association of mutual aid among the clergy, nobles, and people had been established, the bishop returned with much wealth from England. Angered at those responsible for this innovation, for a long time he kept away from the city. . . .

The next day—that is, on Thursday—when the bishop and Archdeacon Gautier were engaged after the noon offices in collecting money, suddenly there arose throughout the city the tumult of men shouting, "Commune!" Then through the nave of the cathedral of Notre-Dame, and through the very door by which Gérard's killers had come and gone, a great crowd of burghers attacked the episcopal palace, armed with rapiers, double-edged swords, bows, and axes, and carrying clubs and lances. As soon as this sudden attack was discovered, the nobles rallied from all sides to the bishop, having sworn to give him aid against such an assault if it should occur. In this rally Guimar the castellan, an older nobleman of handsome presence and guiltless character, armed only with a shield and spear, ran through the church. Just as he entered the bishop's hall, he was the first to fall, struck on the back of the head with a sword by a man named Raimbert, who had been his close friend. Immediately afterward that Renier of whom I spoke before as married to my cousin, rushing to enter the palace, was struck from behind with a spear when he tried to duck under it while poised on the porch of the bishop's chapel. Struck to the ground there, he was soon consumed by the fire of the palace from his groin downward. Adon the *vidame*, sharp in small matters and even keener in important ones, separated from the rest and able to do little by himself among so many, encountered the full force of the attack as he was striving to reach the bishop's palace.[4] With his spear and sword he made such a stand that in a moment he struck down three of those who rushed at him. Then he mounted the dining table in the hall, where he was wounded in the knees and other parts of the body. At last, falling on his knees and striking at his assailants all around him, he kept them off for a long time, until someone pierced his exhausted body with a javelin. After a little he was burned to ashes by the fire in that house.

While the insolent mob was attacking the bishop and howling before the walls of his palace, the bishop and the people who were aiding him fought them off as best they could by hurling stones and shooting arrows. Now, as at all times, he showed great spirit as a fighter; but because he had wrongly and in vain taken up that other sword, he perished by the sword. Unable to resist the reckless assaults of the people, he put on the clothes of one of his servants and fled into the warehouse of the church, where he hid himself in a container. When the cover had been fastened on by a faithful follower, he thought himself safely hidden. As those looking for him ran hither and thither, they did not call out for the bishop but for a felon. They seized one of his pages, but he remained faithful and they could get nothing out of him. Laying hands on another, they learned from the traitor's nod where to look for him. Entering the warehouse and searching everywhere, at last they found him in the following manner.

There was a most pestilent man named Thiégaud, a serf of the abbey of Saint-Vincent. For a long time he was a servant and *prévôt* of Enguerrand of Coucy, who set him over the collection of tolls paid for crossing the bridge at a place called Sort. Sometimes he watched until there were only a few travelers passing and robbed them of all their property; then, so that they could make no complaint against him, he weighted them down and tossed them into the river. How often he had done this, God only knows. Although the number of his thefts and robberies was more than anyone could count, the unrestrained wickedness or his heart was displayed in his hideous face. When he ran afoul of Enguerrand, he committed himself completely to the commune at Laon. He who had before not spared monks or clerks or pilgrims, or, in fact, women, was finally to be the slayer of the bishop. As the leader and instigator of this abominable attack, he searched diligently for the bishop, whom he hated more bitterly than did the rest.

As they sought for him in every vessel, Thiégaud halted in front of the cask where the man was hiding, and after breaking in the head he asked again and again who was there. Hardly able to move his frozen lips under the blows, the bishop said, "A prisoner." Now, as a joke, the bishop used to call this man Isengrin, because he had the look of a wolf and that is what some people commonly

---

[4]A *vidame* (*vicedominus*) was a lay lord who was responsible for protecting and administering ecclesiastical property. At Laon, Gérard of Quierzy had been *avoué* of Saint-Jean of Laon and was succeeded as castellan of that abbey by Roger of Montaigu. Adon the *vidame* seems to have been an episcopal officer. Another important noble of Laon who fought for the bishop was Guimar the castellan.

call wolves. So the scoundrel said to the bishop, "Is this my Lord Isengrin stored away here?" Sinner though he was and yet the Lord's anointed, he was dragged out of the cask by the hair, beaten with many blows, and brought out in the open air in the narrow lane of the cloister before the house of the chaplain Godfrey. As he implored them piteously, ready to swear that he would cease to be their bishop, that he would give them unlimited riches, that he would leave the country, with hardened hearts they jeered at him. Then a man named Bernard of Bruyères raised his sword and brutally dashed out that sinner's brains from his holy head. Slipping between the hands of those who held him, before he died he was struck by someone else with a blow running under his eye sockets and across the middle of his nose. Brought to his end there, his legs were hacked off and many other wounds inflicted. Seeing the ring on the finger of the former bishop and not being able to draw it off easily, Thiégaud cut off the dead man's finger with his sword and took the ring. Stripped naked he was thrown into a corner in front of his chaplain's house. My God, who shall recount the mocking words that were thrown at him by passers-by as he lay there, and with what clods and stones and dirt his corpse was pelted?

READING 3
Regulations for the May Fair at Provins[5]

One of the most famous of all the fairs of France was the May Fair held each year at Provins, southeast of Paris in the region of Champagne. Throughout May and June, merchants from all over Europe plied their wares—cloth, spices, wines—to other merchants, for this was primarily a wholesale rather than retail event.

In general, secular authorities, such as the count of Troyes or the king of France, provided protection, courts of justice, and standardized coinage, weights, and measures (the Troyes weight of precious metals, for example, derives from the nearby Fair of Troyes). In return, the count or king could expect a large cut of the revenues generated at the fair.

This charter, drawn up in 1164 under the guidance of Henry, count of Troyes, sets out some of the agreements between the count and the townspeople of Provins. Keep in mind that this charter shows the concerns only of the count and the townspeople. One can easily imagine letters from tradesmen that complain about the harsh conditions and expense of the lodging in Provins.

[5]From Theodore Evergates, *Feudal Society in Medieval France: Documents from the County of Champagne;* Philadelphia, University of Pennsylvania Press, 1993, pp. 29–30.

In the name of the holy and indivisible Trinity, I, Henry, count palatine of Troyes, to the churches, clerics, knights, townsmen, and all men who have houses within the boundaries of the Fairs of May. In order to assure memory of past acts into the future, it is fitting that letters be carefully drawn up so that malicious purposes do not contravene good intentions. Therefore, since my father, Count Thibaut of good memory, gave you a document establishing the Fairs of May [in 1137], which has unfortunately been lost in a fire, I have revised and reestablished them after hearing the truthful testimony of men who were with my father when he established the fairs.

That most noble prince Thibaut established the boundaries of the fairs which I describe here and order to be retained and not changed by anyone, either through force or presumption: from the tower of [the seneschal] Girard and the houses of Peter "the Purse" [the chamberlain] and Anselm "the Fat" (both of which are within the fair boundaries) extending down the street to the old [town] gate of Jouy (which is located between the house of Saint-Quiriace and the house of Peter "the Devil") and from there directly through the new town to the church of Notre-Dame. Again, from the same tower [of the seneschal] going along Saint John Street, then from the home of Richard of Verdun to the new [town] gate of Chauvigny, passing in front of the prison and through the vacant lot. Whatever is within both the new and old walls and bounded by these streets was established by my illustrious father Count Thibaut, with the consent of your ancestors and of his council of faithful men [his barons], as the location of the Fairs of May. These are the regulations:

[1] No merchant may lodge or transfer his goods or pack horses beyond those boundaries until all the lodges there are filled; at that time, merchants may lodge in the new market where dry-goods merchants are allowed to store and display their goods for sale. The money changers must continue to reside in the old market where they have been residing. If a newly arrived merchant lodges outside the prescribed area before it is filled, he must purge himself by proving that he did not know of this regulation; if he cannot prove his innocence, all his goods, as well as the person who subverted this regulation by renting him lodgings, come under the count's mercy without any [legal] recourse. If the count does not wish to implement this prescribed penalty against transgressors, all of the [confiscated] goods will go for the common use of those to whom the fairs are conceded [the townsmen within the fair boundaries] as compensation for the loss of lodging revenue.

[2] No obstacles my be placed in front of any merchant lodge—not scales, tables, stalls, or chests. The place must be open to allow free passage at night.

[3] Half of the rent of all houses located within the fair boundaries went to my father, and now comes to me, as you and your ancestors conceded. Exception is made for: (a) the houses owned by the hospital which my father exempted so that they could help the poor; (b) the houses which I gave to the chapter of Saint-Jacques for the use of those canons and the poor; and (c) the houses of the chapter of Saint-Quiriace which I have exempted from all customary payments—one

is next to the butchers' hall and the other, formerly owned by Roger "the Leaf," is half owned by Milo, son of the deceased Gerold of Rozay-en-Brie.

My father granted this ordinance to your ancestors, and I likewise have granted it to you and your successors in perpetuity, and I have sealed this letter in order to guarantee its stability. These are the witnesses from Saint-Quiriace: William [canon], my brother; Matthew, dean; Renaud, treasurer; Haice of Plancy; and Master Stephen. These are the witnesses for me: Geoffroy of Joinville,[6] seneschal; Odo of Pougy, constable; Anselm of Traînel, butler; Peter "the Purse," chamberlain; William [of Provins], marshal; Drogo [of Provins] and his brother Peter "the Purse"; Daimbert of Ternantes; and Artaud, chamberlain. Done at Provins in my palace in the year of our Lord 1164. Given [to the townsmen] by William, chancellor.

READING 4

The First Crusade

In August 1071 a Byzantine army led by Emperor Romanus Diogenes was routed by the invading Seljuk Turks under their sultan, Alp Arslan (Reading A). As a result of the Turkish victory, the Byzantines lost Asia Minor, which had for many centuries been the Empire's best source of revenues and soldiers. This was a crippling blow to Byzantium, which appealed to the West—and especially the Western church—for help in repelling the Turks. Western Europe's response came later, and in a much different form, than expected: instead of assistance to Byzantium, Pope Urban II (1088–1099) suggested an expedition that might capture Palestine for Western Christians.

Historians are agreed that Pope Urban delivered a tremendously persuasive and effective speech to the clergy and laity who attended the Council of Clermont in November 1095, thereby launching the First Crusade. But descriptions of the speech differ. Robert the Monk's eyewitness account, presented here (Reading B), is likely to be as accurate as any and is surely the most stirring.

In the third excerpt, the First Crusade is viewed from the perspective of a contemporary Byzantine historian (Reading C). The princess Anna Comnena (1083–c. 1155) was closely connected to the imperial court at Constantinople and was, for a time, heir to the Byzantine throne. Her *Alexiad,* an account of the deeds of her father, Emperor Alexius I, includes an abundance of unique information about the Crusade.

---

[6]Geoffrey was an ancestor of Jean de Joinville, author of the *Life of Louis IX* (Chapter 9, Reading 6B).

The fourth passage details the crusaders' actions when they stormed Jerusalem in 1099 (Reading D). Fulcher of Chartres was present at the Council of Clermont, accompanied the crusaders as far as Edessa, and arrived at Jerusalem shortly after its fall, remaining there for the next twenty years. His chronicle, then, is one of the most reliable sources we have on the entire First Crusade.

The final selection provides a view of the sack of Jerusalem from an Arab perspective (Reading E). Ibn al-Athir (1160–1233) was a prolific historian, his *Perfect History* running to fourteen volumes in its printed version. Originally from Mosul in Mesopotamia (today, Iraq), Ibn al-Athir regarded the events in the Near East with great interest. Although he was born a half century after the events he describes, he and his younger brother were both in the service of the Muslim general Saladin at the time of the Third Crusade.

A.   MICHAEL PSELLUS, THE BATTLE OF MANZIKERT, 1071[7]

With his usual contempt of all advice, whether on matters civil or military, [Romanus] at once set out with his army and hurried to Caesarea. Having reached that objective, he was loath to advance any further and tried to find excuses for returning to Byzantium, not only for his own sake but for the army's. When he found the disgrace involved in such a retreat intolerable, he should have come to terms with the enemy and put a stop to their annual incursions. Instead, whether in desperation, or because he was more confident than he should have been, he marched to the attack without taking adequate measures to protect his rear. The enemy, seeing him advance, decided to lure him on still farther and ensnare him by cunning. They therefore rode on ahead of him and then retired again, as though the retreat was planned. By carrying out this maneuver several times, they succeeded in cutting off some of our generals, who were taken captive.

Now I was aware—though he was not—that the Sultan himself, the king of the Persians and Kurds, Alp Arslan [the Seljuk leader], was present in person with his army, and most of their victories were due to his leadership. Romanus refused to believe anyone who detected the Sultan's influence in these successes. The truth is, he did not want peace. He thought he would capture the barbarian camp without a battle. Unfortunately for him, through his ignorance of military science, he had scattered his forces; some were concentrated round himself, others had been sent off to take up some other position. So, instead of opposing his adversaries with the full force of his army, less than half were actually involved.

[7]From Michael Psellus, *Chronographica*, in *Fourteen Byzantine Rulers*, tr. E. R. A. Sewter; New York, Penguin Books, 1966, pp. 353–356.

Although I cannot applaud his subsequent behavior, it is impossible for me to censure him. The fact is, he bore the whole brunt of the danger himself. His action can be interpreted in two ways. My own view represents the mean between these two extremes. On the one hand, if you regard him as a hero, courting danger and fighting courageously, it is reasonable to praise him; on the other, when one reflects that a general, if he conforms to the accepted rules of strategy, must remain aloof from the battle-line, supervising the movements of his army and issuing the necessary orders to the men under his command, then Romanus's conduct on this occasion would appear foolish in the extreme, for he exposed himself to danger without a thought of the consequences. I myself am more inclined to praise than to blame him for what he did.

However that may be, he put on the full armor of an ordinary soldier and drew sword against his enemies. According to several of my informants he actually killed many of them and put others to flight. Later, when his attackers recognized who he was, they surrounded him on all sides. He was wounded and fell from his horse. They seized him, of course, and the Emperor of the Romans was led away, a prisoner, to the enemy camp, and his army was scattered. Those who escaped were but a tiny fraction of the whole. Of the majority some were taken captive, the rest massacred.

I do not intend at this moment to write of the time spent by the emperor in captivity, or of the attitude adopted towards him by his conqueror. That must wait till later. A few days after the battle, one of those who escaped, arriving before his comrades, brought the terrible news to the city. He was followed by a second messenger, and by others. The picture they painted was by no means distinct, for each explained the disaster in his own fashion, some saying that Romanus was dead, others that he was only a prisoner; some again declared that they had seen him wounded and hurled to the ground, while others had seen him being led away in chains to the barbarian camp. In view of this information, a conference was held in the capital, and the empress considered our future policy. The unanimous decision of the meeting was that, for the time being, they should ignore the emperor, whether he was a prisoner, or dead, and that Eudocia and her sons should carry on the government of the Empire.

B.   POPE URBAN II, SPEECH AT THE COUNCIL OF CLERMONT, NOVEMBER 27, 1095, BY ROBERT THE MONK[8]

Oh, race of Franks, race from across the mountains, race chosen and beloved by God—as shines forth in very many of your works—set apart from all nations by the situation of your country, as well as by your catholic faith and the honor of

---

[8]From Dana C. Munro, *Urban and the Crusades, Translations and Reprints from the Original Sources of European History,* vol. 1, no. 2; Philadelphia, University of Pennsylvania Press, 1895, pp. 5–8.

the holy Church! To you our discourse is addressed and for you our exhortation is intended. We wish you to know what a grievous cause has led us to your country, what peril threatening you and all the faithful has brought us.

From the confines of Jerusalem and the city of Constantinople a horrible tale has gone forth and very frequently has been brought to our ears, namely, that a race from the kingdom of the Persians, an accursed race, a race utterly alienated from God, a generation forsooth which has not directed its heart and has not entrusted its spirit to God, has invaded the lands of those Christians and has depopulated them by the sword, pillage and fire; it has led away a part of the captives into its own country, and a part it has destroyed by cruel tortures; it has either entirely destroyed the churches of God or appropriated them for the rites of its own religion. They destroy the altars, after having defiled them with their uncleanness. They circumcise the Christians, and the blood of the circumcision they either spread upon the altars or pour into the vases of the baptismal font. When they wish to torture people by a base death, they perforate their navels, and dragging forth the extremity of the intestines, bind it to a stake; then with flogging they lead the victim around until the viscera having gushed forth the victim falls prostrate upon the ground. Others they bind to a post and pierce with arrows. Others they compel to extend their necks and then, attacking them with naked swords, attempt to cut through the neck with a single blow. What shall I say of the abominable rape of the women? To speak of it is worse than to be silent. The kingdom of the Greeks is now dismembered by them and deprived of territory so vast in extent that it can not be traversed in a march of two months. On whom therefore is the labor of avenging these wrongs and of recovering this territory incumbent, if not upon you? You, upon whom above other nations God has conferred remarkable glory in arms, great courage, bodily activity, and strength to humble the hairy scalp of those who resist you.

Let the deeds of your ancestors move you and incite your minds to many achievements; the glory and greatness of king Charles the Great, and of his son Louis, and of your other kings, who have destroyed the kingdoms of the pagans, and have extended in these lands the territory of the holy church. Let the holy sepulchre of the Lord our Saviour, which is possessed by unclean nations, especially incite you, and the holy places which are now treated with ignominy and irreverently polluted with their filthiness. Oh, most valiant soldiers and descendants of invincible ancestors, be not degenerate, but recall the valor of your progenitors.

But if you are hindered by love of children, parents and wives, remember what the Lord says in the Gospel, "He that loveth father or mother more than me, is not worthy of me." "Every one that hath forsaken houses, or brethren, or sisters, or father, or mother, or wife, or children, or lands for my name's sake shall receive an hundred-fold and shall inherit everlasting life." Let none of your possessions detain you, no solicitude for your family affairs, since this land which you inhabit, shut in on all sides by the seas and surrounded by the mountain peaks, is too narrow for your large population; nor does it abound in wealth; and it furnishes scarcely food enough for its cultivators. Hence it is that you murder and devour one another, that you wage war, and that frequently you perish by mutual wounds. Let therefore hatred depart from among you, let your quarrels end, let wars cease, and let all dissensions and controversies slumber. Enter upon the road to the Holy Sepulchre; wrest that land from the wicked race, and subject it to yourselves. That land which as the Scripture says "floweth with milk and honey," was given by God into the possession of the children of Israel.

Jerusalem is the navel of the world; the land is fruitful above others, like another paradise of delights. This the Redeemer of the human race has made illustrious by His advent, has beautified by residence, has consecrated by suffering, has redeemed by death, has glorified by burial. This royal city, therefore, situated at the center of the world, is now held captive by His enemies, and is in subjection to those who do not know God, to the Worship of the heathens. She seeks therefore and desires to be liberated, and does not cease to implore you to come to her aid. From you especially she asks succor, because, as we have already said, God has conferred upon you above all nations great glory in arms. Accordingly undertake this journey for the remission of your sins, with the assurance of the imperishable glory of the kingdom of heaven.

When Pope Urban had said these and very many similar things in his urbane discourse, he so influenced to one purpose the desires of all who were present, that they cried out, "It is the will of God! It is the will of God!" When the venerable Roman pontiff heard that, with eyes uplifted to heaven he gave thanks to God and, with his hand commanding silence, said:

Most beloved brethren, to-day is manifest in you what the Lord says in the Gospel, "Where two or three are gathered together in my name there am I in the midst of them." Unless the Lord God has been present in your spirits, all of you would not have uttered the same cry. For, although the cry issued from numerous mouths, yet the origin of the cry was one. Therefore I say to you that God, who implanted this in your breasts, has drawn it forth from you. Let this then be your war-cry in combats, because this word is given to you by God. When an armed attack is made upon the enemy, let this one cry be raised by all the soldiers of God: It is the will of God! It is the will of God!

And we do not command or advise that the old or feeble, or those unfit for bearing arms, undertake this journey; nor ought women to set out at all, without their husbands or brothers or legal guardians. For such are more of a hindrance than aid, more of a burden than advantage. Let the rich aid the needy; and according to their wealth, let them take with them experienced soldiers. The priests and clerks of any order are not to go without the consent of their bishop; for this journey would profit them nothing if they went without permission of those. Also, it is not fitting that laymen should enter upon the pilgrimage without the blessing of their priests.

Whoever, therefore, shall determine upon the holy pilgrimage and shall make his vow to God to that effect and shall offer himself to Him as a living sacrifice, holy, acceptable unto God, shall wear the sign of the cross of the Lord on his forehead or on his breast. When, truly, having fulfilled his vow he wishes to return let him place the cross on his back between his shoulders. Such, indeed, by the two-fold action will fulfill the precept of the Lord, as He commands in the Gospel, "He that taketh not his cross and followeth after me, is not worthy of me."

C.   ANNA COMNENA, THE ARRIVAL OF THE CRUSADERS IN BYZANTIUM, 1096[9]

Alexius had no time to relax before he heard a rumour that countless Frankish armies were approaching: He dreaded their arrival, knowing as he did their uncontrollable passion, their erratic character and their irresolution, not to mention the other peculiar traits of the Kelt,[10] with their inevitable consequences: their greed for money, for example, which always led them, it seemed, to break their own agreements without scruple for any chance reason. He had consistently heard this said of them and it was abundantly justified. So, far from despairing, however, he made every effort to prepare for war if need arose. What actually happened was more far-reaching and terrible than rumour suggested, for the whole of the west and all the barbarians who lived between the Adriatic and the Straits of Gibraltar migrated in a body to Asia, marching across Europe country by country with all their households. The reason for this mass-movement is to be found more or less in the following events. A certain Kelt, called Peter, with the surname Koukoupetros,[11] left to worship at the Holy Sepulchre and after suffering much ill-treatment at the hands of the Turks and Saracens who were plundering the whole of Asia, he returned home with difficulty. Unable to admit defeat, he wanted to make a second attempt by the same route, but realizing the folly of trying to do this alone (worse things might happen to him) he worked out a clever scheme. He decided to preach in all the Latin countries. A divine voice, he said, commanded him to proclaim to all the counts in France that all should depart from their homes, set out to worship at the Holy Shrine and with all their soul and might strive to liberate Jerusalem from the Agarenes.[12] Surprisingly, he was successful. It was as if he had inspired every heart with some divine oracle. Kelts assembled from all parts, one after another, with arms and horses and all the other equipment for war. Full of enthusiasm and ardour they thronged every highway,

[9]From *The Alexiad of Anna Comnena*, tr. E. R. A. Sewter; London, Penguin Classics, 1969, pp. 308–10.
[10]Western crusaders.
[11]This is Peter the Hermit.
[12]The Turks.

and with these warriors came a host of civilians, outnumbering the sand of the sea shore or the stars of heaven, carrying palms and bearing crosses on their shoulders. There were women and children, too, who had left their own countries. Like tributaries joining a river from all directions they streamed towards us in full force, mostly through Dacia. The arrival of this mighty host was preceded by locusts, which abstained from the wheat but made frightful inroads on the vines. The prophets of those days interpreted this as a sign that the Keltic army would refrain from interfering in the affairs of Christians but bring dreadful affliction on the barbarian Ishmaelites,[13] who were the slaves of drunkenness and wine and Dionysos. The Ishmaelites are indeed dominated by Dionysos and Eros; they indulge readily in every kind of sexual licence, and if they are circumcised in the flesh they are certainly not so in their passions. In fact, the Ishmaelites are nothing more than slaves—trebly slaves—of the vices of Aphrodite.

D.   FULCHER OF CHARTRES, THE CAPTURE OF JERUSALEM, 1099[14]

On the following day, at the blast of the trumpets, they undertook the same work more vigorously, so that by hammering in one place with the battering-rams, they breached the wall. The Saracens had suspended two beams before the battlement and secured them by ropes as a protection against the stones hurled at them by their assailants. But what they did for their advantage later turned to their detriment, with God's providence. For when the tower was moved to the wall, the ropes, by which the aforesaid beams were suspended, were cut by falchions, and the Franks constructed a bridge for themselves out of the same timber, which they cleverly extended from the tower to the wall.

Already one stone tower on the wall, at which those working our machines had thrown flaming firebrands, was afire. The fire, little by little replenished by the wooden material in the tower, produced so much smoke and flame that not one of the citizens on guard could remain near it.

Then the Franks entered the city magnificently at the noonday hour on Friday,[15] the day of the week when Christ redeemed the whole world on the cross. With trumpets sounding and with everything in an uproar, exclaiming: "Help, God!" they vigorously pushed into the city, and straightway raised the banner on the top of the wall. All the heathen, completely terrified, changed their boldness to swift flight through the narrow streets of the quarters. The more quickly they fled, the more quickly were they put to flight.

Count Raymond and his men, who were bravely assailing the city in another section, did not perceive this until they saw the Saracens jumping from the top

---

[13]The Turks.

[14]From "Chronicle of Fulcher of Chartres," tr. Martha E. McGinty in *The First Crusade,* ed. Edward Peters; Philadelphia, University of Pennsylvania Press, 1971, pp. 76–79.

[15]July 15, 1099.

of the wall. Seeing this, they joyfully ran to the city as quickly as they could, and helped the others pursue and kill the wicked enemy.

Then some, both Arabs and Ethiopians, fled into the Tower of David; others shut themselves in the Temple of the Lord and of Solomon, where in the halls a very great attack was made on them. Nowhere was there a place where the Saracens could escape the swordsmen.

On the top of Solomon's Temple, to which they had climbed in fleeing, many were shot to death with arrows and cast down headlong from the roof. Within this Temple about ten thousand[16] were beheaded. If you had been there, your feet would have been stained up to the ankles with the blood of the slain. What more shall I tell? Not one of them was allowed to live. They did not spare the women and children.

The Spoils which the Christians Took

After they had discovered the cleverness of the Saracens, it was an extraordinary thing to see our squires and poorer people split the bellies of those dead Saracens, so that they might pick out besants[17] from their intestines, which they had swallowed down their horrible gullets while alive. After several days, they made a great heap of their bodies and burned them to ashes, and in these ashes they found the gold more easily.

Tancred rushed into the Temple of the Lord, and seized much of the gold and silver and precious stones. But he restored it, and returned everything or something of equal value to its holy place. I say, "holy," although nothing divine was practised there at the time when the Saracens exercised their form of idolatry in religious ritual and never allowed a single Christian to enter.

> With drawn swords, our people ran through the city;
> Nor did they spare anyone, not even those pleading for mercy.
> The crowd was struck to the ground, just as rotten fruit
> Falls from shaken branches, and acorns from a wind-blown oak.

The Sojourn of the Christians in the City

After this great massacre, they entered the homes of the citizens, seizing whatever they found in them. It was done systematically, so that whoever had entered the home first, whether he was rich or poor, was not to be harmed by anyone else in any way. He was to have and to hold the house or palace and whatever he had found in it entirely as his own. Since they mutually agreed to maintain this rule, many poor men became rich.

---

[16]Not all accounts agree with this high number.

[17]Besants: gold coins, so called because they were originally Byzantine. Saracen besants were dinars of the same value as the Byzantine coins.

Then, going to the Sepulchre of the Lord and His glorious Temple, the clerics and also the laity, singing a new song unto the Lord in a high-sounding voice of exultation, and making offerings and most humble applications, joyously visited the Holy Place as they had so long desired to do.

Oh, time so longed for! Oh, time remembered among all others! Oh, deed to be preferred before all deeds! Truly longed for, since it had always been desired by all worshippers of the Catholic faith with an inward yearning of the soul. This was the place, where the Creator of all creatures, God made man, in His manifold mercy for the human race, brought the gift of spiritual rebirth. Here He was born, died, and rose. Cleansed from the contagion of the heathen inhabiting it at one time or another, so long contaminated by their superstition, it was restored to its former rank by those believing and trusting in Him.

And truly memorable and rightly remembered, because those things which the Lord God our Jesus Christ, as a man abiding among men on earth, practised and taught have often been recalled and repeated in doctrines. And, likewise, what the Lord wished to be fulfilled, I believe, by this people so dear, both His disciple and servant and predestined for this task, will resound and continue in a memorial of all the languages of the universe to the end of the ages.

E.   IBN AL-ATHIR, THE CAPTURE OF JERUSALEM, 1099[18]

Taj ad-Daula Tutūsh was the Lord of Jerusalem but had given it as a feoff to the amīr Suqmān ibn Artūq the Turcoman. When the Franks defeated the Turks at Antioch the massacre demoralized them, and the Egyptians, who saw that the Turkish armies were being weakened by desertion, besieged Jerusalem under the command of al-Afdal ibn Badr al-Jamali. Inside the city were Artūq's sons, Suqmān and Ilghazi, their cousin Sunij and their nephew Yaquti. The Egyptians brought more than forty siege engines to attack Jerusalem and broke down the walls at several points. The inhabitants put up a defence, and the siege and fighting went on for more than six weeks. In the end the Egyptians forced the city to capitulate, in sha'bān 489/August 1096.[19] Suqmān, Ilghazi and their friends were well treated by al-Afdal, who gave them large gifts of money and let them go free. They made for Damascus and then crossed the Euphrates. Suqmān settled in Edessa and Ilghazi went on into Iraq. The Egyptian governor of Jerusalem was a certain Iftikhār ad-Daula, who was still there at the time of which we are speaking.

After their vain attempt to take Acre by siege, the Franks moved on to Jerusalem and besieged it for more than six weeks. They built two towers, one of which, near Sion, the Muslims burnt down, killing everyone inside it. It had

---

[18]From Francesco Gabrieli, *Arab Historians of the Crusades*, tr. E. J. Cotello; Berkeley, University of California Press, 1969, pp. 10–11.
[19]The correct date is August 1098.

scarcely ceased to burn before a messenger arrived to ask for help and to bring the news that the other side of the city had fallen. In fact Jerusalem was taken from the north on the morning of Friday 22 sha'bān 492/15 July 1099. The population was put to the sword by the Franks, who pillaged the area for a week. A band of Muslims barricaded themselves into the Tower of David and fought on for several days. They were granted their lives in return for surrendering. The Franks honoured their word, and the group left by night for Ascalon. In the Masjid al-Aqsa the Franks slaughtered more than 70,000 people, among them a large number of Imams and Muslim scholars, devout and ascetic men who had left their homelands to live lives of pious seclusion in the Holy Place. The Franks stripped the Dome of the Rock of more than forty silver candelabra, each of them weighing 3,600 drams, and a great silver lamp weighing forty-four Syrian pounds, as well as a hundred and fifty smaller silver candelabra and more than twenty gold ones, and a great deal more booty. Refugees from Syria reached Baghdād in ramadan, among them the qadi Abu Sa'd al-Hárawi. They told the Caliph's ministers a story that wrung their hearts and brought tears to their eyes. On Friday they went to the Cathedral Mosque and begged for help, weeping so that their hearers wept with them as they described the sufferings of the Muslims in that Holy City: the men killed, the women and children taken prisoner, the homes pillaged. Because of the terrible hardships they had suffered, they were allowed to break the fast.

READING 5

Bernard of Clairvaux, On the Knights Templars[20]

St. Bernard of Clairvaux (1090–1153) was the foremost figure among the first generation of Cistercian monks. He was an ardent and outspoken advocate of the Second Crusade, and a contributor to the writing of the Rule of the Knights Templars—an order of crusaders who took monastic vows. In these and other ways, Bernard demonstrated his devotion to the crusading movement at its most zealous. St. Bernard led the order of Clairvaux, the great reforming monastic order of the twelfth century. Bernard sought to assert the place of traditional Christian values in the rapidly changing world of the twelfth century. In this passage, he offers his vision of the Knights Templars, an order of warrior-monks whose self-appointed task was to defend Jerusalem.

---

[20]From *The Records of Medieval Europe,* ed. Carolly Erickson; New York, Anchor Books, 1971, pp. 184–186.

A new kind of knighthood is now heard of in the land; it has arisen in that region once visited by the Rising Star from on high, and from whence he drove out the princes of darkness with the strength of his hand—where even now with the hands of his worthies he is crushing their minions, sons of disloyalty, and driving them out, and is accomplishing the redemption of his people, raising again the trumpet of our salvation in the house of his son David. . . .

He is a fearless knight, in truth, and secure on all sides, who, as he has girded his body with iron, so has girded his soul with the shield of faith. Surely, fortified with both these weapons, he fears neither demon nor man. Nor does he who desires to die fear death. For what should he fear in living or in dying, for whom to live is Christ, to die is gain?[21] To be sure, he stands faithfully and willingly for Christ; but he desires even more to be dissolved and be with Christ, for this is better. . . .

Of Worldly Knighthood

What end and reward therefore does it have, this worldly—I do not say knighthood [*militia*] but roguery [*malitia*]—if as a murderer a man sins mortally and when killed, perishes eternally? . . . You [worldly knights] cover your horses with silks; you have I know not what little cloths hanging from your cuirasses; you paint your lances, shields and saddles; you encrust your reins and spurs with gold, silver and gems; and in this splendor, with shameful fury, impudently oblivious, you race on to your death. Are these the trappings of a military man, or are they rather womanly ornaments? . . .

Of the New Knighthood

The knight of Christ, I say, is safe in slaying, safer if he is slain. He is accountable to himself when he is slain, to Christ when he slays. "For he beareth not the sword in vain: for he is the minister of God, a revenger to execute wrath upon him that doeth evil, to praise him that doeth good."[22] For when he kills a malefactor, he does not commit homicide but, I might say, malicide, and is clearly reputed to be the vindicator of Christ, bringing punishment to evildoers, and praise in truth to good men. Moreover, when he is himself killed, it is known that he does not perish, but triumphs. The death he inflicts is Christ's gain; the death he dies, his own. The Christian is glorified; in the death of a Christian, the liberality of the King is shown, when the knight is led to his reward.

[21]Philippians 1:21.
[22]Romans 13:4.

STUDY QUESTIONS

A What impact did commercialization have on the traditional bonds of European society?

B Do commercial motives link all the Readings in this chapter?

C What images did Westerners have of foreigners or "the other" in this period?

Reading 1: The Customs of Newcastle-upon-Tyne

What are the broad areas of concern over which the townspeople wanted to protect their rights? Why would King Henry II have granted these rights?

Reading 2: Guibert of Nogent, On the Revolt of the Laon Commune

What seem to have been the reasons for the civic rebellion at Laon? Can you detect any class biases on the part of the author?

Reading 3: Regulations for the May Fair at Provins

As in Reading 1, why were commerical activities so minutely regulated? As in Reading 1, why was it important to note that these regulations dated from a previous generation and were not a recent invention?

Reading 4: The First Crusade

Based on Robert the Monk, what image do the Crusaders have of themselves? What image do the Byzantines and Muslims have of the Crusaders? Based on the selections here, what motives impelled Westerners to go on the Crusade? What motives led to the massacre of Jerusalem?

Reading 5: Bernard of Clairvaux, On the Knights Templars

What are the differences between the traditional knighthood and the new knighthood? How do Bernard's views help explain the Crusading fervor of the day?

CHAPTER 6

🔯 A VISUAL PORTFOLIO

This chapter violates the chronological limits of Part Two, "The High Middle Ages," in order to include visual, as opposed to written, sources. These sources range widely in time and in scope; yet they are as revealing of the Middle Ages as a law code or a philosophical treatise.

Just as a skyscaper hints at the values of the modern age—great engineering abilities, an obsession with size, corporate ownership—so the architectural structures shown here can act as a window into the medieval age. To take but one example, the façade of the monastery of St.-Jouin-de-Marnes (illustration 12) suggests medieval Europe's newfound sense of self-confidence, its religion-centeredness, and its love of ancient Rome (look closely at the round arches and the columns on the Arch of Constantine in illustration 1).

The extensive introductory notes will help orient the viewer toward a clearer understanding of each of the illustrations in turn. But in all cases, we encourage the student to consider, as with the written sources, the artist's intent, the artist's audience, and the limitations under which the artist labored.

1.   THE ARCH OF CONSTANTINE

This great monument was erected near the Colosseum between A.D. 312 and 315, at the command of the Roman Senate, to commemorate Constantine's decisive victory over his rival Maxentius in the battle of the Milvian Bridge (see pp. 7–8). The victory enabled Constantine to enter Rome and gave him sole rule over the Western Empire. His success was widely attributed to his acceptance of the Christian God prior to the battle, but the exact time and circumstances of Constantine's conversion have been much debated and remain unresolved. There are no signs of Christian influences in the sculpture on the arch—much of which was snatched from earlier monuments honoring the pagan emperors Trajan, Hadrian, and Marcus Aurelius. The structure is one of many triumphal arches erected during the imperial centuries, in Rome and its provinces, to honor the deeds of emperors. Most such arches have perished, but the arch of Constantine was preserved during subsequent Christian centuries because of his renown as the first Christian emperor. Several pagan "nikes" ("winged victories"), one of them hovering over the main battle scene, were thought by later Christians to be angels.

2.   GOLD BROOCH
FROM CHILDERIC'S BURIAL

The early Germanic peoples produced little in the way of monumental architecture or sculpture, but excelled in the making of smaller objects of art—ornaments, implements, and weapons. Shown here are several different views of a gold brooch, late Roman in style but probably of Frankish manufacture, found in the tomb of the early Frankish King Childeric I (d. 481 or 482), father of the first Christian king of the Franks, Clovis I. The brooch is of a type that was commonly worn on the right shoulder by high Roman officials—many of whom, by the later fifth century, were also, and primarily, Germanic war leaders.

The tomb was discovered near Tournai (modern Belgium) in 1653, with a treasure of precious objects: gold and garnet belt and weapon fittings, a Frankish war axe, a golden arm ring, a golden bull's head, an abundance of golden bees (perhaps to decorate the royal harness), about a hundred Byzantine gold coins, and a seal ring bearing a royal portrait with the identifying inscription, *Childerici Regis*—"King Childeric." In 1655 the French archaeologist Jacques Chifflet published a description of these treasures in a work that is particularly valuable to us because in 1831 virtually all the tomb's contents were stolen by an unknown thief. Most of them, including the brooch shown here (from Chifflet's engraving), have never been recovered. Chifflet believed wrongly that the object was a writing stylus, and he depicted it as such at the bottom of the engraving. Above the hand holding the "stylus," the brooch is shown disassembled (left), complete (center), and with its prong folded inward (right).

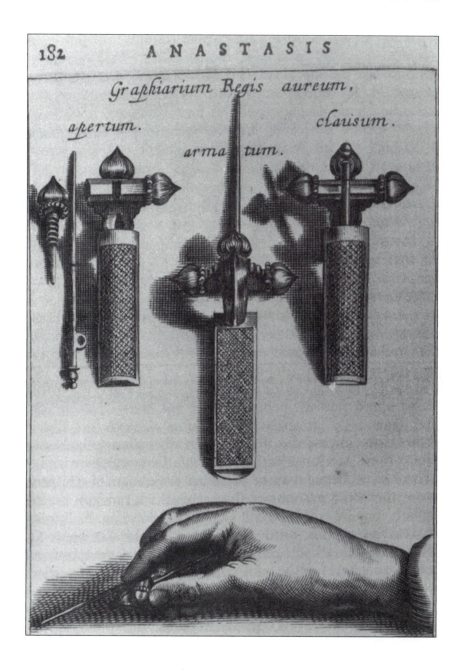

3.   OUTLINE OF THE SUTTON HOO BURIAL SHIP

In 1939 a spectacular assortment of precious objects dating from the seventh century was discovered at Sutton Hoo in southeastern England. They had been placed in an immense burial ship some eighty-nine feet in length, which served as the tomb of a extraordinarily wealthy person. The wooden hull of the ship has rotted entirely away, but the rivets remain, along with the stains of the original planks and beams, pictured here. The burial ship was surmounted by a wooden-roofed chamber in which a large coffin and an abundance of treasure had been placed. The great ship had been hauled from a river to the top of a bluff some hundred feet above, where it was placed in a trench. Attendants had then filled in the trench and heaped a large earthen mound over the ship. Although the mound was clearly visible for a considerable distance, it remained undisturbed until the discovery in 1939.

Because the Sutton Hoo ship, unlike Childeric's tomb, contained no signet ring or other inscription, its occupant cannot be positively identified. A number of scholars, however, strongly suspect that the ship was the tomb of King Redwald of East Anglia (d. c. 625), who reigned in the second decade of the seventh century and was recognized as the dominant king in southern England in his time. The dates on the coins found in the ship were consistent with what we know of the dates of King Redwald's reign, and the magnificence of the treasure suggests a royal burial. Among the precious objects—designed to sustain, defend, adorn, and amuse a great prince during his posthumous sojourn—are an abundance of gold and silver jewelry and plate, a lyre, dice, drinking horns, an assortment of Frankish gold coins, and a small arsenal of weapons and armor, including a beautifully wrought sword, a battle axe, a coat of mail, an impressive selection of spears, and a marvelously well-preserved shield and helmet. The splendor of these artifacts—now displayed in the British Museum— demonstrates clearly that a seventh-century Anglo-Saxon of princely status could live and die in prodigious opulence.

Perhaps the most memorable treasure in the Sutton Hoo collection is a hanging bowl with an enamel fish mounted to swivel on a pedestal inside it—seemingly a rudimentary version of a floating magnetic compass, possibly intended to provide the burial ship the latest navigational technology for its voyage to Valhalla.

4.   ST. LUKE, FROM THE GOSPELS OF ST. CHAD

During the seventh and eighth centuries, a remarkable artistic style, known as Hiberno-Saxon (i.e., Irish-English), flourished in Ireland and northern England. This style was a vehicle for an outpouring of masterpieces in metalwork, sculpture, and manuscript decoration. It combined the exuberant abstract, curvilinear designs traditional in Irish-Celtic art with similarly abstract interlace and rectilinear patterns characteristic of Germanic jewelry and metalwork, carried by the Anglo-Saxons into Britain. The work of Irish Christian missionaries in late sixth- and seventh-century northern England, who converted much of pagan Northumbria and established the great monastery of Lindisfarne on an offshore island, resulted in the merging of the Celtic and Germanic/Anglo-Saxon artistic traditions into the Hiberno-Saxon style.

As essential tools for their work of evangelism, Celtic missionaries produced a number of richly illustrated books containing copies of the four Gospels—the accounts of Jesus' life by Saints Matthew, Mark, Luke, and John. Shown here is a highly stylized depiction of St. Luke from the *Gospels of St. Chad* (eighth century). Although Hiberno-Celtic artists excelled in intricate abstract designs of great vitality and genius, naturalistic depictions of human beings were not in their artistic repertoire. As the art historian Kenneth Clark put it, "When a man appears he cuts a very poor figure." Most likely, the St. Chad artist was not at all interested in rendering a faithful human portrait but preferred to depict St. Luke's body as a configuration of stylized, curvilinear patterns analogous to the abstract designs he was accustomed to drawing elsewhere.

The figure of St. Luke is rich in symbolism. In his hands, he holds two crossed ceremonial staffs, perhaps representing two versions of the biblical Tree of Life. Astride his rock-solid halo is the winged ox that traditionally symbolizes St. Luke in Christian art. The ox's staring eyes are almost as mesmerizing as those of Luke himself.

5.   ST. MATTHEW, FROM THE EBBO GOSPELS

In contrast to the Hiberno-Saxon illuminator of the *Gospels of St. Chad,* artists at the court of Charlemagne (768–814) were largely successful in recapturing the naturalistic style of Classical Antiquity. Their success constitutes one aspect of the classicizing spirit of late eighth- and ninth-century Francia that marked the Carolingian Renaissance. By about 820, when the *Ebbo Gospels* were produced at the great Frankish cultural center of Reims, Carolingian illuminators had moved beyond mere repetition of Classical forms to a conscious and highly dramatic reinterpretation of them. The depiction of the evangelist St. Matthew from the *Ebbo Gospels* is obviously far more naturalistic than that of St. Luke from the *Gospels of St. Chad* (see illustration 4), but it is also enlivened with a nervous energy unknown to Classical Roman art. St. Matthew and the landscape around him seem agitated by a divine force—a kind of wind from heaven. As one art historian expresses it, the artist has transformed the evangelist from a placid Roman writer "into a man seized with the frenzy of divine inspiration, an instrument for recording the Word of God." Matthew's symbol in Christian art, a man with wings, appears inconspicuously in the upper right-hand corner of the scene rather than astride the evangelist's head as in the more abstract portrayal of Luke in the *Gospels of St. Chad.* Judging from Matthew's intensity, he might well have shaken the winged man off.

The Ebbo style, still Classical but animated with new energy, continued to influence Carolingian art throughout much of the ninth century. It gave way eventually to new forms of expression associated with the Saxon dynasty of German kings and Holy Roman emperors, a style known as Ottonian after the three Ottos—father, son, and grandson—who ruled Germany through much of the tenth century.

6.   OTTO III IN MAJESTY, FROM THE AACHEN GOSPELS, c. 1000

This stately illumination, a characteristic product of the Ottonian Renaissance, depicts the Holy Roman emperor Otto III in more than earthly glory. Otto is presented here as Christ's representative on earth, occupying the upper central position normally reserved for Christ in such depictions. Otto is thus transformed into a kind of embodiment for Christ himself. The emperor is enthroned, held up by the embodiment of the earth; Otto in turn holds the orb that symbolizes the earth over which he rules. Kings, princes, and prelates do the emperor reverence, while above them the four evangelists (left to right: Luke as a winged ox, Matthew as a winged man, John as an eagle, and Mark as a winged lion) hold a veil separating the earthly parts of the emperor's body from the heavenly parts. (At his coronation, he received holy anointment on his shoulders and head.) At the top center, God's hand places the crown on Otto's head, emphasizing the imperial doctrine that the emperor's authority comes not through the pope but directly from the divine source. (Compare Liudprand's description of Otto II's coronation, pp. 146–149.)

7.   ST. MICHAEL'S ABBEY, HILDESHEIM, c. 1001–1033

This ancient church was begun in the reign of Emperor Otto III. As a consequence of nearly ten centuries of wear and tear, including ruinous damage during World War II, it has been heavily and repeatedly reconstructed. Nevertheless, it retains much of its original character and is generally regarded as the finest surviving example of Ottonian architecture. It was built by Bernward, bishop of Hildesheim in Saxony, as the church of the Benedictine abbey of St. Michael's, which he founded in his episcopal city (c. 1001). Bishop Bernward was an art lover and a traveler who had viewed the impressive late-antique basilicas in Rome—Santa Maria Maggiore, St. Paul's outside the Walls, Old St. Peter's, St. John's Lateran, and others. Like them, and like many Carolingian churches, St. Michael's was built on the basilica plan, with a three-aisle nave and choir ending in a semicircular apse, and a wooden ceiling (the present ceiling is from the thirteenth century). Bernward's church is unusual, however, in having two apses, one at either end of the church, and two identical pairs of transepts. The interior decoration is elaborate for its time, the aisles are supported by alternating round columns and square pillars, and the huge, striped transverse arches in the nave anticipate the Romanesque style that would develop later in the eleventh century. The large expanse of blank wall between the aisle arcades and the clearstory windows far above them adds to the harmony and clarity that characterize this masterpiece of Ottonian, pre-Romanesque art.

Not far from St. Michael's church is a remarkable rose bush, reputed to be a thousand years old—as old as St. Michael's itself. Even if, as some suspect, the plant is only a few hundred years old and not a thousand, it is nevertheless well worth the walk from St. Michael's through the pleasant streets of Hildesheim to view what may be the oldest rose bush in Europe.

8.   CASTLE RISING, NORFOLK, ENGLAND

This castle was built in the reign of King Stephen of England, around 1139, by William of Albini earl of Sussex, former Master Butler of Henry I (died 1135), who married King Henry's widow, Adeliza of Louvain. William of Albini built his great castle ("fit for a queen," as one observer put it) atop an earlier mound of vast proportions that had originally been intended to support a palisaded wooden tower of the "motte and bailey" type such as the Normans had erected in great number during the decades following the Norman Conquest of 1066. The bailey is the square enclosure at ground level, directly in front of the motte (i.e., slightly to the left of it in the photo). It originally contained a great hall and other domestic buildings, all of which have perished.

Some two generations after the heyday of motte and bailey castles, William of Albini built a much more sophisticated, stone castle atop the great motte, which was itself extended in later years. Only 50 feet high, the stone castle is scarcely visible from the ground because of the high ringwork surrounding it. But the structure is much longer and broader than its 50-foot height and is quite unlike the usual stone towers of its time. Known as a "hall keep," it consists of a two-storied great hall (abutted by a kitchen) and a great chamber with a chapel next to it—both on the second story (the first story being used for storage). The castle keep was approached by a path running from an outer ward through a gate-house (left). The great ringwork surrounding the keep originally enclosed other residential buildings as well and would have protected this unusually luxurious and elegant stone structure from attack. The earthwork dominated a small, planned village that flourishes to this day.

When the Albini line died out in the mid-thirteenth century, Castle Rising passed to the monarchy. In the fourteenth century, King Edward III granted it to his mother, Queen Isabella. For although he deprived her of power for betraying her royal husband (Edward III's father), King Edward II, he nevertheless permitted her to live on in luxury at Castle Rising. It then passed to Edward III's son, the Black Prince. By Elizabethan times it was falling into ruin. As it stands today, it is better preserved than most castles of its time but, lacking all its floors and its roof, it is no longer fit for a queen.

9. CLUNY III, FLOOR PLAN

The abbey of Cluny in Burgundy was founded in 909 by Duke William of Aquitaine who, in his foundation charter, renounced his ducal right to appoint abbots and left the decision to the monks and who granted the proprietorship of the abbey to the papacy. Although the tenth-century popes lacked the power to protect religious establishments outside the environs of central Italy, abbots of Cluny would later use their relationship with the papacy to win independence from the jurisdiction of local bishops over their abbey and its increasingly numerous and far-flung dependent priories.

Under a series of talented, saintly, and long-lived abbots, Cluny became an internationally celebrated focal point of monastic reform. Its monks adhered strictly to the Benedictine rule as interpreted and elaborated by the Carolingian monastic reformer St. Benedict of Aniane. The Cluniacs embellished these pious traditions with a new emphasis on around-the-clock prayers, psalms, and masses for dead benefactors and friends. Cluny's piety and majestic liturgical observances were admired far and wide, with the result that an increasing number of religious houses submitted or were granted to it as dependent priories subject to the abbot of Cluny. By the beginning of the twelfth century, Cluniac priories numbered in the hundreds, and Cluny had become the foremost abbey in Western Europe.

The growth of Cluny from its humble beginnings in 909 necessitated a series of rebuilding programs. Later in the tenth century, the original church gave way to a larger one, known to architectural historians as Cluny II, and around 1085, work commenced on Cluny III. This new church, the building of which continued far into the twelfth century, was a vast and imposing edifice, the largest in medieval Western Europe, and featured the earliest systematic use of pointed arches—which were to become a significant feature of Gothic architecture. Kings and magnates, from England to the Iberian peninsula, contributed to the building fund for this greatest of all churches. Cluny III stood until the French Revolution, at which time it was converted into a stone quarry and largely demolished. Only the great north transept remains to suggest to modern visitors the immensity of the original structure.

The floor plan of Cluny shows the monastery—church and domestic buildings—as of the mid-twelfth century. The church, Cluny III, is at the left. At the top, angled downward, is the infirmary complex. Below that, the top tier of rooms includes a warming room, the chapter house (where the monastic congregation met), the treasury, the monks' dormitory, and latrines. Below are the cloister, refectory (dining room), and novices' cloister. The remaining structures include a wine cellar, a kitchen, a bakery, guest houses, and stables. The overall plan, which resembles those of other large abbeys, makes clear that the monastic community provided for a wide variety of human needs, both spiritual and physical.

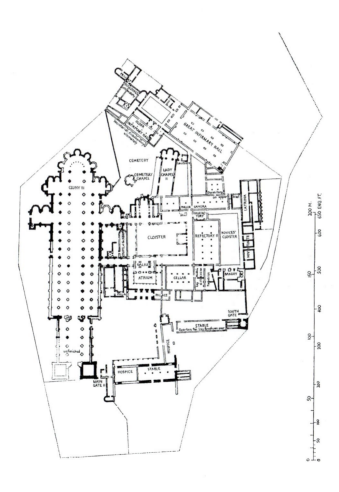

10.   ST.-GENIS-DES-FONTAINES, CARVED LINTEL, c. 1040

This simple carving of Christ in majesty flanked by angels and apostles is probably the earliest work of sculpture in medieval France. It is dated by inscription to 1020 (although some art historians suspect that it was actually of a somewhat later date) and occupies the lintel above the central portal of the small parish church of St.-Genis-des-Fontaines, a village in Languedoc (southwestern France) nestled in the Pyrenees near the Spanish border. The overall design of the sculpture can be traced back through carved ivories to the decorative schemes of early Christian and pagan sarcophagi (stone coffins).

The carving at St.-Genis-des-Fontaines is plain, two-dimensional, and altogether unpretentious compared with later Romanesque sculpture (see illustration 11, from about a century later). But like all subsequent sculpture until the later twelfth century, the figures are in low relief. Freestanding statues remained unknown to Romanesque sculptors and came only with the advent of the Gothic style.

211

11.   AUTUN, CARVED CAPITAL OF JUDAS' SUICIDE, GISLEBERTUS

The sculpture that ornaments the tympanum and capitals of the cathedral of Autun in Burgundy dates from about 1125 to 1135 and was evidently the work, in whole or in part, of a sculptor named Gislebertus (Gislebert or Gilbert). We know absolutely nothing about this person except the fact that he "signed" his Last Judgment scene on the tympanum of the central portal with the carved words *Gislebertus hoc fecit,* "Gislebert made this." Nevertheless, on the basis of his work at Autun, and probably at the nearby abbey of Vézelay as well, he is regarded as one of the foremost masters of Romanesque art.

Like all Romanesque sculpture, the works of Gislebertus are in relief rather than freestanding. But much of his work is in high relief and achieves a psychological impact and sense of three-dimensionality. These effects are well exemplified in his *Suicide of Judas,* carved on a capital atop one of the columns at the south wall of Autun Cathedral. Judas, his mouth open in despair, has hung himself on a rope attached to a tree, while two hideously ugly winged demons with similarly open mouths pull him downward. Attached to the rope (left center) is a round object that probably represents the purse containing the thirty pieces of silver that Judas received for betraying Jesus. In the society from which this sculpture emerged, the act of betraying one's lord was perhaps the worst of all evils, and Judas was seen as the ultimate betrayer.

12.   ST.-JOUIN-DE-MARNES, ROMANESQUE FACADE

The abbey church of St.-Jouin-de-Marnes in Poitou (west central France), begun about 1095, is a splendid example of the Romanesque (Roman-like) style that flourished between 1050 and 1150, giving way in the second half of the twelfth century to Gothic. Its striking facade dates from about 1130, concurrent with Gislebertus's Autun.

Romanesque architecture is characterized by a basilica floor plan of nave and side aisles, round Classical arches, massive walls, small windows (relative to the subsequent Gothic style), and, especially in the generation centering on 1130, an elaborately sculpted central portal of multiple recessed arches resting on clustered columns (colonnettes), symbolizing the threshold of heaven. The facade of St.-Jouin-de-Marnes, like other Romanesque facades of its era, is divided by heavy multiple columns into three parts, which correspond to the interior nave and side aisles. Above the central window of the facade is a group of figures carved in relief, representing the Last Judgment. Note, too, the three entrance arches, which are reminiscent of the Arch of Constantine (illustration 1) and therefore evoke Constantine's triumph over paganism.

The province of Poitiers contains a marvelous abundance of Romanesque churches, owing to its economic prosperity during much of the twelfth century. In the thirteenth century, the center of French politics and economic growth shifted northward to the region around Paris, leaving the Poitevins too poor to demolish their Romanesque churches and rebuild them in the newly fashionable Gothic style.

13.   LAON CATHEDRAL, FACADE

This majestic early Gothic cathedral rises from the northern French hilltop town of Laon. Begun in 1165 and completed in 1235, it replaced a Romanesque edifice that was consumed by fire in the Laon communal rebellion of 1112 (see pp. 175–178). The facade of the new cathedral displays distinct similarities to the Romanesque facade of St.-Jouin-de-Marnes (illustration 12) but striking differences as well. Like St.-Jouin, Laon Cathedral has a large central portal with smaller portals on either side, corresponding to the basilica floor plan of the interior with a large nave and two side aisles. And the tripartite scheme, as at St.-Jouin, extends upward to provide an architectural framework for the entire facade. Similarly, horizontal elements on the Laon facade delineate, much more clearly than at St.-Jouin, the divisions of the interior nave elevation pictured in illustration 14. Indeed, as in other Gothic churches of the era, the Laon facade goes far beyond its Romanesque predecessors in integrating all its architectural and decorative details into a remarkably balanced and intelligible unity of overall design.

There are, however, significant differences between Laon and St.-Jouin. The arches at Laon, no longer perfectly round, are beginning to point (much more noticeably in the interior). The two west towers are tremendously more dominant than those at St.-Jouin. They rise upward some 182 feet, and from their upper stages, colossal stone oxen look out over the city and surrounding countryside—placed there perhaps to honor the beasts that dragged stones for the cathedral up the steep hill atop which the city is built. (One tradition alleges that the oxen hauled the stones up the hill of their own accord.) Unlike Romanesque figures, always carved in relief, the Laon oxen are freestanding, as are the rows of figures (much restored) within the huge portals. The sculptural group in the main portal depicts the coronation of the Virgin Mary, whose statue stands against the slender pillar dividing the two central doors. The rose window above the main portal was not a Gothic innovation; a number of twelfth-century Romanesque churches had rose windows as well. Nevertheless, they became a characteristic feature of Gothic churches and were much elaborated by architects of the thirteenth century and thereafter. Particularly stunning examples are to be found at Chartres Cathedral and in the north and south transepts of Notre Dame, Paris.

14.   LAON CATHEDRAL, NAVE ELEVATION

At the time that builders were constructing the nave of Laon Cathedral, from about 1175 to 1190, Gothic architecture was still in the experimental stage. The Laon nave, with its four-story elevation, was decisively Gothic in style—with pointed arches, upward-thrusting colonnettes, and stone ribs crisscrossing the vault. But it had not yet achieved the classic high Gothic style inaugurated at Chartres beginning in the mid-1190s, with its three-story elevation featuring arcade arches and huge clearstory windows in equal proportion, separated by a slender "triforium" similar to Laon's third story. Chartres became the model, and the three-story elevation characterized virtually all subsequent Gothic churches (see, for example, illustration 16, Prague Cathedral).

Another transitional feature at Laon is the thickness of the arcade columns. In the high Gothic churches that followed, the columns became thinner and more delicate, as architects strove to reduce stone surfaces and make windows larger and larger. Slender columns, vault ribs, and the addition of flying buttresses in the early thirteenth century enabled architects to support the downward and outward thrust of stone vaulting without the necessity of thick walls. Instead, they created structures that were, in essence, stone skeletons with walls of lustrous, colored glass. The architects of Laon Cathedral had not yet attained that ideal, but they were approaching it. And their younger contemporaries would achieve it at Chartres, Reims, Amiens, and other great cathedrals of the thirteenth century.

15.   NOTRE DAME CATHEDRAL, PARIS, THE ST. ANNE PORTAL

The cathedral of Notre Dame, Paris, like the many other French cathedrals dedicated to Notre Dame, bears witness to the growing strength of the cult of the Virgin Mary in high medieval France. Pictured here is the St. Anne portal, to the south of the central portal. St. Anne and St. Joachim were believed to be Mary's mother and father. St. Anne had long believed herself to be barren; the sculpture on the lower lintel depicts Anne and Joachim's sorrow over their childless marriage, the announcement by an angel that Anne would bear a child after all, the birth of the Virgin Mary, her marriage to Joseph, and their journey to Nazareth. The upper lintel portrays the events preceding Jesus's birth (Annunciation and Visitation) and the Nativity in Bethlehem. On the tympanum above, Mary has been crowned Queen of Heaven and sits in glory with the infant Jesus on her lap, flanked by angels, a king of France (Louis VII), and two high officers of state doing reverence to her.

The entire west facade of Notre Dame, Paris—badly damaged over the years by the ravages of rogue Protestants and revolutionaries—underwent heavy-handed restorations in the late nineteenth century. Although the St. Anne tympanum retains its medieval theme and iconography, much of the sculpture has been insensitively restored or altogether redone in a style that "authorities" at the time believed to be medieval. Although the ensemble is more or less authentic, beware of the details!

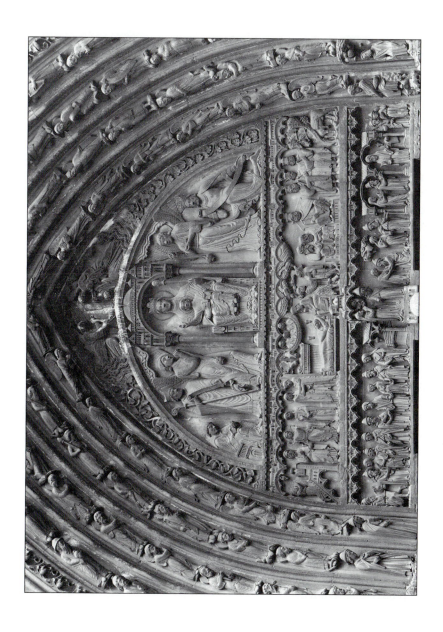

221

16. PRAGUE CATHEDRAL, LATE GOTHIC VAULTING, 1344–1385

Contrary to common belief, the architects and sculptors of medieval Europe were not all anonymous. We know the names of many of them— Gislebertus of Autun, for example (illustration 11), and the architects of such celebrated cathedrals as Amiens, Canterbury, and Prague. The chief architect of Prague Cathedral was Peter Parler, a member of a distinguished family of architects active in south Germany and the Rhinelands. The cathedral was dedicated to the early Christian martyr St. Vitus, about whom nothing certain is known except that his name came to be associated, quite unfairly, with the later medieval practice of frenzied, screaming, convulsive dancing that bordered on mass hysteria and alarmed the public authorities.

Prague Cathedral—with its three-story elevation, great height, huge windows, and pointed arches—is French in overall design. It illustrates the fact that during the thirteenth and fourteenth centuries, the Gothic style, which had originated in the region around Paris, had become international. Besides Prague, one encounters French Gothic churches in such far-flung places as Uppsala, Cologne, and Westminster. Like many Western European churches built since the 1240s, Prague Cathedral was constructed in a style called Rayonnant Gothic (named for the radiating character of its immense rose windows). On the model of its earliest exemplars—structures such as La Sainte-Chapelle, the transept facades of Notre Dame, Paris, and the nave and upper choir of St.-Denis—Rayonnant Gothic churches strove to carry to its ultimate extent the Gothic idea of window walls supported by a slender stone skeleton of columns, vault ribs, and flying buttresses. Prague Cathedral typifies this style with its immense clearstory windows and, just beneath them, its glazed (glass-backed) triforium. The side aisles are illuminated by windows of comparable size (not shown here). Like other late medieval churches, the vaults of Prague Cathedral are crossed and supported by increasingly complex patterns of vault ribs. But the particular arrangement of vault ribs at Prague is a unique and characteristic product of Peter Parler's inventiveness and love of decorative exuberance.

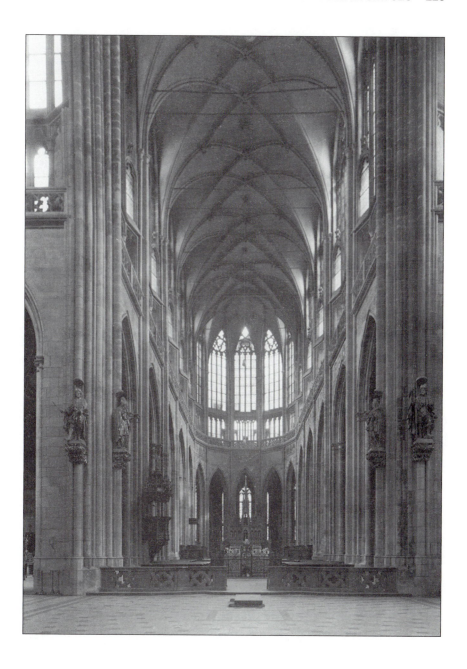

17.   MAP OF FLORENCE, ITALY[1]

Like many medieval cities, Florence traced its origins to the Romans. The town was laid out at the time of Octavian (c. 41 B.C.) in the fashion of a Roman military camp, namely a walled enclosure with a grid pattern in a north-south orientation. The original walls of this Roman town can still be seen in the center of this map of Florence drawn up by Stefano Bonsignori in 1584. The large cathedral—S. Maria del Fiore, begun in 1294 and capped off with Brunileschi's famous dome—is located in the northeast corner of the city, originally doubtless the site of a Roman temple. Further inspection shows a second grid pattern that can be seen stretching north from the Arno River, turned 31 degrees from the original city grid. This, too, was laid out by the Romans as part of a process of centuriation, or parceling out the lands for farming in a very regular system of rectangular plots, in this case the axis of which is the river itself.

As a result of the twelfth century commercial revolution, the Florentines had outgrown the Roman core and so established a new wall, including for the first time a small area south of the Arno, completed by 1285 (depicted on the map with dashed lines). By this time the population of Florence was fast approaching 50,000 inhabitants who were probably already cramped in the new 197 acres of territory. Thus, the town fathers built another wall, further out, encompassing 1,556 acres. This new wall, completed in 1335 (marked by dashes and dots), included room to expand, again on both sides of the river. But because of the population decline from the plague (see Boccacio's description in Chapter 11, Reading 1), much of the land went unsettled, remaining fields until the 1800s. This rural area immediately surrounding the city, or *contado,* was quite important to the Florentines, for the great merchants acquired estates there, which they actively supervised and which provided a good deal of Florence's agricultural wealth.

Finally, the late medieval trace italienne bastion, the star-shaped fortress on the North, reflects the development of gunpowder artillery, which essentially obviated the necessity for any additional walls.

---

[1]Map by Stefano Bonsignori from Gene Brucker, *Florence: The Golden Age, 1138–1737;* University of California Press, 1998, p. 24.

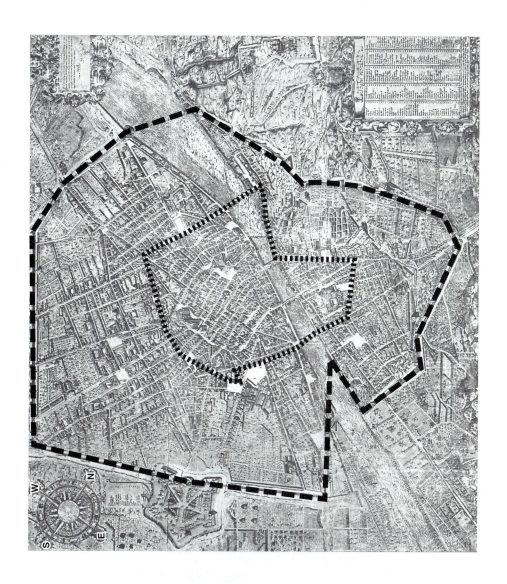

18.   PEÑAFIEL CASTLE, SPAIN

This majestic bastion of the Spanish *Reconquista* rises like a stone battleship from a high and narrow spine of land in north central Castile. "Peñafiel" means "the faithful rock," and the ridge on which the present castle stands is obviously a natural defensive site of major importance. It was fortified as early as the mid-tenth century, when it stood as an advanced Christian outpost against the Muslims. The celebrated Muslim leader Almanzor captured it in 995, but in 1013 it was retaken by Christians, who built a castle and new walls atop the ridge. During the years that followed, Peñafiel was strengthened and refortified on several occasions. The present castle, built on the site of these older fortifications, dates in part from the early fourteenth century but principally from the mid-fifteenth. Even then it remained a military stronghold rather than a permanent residence; it was all but impregnable but lacked the spaciousness and comforts of a noble palace. With its great fifteenth-century keep rising from amidst its battlemented curtain walls, Peñafiel marks the culmination of medieval military architecture, secure against the assaults of arrows, battering rams, firebrands, and stone missiles, yet vulnerable to the cannon that was transforming warfare in the late Middle Ages.

19. PEÑAFIEL CASTLE, GROUND PLAN

This ground plan amplifies the depiction of Peñafiel castle, showing the outline of the castle lying shiplike astride its elongated hill. The constituent elements of Peñafiel's defensive system are identified here, from the inner ward above the keep to the outer ward beneath it. The diagram also shows, as the preceding photograph does not, that the keep and inner ward were defended by a moat, and that a walled town extended downward from the castle and depended on it for protection.

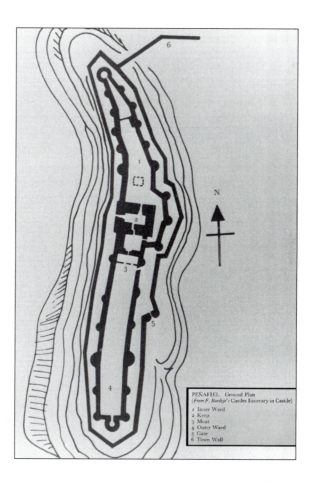

PEÑAFIEL Ground Plan
(From F. Bordeje's Castles Itinerary in Castile)

1 Inner Ward
2 Keep
3 Moat
4 Outer Ward
5 Gate
6 Town Wall

20.   BASILICA OF SAN FRANCESCO, ASSISI, POPE INNOCENT III'S DREAM

A celebrated cycle of twenty-eight frescoes depicting episodes in the life of St. Francis adorns the upper basilica of a great church built in his honor, San Francesco in Assisi. The frescoes probably date from the 1290s and are usually attributed, quite plausibly, to the great medieval artist Giotto, assisted by apprentices. The iconography of this cycle is derived from what was at the time Francis' official biography, written by the minister general of the Franciscan order, the eminent scholar St. Bonaventure, and authorized by a general chapter of the Franciscan community. During the generation between St. Francis' death in 1226 and Bonaventure's biography in 1260 to 1263, oral traditions had enriched Francis' life with a fertile growth of legends, some of them possibly true, others most unlikely. Bonaventure pruned many of these legendary accretions from his biography but retained others.

One of the more memorable and less likely legends preserved by Bonaventure appears in the San Francesco cycle in a fresco probably painted by Giotto himself. It illustrates a dream of Pope Innocent III that is said to have occurred just before St. Francis and a small band of disciples met the pope for the first time and petitioned him to authorize their way of life. As head of a powerful and wealthy church, Innocent would have been unlikely, so it was thought, to approve the Franciscan mission of apostolic poverty and unsupervised preaching were it not for the dream. In it, Innocent, who had been deeply troubled by the spread of the Albigensian heresy, saw his magnificent papal residence, the Lateran Palace, tilting and about to collapse until a brown-robed giant placed his shoulder against it and kept it from falling. When Innocent awakened and, shortly afterwards, received the little band of Franciscans into his presence, he recognized St. Francis as the giant in his dream.

That Innocent actually had such a dream we can well doubt. Whether or not he regarded Francis as a possible antidote to the Albigensian threat, we cannot know. But despite some misgivings, the pope responded to Francis's petition by endorsing his mission.

21.   A LADY AND HER LOVER, THE MINNESÄNGER MANUSCRIPT, HEIDELBURG

This illumination, from a fourteenth-century document known as the *Minnesänger Manuscript* and preserved in the library of Heidelburg University, bears on the subject of courtly love. It depicts a lady mounted on a rather morose-looking horse, visiting her knightly lover, who leans out of the window of a castle tower. The lady is binding the hands of her lover with threads of gold, symbolizing the depth of their mutual affection.

22.   A WOMAN ARTIST AT WORK

Medieval women participated in many professions and activities that
would be reserved to men in later ages: trade, banking, the direction of
business enterprises, textile manufacturing, brewing, tax collecting, money
lending, illuminating and copying books, managing hotels and taverns, and
a variety of other activities. This illustration, from a French manuscript of
the second half of the fifteenth century, demonstrates that women also
played a role as artists in the Middle Ages. Here, an artist is shown with her
brush and palette, lavishing close attention on her female subject.

23.   THE MONTH OF MARCH, FROM A BOOK OF HOURS

In the late Middle Ages books of hours became a popular fashion of devotion. They highlighted saints days, favorite psalms, and events from the life of Christ, serving as a compact and personalized form of liturgical calendar (note the zodiacal signs, phases of the moon, and days of the month in the semicircle at the top of the painting). Most of these books of hours were sumptuously illustrated, as wealthy families commissioned the best artists available. John, the Duke of Berry (1360–1416) selected the talented Limbourg brothers to illuminate his *Tres Riches Heures,* the page here depicting the month of March.

It is customary to see illustrations from the books of hours as windows into the life of the medieval elite, which they are. Some of them, though, reveal a great deal about daily life of the peasantry. Certainly the castle of Lusignan anchors the scene, and the fanciful winged dragon hovering atop one of the castle towers is an allusion to a story told about the Berry family. But the foreground is dominated by peasants at their spring labors— shepherding, tending vines, and planting—actions that went on virtually unremarked by the nobility throughout the Middle Ages.

At the forefront we find a ploughman. The peasant is an old man in tattered clothes, guiding the plow with his left hand while goading the oxen with the stick in his right hand. By the high Middle Ages the heavy plow (as opposed to the earlier scratch plow) had become the common vehicle for attacking the soil. It was a complex invention that included a blade (the coulter) to slice the earth, a second blade set at right angles to the first (the ploughshare) to slice the sod at root level, and a strong piece of wood (the moldboard) to turn the turf over. The wheels aided the pulling action but were mostly used to guide the depth of the plow blade. The heavy plow was essential to the prosperity of most of France, England, and Germany, because—when used with teams of oxen or horses—it alone could break the thick soils of northern Europe.

This painting shows a growing appreciation for the ploughman. In the early Middle Ages the ploughman, if he was mentioned at all, was associated with Cain, the lowly tiller of the earth and slayer of the more noble shepherd, his brother Abel. But late medieval authors such as Geoffrey Chaucer called him "an honest worker, good and true, living in peace and perfect charity," and William Langland even likened his fictional hero Piers the Ploughman to Christ himself.

STUDY QUESTIONS

Visual documents cannot be approached in precisely the same way as written sources, so the questions for this chapter adopt a different format.

A Roman influences were important to many aspects of medieval life, including architecture. Based on the Arch of Constantine (illustration 1), what Roman influences are found in illustrations 12, 13, and 14?

B In the West we are conditioned to seeing the human form in its Classical rendering. Which manuscript paintings in illustrations 4, 5, and 6 are most successful in capturing Classical conventions? How can we explain the increasing Classicism of medieval painting? Does illustration 4 in any way succeed at presenting a compelling portrait of Saint Luke?

C Human burials often end up preserving items that the deceased valued most highly. In illustrations 2 and 3, how do we explain the value of something as tiny as a brooch and as large as a ship?

D One of the main functions of a medieval church was to act as a setting for numerous liturgical activities (e.g., the divine offices, the mass, holy day processions, etc.). To what degree do the church structures as shown in illustrations 7, 9, 14, and 16 reinforce liturgical purposes?

E Another function of a medieval church was to help educate a Christian population by illustrating various theological tenets (e.g., the importance of light as a divine essence). To what degree do illustrations 9, 10, 11, 12, 13, 14, 15, 16, and 20 reinforce theological beliefs?

F Based on illustrations 8, 17, 18, and 19, how did military defensive capabilities improve over time?

G By the fourteenth century painting had become more self-assured. How do illustrations 21, 22, and 23 reveal more refined aspects of medieval civilization? What do these illustrations say about views of human labor? About changing roles for women and for peasants? How do illustrations 21 and 22 in particular show a more introspective society?

⊠ NEW PATHS TO GOD: MONKS AND PHILOSOPHERS

The foundations of medieval Christianity had been established in a world that was poor, rural, and isolated. But by the High Middle Ages, it was apparent that these conditions had changed, as the new age saw the rapid creation of wealth, the development of towns, and extensive contact with foreign cultures. The response by Christian institutions was as varied as the stimuli: reaction, assimilation, reform, renovation.

For example, the Cistercians (Reading 1)—whose greatest representative in the twelfth century, St. Bernard, abbot of Clairvaux (Reading 1B), we encountered in Chapter 5—constituted a drastically reformed version of Benedictine monasticism. St. Hildegard was one of the most famous mystics of her day (Reading 2A). Francis of Assisi, perhaps the most beloved saint of the High Middle Ages, broke with the cloistered tradition of Benedictine monasticism altogether, and his order refused gifts of manors. St. Francis himself was an unassuming, impetuous person. The Franciscan Rule of 1223 (Reading 3) reflects an effort by the papacy to provide Francis's followers with a logical organizational structure alien to Francis himself but perhaps necessary for the survival of his order. Francis was a town dweller, and he and his followers placed strong emphasis on preaching and serving in towns. Like the Franciscans, the Dominicans chose to live in the world, away from the shelter of a monastery, and to preach to the laity (Reading 4). The intense urban piety that inspired the Franciscans and Dominicans also gave rise to the first major heretical movements since late Antiquity. The Albigensians and Waldensians, although condemned by the papacy, flourished in the towns of southern Europe (Readings 5 and 6). Against them and others, the cause of Catholic orthodoxy was upheld and strongly asserted at the Fourth Lateran Council (1215), convened and chaired by the ablest pope of the High Middle Ages, Innocent III (Reading 7).

Many of the same impulses that transformed Christian institutions in the period also affected academic theology. St. Anselm, the most important speculative philosopher of his generation, was—like St. Bernard—a monk of deep piety, penetrating intellect, and political acumen. Anselm's ontological proof of God (Reading 8) may seem at first sight a bit silly, but it is not easily dismissed. Anselm sought to uncover the deepest meanings locked within our knowledge and belief; others looked for a new basis for understanding. This trend was first evident among Muslim scholars (Reading 9). Our excerpt from Peter Abelard's *Sic et Non* (Reading 10) bears witness to a similar spirit of intellectual debate in the urban schools of Europe, although Abelard carried the idea of debate farther than most. In Thomas Aquinas the themes seem to run together: Thomas was a Dominican who carried out his most celebrated work in Paris; his theology showed great sensitivity to ancient authors, especially Aristotle, and to Muslim philosophers; and he managed to be flexible without compromising the basic tenets of Christianity (Reading 11). St. Thomas Aquinas has traditionally been regarded as the spokesperson of thirteenth-century Catholic theology, but he was opposed by theologians in his own day and several of his opinions were condemned among the philosophical positions rejected by Etienne Tempier, bishop of Paris, in 1277, three years after Aquinas's death (Reading 12). The final passage, by the Franciscan William of Ockham, concerns "universals," one of the central thematic problems of high medieval philosophy. Ockham, working within the strictures established by Tempier, demonstrates the chill that fourteenth-century skepticism, as exemplified in Ockham, cast on the heady optimism of thirteenth-century scholasticism (Reading 13).

READING 1

The Cistercians

Clairvaux, one of the earliest Cistercian daughter houses, had the celebrated St. Bernard (1090–1153) as its first abbot. This contemporary description by William of St. Thierry (d. 1142), friend and biographer of St. Bernard, captures the mood of Clairvaux in its early years, although perhaps in a slightly idealized fashion.

Saint Bernard, the driving force behind the Cistercian order, wrote numerous letters. He gave advice—both solicited and unsolicited—to the rich and famous of Europe. Like an Old Testament prophet he railed against injustices. He also wrote simple letters of introduction, such as the letter in document B to the abbot of a house of regular canons at Troyes. The letter shows Bernard's concern for even the humblest monks and his keen psychological insight into his fellow man (and, in the case of Reading 2, his fellow woman). The epistle also indicates the emphasis on manual labor for which the Cistercians were famous and which separated them from other orders such as Cluny.

A.   WILLIAM OF ST. THIERRY, A DESCRIPTION OF CLAIRVAUX[1]

At the first glance as you entered Clairvaux by descending the hill you could see that it was a temple of God; and the still, silent valley bespoke, in the modest simplicity of its buildings, the unfeigned humility of Christ's poor. Moreover, in this valley full of men, where no one was permitted to be idle, where one and all were occupied with their allotted tasks, a silence deep as that of night prevailed. The sounds of labor, or the chants of the brethren in the choral service, were the only exceptions. The orderliness of this silence, and the report that went forth concerning it, struck such a reverence even into secular persons that they dreaded breaking it—I will not say by idle or wicked conversation, but even by proper remarks. The solitude, also, of the place—between dense forests in a narrow gorge of neighboring hills—in a certain sense recalled the cave of our father St. Benedict,[2] so that while they strove to imitate his life, they also had some similarity to him in their habitation and loneliness. . . .

[1]From *A Source Book of Mediaeval History,* ed. Frederic Austin Ogg; New York, American Book Company, 1907, pp. 258–260.
[2]The famous founder of the monastery of Monte Cassino and the compiler of the Benedictine Rule.

Although the monastery is situated in a valley, it has its foundations on the holy hills, whose gates the Lord loveth more than all the dwellings of Jacob. Glorious things are spoken of it, because the glorious and wonderful God therein worketh great marvels. There the insane recover their reason, and although their outward man is worn way, inwardly they are born again. There the proud are humbled, the rich are made poor, and the poor have the Gospel preached to them, and the darkness of sinners is changed into light. A large multitude of blessed poor from the ends of the earth have there assembled, yet have they one heart and one mind; justly, therefore, do all who dwell there rejoice with no empty joy. They have the certain hope of perennial joy, of their ascension heavenward already commenced. In Clairvaux, they have found Jacob's ladder, with angels upon it; some descending, who so provide for their bodies that they faint not on the way; others ascending, who so rule their souls that their bodies hereafter may be glorified with them.

For my part, the more attentively I watch them day by day, the more do I believe that they are perfect followers of Christ in all things. When they pray and speak to God in spirit and in truth, by their friendly and quiet speech to Him, as well as by their humbleness of demeanor, they are plainly seen to be God's companions and friends. When, on the other hand, they openly praise God with psalms, how pure and fervent are their minds, is shown by their posture of body in holy fear and reverence, while by their careful pronunciation and modulation of the psalms, is shown how sweet to their lips are the words of God—sweeter than honey to their mouths. As I watch them, therefore, singing without fatigue from before midnight to the dawn of day, with only a brief interval, they appear a little less than the angels, but much more than men. . . .

As regards their manual labor, so patiently and placidly, with such quiet countenances, in such sweet and holy order, do they perform all things, that although they exercise themselves at many works, they never seem moved or burdened in anything, whatever the labor may be. Whence it is manifest that that Holy Spirit worketh in them who disposeth of all things with sweetness, in whom they are refreshed, so that they rest even in their toil. Many of them, I bear, are bishops and earls, and many illustrious through their birth or knowledge; but now, by God's grace, all distinction of persons being dead among them, the greater any one thought himself in the world, the more in this flock does he regard himself as less than the least. I see them in the garden with hoes, in the meadows with forks or rakes, in the fields with scythes, in the forest with axes. To judge from their outward appearance, their tools, their bad and disordered clothes, they appear a race of fools, without speech or sense. But a true thought in my mind tells me that their life in Christ is hidden in the heavens. Among them I see Godfrey of Peronne, Raynald of Picardy, William of St. Omer, Walter of Lisle, all of whom I knew formerly in the old man, whereof

I now see no trace, by God's favor. I knew them proud and puffed up; I see them walking humbly under the merciful hand of God.

B.   LETTER OF BERNARD OF CLAIRVAUX TO THE ABBOT OF TROYES[3]

To his friend and fellow-servant Lord W. Abbot of the Canons Regular at Troyes, greetings in the Lord, from Brother Bernard, the unprofitable servant of the church of Clairvaux.

   I have persuaded this cleric (the bearer of this letter), who desires to leave the world and remain with us, to come instead to you, because I fear that the hardness of our life would break him. I therefore commend him to you as one well known to all of us here, excellently behaved, and highly cultured; in short, as a servant of God whom I believe will be, by God's grace, a great comfort to you. I am very fond of him and am sending him to you as much for your sake as for his, since I would gladly keep him here on account of his virtuous life, but for the fact that, delicate and unused to manual work as he is, I fear to receive him. Farewell.

READING 2

Hildegard of Bingen, Letter to Bernard of Clairvaux, with Reply

St. Hildegard (1098–1179), a German noble and Benedictine abbess, was recognized and widely admired by her contemporaries as a marvelously gifted polymath: a prophet, composer, poet, theologian, physician, and mystic. She wrote numerous letters, medical essays, mystical treatises, and poetic works set to her own music (a modernized version of her hymns, "Visions," made top-forty charts in 1994, and her *Ordo Virtutum,* a highly innovative and extremely beautiful musical morality play, is often performed and spendidly recorded). Hildegard began receiving mystical visions when she was a young girl, and they shaped her understanding of theology. Since it was potentially dangerous in the Middle Ages to be an "unauthorized" mystic (and remains so today), St. Hildegard, in this letter, seeks support for her visions from one of the most influential churchmen of her time, St. Bernard of Clairvaux (see pp. 189–190). Bernard's brief response makes it clear that he was convinced of their legitimacy.

---

[3]From *The Letters of St. Bernard of Clairvaux,* tr. Bruno Scott James; Chicago, Henry Regnery Co., 1953, p. 440.

A.   HILDEGARD TO BERNARD, ABBOT OF CLAIRVAUX, c. 1147[4]

O venerable father Bernard, I lay my claim before you, for, highly honored by God, you bring fear to the immoral foolishness of this world and, in your intense zeal and burning love for the Son of God, gather men [cf. Luke 5:10] into Christ's army to fight under the banner of the cross against pagan savagery.[5] I beseech you in the name of the Living God to give heed to my queries.

Father, I am greatly disturbed by a vision which has appeared to me through divine revelation, a vision seen not with my fleshly eyes but only in my spirit. Wretched, and indeed more than wretched in my womanly condition, I have from earliest childhood seen great marvels which my tongue has no power to express but which the Spirit of God has taught me that I may believe. Steadfast and gentle father, in your kindness respond to me, your unworthy servant, who has never, from her earliest childhood, lived one hour free from anxiety. In your piety and wisdom look in your spirit, as you have been taught by the Holy Spirit, and from your heart bring comfort to your handmaiden.

Through this vision which touches my heart and soul like a burning flame, teaching me profundities of meaning, I have an inward understanding of the Psalter, the Gospels, and other volumes. Nevertheless, I do not receive this knowledge in German. Indeed, I have no formal training at all, for I know how to read only on the most elementary level, certainly with no deep analysis. But please give me your opinion in this matter, because I am untaught and untrained in exterior material, but am only taught inwardly, in my spirit. Hence my halting, unsure speech.

When I hear from your pious wisdom, I will be comforted. For with the single exception of a certain monk in whose exemplary life I have the utmost confidence, I have not dared to tell these things to anyone, since there are so many heresies abroad in the land, as I have heard. I have, in fact, revealed all my secrets to this man, and he has given me consolation, for these are great and fearsome matters.

Now, father, for the love of God, I seek consolation from you, that I may be assured. More than two years ago, indeed, I saw you in a vision, like a man looking straight into the sun, bold and unafraid. And I wept, because I myself am so timid and fearful. Good and gentle father, I have been placed in your care so that you might reveal to me through our correspondence whether I should speak these things openly or keep my silence, because I have great anxiety about this vision with respect to how much I should speak about what I have seen and

---

[4]From *The Letters of Hildegard of Bingen,* tr. Joseph L. Baird and Radd K. Ehrman; New York, Oxford University Press, 1994, pp. 27–28, 31.

[5]A reference to the Second Crusade, which Bernard had helped set in motion.

heard. In the meantime, because I have kept silent about this vision, I have been laid low, bedridden in my infirmities, and am unable to raise myself up.

Therefore, I weep with sorrow before you. For in my nature, I am unstable because I am caught in the winepress, that tree rooted in Adam by the devil's deceit which brought about his exile into this wayward world. Yet, now, rising up, I run to you. And I say to you: You are not inconstant, but are always lifting up the tree, a victor in your spirit, lifting up not only yourself but also the whole world unto salvation. You are indeed the eagle gazing directly at the sun.

And so I beseech your aid, through the serenity of the Father and through His wondrous Word and through the sweet moisture of compunction, the Spirit of truth [cf. John 14:17; 16:13], and through that holy sound, which all creation echoes, and through that same Word which gave birth to the world, and through the sublimity of the Father, who sent the Word with sweet fruitfulness into the womb of the Virgin, from which He soaked up flesh, just as honey is surrounded by the honeycomb. And may that Sound, the power of the Father, fall upon your heart and lift up your spirit so that you may respond expeditiously to these words of mine, taking care, of course, to seek all these things from God—with regard to the person or the mystery itself—while you are passing through the gateway of your soul, so that you may come to know all these things in God. Farewell, be strong in your spirit, and be a mighty warrior for God. Amen.

B. ABBOT BERNARD OF CLAIRVAUX TO HILDEGARD

Brother Bernard, called Abbot of Clairvaux, offers to Hildegard, beloved daughter in Christ, whatever the prayer of a sinner can accomplish.

It is perhaps to be attributed to your humility that you appear to have a higher regard for our poor abilities than I myself would admit. All the same, I have made some effort to respond to your letter of love, although the press of business forces me to respond more briefly than I would have liked.

We rejoice in the grace of God which is in you. And, further, we most earnestly urge and beseech you to recognize this gift as grace and to respond eagerly to it with all humility and devotion, with the knowledge that "God resisteth the proud, and giveth grace to the humble" [James 4:6; I Pet. 5:5]. But, on the other hand, when the learning and the anointing (which reveals all things to you) are within, what advice could we possibly give?

And so we ask all the more, and humbly beseech, that you remember us before God, and not only us but also those who are bound to us in spiritual community.

READING 3

St. Francis, The Rule[6]

St. Francis (1181–1226), son of a cloth merchant of the Italian hillside town of Assisi, founded a religious order that differed significantly from traditional Benedictine monasticism. His followers, the Friars Minor (Lesser Brothers) were bound to both individual and corporate proverty. Instead of being cloistered in a monastery, they worked and preached in the outside world, particularly in cities. In 1210 Francis won the provisional approval of Pope Innocent III for his brief, simple Rule consisting of carefully chosen quotations from the Bible. The Franciscan order grew so swiftly during the following decade that the original Rule of 1210 no longer sufficed. The more elaborate Rule of 1223, issued in Francis's name, was prepared by others under the authorization of Innocent's successor, Pope Honorius III. It preserves Francis's basic ideals but frames them in a much more coherent organizational structure with appropriate jurisdictional safeguards. The document should be read with an effort to untangle the original ideals from the later structure.

1. This is the rule and life of the Minor Brothers, namely, to observe the holy gospel of our Lord Jesus Christ by living in obedience, in poverty, and in chastity. Brother Francis promises obedience and reverence to Pope Honorius and to his successors who shall be canonically elected, and to the Roman Church. The other brothers are bound to obey brother Francis, and his successors.

2. If any, wishing to adopt this life, come to our brothers [to ask admission], they shall be sent to the provincial ministers, who alone have the right to receive others, into the order. The provincial ministers shall carefully examine them in the catholic faith and the sacraments of the church. And if they believe all these and faithfully confess them and promise to observe them to the end of life, and if they have no wives, or if they have wives, and the wives have either already entered a monastery, or have received permission to do so, and they have already taken the vow of chastity with the permission of the bishop of the diocese [in which they live], and their wives are of such an age that no suspicion can rise against them, let the provincial ministers repeat to them the word of the holy gospel, to go and sell all their goods and give to the poor [Matt. 19:21]. But if they are not able to do so, their good will is sufficient for them. And the brothers and provincial ministers shall not be solicitous about the temporal possessions of

[6]From *A Source Book for Mediaeval History,* ed. and tr. O. J. Thatcher and E. H. McNeal; New York, Charles Scribner's Sons, 1905, pp. 498–504.

those who wish to enter the order; but let them do with their possessions whatever the Lord may put into their minds to do. Nevertheless, if they ask the advice of the brothers, the provincial ministers may send them to God-fearing men,
at whose advice they may give their possessions to the poor. The ministers shall
give them the dress of a novice, namely: two robes without a hood, a girdle,
trousers, a hood with a cape reaching to the girdle. But the ministers may add to
these if they think it necessary. After the year of probation is ended they shall be
received into obedience [that is, into the order], by promising to observe this
rule and life forever. And according to the command of the pope they shall
never be permitted to leave the order and give up this life and form of religion.
For according to the holy gospel no one who puts his hand to the plough and
looks back is fit for the kingdom of God [Luke 9:62]. And after they have promised obedience, those who wish may have one robe with a hood and one without
a hood. Those who must may wear shoes, and all the brothers shall wear common clothes, and they shall have God's blessing if they patch them with coarse
cloth and pieces of other kinds of cloth. But I warn and exhort them not to despise nor judge other men who wear fine and gay clothing, and have delicious
foods and drinks. But rather let each one judge and despise himself.

3. The clerical brothers shall perform the divine office according to the rite
of the holy Roman church, except the psalter, from which they may have bre-
viaries. The lay brothers shall say 24 Paternosters at matins, 5 at lauds, 7 each at
primes, terces, sexts, and nones, 12 at vespers, 7 at completorium, and prayers
for the dead. And they shall fast from All Saints' day [November 1] to Christmas. They may observe or not, as they choose, the holy Lent which begins at
epiphany [January 6] and lasts for 40 days, and which our Lord consecrated by
his holy fasts. Those who keep it shall be blessed of the Lord, but those who do
not wish to keep it are not bound to do so. But they shall all observe the other
Lent [that is, from Ash Wednesday to Easter]. The rest of the time the brothers
are bound to fast only on Fridays. But in times of manifest necessity they shall
not fast. But I counsel, warn, and exhort my brothers in the Lord Jesus Christ
that when they go out into the world they shall not be quarrelsome or con-
tentious, nor judge others. But they shall be gentle, peaceable, and kind, mild
and humble, and virtuous in speech, as is becoming to all. They shall not ride on
horseback unless compelled by manifest necessity or infirmity to do so. When
they enter a house they shall say, "Peace be to this house." According to the
holy gospel, they may eat of whatever food is set before them.

4. I strictly forbid all the brothers to accept money or property either in person or through another. Nevertheless, for the needs of the sick, and for clothing
the other brothers, the ministers and guardians may, as they see that necessity requires, provide through spiritual friends, according to the locality, season, and
the degree of cold which may be expected in the region where they live. But, as
has been said, they shall never receive money or property.

5. Those brothers to whom the Lord has given the ability to work shall work faithfully and devotedly, so that idleness, which is the enemy of the soul, may be excluded and not extinguish the spirit of prayer and devotion to which all temporal things should be subservient. As the price of their labors they may receive things that are necessary for themselves and the brothers, but not money or property. And they shall humbly receive what is given them, as is becoming to the servants of God and to those who practise the most holy poverty.

6. The brothers shall have nothing of their own, neither house, nor land, not anything, but as pilgrims and strangers in this world, serving the Lord in poverty and humility, let them confidently go asking alms. Nor let them be ashamed of this, for the Lord made himself poor for us in this world. This is that highest pitch of poverty which has made you, my dearest brothers, heirs and kings of the kingdom of heaven, which has made you poor in goods, and exalted you in virtues. Let this be your portion, which leads into the land of the living. Cling wholly to this, my most beloved brother, and you shall wish to have in this world nothing else than the name of the Lord Jesus Christ. And wherever they are, if they find brothers, let them show themselves to be of the same household, and each one may securely make known to the other his need. For if a mother loves and nourishes her child, how much more diligently should one nourish and love one's spiritual brother? And if any of them fall ill, the other brothers should serve them as they would wish to be served.

7. If any brother is tempted by the devil and commits a mortal sin, he should go as quickly as possible to the provincial minister, as the brothers have determined that recourse shall be had to the provincial ministers for such sins. If the provincial minister is a priest, he shall mercifully prescribe the penance for him. If he is not a priest, he shall, as may seem best to him, have some priest of the order prescribe the penance. And they shall guard against being angry or irritated about it, because anger and irritation hinder love in themselves and in others.

8. All the brothers must have one of their number as their general minister and servant of the whole brotherhood, and they must obey him. At his death the provincial ministers and guardians shall elect his successor at the chapter held at Pentecost, at which time all the provincial ministers must always come together at whatever place the general minister may order. And this chapter must be held once every three years, or more or less frequently, as the general minister may think best. And if at any time it shall be clear to the provincial ministers and guardians that the general minister is not able to perform the duties of his office and does not serve the best interests of the brothers, the aforesaid brothers, to whom the right of election is given, must, in the name of the Lord, elect another as general minister. After the chapter at Pentecost, the provincial ministers and guardians may, each in his own province, if it seems best to them, once in the same year convoke the brothers to a provincial chapter.

9. If a bishop forbids the brothers to preach in his diocese, they shall obey him. And no brother shall preach to the people unless the general minister of the brotherhood has examined and approved him and given him the right to preach. I also warn the brothers that in their sermons their words shall be chaste and well chosen for the profit and edification of the people. They shall speak to them of vices and virtues, punishment and glory, with brevity of speech, because the Lord made the word shortened over the earth [Rom. 9:28].

10. The ministers and servants shall visit and admonish their brothers and humbly and lovingly correct them. They shall not put any command upon them that would be against their soul and this rule. And the brothers who are subject must remember that for God's sake they have given up their own wills. Wherefore I command them to obey their ministers in all the things which they have promised the Lord to observe and which shall not be contrary to their souls and this rule. And whenever brothers know and recognize that they cannot observe this rule, let them go to their ministers, and the ministers shall lovingly and kindly receive them and treat them in such a way that the brothers may speak to them freely and treat them as lords speak to, and treat, their servants. For the ministers ought to be the servants of all the brothers. I warn and exhort the brothers in the Lord Jesus Christ to guard against all arrogance, pride, envy, avarice, care, and solicitude for this world, detraction, and murmuring. And those who cannot read need not be anxious to learn. But above all things let them desire to have the spirit of the Lord and his holy works, to pray always to God with a pure heart, and to have humility, and patience in persecution and in infirmity, and to love those who persecute us and reproach us and blame us. For the Lord says, "Love your enemies and pray for those who persecute and speak evil of you" [cf. Matt. 5:44]. "Blessed are they who suffer persecution for righteousness' sake, for theirs is the kingdom of heaven" [Matt. 5:10]. He that endureth to the end shall be saved [Matt. 10:22].

11. I strictly forbid all the brothers to have any association or conversation with women that may cause suspicion. And let them not enter nunneries, except those which the pope has given them special permission to enter. Let them not be intimate friends of men or women, lest on this account scandal arise among the brothers or about brothers.

12. If any of the brothers shall be divinely inspired to go among Saracens and other infidels they must get the permission to go from their provincial minister, who shall give his consent only to those who he sees are suitable to be sent. In addition, I command the ministers to ask the pope to assign them a cardinal of the holy Roman church, who shall be the guide, protector, and corrector of the holy church, and steadfast in the catholic faith, they may observe poverty, humility, and the holy gospel of our Lord Jesus Christ, as we have firmly promised to do. Let no man dare act contrary to this confirmation.

READING 4

Humbert of Romans, On the Formation of Preachers[7]

While both the Dominicans and the Franciscans shared certain aims such as corporate poverty and ministry to the poor, the Dominicans in particular emphasized preaching—an attribute that was embedded in their name— the Order of the Preachers. Humbert of Romans (1194–1277), for a time the Master of the Order, wrote a treatise, *On the Formation of Preachers,* that was much more than a mere how-to manual. It was a calling and even "a legitimate nucleus for a whole way of life." This selection highlights the importance of study and education in the effective composition of a sermon, values for which the Dominicans became duly famous as educators, theologians, and even inquisitors. It was no accident that one of the greatest medieval theologians—Thomas Aquinas (see Reading 9)—was a Dominican. Note in the selection's first paragraph the *sic et non* approach to argumentation, a technique that grew out of the university milieu. Indeed, much of Humbert's advice is as useful to lecturing as to preaching.

Though a grace of preaching is strictly had by God's gift, a sensible preacher still ought to do what he can to ensure that his preaching is commendable, by carefully studying what he has to preach. "The seven angels who held the seven trumpets prepared themselves to play their trumpets" (Apoc. 8:6). According to the Gloss, this means "all those who preach in imitation of the apostles." Against this, Matthew 10:19 says, "Do not consider what you are going to say." But the apostles were privileged in their preaching; those who are not so privileged are permitted to think out what to say beforehand. So Jerome says, in his comment on Ezekiel 3:1, "Eat the book": "The words of God should be stored up in our hearts and carefully examined, and only then proffered to the people."

Now there are some preachers whose preparatory study is either all devoted to subtleties, with a view to producing an intricate web of subtleties, or, at other times, it is exclusively devoted to looking for novelties, their intention, like that of the Athenians, being always to find something new to say. At other times they occupy themselves entirely with philosophical points, wanting only to win renown for their tongues. But a good preacher's concern is rather to study what is useful. When he goes back over a sermon he has prepared, he will cut out whatever strikes him as less useful and retain only what is really useful, like the apostle, who say, "You know that from the first day I entered Asia, I have not held back from you anything useful, but have declared it all to you" (Acts 20:18–20).

[7]From *Early Dominicans, Selected Writings,* ed. Simon Tugwell; New York, Paulist Press, 1982, pp. 205–208.

There are others who work hard to find a lot to say, multiplying the sections of their sermons or using too many distinctions or producing long lists of authorities or strings of arguments or illustrations; or they look for lots of different words all meaning the same thing, or they repeat the same ideas over and over again, or they produce interminable prothemes or expound a single word in all kinds of different senses. All of these are serious faults in a sermon. A reasonable amount of rain is good for the fruitfulness of the earth, but too much just swamps it. A moderate amount of food is good for the stomach, but too much revolts it. A short act of worship encourages devotion, but one that is too long just sends people to sleep. So concise preaching is useful, but it becomes useless if it goes on too long. So a good, intelligent preacher ought not to devote his attention to having a lot to say, he should rather study how to contain what he says within a reasonable limit. And if he finds that he has thought of too many things to say, he should cut back what is less useful, so that he will be giving the household a reasonable measure of wheat, like a good steward (Luke 12:42), not the whole crop that he can get hold of.

There are some people who either use nothing but arguments to make what they are saying more convincing, or else nothing but anecdotes or else nothing but authorities. It is much better to use all three, so that someone who does not respond to the one may be moved by one of the others. There are many people who respond more to one than to the others.

When these three all work together, the hook of preaching has a strong triple line attached to it, and that is a line which no fish can easily break.

We can gather from all of this that when a good preacher is working on his sermon, he should first make sure what he proposes to say is useful, like a good host making sure that the food he gets prepared for his guests is good. Then, out of such useful material, he should aim to prepare something which is not immoderately long just as a good host does not serve up absolutely everything that can be found at the butcher's, however fond he is of his guests, but he takes a moderate amount from what is best there. And thirdly he should consider how to make what he is going to say more persuasive, like a host ensuring that a meal is prepared carefully and tastefully, so that his guests will get more pleasure out of eating it and digest it with less difficulty.

Then there are some people who apply a great deal of ingenuity to finding strange texts for the sermons they are going to preach, like the man who was going to preach on the apostles Pete and Paul, and took Numbers 3:20 as his text, "The sons of Merari were Moholi and Musi." But such extraneous texts can usually only be adapted to the subject of the sermon with a considerable degree of inappropriate twisting of the sense, and they are more likely to make people laugh at the sermon than they are to edify them.

On the other hand, there are some preachers so intent on finding a text to suit the day that this very concern for appropriateness makes them overlook the criterion of usefulness, so that they take texts which contain little or nothing that is of any use to their audience. People like this should be called church cantors rather than preachers of Christ. It is the job of the church's cantors to chant the texts which are proper to the season or the feast, without regard to whether the sense of what they are singing is useful to those who listen to it or not.

Others again take a text so short that there is only one point contained in it, like people who give their guests a meal of only one dish.

Others take a longer text, containing several points, of which some are not very useful, and then give a long commentary on every little detail, whether or not it contains anything useful. That is rather like wanting to make a meal out of a cow and preparing one dish from the horns, one from the skin, another from the hoofs, and so on till the cow was quite used up. That is not a sensible way to cook. A sensible cook would make a meal out of the best parts of the animal and leave the rest.

Then there are others who take a text which contains many useful points, but spend so long expounding the first one or two points that they cannot deal with any of the others. They are like boorish people who give you such a large helping of the first course of a meal and make it go on so long that you cannot eat anything of the other courses, even though they may actually be better than the first. Hosts who are gentlemen do just the opposite. They give you many different courses, but only give you a little of each one. This style of eating is far more agreeable to the guests.

So a preacher ought to abandon all such abuses and devote his careful attention to finding a text which clearly fits his subject and which contains something useful which is adapted to his audience, and not just one point but several; and if it contains anything which is not so useful, he should give little or no time to developing it.

There are also some preachers who do not have the mental capacity to produce decent sermons themselves, but who will not stoop to studying what other people have said, insisting on saying only what they can discover for themselves. They are like people who insist on providing only bread that they have made themselves, even though they are not good bakers. This is the opposite of what we find in the gospel, where the Lord ordered bread to be distributed by the disciples: they had not made it themselves, it had already been made by somebody else (Mark 6:37ff).

I have been told that once Pope Innocent (under whom the Lateran Council was held) was to preach on some great feast. Now he was a highly educated man, but even so he had someone stand by him with St. Gregory's homily for that feast, and he preached it word for word, turning it from Latin into the vernacular, and when he could not remember what came next he asked the man with the text there to remind him. When he was asked afterwards why he had done this, when he was quite capable of finding plenty of new things to say for himself, he said that he had done it as a rebuke and lesson for people who thought it was beneath them to use other people's words in their sermons.

Then again there are others who are quite clever and intelligent enough, but who are so confident in their own cleverness that they ignore the saints' comments on Holy Scripture and rely on their own exegesis. As Jerome says, "They disdain to find out what the prophets and the apostles really meant. They fit texts to their own view which do not really fit, forcing reluctant scriptures to serve their own purposes." They are like people who imagine that bells they hear chiming are saying whatever they themselves happen to be thinking of. To quote Jerome again, "They suppose that whatever they may say is the law of God."

There are others who are more interested in their literary style than in the content of what they are saying. That is like being more interested in the beauty of the dishes in which food is served than in the food itself. As Augustine says in the *Confessions,* "I learned that wisdom and foolishness are like useful and useless kinds of food, and that elegant and inelegant words are like elegant and inelegant dishes: you can serve either kind of food in either kind of dish."

So a wise preacher should abandon these three faults, and study what others have said about the bible, and rely more on the saints' interpretations than on his own, and prefer good content in what he says to good style.

READING 5

The Albigensian Heresy[8]

This account, written between 1208 and 1213, antedates the Fourth Lateran Council (Reading 7) by only a few years and helps explain the council's severely anti-Albigensian stance. Although it is more nearly a diatribe than an objective work of investigative reporting, it does make clear that, by Catholic standards, the Albigensian (or Cathar) beliefs were quite exotic. Blending Christian ideas with the religious dualism of ancient Persia, the Albigensians appear to have been not only anti-Catholic but anti-Semitic as well.

The question remains, To what extent can a document of this sort be trusted? Could one trust an analysis of the United States government in an Iraqi government newspaper? Or a discussion of Catholic doctrine written by an Albigensian? The answer is not simple. Perhaps one might expect such hostile testimony to be more or less accurate in its general outline but selective or deceptive in detail. To what degree does the following document provide a believable picture?

[8]From *Heresies of the High Middle Ages,* ed. Walter L. Wakefield and Austin P. Evans; New York, Columbia University Press, 1969, pp. 231–235. Reprinted by permission.

The group of heretics inhabiting our region, that is to say, the dioceses of Narbonne, Béziers, Carcassonne, Toulouse, Albi, Rodez, Cahors, Agen, and Perigueux [all in southern France], believe and have the effrontery to say that there are two gods, that is, a good God and a strange god, using the text of Jeremiah: "As you have forsaken me," He said, "and served a strange god in your own land, so you shall serve strangers in a land not your own." The present world and all that is visible therein, they declare, were created and made by the malign god, for they show by whatever arguments they can command that these are evil. Of the world they say that it is "wholly seated in wickedness," and that "a good tree cannot bring forth evil fruit, neither can an evil tree bring forth good fruit." They hold that all good things come from the good God and from the evil one all evil things. The Mosaic law, they say, was imparted by the evil god, for they cite from the words of the Apostle, "The Law is one of sin and death" and "worketh wrath." They declare that when Christ gave the bread of His disciples, He told them, "Take ye and eat," and, touching Himself with His hand, said, "This is my body"; wherefore they do not believe that anyone consecrates the Host. They speak slightingly of marriage of the flesh because Christ said, "Whoever shall look on a woman," and so on. They reject baptism of children performed with actual water because children do not have faith, for which they cite the Gospel, "He that believeth not shall be condemned." They do not believe in the resurrection of the bodies of this world, for Paul said, "Flesh and blood cannot possess the kingdom of God." Whatever is ritually observed in the Church Universal they call vain and absurd, for they hold that doctrine to be a thing of men and without basis, whereby one worships God in vain.

In their secret meetings their elders recount that the wicked god first fashioned his creatures and at the beginning of his act of creation, made four beings, two male and two female, a lion and a bee-eater, an eagle and a spirit. The good God took from him the spirit and the eagle and with them He produced the things which He made. After a long time, the malign god, enraged by his spoliation, sent a certain son of his, whom they call Melchizedek, Seir, or Lucifer, with a great and splendid host of men and women to the court of the good God, to find whether guile might not avenge his father for his own. And on beholding him distinguished in beauty and intelligence, the good God appointed him prince, priest, and steward over His own people, and through him gave a testament to the people of Israel. In the absence of the Lord, he beguiled the people into disbelief of the truth, promising them that much more, better, and delightful things than those which they had in their own land would be given them in his. They yielded to his blandishments, spurning their God and the testament given them. He bore away some of them and scattered them throughout his realms. The more noble, a designation which these people took to themselves, he sent into this world, which they call the last lake, the farthest earth, and the deepest hell. He sent the souls, so they say, leaving the bodies prostrate in the desert, abandoned by the spirits, for as John says in the Apocalypse, "The great dragon, that old serpent, devil and Satan, struck with his tail the third part of the stars and dashed them to earth." Such, they say, are "the sheep which are lost of the house of Israel," to whom Christ was sent, as He himself says in the Gospel: "The Son of man is come to seek and to save that which was lost"; and also, "The Son of man came not to destroy souls but to save." That Seir, as they assert, was the father of the lawgiver, for which they cite in the Law: "The Lord came from Sinai, and from Seir he was born to us"; and in Ezechiel, "Son of man, set thy face against Mount Seir, and prophesy concerning it, and say to it: Behold, Mount Seir, and I will make thee desolate and waste. I will destroy thy cities and thou shalt be desolate; and thou shalt know that I am the Lord, because thou hast been an everlasting enemy and hast shut up the children of Israel in the hands of the sword." Also, they say that the malign god exists without beginning or end, and rules as many and as extensive lands, heavens, people and creatures as the good God. The present world, they say, will never pass away or be depopulated. They have the daring to assert that the Blessed Mary, mother of Christ, was not of this world. For they say in their secret meetings that Christ, in whom they hope for salvation, was not in this world except in a spiritual sense within the body of Paul, citing Paul himself: "Do you seek a proof of Christ that speaketh in me?" For they say that Paul, "sold under sin," brought the Scriptures into this world and was held prisoner, that he might reveal the ministry of Christ.

For they believe that Christ was born in the "land of the living," of Joseph and Mary, whom they say were Adam and Eve; there He suffered and rose again; thence He ascended to His Father; there He did and said all that was recorded of Him in the New Testament. With this testament, and with His disciples, His father and mother, He passed through seven realms, and thence freed His people. In that land of the living, they believe, there are cities and outside them castles, villages and woodlands, meadows, pastures, sweet water and salt, beasts of the forest and domestic animals, dogs and birds for the hunt, gold and silver, utensils of various kinds, and furniture. They also say that everyone shall have his wife there and sometimes a mistress. They shall eat and drink, play and sleep, and do all things just as they do in the world of the present. And all will be, as they say, well pleasing to God when "the saints shall rejoice in glory; they shall be joyful in their beds," and when they shall have "two-edged swords in their hands to execute vengeance upon the nations," and when the children of Zion shall praise His name in choir and with the timbrel, for "this glory will be to all his saints." For God himself, they say, has two wives, Collam and Colibam, and from the He engendered sons and daughters, as do humans. On the basis of this belief, some of them hold there is no sin in man and woman kissing and embracing each other, or even lying together for intercourse, nor can one sin in doing so for payment.

They also believe that when the soul leaves the human body, it passes to another body, either of a human or of a beast, unless the person shall have died while under their instruction. If, however, he shall have died while continuing steadfast among them, they say that the soul goes to a new earth, prepared by God for all the souls that are to be saved, where it finds clothing, that is, the body prepared for it by its own father and mother. There all await the general resurrection which they shall experience, so they say, in the land of the living, with all their inheritance which they shall recover by force of arms. For they say that until then they shall possess that land of the malign spirit and shall make use of the clothing of the sheep, and shall eat the good things of the earth, and shall not depart thence until all Israel is saved. Also they teach in their secret meetings that Mary Magdalen was the wife of Christ. She was the Samaritan woman to whom He said, "Call thy husband." She was the woman taken in adultery, whom Christ set free lest the Jews stone her, and she was with Him in three places, in the temple, at the well, and in the garden. After the Resurrection, He appeared first to her. They say that John the Baptist is one of the chief malign spirits.

READING 6
The Waldensian Heresy[9]

The same questions should be asked of this source as of the previous one. The author, Rainier Sacconi (fl. 1245), was an inquisitor, and his testimony can therefore be expected to be both well informed and unsympathetic. Compare the canon of the Fourth Lateran Council (Reading 7) relating to the priest's role in the consecration of the eucharist.

The doctrines described here were first promulgated in the later twelfth century by a townsman of Lyons (southern France) named Valdes, or "Waldo." He and his followers are customarily called Waldensians by modern historians but were known at the time as the "Poor Men of Lyons." Which of the two doctrines, Waldensian or Albigensian, came closest to anticipating modern Protestant beliefs?

We have said enough of the heresy of the Cathars. Now let us turn to that of the *Leonistae,* or Poor Men of Lyons. They are divided into two parts, the Poor Men from North of the Alps [*Pauperes Ultramontani*] and the Poor Men of Lombardy, the latter being descended from the former.

The first, the Poor Men from across the Alps, say that the New Testament prohibits all swearing as mortal sin. They also reject secular justice, on the

[9]From *The Birth of Popular Heresy,* (Documents of Medieval History Series), ed. and tr. R. I. Moore; London, Edward Arnold, Ltd., 1975, pp. 144–145. Reprinted by permission.

ground that kings, princes and potentates ought not to punish evil-doers. They say that an ordinary layman may consecrate the body of the Lord, and I believe that they apply this to women as well for they have never denied it to me. They allege that the Roman Church is not the Church of Jesus Christ.

The Poor Men of Lombardy agree with the others about swearing and secular justice. On the eucharist they are even worse, holding that it may be consecrated by any man who is not in mortal sin. They say that the Roman Church is a church of evil, the beast and harlot which are found in the Book of Revelations, and that it is no sin to eat meat during Lent or on Friday against the precept of the Church, if it is done without offence to others.

They also say that the Church of Christ remained in bishops and other prelates until St. Sylvester, and failed in him, until they themselves restored it, though they do say there have always been some who have feared God and been saved. They believe that children can be saved without baptism.

This work was faithfully compiled by Brother Rainier in A.D. 1250. Deo Gratias.

READING 7

A Canon from the Fourth Lateran Council[10]

In 1215 Pope Innocent III presided over a universal council of the Church at his Lateran basilica in Rome. More than 1,200 prelates attended, including the patriarchs of Jerusalem and recently conquered Constantinople, along with envoys from all the kingdoms and major principalities of Christendom. The canons (decrees) of the Fourth Lateran Council reflect the efforts of the high medieval papacy to reform, systematize, and standardize religious practice throughout Europe. Among other things, clerical dress was standardized; bishops were ordered to preach regularly and to maintain schools; priests were forbidden to participate in judicial ordeals and to charge fees for performing sacraments; lay people were commanded to do penance and receive the eucharist at least once a year.

The excerpt below illustrates the Church's concern over the spread of the Albigensian and Waldensian heresies, with their denial of papal authority and of the priesthood's exclusive power to perform the sacrament of the eucharist. Notice the emphasis on combating heresy by force, through the Albigensian Crusade (then in full gallop) and accompanying judicial proceedings. The Church's response to heresy bears some similarity to the response of modern states to treason.

---

[10]From *Disciplinary Decrees of the General Councils*, ed. and tr. H. J. Schroeder, St. Louis, B. Herder Book Co., 1937, pp. 242–244.

CANON 3

We excommunicate and anathematize every heresy that raises itself against the holy, orthodox and Catholic faith which we have above explained; condemning all heretics under whatever name they may be known, for while they have different faces, they are nevertheless bound to each other by their tails, since in all of them vanity is a common element. Those condemned, being handed over to the secular rulers or their bailiffs, let them be abandoned, to be punished with due justice, clerics being first degraded from their orders. As to the property of the condemned, if they are laymen, let it be confiscated; if clerics, let it be applied to the churches from which they received revenues. But those who are only suspected, due consideration being given to the nature of the suspicion and the character of the person, unless they prove their innocence by a proper defense, let them be anathematized and avoided by all until they have made suitable satisfaction; but if they have been under excommunication for one year, then let them be condemned as heretics. Secular authorities, whatever office they may hold, shall be admonished and induced and if necessary compelled by ecclesiastical censure, that as they wish to be esteemed and numbered among the faithful, so for the defense of the faith they ought publicly to take an oath that they will strive in good faith and to the best of their ability to exterminate in the territories subject to their jurisdiction all heretics pointed out by the Church; so that whenever anyone shall have assumed authority, whether spiritual or temporal, let him be bound to confirm this decree by oath. But if a temporal ruler, after having been requested and admonished by the Church, should neglect to cleanse his territory of this heretical foulness, let him be excommunicated by the metropolitan and the other bishops of the province. If he refuses to make satisfaction within a year, let the matter be made known to the supreme pontiff, that he may declare the ruler's vassals absolved from their allegiance and may offer the territory to be ruled by Catholics, who on the extermination of the heretics may possess it without hindrance and preserve it in the purity of faith; the right, however, of the chief ruler is to be respected so long as he offers no obstacle in this matter and permits freedom of action. The same law is to be observed in regard to those who have no chief rulers (that is, are independent). Catholics who have girded themselves with the cross for the extermination of the heretics shall enjoy the indulgences and privileges granted to those who go in defense of the Holy Land.

We decree that those who give credence to the teachings of the heretics, as well as those who receive, defend, and patronize them, are excommunicated; and we firmly declare that after any one of them has been branded with excommunication, if he has deliberately failed to make satisfaction within a year, let him incur *ipso jure* the stigma of infamy and let him not be admitted to public offices or deliberations, and let him not take part in the election of others to such offices or use his right to give testimony in a court of law. Let him also be intestable, that he may not have the free exercise of making a will, and let him be deprived of the right of inheritance. Let no one be urged to give an account to him in any matter, but let him be urged to give an account to others. If perchance he be a judge, let his decisions have no force, nor let any case be brought to his attention. If he be an advocate, let his assistance by no means be sought. If a notary, let the instruments drawn up by him be considered worthless, for, the author being condemned, let them enjoy a similar fate. In all similar cases we command that the same be observed. If, however, he be a cleric, let him be deposed from every office and benefice, that the greater the fault the graver may be punishment inflicted.

If any refuse to avoid such after they have been ostracized by the Church, let them be excommunicated till they have made suitable satisfaction. Clerics shall not give the sacraments of the Church to such pestilential people, nor shall they presume to give them Christian burial, or to receive their alms or offerings; otherwise they shall be deprived of their office, to which they may not be restored without a special indult of the Apostolic See. Similarly, all regulars, on whom also this punishment may be imposed, let their privileges by nullified in that diocese in which they have presumed to perpetrate such excesses.

But since some, under "the appearance of godliness, but denying the power thereof," as the Apostle says (II Tim. 3:5), arrogate to themselves the authority to preach, as the same Apostle says: "How shall they preach unless they be sent?" (Rom. 10:15), all those prohibited or not sent, who, without the authority of the Apostolic See or of the Catholic bishop of the locality, shall presume to usurp the office of preaching either publicly or privately, shall be excommunicated and unless they amend, and the sooner the better, they shall be visited with a further suitable penalty. We add, moreover, that every archbishop or bishop should himself or through his archdeacon or some other suitable persons, twice or at least once a year make the rounds of his diocese in which report has it that heretics dwell, and there compel three or more men of good character or, if it should be deemed advisable, the entire neighborhood, to swear that if anyone know of the presence there of heretics or others holding secret assemblies, or differing from the common way of the faithful in faith and morals, they will make them known to the bishop. The latter shall then call together before him those accused, who, if they do not purge themselves of the matter of which they are accused, or if after the rejection of their error they lapse into their former wickedness, shall be canonically punished. But if any of them by damnable obstinacy should disapprove of the oath and should perchance be unwilling to swear, from this very fact let them be regarded as heretics.

We wish, therefore, and in virtue of obedience strictly command, that to carry out these instructions effectively the bishops exercise through their dioceses a scrupulous vigilance if they wish to escape canonical punishment. If from sufficient evidence it is apparent that a bishop is negligent or remiss in cleansing his diocese of the ferment of heretical wickedness, let him be deposed from the episcopal office and let another, who will and can confound heretical depravity, be substituted.

READING 8
St. Anselm, The Ontological Argument[11]

A native of northwestern Italy, St. Anselm (d. 1109) migrated to Normandy to become a monk, and later an abbot, of the monastery of Bec. In 1093 he became archbishop of Canterbury and was twice exiled as a result of conflicts with the Anglo-Norman monarchy over ecclesiastical liberties.

Anselm was a devotee of St. Augustine (d. 430), who was himself influenced by Plato's doctrine of the superiority of meditation to observation. Notice that Anselm's ontological argument is more nearly a meditation—"faith seeking understanding," in Anselm's words—than a formal proof, and that it depends on pure reason rather than on the workings of the physical world. One must bear in mind that Anselm is addressing monks rather than students or skeptics. He is writing to believers, with the aim of helping them understand more fully the faith to which they have already committed their lives.

After I had published, at the solicitous entreaties of certain brethren, a brief work (the *Monologion)* as an example of meditation on the grounds of faith, in the person of one who investigates, in a course of silent reasoning with himself, matters of which he is ignorant; considering that this book was knit together by the linking of many arguments, I began to ask myself whether there might be found a single argument which would require no other for its proof than itself alone; and alone would suffice to demonstrate that God truly exists, and that there is a supreme good requiring nothing else, which all other things require for their existence and well-being; and whatever we believe regarding the divine Being.

Although I often and earnestly directed my thought to this end, and at some times that which I sought seemed to be just within my reach, while again it wholly evaded my mental vision, at last in despair I was about to cease, as if from the search for a thing which could not be found. But when I wished to exclude this thought altogether, lest, by busying my mind to no purpose, it should keep me from other thoughts, in which I might be successful; then more and more, though I was unwilling and shunned it, it began to force itself upon me, with a kind of importunity. So, one day, when I was exceedingly wearied with resisting its importunity, in the very conflict of my thoughts, the proof of which I had despaired offered itself, so that I eagerly embraced the thoughts which I was strenuously repelling.

[11]From *The Basic Writings of St. Anselm,* tr. S. N. Deane; La Salle, Ill., The Open Court Publishing Co., 1903, pp. 1–11.

Thinking, therefore, that what I rejoiced to have found, would, if put in writing, be welcome to some readers, of this very matter, and of some others, I have written the following treatise, in the person of one who strives to lift his mind to the contemplation of God, and seeks to understand what he believes. In my judgment, neither this work nor the other, which I mentioned above, deserved to be called a book, or to bear the name of an author; and yet I thought they ought not to be sent forth without some title by which they might, in some sort, invite one into whose hands they fell to their perusal. I accordingly gave each a title, that the first might be known as, An Example of Meditation on the Grounds of Faith, and its sequel as, Faith Seeking Understanding.

Be it mine to look up to thy light, even from afar, even from the depths. Teach me to seek thee, and reveal thyself to me when I seek thee, for I cannot seek thee, except thou teach me, nor find thee, except thou reveal thyself. Let me seek thee in longing, let me long for thee in seeking; let me find thee in love, and love thee in finding. Lord, I acknowledge and I thank thee that thou hast created me in this thine image, in order that I may be mindful of thee, may I conceive of thee, and love thee; but that image has been so consumed and wasted away by vices, and obscured by the smoke of wrongdoing, that it cannot achieve that for which it was made, except thou renew it, and create it anew. I do not endeavor, O Lord, to penetrate thy sublimity, for in no wise do I compare my understanding with that; but I long to understand in some degree thy truth, which my heart believes and loves. For I do not seek to understand that I may believe, but I believe in order to understand. For this also I believe—that unless I believed, I should not understand.

And so, Lord, do thou, who dost give understanding to faith, give me, so far as thou knowest it to be profitable, to understand that thou art as we believe; and that thou art that which we believe. And, indeed, we believe that thou art a being than which nothing greater can be conceived. Or is there no such nature, since the fool hath said in his heart, there is no God (Psalms 14:1)? But, at any rate, this very fool, when he hears of this being of which I speak—a being than which nothing greater can be conceived—understands what he hears, and what he understands is in his understanding; although he does not understand it to exist.

For, it is one thing for an object to be in the understanding, and another to understand that the object exists. When a painter first conceives of what he will afterwards perform, he has it in his understanding, but he does not yet understand it to be, because he has not yet performed it. But after he has made the painting, he both has it in his understanding, and he understands that it exists, because he has made it.

Hence, even the fool is convinced that something exists in the understanding, at least, than which nothing greater can be conceived. For, when he hears of this, he understands it. And whatever is understood, exists in the understanding. And assuredly that, than which nothing greater can be conceived, cannot exist in the understanding alone. For, suppose it exists in the understanding alone: then it can be conceived to exist in reality; which is greater.

Therefore, if that, than which nothing greater can be conceived, exists in the understanding alone, the very being, than which nothing greater can be conceived, is one, than which a greater can be conceived. But obviously this is impossible. Hence, there is no doubt that there exists a being, than which nothing greater can be conceived, and it exists both in the understanding and in reality.

And it assuredly exists so truly, that it cannot be conceived not to exist. For, it is possible to conceive of a being which cannot be conceived not to exist; and this is greater than one which can be conceived not to exist. Hence, if that, than which nothing greater can be conceived, can be conceived not to exist, it is not that, than which nothing greater can be conceived. But this is an irreconcilable contradiction. There is, then, so truly a being than which nothing greater can be conceived to exist, that it cannot even be conceived not to exist; and this being thou art, O Lord, our God.

So truly, therefore, dost thou exist, O Lord, my God, that thou canst not be conceived not to exist; and rightly. For, if a mind could conceive of a being better than thee, the creature would rise above the Creator; and this is most absurd. And, indeed, whatever else there is, except thee alone, can be conceived not to exist. To thee alone, therefore, it belongs to exist more truly than all other beings, and hence in a higher degree than all others. For, whatever else exists does not exist so truly, and hence in a less degree it belongs to it to exist. Why, then, has the fool said in his heart, there is no God (Psalms 14:1), since it is so evident, to a rational mind, that thou dost exist in the highest degree of all? Why, except that he is dull and a fool?

But how has the fool said in his heart what he could not conceive; or how is it that he could not conceive what he said in his heart—since it is the same to say in the heart, and to conceive?

But, if really, nay, since really, he both conceived, because he said in his heart; and did not say in his heart, because he could not conceive; there is more than one way in which a thing is said in the heart or conceived. For, in one sense, an object is conceived, when the word signifying it is conceived; and in another when the very entity, which the object is, is understood.

In the former sense, then, God can be conceived not to exist; but in the latter, not at all. For no one who understands what fire and water are can conceive fire to be water, in accordance with the nature of the facts themselves, although this is possible according to the words. So, then, no one who understands what God is can conceive that God does not exist; although he says these words in his heart, either without any, or with some foreign, signification. For, God is that than which a greater cannot be conceived. And he who thoroughly understands this, assuredly understands that this being so truly exists, that not even in concept can it be nonexistent. Therefore, he who understands that God so exists, cannot conceive that he does not exist.

I thank thee, gracious Lord, I thank thee; because what I formerly believed by thy bounty, I now so understand by thine illumination, that if I were unwilling to believe that thou dost exist, I should not be able to understand this to be true.

What art thou, then, Lord God, than whom nothing greater can be conceived? But what art thou, except that which, as the highest of all beings' alone exists through itself, and creates all other things from nothing? For, whatever is not this is less than a thing which can be conceived of. But this cannot be conceived of thee. What good, therefore, does the supreme God lack, through which every good is? Therefore, thou art just, truthful, blessed, and whatever it is better to be than not to be. For it is better to be just than not just; better to be blessed than not blessed.

READING 9

Al-Ghazali, Deliverance from Error[12]

Medieval Europe owed a massive cultural debt to Islamic civilizations. Rhymed poetry, algebra, the pointed arch that made Gothic architecture possible, even chivalry, all had some roots in Muslim cultures. Just as significant were the ideas that Islam nurtured and transmitted: Indic numerals (our familiar counting system), medieval Jewish thought, and vast amounts of classical literature, especially the works of Aristotle, arrived in Europe through Muslim intermediaries.

The contributions of Muslim philosophers were one germ of the revival of speculative thought in the West. Islam, like Christianity, was monotheistic, and insisted on a single deity who created the universe out of divine will alone; and, like Christianity, Islamic philosophers puzzled over the relationship between sacred revelation and human observation. Finally, Islam, too, inherited the classical legacy of Plato and Aristotle, whose careful and imposing world views were as satisfying as those of religious authorities, but vastly different. The consequence was doubt, speculation, creativity, and insight.

Abu Hamed al-Ghazali (1058–1111) is one such philosopher-theologian. More than a half millennium before René Descartes wrote his celebrated *Discourse on Method,* with its exploration of systematic doubt, al-Ghazali engaged in the same process. Al-Ghazali's approach to problems of doubt and certainty invites comparisons to both Anselm and Abelard.

---

[12]From W. Montgomery Watt, *The Faith and Practice of Al-Ghazali;* Chicago, Kazi Publications, 1982, pp. 19–26.

You must know—and may God most high perfect you in the right way and soften your hearts to receive the truth—that the different religious observances and religious communities of the human race and likewise the different theological systems of the religious leaders, with all the multiplicity of sects and variety of practices, constitute ocean depths in which the majority drown and only a minority reach safety. . . .

From my early youth, since I attained the age of puberty before I was twenty, until the present time when I am over fifty, I have ever recklessly launched out into the midst of these ocean depths, I have ever bravely embarked on this open sea, throwing aside all craven caution; I have poked into every dark recess, I have made an assault on every problem, I have plunged into every abyss, I have scrutinized the creed of every sect, I have tried to lay bare the inmost doctrines of every community. All this have I done that I might distinguish between true and false, between sound tradition and heretical innovation. . . .

To thirst after a comprehension of things as they really are was my habit and custom from a very early age. It was instinctive with me, a part of my God-given nature, a matter of temperament and not of my choice or contriving. Consequently as I drew near the age of adolescence the bonds of mere authority ceased to hold me and inherited beliefs lost their grip upon me . . . I therefore said within myself: "To begin with, what I am looking for is knowledge of what things really are, so I must undoubtedly try to find what knowledge really is." It was plain to me that sure and certain knowledge is that knowledge in which the object is disclosed in such a fashion that no doubt remains along with it, that no possibility of error or illusion accompanies it, and that the mind cannot even entertain, such a supposition. Certain knowledge must also be infallible. . . . After these reflections I knew that whatever I do not know in this fashion and with this mode of certainty is not reliable and infallible knowledge; and knowledge that is not infallible is not certain knowledge.

Thereupon I investigated the various kinds of knowledge I had, and found myself destitute of all knowledge with this characteristic of infallibility except in the case of sense-perception and necessary truths. . . . I proceeded therefore with extreme earnestness to reflect on sense-perception and on necessary truths, to see whether I could make myself doubt them. The outcome of this protracted effort to induce doubt was that I could no longer trust sense-perception.

When these thoughts had occurred to me and penetrated my being, I tried to find some way of treating my unhealthy condition; but it was not easy. Such ideas can only be repelled by demonstration; but a demonstration needs a combination of first principles; since this is not admitted, however, it is impossible to make the demonstration. The disease was baffling, and lasted almost two months, during which I was a skeptic in fact though not in theory nor in outward expression. At length God cured me of the malady; my being was restored to health and an even balance; the necessary truths of the intellect became once more accepted, as I regained confidence in their certain and trustworthy character.

This did not come about by systematic demonstration or marshaled argument, but by a light which God most high cast into my breast. That light is the key to the greater part of knowledge. Whoever thinks that the understanding of things Divine rest upon strict proofs has in his thought narrowed down the wideness of God's mercy. When the Messenger of God (peace be upon him) was asked about "enlarging" and its meaning in the verse, "Whenever God wills to guide a man, He enlarges his breast for Islam" [Koran 6:125], he said, "It is a light which God most high casts into the heart, and from that light must be sought an intuitive understanding of things Divine. That light at certain times gushes from the spring of Divine generosity, and for it one must watch and wait—as Muhammad (peace be upon him) said: "In the days of your age your Lord has gusts of favour; then place yourselves in the way of them.""

READING 10
Peter Abelard, Sic et Non[13]

Peter Abelard's (1079–1142) *Sic et Non* ("Yes and No") intrigued his students and deeply annoyed many of his conservative contemporaries by pitting divergent authoritative opinions—from the Bible, Church fathers, and papal councils—against one another. The reconciliation of divergent opinions was to become a basic methodology in both medieval theology and medieval law. Abelard, however, got into trouble by declining to reconcile the contradictory views that he set forth, leaving it to his students to resolve such issues as whether anything happens by chance, whether it is permissible to lie, and whether sin is pleasing to God. Abelard's use of reason to refine faith is characteristic of medieval scholasticism.

Among the many words of the holy fathers some seem not only to differ from one another but even to contradict one another. Hence it is not presumptuous to judge concerning those by whom the world itself will be judged. Bearing in mind our foolishness, we believe that our understanding is defective rather than the writings of those to whom truth himself said, "It is not you who speak but the spirit of your father who speaks in you." Why should it seem surprising if we, lacking the guidance of the holy spirit, fail to understand them?

Our achievement of understanding is impeded especially by unusual modes of expression and by the different significances that can be attached to one and

---

[13]From Peter Abelard, *Sic et Non (Yes and No) 1138,* ed. and tr. Brian Tierney, *Sources of Medieval History,* 4th edition; New York, Alfred Knopf, 1983, pp. 172–175.

the same word. We must also take special care that we are not deceived by corruptions of the text or by false attributions when sayings of the fathers are quoted that seem to differ from the truth or to be contrary to it; for many apocryphal writings are set down under names of saints to enhance their authority, and even the texts of the divine scripture are corrupted by the errors of scribes. If, in scripture, anything seems absurd, you are not permitted to say, "The author of this book did not hold the truth," but rather that the book is defective or that the interpreter erred or that you do not understand. But if anything seems contrary to truth in the works of later authors, the reader or auditor is free to judge, so that he may approve what is pleasing and reject what gives offence, unless the matter is established by certain reason or canonical authority.

In view of these considerations we have undertaken to collect various sayings of the fathers that give rise to questioning because of their apparent contradictions. Assiduous and frequent questioning is indeed the first key to wisdom. For by doubting we come to inquiry; and through inquiring we perceive the truth.

READING 11

St. Thomas Aquinas, The Existence of God[14]

St. Thomas Aquinas (c. 1225–1274) was a Dominican friar who became the greatest of the scholastic philosophers. He was a prolific writer, whose most important work was the reconciling of pagan philosophies, especially those of Averroes and Aristotle, with Christian thought. The following passage gives "the five ways of St. Thomas," five proofs for the existence of God. The arguments rest largely on observation, not on introspection as Anselm's ontological argument does (see pp. 256–259). This passage offers a sketch of Thomas's methodical approach and demonstrates his careful mix of natural reason and revealed religion.

ARTICLE 1.   IS IT SELF-EVIDENT THAT THERE IS A GOD?

I maintain then that the proposition "God exists" is self-evident in itself, for, as we shall see later, its subject and predicate are identical, since God is his own existence. But, because what it is to be God is not evident to us, the proposition is not self-evident to us, and needs to be made evident. This is done by means of

[14]From Thomas Aquinas, *Summa Theologiae,* ed. Thomas Gilby, O.P.; New York, Image Books, 1969, pp. 64–70.

things which, though less evident in themselves, are nevertheless more evident to us, by means, namely, of God's effects.

The awareness that God exists is not implanted in us by nature in any clear or specific way. Admittedly, man is by nature aware of what by nature he desires, and he desires by nature a happiness which is to be found only in God. But this is not, simply speaking, awareness that there is a God, any more than to be aware of someone approaching is to be aware of Peter, even should it be Peter approaching: many, in fact, believe the ultimate good which will make us happy to be riches, or pleasure, or some such thing.

Someone hearing the word "God" may very well not understand it to mean "that than which nothing greater can be thought," indeed, some people have believed God to be a body. And even if the meaning of the word "God" were generally recognized to be "that than which nothing greater can be thought," nothing thus defined would thereby be granted existence in the world of fact, but merely as thought about. Unless one is given that something in fact exists than which nothing greater can be thought—and this nobody denying the existence of God would grant—the conclusion that God in fact exists does not follow.

ARTICLE 2.   CAN IT BE MADE EVIDENT?

The truths about God which St. Paul says we can know by our natural powers of reasoning—that God exists, for example—are not numbered among the articles of faith, but are presupposed to them. For faith presupposes natural knowledge, just as grace presupposes nature and all perfections presuppose that which they perfect. However, there is nothing to stop a man accepting on faith some truth which he personally cannot demonstrate, even if that truth in itself is such that demonstration could make it evident.

Effects can give comprehensive knowledge of their cause only when commensurate with it: but, as we have said, any effect whatever can make it clear that a cause exists. God's effects, therefore, can serve to demonstrate that God exists, even though they cannot help us know him comprehensively for what he is.

ARTICLE 3.   IS THERE A GOD?

[Objections to the affirmative:]

1. It seems that there is no God. For if, of two mutually exclusive things, one were to exist without limit, the other would cease to exist. But by the word "God" is implied some limitless good. If God then existed, nobody would ever encounter evil. But evil is encountered in the world. God therefore does not exist.

2. Moreover, if a few causes fully account for some effect, one does not seek more. Now it seems that everything we observe in this world can be fully

accounted for by other causes, without assuming a God. Thus natural effects are explained by natural causes, and contrived effects by human reasoning and will. There is therefore no need to suppose that a God exists.

[Reply: There are five ways in which one can prove that there is a God.]

The first and most obvious way is based on change. Some things in the world are certainly in process of change: this we plainly see. Now anything in process of change is being changed by something else. This is so because it is characteristic of things in process of change that they do not yet have the perfection toward which they move, though able to have it; whereas it is characteristic of something causing change to have that perfection already. For to cause change is to bring into being what was previously only able to be, and this can only be done by something that already is: thus fire, which is actually hot, causes wood, which is able to be hot, to be become actually hot, and in this way causes change in the wood. Now the same thing cannot at the same time be both actually X and potentially X, though it can be actually X and potentially Y: the actually hot cannot at the same time be potentially hot, though it can be potentially cold. Consequently, a thing in process of change cannot itself cause that same change; it cannot change itself. Of necessity therefore anything in process of change is being changed by something else. Moreover, this something else, if in process of change, is itself being changed by yet another thing; and this last by another. Now we must stop somewhere, otherwise there will be no first cause of the change, and, as a result, no subsequent causes. For it is only when acted upon by the first cause that the intermediate causes will produce the change: if the hand does not move the stick, the stick will not move anything else. Hence one is bound to arrive at some first cause of change not itself being changed by anything, and this is what everybody understands by God.

The second way is based on the nature of causation. In the observable world causes are found to be ordered in series; we never observe, nor ever could, something causing itself; for this would mean it preceded itself, and this is not possible. Such a series of causes must however stop somewhere; for in it an earlier member causes an intermediate and the intermediate a last (whether the intermediate be one or many). Now if you eliminate a cause you also eliminate its effects, so that you cannot have a last cause, nor an intermediate one, unless you have a first. Given therefore no stop in the series of causes, and hence no first cause, there would be no intermediate causes either, and no last effect, and this would be an open mistake. One is therefore forced to suppose some first cause, to which everyone gives the name "God."

The third way is based on what need not be and on what must be, and runs as follows. Some of the things we come across can be but need not be; for we find them springing up and dying away, thus sometimes in being and sometimes not. Now everything cannot be like this, for a thing that need not be, once was not;

and if everything need not be, once upon a time there was nothing. But if that were true there would be nothing even now, because something that does not exist can only be brought into being by something already existing. So that if nothing was in being nothing could be brought into being, and nothing would be in being now, which contradicts observation. Not everything therefore is the sort of thing that need not be; there has got to be something that must be. Now a thing that must be, may or may owe this necessity to something else. But just as we must stop somewhere in a series of causes, so also in the series of things which must be and owe this to other things. One is forced therefore to suppose something which must be, and owes this to no other thing than itself; indeed it itself is the cause that other things must be.

The fourth way is based on the gradation observed in things. Some things are found to be more good, more true, more noble, and so on, and other things less. But such comparative terms describe varying degrees of approximation to a superlative; for example, things are hotter and hotter the nearer they approach what is hottest. Something, therefore, is the truest and best and most noble of things, and hence the most fully in being; for Aristotle says that the truest things are the things most fully in being. Now when many things possess some property in common, the one most fully possessing it causes it in the others; here, to use Aristotle's example, the hottest of all things, causes all other things to be hot. There is something therefore which causes in all other things their being, their goodness, and whatever other perfection they have. And this we call "God."

The fifth way is based on the guidedness of nature. An orderedness of actions to an end is observed in all bodies obeying natural laws, even when they lack awareness. For their behavior hardly ever varies, and will practically always turn out well; which shows that they truly tend to a goal, and do not merely hit it by accident. Nothing however that lacks awareness tends to a goal, except under the direction of someone with awareness and with understanding; the arrow, for example, requires an archer. Everything in nature, therefore, is directed to its goal by someone with intelligence, and this we call God.

Hence:

1. As Augustine says, since God is supremely good, he would not permit any evil at all in his works, unless he were sufficiently almighty and good to bring good even from evil. It is therefore a mark of the limitless goodness of God that he permits evils to exist, and draws from them good.

2. Natural causes act for definite purposes under the direction of some higher cause, so that their effects must also be referred to God as the first of all causes. In the same manner contrived effects must likewise be referred back to a higher cause than human reasoning and will, for these are changeable and can cease to be, and, as we have seen, all changeable things and things that can cease to be require some first cause which cannot change and of itself must be.

READING 12

Etienne Tempier, The Condemnations of 1277[15]

Among the conservative churchmen concerned about the juxtaposition of philosophical speculation and Christian belief was Etienne Tempier, bishop of Paris (1267–1288) in Aquinas's lifetime. Tempier grew so alarmed—as he explains in this document—that he thought it necessary to rein in the academic free-for-all at Paris and to place restrictions on what could and could not be discussed and debated. Although the condemnations applied primarily to other theologians, some of whose philosophical inquiries led to conclusions contrary to Christian revelation, the philosophical system of Thomas Aquinas himself, despite his effort to reconcile Christianity and Greek logic, was not immune to Tempier's prohibitions. In addition to showing the conservative reaction against pure speculation, the condemnations also highlight the richness of ideas in the theology faculty.

Stephen[16] by divine permission unworthy servant of the church of Paris, sends greetings in the Son of the glorious Virgin to all those who will read this letter:

We have received frequent reports, inspired by zeal for the faith, on the part of important and serious persons to the effect that some students of the arts in Paris are exceeding the boundaries of their own faculty and are presuming to treat and discuss, as if they were debatable in the schools, certain obvious and loathsome errors. Those students are not hearkening to the admonition of Gregory, "Let him who would speak wisely exercise great care, lest by his speech he disrupt the unity of his listeners," particularly when in support of the aforesaid errors they adduce pagan writings that—shame on their ignorance—they assert to be so convincing that they do not know how to answer them. For they say that these things are true according to philosophy but not according to the Catholic faith, as if there were two contrary truths and as if the truth of Sacred Scripture were contradicted by the truth in the sayings of the accursed pagans.

Lest, therefore, this unguarded speech lead simple people into error, we, having taken counsel with the doctors of Sacred Scripture and other prudent men, strictly forbid these and like things and totally condemn them.

That there is no more excellent state than to study philosophy.

That the only wise men in the world are the philosophers.

---

[15]From Arthur Hyman and James J. Walsh, *Philosophy in* the *Middle Ages;* Indianapolis, Hackett Publishing Company, 1973, pp. 542–549.

[16]"Etienne" is French for "Stephen."

That one should not hold anything unless it is self-evident or can be manifested from self-evident principles.

That man should not be content with authority to have certitude about any question.

That our intellect by its own natural power can attain to a knowledge of the first cause—this does not sound well and is erroneous if what is meant is immediate knowledge.

That we can know God by his essence in this mortal life.

That nothing can be known about God except that He is, or His existence.

That what is impossible absolutely speaking cannot be brought about by God or by another agent—this is erroneous if we mean "impossible according to nature."

That God could not move the heaven in a straight line, the reason being that He would then leave a vacuum.

That God cannot produce the effect of a secondary cause without the secondary cause itself.

That the world, although it was made from nothing, was not newly made and, although it passed from nonbeing to being, the nonbeing did not precede being in duration but only in nature.

That it is impossible to refute the arguments of the Philosopher [Aristotle] concerning the eternity of the world unless we say that the will of the first being embraces incompatibles.

That nothing happens by chance, but everything comes about by necessity, and that all the things that will exist in the future will exist by necessity.

That forms are not divided except through matter.

That the soul is inseparable from the body, and that the soul is corrupted when the harmony of the body is corrupted.

That our will is subject to the power of the heavenly bodies.

That in all his actions man follows his appetite, and always the greater appetite.

That after a conclusion has been reached about something to be done, the will does not remain free, and that punishments are provided by law only for the correction of ignorance and in order that the correction may be a source of knowledge for others.

That happiness is had in this life and not in another.

That raptures and visions are caused only by nature.

That the Christian law impedes learning.

That there are fables and falsehoods in the Christian law just as in others.

That one does not know anything more by the fact that he knows theology.

That the teachings of the theologian are based on fables.

That the natural philosopher has to deny absolutely the newness of the world because he bases himself on natural causes and natural reasons, whereas the faithful can deny the eternity of the world because he bases himself on supernatural causes.

That a philosopher must not concede the resurrection to come, because it cannot be investigated by reason—this is erroneous because even a philosopher must "bring his mind into captivity to the obedience of Christ" [11 Cor. 10:5].

READING 13

William of Ockham, Universals[17]

The English Franciscan philosopher William of Ockham (c. 1290–1349) was deeply skeptical of the intellectual synthesis of faith and reason forged by Thomas Aquinas and other high medieval theologians. His skepticism extended to the issue of "universals," which had occasioned philosophical debate since the time of the ancient Greeks: Does our *idea* of dog or cat or woman or man exist independent of the actual *thing?* Plato argued for the independent existence of the idea, and he was followed by St. Augustine (and by Augustine's intellectual followers) who argued that these were the templates God used in the creation of the world. Aristotle, on the other hand, believed that universals do not exist as separate entities but only in particular, concrete manifestations of the universal idea; i.e., the human mind acquires the idea of "dogness"—of the ideal dog—by a process of abstraction: we observe a number of individual dogs and determine what they have in common. In short, the universal does exist, but only in the particular. This was the view of such high medieval Aristotelians as Thomas Aquinas. Ockham argues, on the other hand, that universals do not exist at all. They are mere names. This problem had vexed philosophers for centuries: Ockham here poses the question in a new way that leads directly to his elegant solution.

I am enquiring now, whether this universal is something real from the part of the thing which is outside of the soul. All whom I meet agree by saying that the entity which is somehow universal is really in the individual, although some say that it is distinguished only formally, and some that it is not distinguished at all according to the nature of the thing, but only according to reason. All these opin-

[17]From Anne Fremantle, *The Age of Belief;* New York, Signet Books, 1954, pp. 208–209.

ions coincide in that the universals are allowed to exist somehow away from the thing, so that their universality is held to be really present in the singular objects themselves. This latter opinion is simply false and absurd. Against this is my case. There is no unitary, unvaried or simple thing in a multiplicity of singular things, nor in any kind of created individuals, together and at the same time. If such a thing were allowed, it would be numerically one, therefore it would not be in singular objects nor would it be of their essence. But the singular and the universal thing are themselves two things, really distinct and equally simple, therefore if the singular thing is numerically one, the universal thing will be numerically one also.

If humanity were different from particular individuals and a part of their essence, one and the same invariable thing would be in many individuals, and so this same numerically one and invariable thing would be at different places, which is false. In the same way, that same invariable thing would, say, be condemned in Judas and saved in Christ, and hence, there would be something condemned and miserable in Christ, which is absurd.

To conclude, I say that there is no such thing as a universal, intrinsically present in the things to which it is present. No universal, except that which is such by voluntary agreement, is existent in any way outside of the soul, but everything that can be predicated of many things is by its nature in the mind either psychologically or logically.

STUDY QUESTIONS

A Different monastic orders had different callings. What were the main emphases that separated the Cistercians, the Franciscans, and the Dominicans?
B How is the rise of heresy linked to new monastic orders and new theological speculation?
C At some point, almost all the ideas and movements discussed in this chapter were considered suspect by church authorities. Why? What is dangerous here?

Reading 1: The Cistercians

Why did the Cistercians seek out marginal lands on which to build their communities? In most monasteries the Opus Dei (the Work of God) meant the performance of the liturgical offices, but based on documents A and B, what was the second sense of the term used by the Cistercians?

Reading 2: Hildegard of Bingen, Letter to Bernard of Clairvaux, with Reply

Both Hildegard and Bernard were voluminous letter writers. Do you have any hints here about who the intended audience was for their letters? Were they writing solely to their addressees?

Reading 3: St. Francis, The Rule, 1223

In what ways are Franciscan ideals of poverty, chastity, and obedience different from or similar to the Benedictine interpretation? According to the Rule of 1223, which values of the Christian life merit the most attention?

Reading 4: Humbert of Romans, On the Formation of Preachers

What does Humbert see as the main mistakes preachers make? Why was correct preaching so important to Humbert?

Reading 5: The Albigensian Heresy

What specific tenets of the Albigensian heresy seem to be reworkings of Old and New Testament theology, and which seem to come from elsewhere?

Reading 6: The Waldensian Heresy

Do you find overlapping ideas between the Albigensians and Waldensians, or do the heresies seem to derive from separate causes?

Reading 7: A Canon from the Fourth Lateran Council, 1215

In what specific ways is this canon a direct response to the Albigensian and Waldensian heresies?

Reading 8: St. Anselm, The Ontological Argument

This is a subtle argument, based on a logician's trick: if you can't prove something directly, prove that its opposite is false. How does this work in Anselm's case?

Reading 9: Al-Ghazali, Deliverance from Error

What is the "problem of doubt" as al-Ghazali expresses it? What is his solution? How does he reconcile doubt and faith?

Reading 10: Peter Abelard, Sic et Non

What is the "problem of doubt" as Abelard expresses it? What is his solution? Does this passage suggest why Abelard fell afoul of church authorities?

Reading 11: St. Thomas Aquinas, The Existence of God

Aquinas, like Anselm, is trying to demonstrate the existence of God. How does his approach differ from Anselm's? In what ways does Aquinas still leave room for faith and revelation?

Reading 12: Etienne Tempier, The Condemnations of 1277

What sorts of ideas were being debated in Paris in 1277? Why were these condemned? Can you find these errors in the authors you have read in this chapter? What is left for philosophy to study after these subjects have been ruled to be off limits?

Reading 13: William of Ockham, Universals

Ockham is concerned with universals only as humans understand them, not—unlike earlier philosophers—with how God may understand them. How does that change his approach to the problem? In what ways is Ockham opening a door to doubt?

CHAPTER **8**

◉ WORLDS IN COLLISION: PAPACY AND EMPIRE

In the mid-eleventh century, as the High Middle Ages dawned, the papacy was just beginning to emerge as an international force, whereas the kings of Germany (Holy Roman emperors) were at the height of their power. Emperor Henry III appointed popes as readily as he appointed the bishops of his own German kingdom. But with Henry III's premature death, reformers at the papal court took advantage of a weak imperial regency government to assert papal independence from imperial control (Reading IA). Subsequently, the fiery reformer Pope Gregory VII, gripped by the ideal of a papal monarchy asserting its authority over kings, princes, and bishops, struggled fiercely against Henry III's son and successor, Henry IV (Readings IB–IF). Gregory was determined to abolish the traditional royal/imperial privilege of appointing bishops and abbots at will, and Henry IV was equally determined to preserve it. The specific problem of investitures was finally resolved in the Concordat of Worms of 1122 (Reading IG). But the resulting papal-imperial conflict continued to fester (Reading IH).

The incident at Besançon (Reading 2) is an excellent illustration of the relationship between papacy (a *very* strong pope: Hadrian IV) and empire (a *very* strong emperor: Frederick Barbarossa). Reading 3, by the most powerful of all medieval popes, Innocent III, illustrates the papal ideology at its height. It was Innocent III who placed the gifted monarch Frederick II on the imperial throne, much to the regret of subsequent popes. Salimbene's account of Frederick II gives a glimpse of why he impressed, amazed, and frightened his contemporaries—especially the Italian clergy, who feared the dreams and plans of this able emperor (Reading 4). Finally, the passage from Dante's *De Monarchia*—supporting the authority of the Holy Roman Empire—takes explicit exception to Pope Innocent III's "sun-moon" analogy and indicates that papal ideology had able and articulate critics (Reading 5).

READING 1

Documents of the Investiture Controversy, 1059–1122[1]

A.   THE PAPAL ELECTION DECREE OF 1059

Despite a characteristically medieval effort to seek historical precedents for their act, Pope Nicholas II (1059–1061) and his reform cardinals revolutionized the papal election process. Traditionally, popes had been selected either by the king/emperor or by factions among the Roman nobility. But the reformers were determined to terminate lay control of ecclesiastical appointments, and they began at the top. Henry IV was still a child in 1059, but the reformers correctly anticipated that the German imperial court would bitterly oppose this papal declaration of independence. They address the problem in clauses 5 and 6.

In the name of the Lord God, our Saviour Jesus Christ, in the 1059th year from his incarnation, in the month of April, in the 12th indiction, in the presence of the holy gospels, the most reverend and blessed apostolic pope Nicholas presiding in the Lateran patriarchal basilica which is called the church of Constantine. . . .

Fortified by the authority of our predecessors and the other holy fathers, we decide and declare:

1. On the death of a pontiff of the universal Roman Church, first, the cardinal bishops, with the most diligent consideration, shall elect a successor; then they shall call in the other cardinal clergy [to ratify their choice], and finally the rest of the clergy and the people shall express their consent to the new election.

2. In order that the disease of venality may not have any opportunity to spread, the devout clergy shall be the leaders in electing the pontiff, and the others shall acquiesce. And surely this order of election is right and lawful, if we consider either the rules or the practice of various fathers, or if we recall that decree of our predecessor, St. Leo, for he says: "By no means can it be allowed that those should be ranked as bishops who have not been elected by the clergy, and demanded by the people, and consecrated by their fellow-bishops of the province with the consent of the metropolitan." But since the apostolic seat is above all the churches in the earth, and therefore can have no metropolitan over it, without doubt the cardinal bishops perform in it the office of the metropolitan, in that they advance the elected prelate to the apostolic dignity [that is, choose, consecrate, and enthrone him].

[1]From *A Source Book for Mediaeval History,* ed. and tr. O. J. Thatcher and E. H. McNeal; New York, Charles Scribner's Sons, 1905, pp. 128–131, 136–138, 151–156, 160–161, 164–166.

3. The pope shall be elected from the church in Rome, if a suitable person can be found in it, but if not, he is to be taken from another church.

4. In the papal election—in accordance with the right which we have already conceded to Henry and to those of his successors who may obtain the same right from the apostolic see—due honor and reverence shall be shown our beloved son, Henry, king and emperor elect [that is, the rights of Henry shall be respected].

5. But if the wickedness of depraved and iniquitous men shall so prevail that a pure, genuine, and free election cannot be held in this city, the cardinal bishops with the clergy and a few laymen shall have the right to elect the pontiff wherever they shall deem most fitting.

6. But if after an election any disturbance of war or any malicious attempt of men shall prevail so that he who is elected cannot be enthroned according to custom in the papal chair, the pope elect shall nevertheless exercise the right of ruling the holy Roman Church, and of disposing of all its revenues, as we know St. Gregory did before his consecration.

But if anyone, actuated by rebellion or presumption or any other motive, shall be elected or ordained or entroned in a manner contrary to this our decree, promulgated by the authority of the synod, he with his counsellors, supporters, and followers shall be expelled from the holy Church of God by the authority of God and the holy apostles Peter and Paul, and shall be subjected to perpetual anathema as Antichrist and the enemy and destroyer of all Christianity; nor shall he ever be granted a further hearing in the case, but he shall be deposed without appeal from every ecclesiastical rank which he may have held formerly. Whoever shall adhere to him or shall show him any reverence as if he were pope, or shall aid him in any way, shall be subject to like sentence. Moreover, if any rash person shall oppose this our decree and shall try to confound and disturb the Roman Church by his presumption contrary to this decree, let him be cursed with perpetual anathema and excommunication, and let him be numbered with the wicked who shall not arise on the day of judgment. Let him feel upon him the weight of the wrath of God the Father, the Son, and the Holy Spirit, and let him experience in this life and the next the anger of the holy apostles, Peter and Paul, whose Church he has presumed to confound. Let his habitation be desolate and let none dwell in his tents [Ps. 69:25]. Let his children be orphans and his wife a widow. Let him be driven forth and let his sons beg and be cast out from their habitations. Let the usurer take all his substance and let others reap the fruit of his labors. Let the whole earth fight against him and let all the elements be hostile to him, and let the powers of all the saints in heaven confound him and show upon him in this life their evident vengeance. But may the grace of omnipotent God protect those who observe this decree and free them from the bonds of all their sins by the authority of the holy apostles Peter and Paul.

B. GREGORY VII, DICTATUS PAPAE

These twenty-seven points were compiled at the papal court around 1075 at the instigation of Pope Gregory VII (1073–1085). The *Dictatus Papae* (Dictates of the Pope) were not made public, but were probably intended as a guide to papal lawyers. Few of the claims were new, yet together they constitute a silent manifesto for the Gregorian idea of papal monarchy. Gregory VII took these claims very seriously and made them the basis of his international policy. A careful reading will explain why Gregory's opponents included bishops as well as kings.

1. That the Roman church was established by God alone.

2. That the Roman pontiff alone is rightly called universal.

3. That he alone has the power to depose and reinstate bishops.

4. That his legate, even if he be of lower ecclesiastical rank, presides over bishops in council, and has the power to give sentence of deposition against them.

5. That the pope has the power to depose those who are absent [i.e., without giving them a hearing].

6. That, among other things, we ought not to remain in the same house with those whom he has excommunicated.

7. That he alone has the right, according to the necessity of the occasion, to make new laws, to create new bishoprics, to make a monastery of a chapter of canons, and vice versa, and either to divide a rich bishopric or to unite several poor ones.

8. That he alone may use the imperial insignia.

9. That all princes shall kiss the foot of the pope alone.

10. That his name alone is to be recited in the churches.

11. That the name applied to him belongs to him alone.

12. That he has the power to depose emperors.

13. That he has the right to transfer bishops from one see to another when it becomes necessary.

14. That he has the right to ordain as a cleric anyone from any part of the church whatsoever.

15. That anyone ordained by him may rule [as bishop] over another church, but cannot serve [as priest] in it, and that such a cleric may not receive a higher rank from any other bishop.

16. That no general synod may be called without his order.

17. That no action of a synod and no book shall be regarded as canonical without his authority.

18. That his decree can be annulled by no one, and that he can annul the decrees of anyone.

19. That he can be judged by no one.

20. That no one shall dare to condemn a person who has appealed to the apostolic seat.

21. That the important cases of any church whatsoever shall be referred to the Roman Church [that is, to the pope].

22. That the Roman Church has never erred and will never err to all eternity, according to the testimony of the holy scriptures.

23. That the Roman pontiff who has been canonically ordained is made holy by the merits of St. Peter, according to the testimony of St. Ennodius, bishop of Pavia, which is confirmed by many of the holy fathers, as is shown by the decrees of the blessed pope Symmachus.

24. That by his command or permission subjects may accuse their rulers.

25. That he can depose and reinstate bishops without the calling of a synod.

26. That no one can be regarded as catholic who does not agree with the Roman Church.

27. That he has the power to absolve subjects from their oath of fidelity to wicked rules.

C.   GREGORY VII, DECREE AGAINST LAY INVESTITURE

Investiture was the formal installation ceremony in which new prelates were given the insignia of their offices. An incoming bishop or abbot would receive a ring and a staff, symbolic of his "marriage" to the church and his role as shepherd of his flock. It had long been customary for churchmen to receive their investiture from lay lords. Bishops and abbots were normally invested by their territorial princes—counts, dukes, kings, or the Holy Roman emperor. The papal reform party condemned this practice as the key symbolic expression of lay control over ecclesiastical appointments. Lay investiture was first prohibited at the Roman Lenten Synod of 1059, which also promulgated the Papal Election Decree. For a time the investiture issue was largely ignored and forgotten. But Gregory VII issued a second investiture ban at a Roman synod in 1075, and subsequent papal synods legislated against the practice repeatedly. The following document, a product of Gregory VII's synod of 1078, is probably quite similar to the investiture decree of 1075, which no longer survives.

Since we know that investitures have been made by laymen in many places, contrary to the decrees of the holy fathers, and that very many disturbances injurious to the Christian religion have thereby arisen in the Church, we therefore decree: that no clergyman shall receive investiture of a bishopric, monastery, or church from the hand of the emperor, or the king, or any lay person, man or

278 PART TWO: THE HIGH MIDDLE AGES

woman. And if anyone has ventured to receive such investiture, let him know
that it is annulled by apostolic authority, and that he is subject to excommunication until he has made due reparation.

D. HENRY IV, DEPOSITION OF GREGORY VII

The Holy Roman emperors depended heavily on the support of powerful
and loyal bishops. Accordingly, Gregory VII's energetic opposition to the
appointment of churchmen by laymen earned him the fierce opposition of
Henry IV (1056–1106) and his handpicked bishops. When Gregory
suspended some of them, Henry responded by convening a synod at
Worms in January 1076 and dispatching a letter to Gregory under his
prepapal name, Hildebrand.

Henry, king not by usurpation, but by the holy ordination of God, to Hildebrand, not pope, but false monk.

This is the salutation which you deserve, for you have never held any office
in the church without making it a source of confusion and a curse to Christian
men instead of an honor and a blessing. To mention only the most obvious cases
out of the many, you have not only dared to touch the Lord's anointed, the archbishops, bishops, and priests; but you have scorned them and abused them, as if
they were ignorant servants not fit to know what their master was doing. This
you have done to gain favor with the vulgar crowd. You have declared that the
bishops know nothing and that you know everything; but if you have such great
wisdom you have used it not to build but to destroy. Therefore we believe that
St. Gregory, whose name you have presumed to take, had you in mind when he
said: "The heart of the prelate is puffed up by the abundance of subjects, and he
thinks himself more powerful than all others." All this we have endured because
of our respect for the papal office, but you have mistaken our humility for fear,
and have dared to make an attack upon the royal and imperial authority which
we received from God. You have even threatened to take it away, as if we had
received it from you, and as if the empire and kingdom were in your disposal
and not in the disposal of God. Our Lord Jesus Christ has called us to the government of the empire, but he never called you to the rule of the Church. This is
the way you have gained advancement in the Church: through craft you have obtained wealth; through wealth you have obtained favor; through favor, the power
of the sword; and through the power of the sword, the papal seat, which is the
seat of peace; and then from the seat of peace you have expelled peace. For you
have incited subjects to rebel against their prelates by teaching them to despise
the bishops, their rightful rulers. You have given to laymen the authority over
priests, whereby they condemn and depose those whom the bishops have put

over them to teach them. You have attacked me, who, unworthy as I am, have yet been appointed to rule among the anointed of God, and who, according to the teaching of the fathers, can be judged by no one save God alone, and can be deposed for no crime except infidelity. For the holy fathers in the time of the apostate Julian did not presume to pronounce sentence of deposition against him, but left him to be judged and condemned by God. St. Peter, himself said: "Fear God, honor the king" [1 Pet. 2:17]. But you, who fear not God, have dishonored me, whom He hath established. St. Paul, who said that even an angel from heaven should be accursed who taught any other than the true doctrine, did not make an exception in your favor, to permit you to teach false doctrines. For he says: "But though we, or an angel from heaven, preach any other gospel unto you than that which we have preached unto you, let him be accursed" [Gal. 1:8]. Come down, then, from that apostolic seat which you have obtained by violence; for you have been declared accursed by St. Paul for your false doctrines and have been condemned by us and our bishops for your evil rule. Let another ascend the throne of St. Peter, one who will not use religion as a cloak of violence, but will teach the life-giving doctrine of that prince of the apostles. I, Henry, king by the grace of God, with all my bishops, say unto you: "Come down, come down, and be accursed through all the ages."

E.   BISHOPS OF GERMANY, LETTER TO GREGORY VII

At the same moment that Henry denounced Pope Gregory (Reading 1D), the German bishops drew up their own letter of condemnation. The bishops saw the pope as the first among equals, not as their overlord. Yet Gregory had directly intervened into what they perceived as their own internal affairs. Moreover, many of them had been invested by the emperor, whom they therefore saw as a natural ally against the novelties being introduced by Gregory.

Siegfried archbishop of Mainz, Udo bishop of Trier, William bishop of Utrecht, etc., etc., (a list of names of twenty-six bishops in all), to brother Hildebrand.

At first when you made yourself pope we thought it better to ignore the illegality of your action and to submit to your rule, in the hope that you would redeem your bad beginning by a just and righteous government of the church, although we realized even then the enormity of the sin which you had committed. But now the lamentable condition of the whole church shows us only too well how we were deceived in you; your violent entrance into office was but the first in a series of wicked deeds and unjust decrees. Our Lord and Redeemer has said, in more places than we can well enumerate here, that love and gentleness are the marks of his disciples, but you are known for your pride, your ambition, and your love of strife. You have introduced worldliness into the church; you have desired a great name rather than a reputation for holiness; you have made a schism in the church and offended its members, who before your time were living together in peace and charity. Your mad acts have kindled the flame of discord which now rages in the churches of Italy, Germany, France, and Spain. The bishops have been deprived of their divine authority, which rests upon the grace of the Holy Spirit received through ordination, and the whole administration of ecclesiastical matters you have given to rash and ignorant laymen. There is nowhere in the church today a bishop or a priest who does not hold his office through abject acquiescence in your ambitious schemes.

The order of bishops, to whom the government of the church was intrusted by the Lord, you have thrown into confusion, and you have disturbed that excellent coordination of the members of Christ which Paul in so many places commends and inculcates, while the name of Christ has almost disappeared from the earth; and all this through those decrees in which you glory. Who among men is not filled with astonishment and indignation at your claims to sole authority, by which you would deprive your fellow-bishops of their coordinate rights and powers? For you assert that you have the authority to try any one of our parishioners for any sin which may have reached your ears even by chance report, and that no one of us has the power to loose or to bind such a sinner, but that it belongs to you alone or to your legate. Who that knows the scriptures does not perceive the madness of this claim?

Since, therefore, it is now apparent that the church of God is in danger of destruction through your presumption, we have come to the conclusion that this state of things can no longer be endured, and we have determined to break our silence and to make public the reasons why you are unfit and have always been unfit to rule the church as pope. These are the reasons:

In the first place, in the reign of Emperor Henry III of blessed memory, you bound yourself by oath never to accept the papacy or to permit anyone else to accept it during the life of that emperor or of his son without the consent of the emperor. There are many bishops still living who can bear witness to that oath. On another occasion, when certain cardinals were aiming to secure the office, you took an oath never to accept the papacy, on condition that they should all take the same oath. You know yourself how faithfully you have kept these oaths!

In the second place, it was agreed in a synod held in the time of Pope Nicholas II and attended by 125 bishops, that no one, under penalty of excommunication, should ever accept the papacy who had not received the election of the cardinals, the approbation of the people, and the consent of the emperor. You yourself proposed and promoted that decree and signed it with your own hand.

In the third place, you have filled the whole church with the stench of scandal, by association on too intimate terms with a woman who was not a member of your family.[2] We do not wish to base any serious charge on this last accusation; we refer to it because it outrages our sense of propriety. And yet the complaint is very generally made that all the judgments and acts of the papacy are passed on by the women about the pope, and that the whole church is governed by this new female conclave.

And finally, no amount of complaint is adequate to express the insults and outrages you have heaped upon the bishops, calling them sons of harlots and other vile names.

Therefore, since your pontificate was begun in perjury and crime, since your innovations have placed the church of god in the gravest peril, since your life and conduct are stained with infamy; we now renounce our obedience, which indeed was never legally promised to you. You have declared publicly that you do not consider us to be bishops; we reply that no one of us shall ever hold you to be the pope.

F. GREGORY VII, DEPOSITION OF HENRY IV

Gregory responded at the Roman Synod of February 1076 by exercising one of the papal prerogatives that he had claimed in the *Dictatus Papae* (clause 12). He reminded his readers, in the form of a prayer, that the papacy derives its power from the authority granted by Jesus to the Apostle Peter, the first pope and Rome's patron saint.

St. Peter, prince of the apostles, incline thine ear unto me, I beseech thee, and hear me, thy servant, whom thou hast nourished from mine infancy and has delivered from mine enemies that hate me for my fidelity to thee. Thou art my witness, as are also my mistress, the mother of God, and St. Paul thy brother, and all the other saints, that thy holy Roman Church called me to its government against my own will, and that I did not gain thy throne by violence; that I would rather have ended my days in exile than have obtained thy place by fraud or for worldly ambition. It is not by my efforts, but by thy grace, that I am set to rule over the Christian world which was specially entrusted to thee by Christ. It is by thy grace and as thy representative that God has given to me the power to bind and to loose in heaven and in earth. Confident of my integrity and authority, I now declare in the name of omnipotent God, the Father, Son, and Holy Spirit, that Henry, son of the emperor Henry, is deprived of his kingdom of Germany and Italy; I do this by thy authority and in defence of the honor of thy Church,

[2]Matilda countess of Tuscany, who also authored Reading 1H, below.

because he has rebelled against it. He who attempts to destroy the honor of the Church should be deprived of such honor as he may have held. He has refused to obey as a Christian should, he has not returned to God from whom he had wandered, he has had dealings with excommunicated persons, he has done many iniquities, he has despised the warnings which, as thou art witness, I sent to him for his salvation, he has cut himself off from thy Church, and has attempted to rend it asunder; therefore, by thy authority, I place him under the curse. It is in thy name that I curse him, that all people may know that thou art Peter, and upon thy rock the Son of the living God has built his Church, and the gates of hell shall not prevail against it.

G.   CALIXTUS II AND HENRY V, THE CONCORDAT OF WORMS, 1122

After dragging on for several decades, the investiture controversy was settled in 1122 by a compromise between Pope Calixtus II (1119–1124) and Emperor Henry V (1106–1125), Henry IV's son and heir. The settlement drew a distinction between a prelate's spiritual and secular authority: the former was conferred by investiture with ring and staff; the latter, by receipt of the "regalia"—a scepter symbolizing territorial lordship. The Concordat of Worms was followed by a generation of peace between empire and papacy.

1. Calixtus, bishop, servant of the servants of God, to his beloved son, Henry, by the grace of God emperor of the Romans, Augustus.

We hereby grant that in Germany the elections of the bishops and abbots who hold directly from the crown shall be held in your presence, such elections to be conducted canonically and without simony or other illegality. In the case of disputed elections you shall have the right to decide between the parties, after consulting with the archbishop of the province and his fellow-bishops. You shall confer the regalia of the office upon the bishop or abbot elect by giving him the scepter, and this shall be done freely without exacting any payment from him; the bishop or abbot elect on his part shall perform all the duties that go with the holding of the regalia.

In other parts of the empire the bishops shall receive the regalia from you in the same manner within six months of their consecration, and shall in like manner perform all the duties that go with them. The undoubted rights of the Roman Church, however, are not to be regarded as prejudiced by this concession. If at any time you shall have occasion to complain of the carrying out of these provisions, I will undertake to satisfy your grievances as far as shall be consistent with my office. Finally, I hereby make a true and lasting peace with you and with all of your followers, including those who supported you in the recent controversy.

2. In the name of the holy and undivided Trinity.

For the love of God and his holy Church and of Pope Calixtus, and for the salvation of my soul, I, Henry, by the grace of God, emperor of the Romans, Augustus, hereby surrender to God and his apostles, Sts. Peter and Paul, and to the holy Catholic Church, all investiture by ring and staff. I agree that elections and consecrations shall be conducted canonically and shall be free from all interference. I surrender also the possessions and regalia of St. Peter which have been seized by me during this quarrel, or by my father in his lifetime, and which are now in my possession, and I promise to aid the Church to recover such as are held by any other persons. I restore also the possessions of all other churches and princes, clerical or secular, which have been taken away during the course of this quarrel, which I have, and promise to aid them to recover such as are held by any other persons.

Finally, I make true and lasting peace with Pope Calixtus and with the holy Roman Church and with all who are or have ever been of his party. I will aid the Roman Church whenever my help is asked, and will do justice in all matters in regard to which the Church may have occasion to make complaint.

All these things have been done with the consent and advice of the princes whose names are written below: Adelbert, archbishop of Mainz; Frederick, archbishop of Cologne, etc.

H.   MATILDA OF TUSCANY, GRANT TO THE PAPACY, 1102

Matilda (1046–1115), countess of Tuscany, was an important participant in the investiture controversy. She played a principal role in the episode at Canossa in 1077, providing refuge to her cherished friend Pope Gregory VII (Canossa was Matilda's own castle) when Emperor Henry IV approached seeking forgiveness, but she was also one of those present who interceded on Henry's behalf. The grant below indicates how the papal-imperial conflict touched upon the fate of the county of Tuscany. Matilda, who was childless, endeavored to grant the papacy the lordship of her vast holdings extending across great stretches of northern Italy. Many years later, she reconciled with the empire, and at her death in 1115, she bequeathed the lordship of her lands to Henry IV's son and heir, Henry V. The papal-imperial dispute over these lands was eventually resolved in an agreement that left the lordship of Matilda's lands to the emperor and the overlordship to the pope.

In the name of the holy and undivided Trinity. . . . In the time of Gregory VII, in the Lateran palace, in the chapel of the holy cross, in the presence of [witnesses], . . . I, Matilda, by the grace of God countess, for the salvation of my

soul and the souls of my parents, gave to the church of St. Peter and to Gregory VII all my possessions, present and future, by whatever title I may hold them.
I gave all my lands in Italy and Germany, and I had a document drawn up to that
effect. But now the document has disappeared, and I fear that my gift may be
questioned. Therefore, I, countess Matilda, again give to the church of Rome,
through Bernard, cardinal and legate of the same holy church of Rome, just as I
did in the time of Gregory VII, all my possessions, present and future, in both Italy
and Germany, by whatever right I hold them, for the salvation of my soul and the
souls of my parents. All these possessions, which belong to me, with all that pertains to them, in all their entirety, I give to the said church of Rome, and by this
deed of gift I confirm the church in the possession of them. As symbols and evi-
dences that I have surrendered these lands I have given a knife, a knotted straw, a
glove, a piece of sod, and a twig from a tree.

READING 2

Otto of Freising, The Incident at Besançon[3]

Pope Hadrian IV (1154–1159), born Nicholas Breakspear, was the only
English pope in the history of the Catholic Church and one of the most
gifted popes of the twelfth century. His letter (1157) to the great Holy
Roman emperor Frederick II, "Barbarossa," is a deft blend of affection and
disapproval. The letter appears verbatim in Otto of Freising's *The Deeds of
Frederick Barbarossa*. Although Otto's account is pro-imperial (he was in
fact Barbarossa's uncle), like many talented historians Otto was careful to
include original documents in his work.

"Bishop Hadrian, the servant of the servants of God, to his beloved son Frederick, the illustrious emperor of the Romans, greeting and apostolic benediction.

"We recollect having written, a few days since, to the Imperial Majesty, of
that dreadful and accursed deed, an offense calling for atonement, committed in
our time, and hitherto, we believe, never attempted in the German lands. In re-
calling it to Your Excellency, we cannot conceal our great amazement that even
now you have permitted so pernicious a deed to go unpunished with the severity
it deserves. For how our venerable brother E[skil], archbishop of Lund, while returning from the apostolic see, was taken captive in those parts by certain god-

---

[3]From Otto of Freising, *The Deeds of Frederick Barbarossa,* tr. C. C. Mierow; New York,
W. W. Norton, 1966. pp. 181–184.

less and infamous men—a thing we cannot mention without great and heartfelt sorrow—and is still held in confinement; how in taking him captive, as previously mentioned, those men of impiety, a seed of evildoers, children that are corrupters, drew their swords and violently assaulted him and his companions, and how basely and shamefully they treated them, stripping them of all they had. Your Most Serene Highness knows, and the report of so great a crime has already spread abroad to the most distant and remote regions. To avenge this deed of exceptional violence, you, as a man to whom we believe good deeds are pleasing but evil works displeasing, ought with great determination to arise and bring down heavily upon the necks of the wicked the sword which was entrusted by divine providence to you for the punishment of evildoers and for the praise of them that do well, [4] and should most severely punish the presumptuous. But you are reported so to have ignored and indeed been indifferent to this deed, that there is no reason why those men should be repentant at having incurred guilt, because they have long since perceived that they have secured immunity for the sacrilege which they have committed.

"Of the reason for this indifference and negligence we are absolutely ignorant, because no scruple of conscience accuses our heart of having in aught offended the glory of Your Serenity. Rather have we always loved, with sincere affection, and treated with an attitude of due kindness, your person as that of our most dear and specially beloved son and most Christian prince, who, we doubt not, is by the grace of God grounded on the rock of the apostolic confession.

"For you should recall, O most glorious son, before the eyes of your mind, how willingly and how gladly your mother, the Holy Roman Church, received you in another year, with what affection of heart she treated you, what great dignity and honor she bestowed upon you, and with how much pleasure she conferred the emblem of the imperial crown, zealous to cherish in her most kindly bosom the height of Your Sublimity, and doing nothing at all that she knew was in the least at variance with the royal will.

"Nor do we regret that we fulfilled in all respects the ardent desires of your heart; but if Your Excellency had received still greater benefits[5] at our hand (had that been possible), in consideration of the great increase and advantage that might through you accrue to the Church of God and to us, we would have rejoiced, not without reason.

"But now, because you seem to ignore and hide so heinous a crime, which is indeed known to have committed as an affront to the Church universal and to your empire, we both suspect and fear that perhaps your thoughts were directed toward this indifference and neglect on this account: that at the suggestion of a

---

[4]Peter 2:14.

[5]*Beneficia:* the emperor and his attendants took this in its feudal sense of "benefice," thus concluding that the pope claimed overlordship of the empire and taking great offense at this alleged claim.

evil man, sowing tares, you have conceived against your most gracious mother the Holy Roman Church and against ourselves—God forbid!—some displeasure or grievance.

"On this account, therefore, and because of all the other matters of business which we know to impend, we have thought best to dispatch at this time from our side to Your Serenity two of the best and dearest of those whom we have about us, namely, our beloved sons, Bernard, cardinal priest of St. Clement's, and Roland, cardinal priest of St. Mark's and our chancellor, men very notable for piety and wisdom and honor. We very earnestly beseech Your Excellency that you receive them with as much respect as kindness, treat them will all honor, and that whatever they themselves set forth before Your Imperial Dignity on our behalf concerning this and concerning other matters to the honor of God and of the Holy Roman Church, and pertaining also to the glory and exaltation of the empire, you accept without any hesitation as though proceeding from our mouth. Give credence to their words, as if we were uttering them" [September 20, 1157].

When this letter had been read and carefully set forth by Chancellor Rainald in a faithful interpretation, the princes who were present were moved to great indignation, because the entire content of the letter appeared to have no little sharpness and to offer even at the very outset an occasion for future trouble. But what had particularly aroused them all was the fact that in the aforesaid letter it had been stated, among other things, that the fullness of dignity and honor had been bestowed upon the emperor by the Roman pontiff, that the emperor had received from his hand the imperial crown, and that he would not have regretted conferring even greater benefits (*beneficia*) upon him, in consideration of the great gain and advantage that might through him accrue to the Roman Church. And the hearers were led to accept the literal meaning of these words and to put credence in the aforesaid explanation because they knew that the assertion was rashly made by some Romans that hitherto our kings had possessed the imperial power over the City, and the kingdom of Italy, by gift of the popes, and that they made such representations and handed them down to posterity not only orally but also in writing and in pictures. Hence it is written concerning Emperor Lothar, over a picture of this sort in the Lateran palace:

> Coming before our gates, the king vows to safeguard the City, Then, liegeman to the Pope, by him he is granted the crown.

Since such a picture and such an inscription, reported to him by those faithful to the empire, had greatly displeased the prince when he had been near the City in a previous year [1155], he is said to have received from Pope Hadrian, after a friendly remonstrance, the assurance that both the inscription and the picture would be removed, lest so trifling a matter might afford the greatest men in the world an occasion for dispute and discord.

When all these matters were fully considered, and a great tumult and uproar arose from the princes of the realm at so insolent a message, it is said that one of the ambassadors, as though adding sword to flame, inquired: "From whom then does he have the empire, if not from our lord the pope?" Because of this remark, anger reached such a pitch that one of them, namely, Otto, count palatine of Bavaria (it was said), threatened the ambassador with his sword. But Frederick, using his authority to quell the tumult, commanded that the ambassadors, being granted safe-conduct, be led to their quarters and that early in the morning they should set forth on their way; he ordered also that they were not to pause in the territories of the bishops and abbots, but to return to the City by the direct road, turning neither to the right nor the left.

READING 3

Two Letters of Pope Innocent III[6]

These two brief passages illustrate Pope Innocent III's (1198–1215) claims for the power and authority of the papacy.

A. TO ACERBIUS AND THE CLERGY OF TUSCANY, 1198

Innocent III to Acerbius, prior, and to the other clergy in Tuscany.

As God, the creator of the universe, set two great lights in the firmament of heaven, the greater light to rule the day and the lesser light to rule the night [Gen. 1:15, 16], so He set two great dignities in the firmament of the universal church, . . . the greater to rule the day, that is, souls, and the lesser to rule the night, that is, bodies. These dignities are the papal authority and the royal power. And just as the moon gets her light from the sun, and is inferior to the sun in quality, quantity, position, and effect, so the royal power gets the splendor of its dignity from the papal authority.

B. TO THE DUKE OF BOHEMIA, 1204

Although there have been many in Bohemia who have worn a royal crown, yet they never received the papal permission to call themselves king in their documents. Nor have we hitherto been willing to call you king, because you were

---

[6]From *A Source Book for Mediaeval History,* ed. and tr. O. H. Thatcher and E. H. McNeal; New York, Charles Scribner's Sons, 1905, pp. 208, 218.

crowned king by Philip, duke of Suabia, who himself had not been legally crowned, and therefore could not legally crown either you or anyone else. But since you have obeyed us, and deserting the duke of Suabia, have gone over to the illustrious king, Otto, emperor-elect, and he regards you as king, we, at his request and out of consideration of your obedience, are willing hereafter to call you king. Now that you know why this favor has been granted you, strive to shun the vice of ingratitude. And show that you have deserved our favor which we have so graciously shown you, and try also to retain it. See that you are solemnly crowned by Otto as soon as possible.

READING 4

Salimbene, On the Emperor Frederick II[7]

Salimbene (1221–c. 1288) was born five years before the death of Saint Francis (see Chapter 8), became a Franciscan in 1238, and wrote an unofficial but lengthy history of the Order. The impetus for his *Chronicle* was actually the simple request of Salimbene's niece Agnes, herself a nun in the Franciscan Order of the Poor Clares, who wanted to know more about her ancestors "on whose behalf she ought to pray." Salimbene's reply—the *Chronicle*—was part family gossip, part Franciscan lore, and part world history. Salimbene, born into a wealthy family from Parma, encountered many of the movers and shakers of the thirteenth century, including the Emperor Frederick II (1208–1250). Salimbene admired some of the emperor's personal traits, but—with Popes Gregory IX and Innocent IV—criticized Frederick's religious free-thinking.

THE EXCESSES OF FREDERICK II

Of faith in God, Frederick had none; he was crafty, wily, avaricious, lustful, malicious, wrathful; and yet a gallant man at times, when he would show his kindness or courtesy; full of solace, jocund, delightful, and clever. He knew how to read, write, and sing, and to make songs and music. He was pleasing in appearance, and well-formed, but of middle stature. I have seen him, and once I admired him, for on my behalf he wrote to Brother Elias, Minister-General of the

    [7]From G. G. Coulton, *From St. Francis to Dante: Translations of the Chronicle of the Franciscan Salimbene;* London, 1907, pp. 241–244. Revised by David S. Spear.

Friars Minor, to send me back to my father.[8] Moreover, he knew to speak with many and varied tongues, and, to be brief, if he had been rightly Catholic, and had loved God and His Church, he would have had few emperors his equals in the world. . . .

Frederick once cut off a notary's thumb who had spelled his name *Fredericus* instead of *Fridericus*. . . .

He had linguistic experiments performed on infants, bidding foster-mothers and nurses to suckle and bathe the children, but not in any way to speak to them; for he wanted to learn whether they would speak the Hebrew language (which had been mankind's first language), or Greek, or Latin, or Arabic, or perchance the tongue of the parents to whom they had been born. But he labored in vain, for the children could not live without the touch of hands, and gestures, and gladness of countenance, and rewards. . . .

Again, when Frederick saw the Holy Land (which God had so often commended as a land flowing with milk and honey, and most excellent above all lands), it pleased him not, and he said that if the God of the Jews had seen *his* lands of Terra di Lavoro, Calabria, Sicily, and Apulia, then He would not so have commended the land which He promised to the Jews. . . .

His fourth excess was that he sent one Nicholas against his will to the bottom of the Faro. Wanting to know whether Nicholas had indeed gone down to the bottom of the sea or if he had just pretended to do so, Frederick threw in his golden cup where he thought the depth was the greatest. Nicholas dived and found it and brought it back up, whereupon the Emperor marveled. But when he would have sent him down again, Nicholas begged, "Send me not down, I pray you; for the sea is so troubled in that depth that if you send me there, I shall never return." Neverthless the Emperor sent him; so there he perished and never returned. . . . All that I have just written I have heard a hundred times from the Brethren of Messana, who have been close friends of mine, for I had in our Order a cousin, Brother Giacomino de Cassio of Parma, who dwelt at Messana and told me these things. . . .

Once Frederick sealed a man alive in a cask until he died therein, wishing thereby to show that the soul perished utterly, as if he might say the word of Isaiah, "Let us eat and drink, for tomorrow we die." Frederick was an Epicurean: he therefore, partly of himself and partly through his wise men, sought out all that he could find in Holy Scripture which might prove that there was no life

---

[8]At age seventeen Salimbene decided to join the Franciscan order, much to his father's disappointment and horror. His father asked Frederick II to intervene. At the subsequent hearing, Salimbene's father accused the Franciscans of having "bewitched" his son. Salimbene held firm to his convictions, quoting Christ's admonition, "He that loveth father or mother more than Me, is not worthy of Me." The incident is reminiscent of Francis's own Christ-centered convictions and paternal dispute.

after death, as for instance, "Thou shalt destroy them, and not build them up," and again "Their sepulchers shall be their houses for ever." . . .

Sixthly, he fed two men most excellently at dinner, one of whom he sent immediately to sleep, and the other to hunt. That same evening he caused them to be disemboweled in his presence, wishing to know which had digested the better: and it was judged by the physicians in favor of him who had slept.

Seventhly and lastly, being one day in his palace, he asked of Michael Scot the astrologer how far he was from the sky. Michael having provided his answer, the Emperor took him to other parts of the kingdom as if for a journey of pleasure, and kept him there several months. Meanwhile Frederick arranged that his architects and carpenters would secretly lower the whole of the palace hall. Many days afterwards, standing in that same palace with Michael, he asked of him, as if by the way, whether he were indeed so far from the sky as he had said before. Michael reworked his calculations and answered that certainly either the sky had been raised or the earth lowered. And then the Emperor knew that Michael Scot spoke the truth.

READING 5
Dante, De Monarchia[9]

In his treatise *De Monarchia,* the great Florentine writer Dante (1265–1321) urges a world order under the governance of the Holy Roman Empire (rather than the papacy). In this passage, Dante attacks the theory of papal supremacy and, in particular, the metaphor of the empire being symbolized by the moon, shining only by reflecting the sunlike glory of the Church (a favorite metaphor of Pope Innocent III's: see above). Dante's great goal is the establishment, through imperial intervention, of political order in war-torn Italy—and in faction-ridden Florence. Florence, Dante's birthplace, was strife-torn in the era following the fall of Frederick II. The German kings no longer exercised real control; the papacy was too distant and too preoccupied with Roman affairs; and Florentine civic government was split between those who longed for more autonomy and those who wanted firmer external control. These troubled circumstances led Dante, one of the most reflective men of any age, to write this political treatise.

---

[9]From Dante Alighieri, *On World-Government or De Monarchia,* tr. H. W. Schneider; New York, The Liberal Arts Press, 1950, pp. 42–45.

The analogy of sun and moon it not applicable to temporal authority, as if it were reflected from the divine right of spiritual authority.

It is asserted by those against whom the remaining discussion is directed that the Empire's authority is subordinate to the Church's as a workman is under the direction of an architect. They use several different arguments, based some of them on the Holy Scriptures and some on the deeds of either popes or emperors, from whose deeds they make certain theoretical inferences.

They say, in the first place, that, according to Genesis, God created two great luminaries, a greater and a lesser, one to govern the day and the other the night. This, they say, is an allegory for two types of power, spiritual and temporal. Then they argue that as the lesser luminary, the moon, has no light of its own except as it receives it from the sun, so temporal power has no authority except as it is derived from spiritual.

To overthrow this and other arguments of theirs, we should note that, as the Philosopher[10] says in his treatise on *Fallacies,* the way to win an argument is to expose an error. Now since error can occur in both the matter and the form of an argument, there are two kinds of fallacies: assuming what is false or inferring incorrectly. The Philosopher objected to Parmenides and Melissus on both of these grounds, saying, "They admit falsehoods and they don't know how to make syllogisms." Here I include under "false" also improbable opinions, for in questions of probable knowledge they have the force of falsehoods. If the fallacy is formal, the critic must destroy the conclusion by showing that the syllogistic structure has been violated. But if the fallacy is material, it is either a case of assuming what is wholly false or relatively false. If an assumption is wholly false, one of the premises must be denied; if it is relatively false, a distinction must be made.

With this procedure in mind, we can better criticize this and the following arguments if we call attention to two types of fallacious appeals to a mystic interpretation: either looking for it where it does not exist, or accepting a meaning which is improper. Regarding the first type Augustine says in his *City of God:* "Not everything narrated is significant, for the insignificant must be narrated in order to bring out the significant. The ploughshare alone turns the furrow, but the other parts of the plough are also needed." Concerning the second type, too, Augustine has something to say in his *Christian Doctrine,* when he is speaking about those who seek a meaning different from the author's intention and says that they make the same mistake that a traveller makes who leaves the road but finally in his digression arrives at the same point to which the road leads; and he adds, "Such a person should be warned that his bad habit of leaving the road may lead him on to cross-roads and wrong roads." Then he gives the specific reason

---

[10]Dante, like Aquinas and Bishop Tempier, refers to Aristotle as "the Philosopher."

why this is a dangerous way of treating Holy Scripture, saying, "Faith will totter, if the authority of the divine Scriptures vacillates." For my part I would say that if such mistakes arise from ignorance, we should carefully correct and pardon them, as we would a person who is afraid of lions in the clouds; but, if they are committed purposely, such interpreters should be treated not as ignoramuses but more as we would treat a tyrant who does not use public regulations for the common welfare but tries to twist their meaning for his own purposes. O greatest of crimes, to abuse the intention of the eternal Spirit, even if it happens in dreams! For the sin is not against Moses, or David or Job, or Matthew or Paul, but against the Holy Spirit, who speaks through them. For though there may be many writers of the divine word, there is but one who dictates it, namely, God, who was pleased to reveal himself to us by using many pens.

After these preliminary observations I can return to the criticism of the argument according to which the two luminaries signify two types of government, an argument which rests entirely on this analogy. There are two ways of showing that this interpretation of the passage in Genesis is inadmissible. First, since governments are not in the essence of human existence but in its circumstantial conditions of "accidents," God would have been guilty of creating backwards, if he had first created types of government and then had created man, which would be absurd to attribute to God. For he made the two luminaries on the fourth day and man on the sixth, according to the text. Besides, since governments exist to guide men toward specific goals, as we shall show, there would have been no use for them if man had remained in the state of innocence in which he was created. For devices such as governments are remedies for the infirmity of sin. Since man was not only not a sinner on the fourth day but didn't exist at all, God would not have acted in accordance with his goodness if he had devised remedies on the fourth day. For it would be a silly physician who prepared a plaster to apply to the future abscess of an unknown person. It is therefore impossible to maintain that God created governments on the fourth day, and therefore Moses must have meant something different from what they imagine.

But this falsehood can also be destroyed by using the gentler method of exposing a material fallacy, and instead of calling the opponent an out-and-out liar, we can make a distinction which he overlooked. Thus I maintain that from the fact that the moon does not shine brightly unless it receives light from the sun, it does not follow that the moon itself depends on the sun. For one must keep in mind that the being of the moon is one thing, its power another, and its functioning a third. In its being the moon is in no way dependent on the sun, and not even in its power and functioning strictly speaking, for its motion comes directly from the prime mover, some of whose rays shine on it. For it has a little light of its own, as we observe in eclipses, but in order to increase its power and efficacy it gets lights from the sun, where it is plentiful. In like manner, I maintain, temporal power receives from spiritual power neither its being, nor its power or authority, nor even its functioning, strictly speaking, but what it receives is the light of grace, which God in heaven and the pope's blessing on earth cause to shine on it in order that it work more effectively.

Lastly, there is a formal fallacy in their argument, for the predicate of the conclusion is not identical with that of the major premise as it should be. Their argument runs thus: the moon receives light from the sun or spiritual power; the temporal power is the moon; therefore the temporal power receives its authority from the spiritual power. In the major premise it is light that the moon receives and in the conclusion it is authority, which are two quite different things, both as to their substance and their meaning, as I have explained.

STUDY QUESTIONS

A What were the points of the conflict between papacy and empire? Did the two parties share any assumptions?

B What did the two sides fear? What did the two sides want?

C What were the main problems facing the German monarchy? The papacy?

Reading 1: Documents of the Investiture Controversy, 1059–1122

What factors made it difficult, if not impossible, for Gregory VII and Henry IV to reach a compromise? Which of the twenty-seven points of the *Dictatus Papae* did Gregory VII implement during his pontificate? Why did the German bishops denounce the pope? What role did Matilda of Tuscany play in the papal-imperial controversy? What does the settlement—the Concordat of Worms—give to each party? Why is this seen as a victory for the papacy?

Reading 2: Otto of Freising, the Incident at Besançon

Why would seemingly trivial things like using the word *beneficium* or a painting of the Emperor Lothar have aroused such passions?

Reading 3: Two Letters of Pope Innocent III

How are these two letters consonant with other documents relating to Innocent III (in Chapter 7, Reading 7)? Were these theories practical? How could they be put into effect?

Reading 4: Salimbene, On the Emperor Frederick II

Setting aside Frederick's callousness, is there a method to his madness?

Reading 5: Dante, De Monarchia

What is Dante's argument? What influences of Aristotle do you find in this selection?

CHAPTER 9

◪ NEW STATES: ENGLAND AND FRANCE

Europe's economic development, the growth of towns, and the more sophisticated culture that these changes inaugurated had a lasting impact on government. Expansions provided not only the means for the development of government—primarily by making available educated people with more sophisticated financial and judicial skills—it also provided incentive, both material (more money to tax) and cultural (a refined sense of the role of the state).

Royal authority had been growing in England since the Norman Conquest of 1066, when William the Conqueror established tight control of the realm (Reading 1). William I's great-grandson, King Henry II, extended royal power significantly (Reading 2). But in King John's reign, a baronial reaction compelled the monarchy to recognize the traditional rights of the nobility and other free English people in the Magna Carta, the "Great Charter" (Reading 3). The conflict between royal authority and the customary rights of subjects found further expression in the legislation of King Edward I (Reading 4).

Although France lagged somewhat behind England, the documents illustrate the gradual rise of the French Capetian monarchy, from the victory of King Louis VI over Thomas of Marle—portrayed here as a veritable monster of twelfth-century Picardy (Reading 5)—to the cult of kingship of King Louis IX (St. Louis) (Reading 6) and the conflicts between King Philip IV (Philip the Fair) and the papacy (Reading 7). It is significant that by 1300, the kingdom of France was able to challenge—successfully—the papacy itself, and to supplant the empire as the most powerful European state.

READING 1

William the Conqueror Subdues Northern England[1]

For about five years after his victory at the battle of Hastings in 1066, William the Conqueror and his Normans were kept busy eliminating pockets of English resistance and suppressing native rebellions such as the one described here. Edwin and Morcar, the preconquest earls of Mercia and Northumbria, did not fight at Hastings and were therefore permitted for a time to keep their earldoms.

The passage shows some of the ways in which William consolidated his new regime in England. The new stone castle was a particularly effective instrument of colonization. (See pp. 206–07 for an illustration of a fortress nearly contemporary to those mentioned in this document.) The author, Orderic Vitalis (1075–1142), was writing a full generation after the event. His sources, oral and written, were generally trustworthy and he used them carefully. But the account of wanton Norman wives which concludes this excerpt is probably exaggerated. Hugh of Grandmesnil did not forfeit his estates, as Orderic suggests, but became a wealthy landholder in central England and bequeathed his lands to one of his sons. Orderic's account of the Norman Conquest is relatively unbiased since he was himself half English and half French. He described himself as an Englishman but spent his youth and adulthood in the Norman abbey of Saint-Evroul, where he died in 1142.

In that same year (1068), the distinguished youths Edwin and Morcar, the sons of Earl Alfgar, rebelled, and as they were joined by many others the entire kingdom of England was in upheaval. King William, however, made peace: in return for count Edwin subduing his brother and nearly a third of England, William promised him his daughter in marriage. But later, owing to the deceitful counsel of the Normans who are a very envious and covetous people, William denied Edwin the hand of the woman for whom he had waited so long. Quite irritated, the two brothers were incited to open rebellion, and a large number of English and the Welsh soon followed. . . .

[At about this time] Bleddyn king of the Welsh went to the aid of his uncles, bringing a multitude of natives with him. Meeting together, many of the English and Welsh nobles complained about the intolerable injuries and indignities which they had suffered at the hands of the Normans and their companions. Using messengers they succeeded in stirring up the insurgents throughout the is-

[1]From *Orderici Vitalis Ecclesiasticae Historiae*, vol. 2, ed. A. Le Prevost; Paris, Société de l'Histoire de France, 1840, pp. 182–186; tr. David S. Spear.

land, both in secret and in public. All swore to strive against the Normans and regain their former liberties. Trouble broke out first and most viciously in the furthest regions beyond the Humber, with the rebels garrisoning themselves in the forests, marshes, estuaries, and even in some of the towns. The city of York was the most explosive, and not even the archbishop himself dared to try to quiet it. Many of the natives began to live in tents, scorning houses whose comforts they thought would make them soft. Indeed, it was for this reason that the Normans called them savages.

King William decided to examine carefully even the remote areas of the realm and to garrison the most advantageous locations against the excursions of the enemy. These fortifications, which the Normans called castles, were seldom found in England before this, and because of them the English, even though they were exceptionally warlike and fearless, found their position greatly weakened. The king built a castle at Warwick, and brought Henry the son of Roger of Beaumont to hold it. Edwin and Morcar, considering with their men the dangers of battle, then sought William's forgiveness, which they obtained so far as they were able. The king next erected a castle at Nottingham and commended it to William Peverel.

Hearing of these events the people of York were disinclined to continue their uprising, and promptly gave up the keys of the city to the king, along with some hostages. Since he was a little leary of their loyalty he built a castle right in the town itself, which he handed over to some carefully chosen knights. After this Archill, the most powerful of the Northumbrians, made peace with the king, and gave over his son to William as a hostage. The bishop of Durham also went to the king seeking peace for Malcolm king of the Scots, and brought the conditions back to Scotland. Malcolm, although he was counted on by the English contingent and was prepared to wage a vigorous campaign on their behalf, nonetheless remained quiet when he heard the peace terms which were offered him. He promptly sent his messengers back with the bishop of Durham, and swore through them that he would remain faithful to the king. Thus by preferring peace to war he was able both to further his own interest and to please many of his own people. For the Scots, although certainly hardy in battle, love leisure and quiet as well, not wishing to disturb the affairs of their neighbors, and are more inclined towards the Christian faith than the pursuit of arms. The king then withdrew, careful though to build castles at Lincoln, Huntingdon, and Cambridge, and to entrust them to his strongest men.

At this time certain Norman women, terribly inflamed by the passions of lust, sent messengers to their men demanding that they return home, adding that unless they did so quickly they would take other mates. They did not themselves dare to cross over to their husbands since they were unaccustomed to sailing, nor did they wish to seek after them in England since there the men were constantly armed and making daily expeditions in which no small amount of blood was lost on both sides. The king of course wanted to keep his knights with him under such unstable conditions, and consequently he offered them lands, revenues, and positions of great power, promising them even more when the whole kingdom should be free from the threat of the enemy. The barons and knights were at a loss, for as long as the king and their own brothers and friends remained surrounded and in danger, they realized that they would be labelled cowards or out-and-out deserters. Yet if they remained, their wives would pollute their beds with the stain of infidelity and besmirch the reputations of their offspring. Finally Hugh of Grandmesnil, who oversaw the Gewissae, that is the area around Winchester, and his brother-in-law Humphrey of Tilleul who had commanded Hastings ever since the day it was first built, along with many others, reluctantly departed while their king still labored with the enemy. They returned to their lewd wives in Normandy, but in so doing relinquished their lands, and neither they nor their heirs were able to recover them afterwards.

READING 2

Four Writs of Henry II[2]

The writ was perhaps the most effective administrative invention of English history. Simplicity itself, the writ was a royal command to a local official ordering him to do (or refrain from doing) a specific act. (The Latin term for writ, *breve*—brief—also hints at its simplicity). Its roots went back to Anglo-Saxon times, but the writ became formalized during the reign of Henry II (1154–1189). The first three writs here constitute significant extensions of the king's authority over land law. Moreover, by making royal justice more accessible, these legal procedures helped extend the authority of the king and his courts. Not coincidentally, most royal writs were sold to plaintiffs by the crown, thereby increasing royal revenues.

The fourth writ, far from being sold and certainly not a generalized formula, emanates from Henry himself. It deals with a highly personal royal concern, namely Henry's ongoing conflict with Archbishop of Canterbury, Thomas Becket. In 1164 Thomas fled England without the king's permission, in the company of some clerical supporters. Henry addresses the bishops of England, ordering them to cut off the revenues of those clerics who accompanied Becket abroad. Quite apart from the writ's success, the dispute ended badly for both king and archbishop when Becket was murdered in his cathedral in 1170.

---

[2]From Ranulf de Glanvill, *Tractatus de legibus et consuetudinibus regni Angliae,* ed. G. E. Woodbine; New Haven, Conn., Yale University Press, 1932, p. 52; tr. J. W. Leedom.

A. ASSIZE OF MORT D'ANCESTOR

The king to the sheriff, greetings. If G. son of O. will give surety for continuing his claim, then summon by good summoners twelve men, free and legal,[3] from the district of _____ , to be before me or my justices on _____ , ready to acknowledge by oath of O., father of G., was seised in demesne as of fee of one virgate of land in that manor on the day that he died; if he died after my coronation; and whether the aforesaid G. is his closest heir. In the meantime they shall have the view of that land, and you shall write down their names. And summon by good summoners R., who holds that land, to be there in order to hear the determination. And you are to bring the summoners and this writ.

B. ASSIZE OF NOVEL DISSEISIN

The king to the sheriff, greetings. A complaint has been made by N. that R. has unlawfully and without judgment disseised him of his free tenement in _____ since my last crossing to Normandy. And so I command you that if the said N. will give you surety for continuing his claim, to restore to that holding the goods and chattels taken from it, and the said tenement with its chattels is to remain in peace until _____ . In the meantime, have twelve men, free and lawful, from the district view the land, and you shall write down their names. And summon them by good summoners to be before me or my justices, ready to make recognizance concerning it. And place under bond and pledges R., or his bailiff, if he cannot be found, to be there in order to hear their determination. And you are to bring the summoners and this writ.

C. WRIT OF RIGHT

The king of Earl W., greetings. I command you without delay to give full right to N. concerning the ten carucates of land in Middleton, which he claims from you by the service of one knight's fee for all service. And unless you do this so that I hear no more complaint about default of judgment, the sheriff of Nottingham will do it.

D. WRIT TO THE BISHOPS OF ENGLAND (DECEMBER 1164)[4]

You know with what malice Thomas, archbishop of Canterbury, has acted towards me and my kingdom, and how basely he has fled. I therefore command you that his clerks, who were with him after his flight, and the other clerks, who

---

[3]Literally, "law-worthy," it's usually translated as "twelve free and lawful men," or "twelve free and legal men."

[4]From *English Historical Documents,* vol. II, second edition, ed. D. C. Douglas and G. W. Greenaway; New York, Oxford University Press, 1981, p. 790.

have disparaged my honour and the honour of the realm, shall not receive any of the revenues which they have within your bishopric, except by my order. Witness: Richard of Lucy. At Marlborough.

Magna Carta, 1215[5]

King John's difficulties reached their climax with a major baronial uprising in 1215, as a result of which he was forced to issue a comprehensive charter guaranteeing customary feudal and political rights. Magna Carta is concerned primarily with the rectification of past abuses of feudal privileges, but it also discloses the significant overlap of lord-vassal relationships with the emerging constitutional doctrine of limited monarchy and government under the law. John (1199–1216) repudiated Magna Carta shortly after issuing it and died in 1216 in the midst of another baronial rebellion. Magna Carta was reissued repeatedly, with certain variations, during the generations that followed.

John, by the grace of God, king of England, lord of Ireland, duke of Normandy and Aquitaine, and count of Anjou, to the archbishops, bishops, abbots, earls, barons, justiciars, foresters, sheriffs, stewards, servants, and to all his bailiffs and faithful subjects, greetings. Know that we, out of reverence for God and for the salvation of our soul and those of all our ancestors and heirs, for the honour of God and the exaltation of holy church, and for the reform of our realm, on the advice of our venerable fathers, Stephen, archbishop of Canterbury, primate of all England and cardinal of the holy Roman church, [and other bishops and magnates]:

1. In the first place have granted to God, and by this our present charter confirmed for us and our heirs for ever that the English church shall be free, and shall have its rights undiminished and its liberties unimpaired; and it is our will that it be thus observed; which is evident from the fact that, before the quarrel between us and our barons began, we willingly and spontaneously granted and by our charter confirmed the freedom of elections which is reckoned most important and very essential to the English church, and obtained confirmation of it

[5]From *English Historical Documents, vol. 3, 1189–1327,* ed. and tr. Harry Rothwell; London, Eyre & Spottiswoode, 1975, pp. 316–324. Reprinted by permission.

from the lord pope Innocent III; the which we will observe and we wish our heirs to observe it in good faith for ever. We have also granted to all free men of our kingdom, for ourselves and our heirs for ever, all the liberties written below, to be had and held by them and their heirs of us and our heirs.

2. If any of our earls or barons or others holding of us in chief by knight service dies, and at his death his heir be of full age and owe relief he shall have his inheritance on payment of the old relief, namely the heir or heirs of an earl £100 for a whole earl's barony, the heir or heirs of a baron £100 for a whole barony, the heir or heirs of a knight 100s, at most, for a whole knight's fee; and he who owes less shall give less according to the ancient usage of fiefs. . . .

6. Heirs shall be married without disparagement, yet so that before the marriage is contracted those nearest in blood to the heir shall have notice.

7. A widow shall have her marriage portion and inheritance forthwith and without difficulty after the death of her husband; nor shall she pay anything to have her dower or her marriage portion or the inheritance which she and her husband held on the day of her husband's death; and she may remain in her husband's house for forty days after his death, within which time her dower shall be assigned to her.

8. No widow shall be forced to marry so long as she wishes to live without a husband, provided that she gives security not to marry without our consent if she holds of us, or without the consent of her lord of whom she holds, if she holds of another. . . .

10. If anyone who has borrowed from the Jews any sum, great or small, dies before it is repaid, the debt shall not bear interest as long as the heir is under age, of whomsoever he holds; and if the debt falls into our hands, we will not take anything except the principal mentioned in the bond. . . .

12. No scutage or aid shall be imposed in our kingdom unless by common counsel of our kingdom, except for ransoming our person, for making our eldest son a knight, and for once marrying our eldest daughter; and for these only a reasonable aid shall be levied. Be it done in like manner concerning aids from the city of London.

13. And the city of London shall have all its ancient liberties and free customs as well by land as by water. Furthermore, we will and grant that all other cities, boroughs, towns, and ports shall have all their liberties and free customs. . . .

20. A free man shall not be amerced for a trivial offence except in accordance with the degree of the offence, and for a grave offence he shall be amerced in accordance with its gravity, yet saving his way of living; and a merchant in the same way, saving his stock-in-trade; and a villein shall be amerced in the same way, saving his means of livelihood—if they have fallen into our mercy: and none of the aforesaid amercements shall be imposed except by the oath of good men of the neighbourhood.

21. Earls and barons shall not be amerced except by their peers, and only in accordance with the degree of the offence. . . .

27. If any free man dies without leaving a will, his chattels shall be distributed by his nearest kinsfolk and friends under the supervision of the church, saving to every one the debts which the deceased owed him. . . .

30. No sheriff, or bailiff of ours, or anyone else shall take the horses or carts of any free man for transport work save with the agreement of that freeman.

31. Neither we nor our bailiffs will take, for castles or other works of ours, timber which is not ours, except with the agreement of him whose timber it is. . . .

38. No bailiff shall in future put anyone to trial upon his own bare word, without reliable witnesses produced for this purpose.

39. No free man shall be arrested or imprisoned or disseised or outlawed or exiled or in any way victimized, neither will we attack him or send anyone to attack him, except by the lawful judgment of his peers or by the law of the land.

40. To no one will we sell, to no one will we refuse or delay right or justice.

41. All merchants shall be able to go out of and come into England safely and securely and stay and travel throughout England, as well by land as by water, for buying and selling by the ancient and right customs free from all evil tolls, except in time of war and if they are of the land that is at war with us. And if such are found in our land at the beginning of a war, they shall be attached, without injury to their persons or goods, until we, or our chief justiciar, know how merchants of our land are treated who were found in the land at war with us when war broke out; and if ours are safe there, the others shall be safe in our land. . . .

45. We will not make justices, constables, sheriffs or bailiffs save of such as know the law of the kingdom and mean to observe it well.

46. All barons who have founded abbeys for which they have charters of the kings of England or ancient tenure shall have the custody of them during vacancies, as they ought to have. . . .

48. All evil customs connected with forests and warrens, foresters and warreners, sheriffs and their officials, river-banks and their wardens shall immediately be inquired into in each county by twelve sworn knights of the same county who are to be chosen by good men of the same county, and within forty days of the completion of the inquiry shall be utterly abolished by them so as never to be restored, provided that we, or our justiciar if we are not in England, know of it first. . . .

52. If anyone has been disseised of or kept out of his lands, castles, franchises or his right by us without the legal judgment of his peers, we will immediately restore them to him: and if a dispute arises over this, then let it be decided by the judgment of the twenty-five barons who are mentioned below in the clause for securing the peace: for all things, however, which anyone has been

disseised or kept out of without the lawful judgment of his peers by King Henry, our father, or by King Richard, our brother, which we have in our hand or are held by others, to whom we are bound to warrant them, we will have the usual period of respite of crusaders, excepting those things about which a plea was started or an inquest made by our command before we took the cross; when however we return from our pilgrimage, of if by any chance we do not go on it, we will at once do full justice therein. . . .

54. No one shall be arrested or imprisoned upon the appeal of a woman for the death of anyone except her husband. . . .

61. Since, moreover, for God and the betterment of our kingdom and for the better allaying of the discord that has arisen between us and our barons we have granted all these things aforesaid, wishing them to enjoy the use of them unimpaired and unshaken for ever, we give and grant them the underwritten security, namely, that the barons shall choose any twenty-five barons of the kingdom they wish, who must with all their might observe, hold and cause to be observed, the peace and liberties which we have granted and confirmed to them by this present charter of ours, so that if we, or our justiciar, or our bailiffs or any one of our servants offend in any way against anyone or transgress any of the articles of the peace or the security and the offence be notified to four of the aforesaid twenty-five barons, those four barons shall come to us, or to our justiciar if we are out of the kingdom, and, laying the transgression before us, shall petition us to have that transgression corrected without delay. And if we do not correct the transgression, or if we are out of the kingdom, if our justiciar does not correct it, within forty days, reckoning from the time it was brought to our notice or to that of our justiciar if we were out of the kingdom, the aforesaid four barons shall refer that case to the rest of the twenty-five barons and those twenty-five barons together with the community of the whole land shall distrain and distress us in every way they can, namely, by seizing castles, lands, possessions, and in such other ways as they can, saving our person and the persons of our queen and our children, until, in their opinion, amends have been made; and when amends have been made, they shall obey us as they did before. And let anyone in the land who wishes take an oath to obey the orders of the said twenty-five barons for the execution of all the aforesaid matters, and with them to distress us as much as he can, and we publicly and freely give anyone leave to take the oath who wishes to take it and we will never prohibit anyone from taking it. Indeed, all those in the land who are unwilling of themselves and of their own accord to take an oath to the twenty-five barons to help them to distrain and distress us, we will make them take the oath as aforesaid at our command. And if any of the twenty-five barons dies or leaves the country or is in any other way prevented from carrying out the things aforesaid, the rest of the aforesaid twenty-five barons shall choose as they think fit another one in his place, and he shall take the oath like the rest. In all matters the execution of which is committed to these twenty-five barons, if

it should happen that these twenty-five are present yet disagree among themselves about anything, or if some of those summoned will not or cannot be present, that shall be held as fixed and established which the majority of those present ordained or commanded, exactly as if all the twenty-five had consented to it; and the said twenty-five shall swear that they will faithfully observe all the things aforesaid and will do all they can to get them observed. And we will procure nothing from anyone, either personally or through anyone else, whereby any of these concessions and liberties might be revoked or diminished; and if any such thing is procured, let it be void and null, and we will never use it either personally or through another. . . .

63. Wherefore we wish and firmly enjoin that the English church shall be free, and that the men in our kingdom shall have and hold all the aforesaid liberties, rights and concessions well and peacefully, freely and quietly, fully and completely, for themselves and their heirs from us and our heirs, in all matters and in all places for ever, as is aforesaid. An oath, moreover, has been taken, as well on our part as on the part of the barons, that all these things aforesaid shall be observed in good faith and without evil disposition. Witness the abovementioned and many others. Given by our hand in the meadow which is called Runnymede between Windsor and Staines on the fifteenth day of June, in the seventeenth year of our reign.

READING 4

Statutes of Edward I[6]

These documents from the reign of Edward I (1277–1307) illustrate the effort of the royal government to control baronial lands by establishing inquiries to investigate the grounds for baronial rights to jurisdiction over such lands (*Quo Warranto:* "By what warrant?"), and by restricting the process of endless links of subinfeudation (*Quia Emptores*). Predictably, the inquiries *Quo Warranto* led to conflicts between the king and some magnates who had held rights for time out of mind, but who lacked formal proof. This episode recounts one incident in the proceedings, and its importance lies in John of Warenne's response to Edward's justices, which reveals an alternate theory of government for the kingdom.

[6]From *Sources of English Constitutional History,* ed. and tr. Carl Stephenson and Frederick G. Marcham; New York, Harper & Row, 1972, pp. 169, 174; and *The Chronicle of Walter of Guisborough,* Camden Society, vol. 89, 3rd series, ed. Harry Rothwell; London, 1957, p. 216; tr. David S. Spear.

A. QUO WARRANTO (STATUTE OF GLOUCESTER OF 1278)

In the year of grace 1278, the sixth of the reign of King Edward, son of King Henry, at Gloucester in the month of August, the same king, having summoned the more discreet men of his kingdom, both greater and lesser, has made provision for the betterment of his kingdom and the fuller administration of justice, as is demanded by the kingly office. . . .

The sheriffs shall have it commonly proclaimed throughout their bailiwicks—that is to say, in cities, boroughs, trading towns, and elsewhere—that all those who claim to have any franchises by charters of the king's predecessors, kings of England, or by other title, shall come before the king or before the itinerant justices on a certain day and at a certain place to show what sort of franchises they claim to have, and by what warrant[7] [they hold them]. . . . And if those who claim to have such franchises, do not come on the day aforesaid, those franchises shall then be taken into the king's hand by the local sheriff in the name of distress; so that they shall not enjoy such franchises until they come to receive justice.

B. WALTER OF GUISBOROUGH, BARONIAL RESPONSE TO THE STATUTE OF GLOUCESTER

Not long afterwards the king (Edward I) upset some of the magnates of the land by sending out his justiciars to find out by what right (*quo warranto*) they held their lands. If they had no good claim, their lands were seized at once. Among those magnates called to appear before the king's justiciars was (John) Earl of Warenne. When asked by what warrant he held his lands, he produced in their presence an ancient and rusty sword, saying, "Here, my lords, here is my warrant. My ancestors rode beside William the Bastard and conquered their lands by this sword. And by this sword I will defend my lands against anyone who wishes to seize them. For it was not the king himself who conquered and subdued these lands, but our ancestors who were with him as comrades and partners." And the magnates agreed with the Earl of Warenne and with his response, and full of turmoil and dissent they withdrew.

C. QUIA EMPTORES, 1290

Whereas the buyers of lands and tenements belonging to the fiefs of magnates and other men have in times past frequently entered upon their fiefs to the prejudice of the same [lords], because the free-holders of the said magnates and other men have sold their lands and tenements to such purchasers to be held in fee by

---

[7]The Latin phrase here is *quo warranto.*

themselves and their heirs of the feoffors and not of the principal lords of the fiefs, whereby those same principal lords have often lost the escheats, marriages, and wardships of lands and tenements belonging to their fiefs; and whereas this has seemed very hard and burdensome to those magnates and other lords, being in such cases manifest disinheritance: [therefore] the lord king in his parliament at Westminister [held] after Easter in the eighteenth year of his reign . . . , at the suggestion of the magnates of his realm, has granted, provided, and established that henceforth every freeman shall be permitted to sell his land or tenement, or a part of it, at pleasure; yet so that the feoffee shall hold that land or tenement of the same principal lord [of whom the feoffor held] and by the same services and customs by which the feoffor earlier held.

READING 5

Suger, Life of Louis VI[8]

Suger (1081–1151), abbot of the French royal monastery of St.-Denis, was a great admirer of Louis VI (1108–1137), who was himself the strongest king since the Carolingian era, and whom Suger depicts as the ideal Christian peacekeeping monarch. Thomas of Marle, whom Suger clearly dislikes, seems in fact (on the basis of independent evidence) to have been every bit as unpleasant as he is depicted in this passage.

A king is obliged by virtue of his office to crush with his strong right hand the impudence of tyrants. For such men freely provoke wars, take pleasure in plunder, oppress the poor, destroy the churches, and give themselves free reign to do whatsoever they wish. And if left to their own devices, such men are further inflamed, for the forces of evil seek always to crush those who are slipping out of their grip while happily stoking the passions of those whom they hope to hold fast for all eternity.

One such wicked man was Thomas of Marle. For while King Louis was busy fighting in the wars which we mentioned earlier, Thomas ravaged the regions around Laon, Reims, and Amiens. Indeed, the devil encouraged him in these things, for the devil as we know is accustomed to leading fools to their damnation. Thomas devastated the region with the fury of a wolf. No fear of ecclesiastical penalty persuaded him to spare the clergy; no feeling of humility convinced

[8]From Suger, *Vie de Louis VI Le Gros,* ed. Henri Waquet; Paris, Société d'Edition "Les Belles Lettres," 1964, pp. 172–179, tr. David S. Spear.

him to spare the people. Everyone was slaughtered, everything destroyed. He snatched two prize estates from the nuns of Saint-John of Laon. And treating the two castles of Crécy-sur-Serre and Nouvion-Catillon as his own, Thomas equipped them with new ramparts and tall towers. In a word, he transformed them into a dragon's lair and a den of thieves, exposing the nearby inhabitants to the miseries of fire and plunder.

Fed up with the intolerable afflictions of this man, the churchmen of France met together (on December 6, 1114) at a great general council at Beauvais. There they passed a sentence of condemnation against the enemies of Jesus Christ. The venerable papal legate Cuno, bishop of Praeneste, was particularly moved by the numerous pleas of the church and the cries of the orphans and the poor. He drew the sword of Saint Peter against Thomas of Marle, and with the unanimous assent of the council, declared him excommunicated, ripped from him *in absentia* the titles and honors of knighthood, branded him a criminal, and declared him unworthy of being called a Christian.

Heeding the wishes of so great a council, King Louis moved quickly against Thomas. Accompanied by his army and the clergy (to whom the king was ever devoted), he turned at once against the heavily defended castle of Crécy. There, thanks to his men at arms, or should we say on account of divine aid, Louis achieved swift victory. He seized the new towers as if they were no more than the huts of peasants; he drove out the criminals; he piously slaughtered the impious; and as for those who had showed no pity, he in turn showed no pity towards them. Anyone seeing the castle engulfed in flames would have understood that, "His whole world shall join Him in the fight against His frenzied foes." (Wisdom of Solomon 5:21).

Flushed by the success of his decisive victory, the king moved quickly against the other illegally held castle, Nouvion. There he was approached by a man who reported the following: "Please know, your majesty, that this wicked castle is harboring a group of men so despicable that hell alone is worthy of housing them. These are the very men who, when you ordered the commune of Laon to be suppressed, set fire not only to the city but also to the cathedral and several other churches. They martyred all of the nobles in the city who dared to come to the aid of their bishop. Worse, these men brutally murdered Bishop Gaudry himself,[9] defender of the church and anointed of Christ, leaving his naked body exposed to the beasts and birds of prey, and cutting off the very finger which held his episcopal ring. Now these horrible men, advised by the evil Thomas of Marle himself, have seized the castle keep."[10]

---

[9]This is the same unfortunate Gaudry, bishop of Laon, who meets death in Chapter 5, Reading 2 (his name is spelled "Gautier" in that source).

[10]The keep was the central tower of a medieval castle.

Driven now by a double anger, King Louis attacked the illegal castle. He burst the walls asunder, like the gates of hell, freeing the innocent, punishing the guilty most severely, and avenging the injuries of the many. Thirsting for justice, Louis decreed that all those murderers he came across would hang from the gibbet, their bodies left for the kites, the crows, and the vultures to feed upon. They richly deserved this punishment since they had not feared to harm the Lord's anointed.

Having levelled the illegitimate castles, and having restored to the nuns of Saint-John their lost estates, the king turned to deal with the city of Amiens. There a certain tyrant named Adam had fortified himself in the city's keep and had laid waste to the city's churches and neighborhoods. Louis besieged the towel for nearly two years, finally taking it from the defenders. Having taken the tower, he completely destroyed it, bringing peace to the region at last, and thereby carrying out his duties as king, for "it is not for nothing that (rulers) hold the power of the sword" (Romans 13:4). And Louis deprived the evil Thomas and his heirs of the lordship of the city of Amiens forever.

READING 6

Documents Relating to Louis IX[11]

Matthew Paris (c. 1200–c. 1259), a monk of St. Albans Abbey, was an Englishman who, despite his name, was probably neither born nor educated in Paris. He was thus a contemporary but not a countryman of St. Louis. Nevertheless, he was in a position to be well informed about the affairs of Western Christendom: St. Albans was a much visited abbey, a day's journey from London on the main road to the north. Matthew was personally acquainted with Henry III; his queen, Eleanor of Province; and important barons, bishops, and royal officials.

The first passage here illustrates the importance of relics and religious ceremonial in intensifying the sense of holiness associated with the French monarch. The relics described here were among the most significant in Christendom. Whether the cross in question was actually the "true cross" remains a matter of debate, but it did have a verifiable pedigree running back to the fourth century. St. Louis took relics very seriously and was not easily fooled. His "beautiful chapel at Paris" described toward the end of

---

[11]From Matthew Paris, *History of the English,* vol. 1, tr. J. A. Giles; London, Henry G. Bohn, 1852, pp. 324–325, 352; and Joinville and Villehardouin, *Chronicles of the Crusader,* tr. M. R. B. Shaw; New York, Penguin Books, 1982, pp. 188–190.

the selection is known as La Sainte-Chapelle and remains to this day one of the architectural marvels of Europe.

The second selection is from Jean de Joinville's *Life of Saint Louis.* Joinville (1224–1317), a nobleman from Champagne, was personally acquainted with his king, accompanying him on the Seventh Crusade. The incident discussed here, an uprising of Henry III of England and Hugh of Lusignan against Louis IX over control of Poitou, shows Louis's ability to subdue a major rebellion (not unlike Louis VI defeating Thomas de Marle in the previous Reading). Effective kings had to be able to thwart attempts to weaken their power and to reward loyal followers. According to Joinville, Louis was adept at both policies.

The third passage relates to Blanche of Castile (1188–1252). She was the daughter of Alfonso VIII of Castile, the wife of Louis VIII of France (1223–1226), and, most importantly, the mother of Louis IX (1226–1270)– St. Louis. Blanche was a principal formative influence on St. Louis. She instilled in him a deep sense of piety, and she served France with great political astuteness as regent both during Louis's long minority and later when he was abroad on the first of his two crusades. Through most of the intervening years, Blanche was a major adviser to her royal son. A modern French historian has said of her, "To all intents and purposes she may be counted among the kings of France."

A. MATTHEW PARIS, LOUIS IX RECEIVES CERTAIN RELICS

In this year [1241], the holy cross of our Lord, which, after the time of Saladin, had remained at Damietta until the unfortunate battle, in which that city had been first gained and afterwards lost, when it fell into the hands of the Saracens, was brought into the kingdom of France, by the agency of the French king and his mother, Blanche, and by the grace of Christ seconding their pious wishes: they gave a large sum of money in order to obtain possession of the same. When this cross was first sold, it was bought by the Venetians for twenty thousand pounds, and they obtained it from the two sons of J., king of Jerusalem, who wanted money to make war on the Greeks; and afterwards Baldwin pawned it for a still larger sum of money, and lastly sold it to Louis, the French king.

On the Friday next preceding Easter-day, on which day our Lord Jesus Christ was nailed to the life-giving-cross for the redemption of the world, this said cross was carried to Paris from the church of St. Antoine, where it had been placed on a vehicle of some kind, on which the king mounted with the two queens, namely, Blanche of Castile, his mother, and Margaret of Provence, his wife, and his brothers, and in the presence of the archbishops, bishops, abbots, and other religious men, as well as the French nobles, and surrounded by a countless host of people, who were awaiting this glorious sight with great joy of heart, raised the cross above his head with tears, whilst the prelates who were present cried with a loud voice, "Behold the cross of our Lord." After all had worshipped it with due reverence and devotion, the king himself, barefooted, ungirt, and with his head bare, and after a fast of three days, following the example of the noble and august Heraclius,[12] carried it in wool to the cathedral church of Notre Dame at Paris; the brothers of the king, too, after having purified themselves by similar acts of devotion, by confessions, fasting, and prayers, followed him on foot with the two queens.

They also carried the crown of thorns (which divine mercy had, as has been before stated, given to the kingdom of France the year before), and raising it on high on a similar vehicle to the other, presented it to the gaze of the people. Some of the nobles supported the arms of the king and his brothers, whilst carrying this pious burden, lest they should become fatigued by holding their hands constantly raised, and give way beneath this priceless treasure. This was done circumspectly at the wish of the prelates, that so holy a thing might be handled reverently by those whose prudent conduct had gained so much glory, after the example of Heraclius, whom we have before mentioned. When they arrived at the cathedral church, all the bells in the city were set ringing, and after special prayers had been solemnly read, the king returned to his great palace, which is in the middle of the city, carrying his cross, his brothers carrying the crown, and the priests following in a regular procession (a sight more solemn or more joyful than which the kingdom of France had never seen), and each and all then, with clasped hands, glorified God, who thus showed his especial love for the French kingdom above all others, and for affording it to his consolation and protection.

Thus, therefore, our Lord Jesus Christ, the King of kings, the Lord of lords, whose judgments are a great deep, in whose hands are the hearts of kings, giving health to whomsoever he wills, in a short space of time endowed and enriched the kingdom of France with these three precious gifts, namely, the aforesaid crown and cross of our Lord, of which we have now made mention, and the body of the blessed Edmund of Canterbury, the archbishop and confessor, which was now manifestly shining forth with unusual miracles. The French king therefore ordered a chapel of handsome structure, suitable for the reception of his said treasure, to be built near his palace, and in it he afterwards placed the said relics with due honour. Besides these the French king had, in his beautiful chapel at Paris, the garment belonging to Christ, the lance, that is to say, the iron head of the lance, and the sponge, and other relics besides; on which account the

[12]The East Roman emperor (610–641) who liberated the "true cross" from the Persians.

pope granted an indulgence of forty days to all who went to them in the chapel at Paris for the sake of paying their devotions.

B. JOINVILLE, LOUIS IX SUBDUES REBELLION

[In the summer of 1242] the King of England [Henry III] came into Gascony to make war on his fellow monarch. Our saintly king rode out to fight against him with as large a force as he could get together. The King of England and the Comte de la Marche [Hugh of Lusignan] advanced to join battle with him before the castle of Taillebourg, which stands beside a wretched little stream called La Charente, at a point where one cannot cross except by a very narrow stone bridge.

As soon as King Louis reached Taillebourg, and the two armies had come in sight of one another, our men, who were on the side of the stream where the castle stood, spared no efforts to get across to the other side. With great risk to themselves they passed over the stream in boats and on pontoon bridges, to fling themselves on the English. Then a fierce and furious fight began. The king, who saw the way things were turning, rushed headlong into danger with the others; but for every man he had with him when he had crossed the stream, the English had at least twenty. None the less, as God willed, the moment the English saw the king cross over, they lost heart and fled for refuge to Saintes. Some of our men followed them into the city but got entangled in their midst and were taken prisoner.

Those of our people who had been taken at Saintes reported later that they had heard talk of a serious quarrel between the King of England and the Comte de la Marche, in which the king had accused the count of sending for him on the pretext that he would find great support in France. At any rate, on the night of his reverse at Taillebourg the King of England left Saintes and went back to Gascony.

The Comte de la Marche, as one who saw there was no help for it, surrendered to King Louis, and took his wife[13] and children with him to prison. Since he now had the count in his power, the king, in making peace with him, was able to obtain a great part of his land, but how much I cannot say, for I had nothing to do with the matter since at that time I was not as yet a knight. I was told, however, that apart from the land the king thus gained, the Comte de la Marche paid ten thousand *livres parisis* into the royal treasury, and a similar sum every subsequent year.

While I was with the king at Poitiers, I had met a certain knight, called Geoffroy de Rançon, who, so I was told, had been greatly wronged by the Comte de

---

[13]Hugh's wife, Isabella, was the widow of King John of England and therefore the mother of Henry III. After this rebellion she retired to a convent.

la Marche. Because of this he had vowed on the Holy Gospels never to have his hair cut short, as is the custom with knights, but wear it long like a woman's until such time as he should be avenged on the count, either by his own hand or another's. As soon as this knight saw the Comte de la Marche, his wife, and his children kneeling before the king and crying for mercy, he immediately sent for a little stool, and had his hair trimmed there and then, in the presence of the king, the Comte de la Marche, and everyone else who was there.

In the course of his recent campaign against the king of England and the barons King Louis had made many generous gifts of money, as I was told by those who returned from this expedition. But neither on account of such gifts nor on account of expenses incurred in that campaign, nor in any others, either oversea or at home, did he ever demand or accept any monetary aid from his barons, his knights, his men, or any of his fine cities in such a way as to cause complaint. Nor is this to be wondered at; for he acted thus on the advice of the good mother at his side, whose counsels he always followed, and also on the advice of certain wise and worthy men who had remained loyal servants of the crown since the time of his father and his grandfather.

C.   MATTHEW PARIS, THE DEATH OF QUEEN BLANCHE

About this same time, namely on the first Sunday of our Lord's Advent, which fell on the first day of the month [1252], died that lady of all ladies of this world, Blanche, the mother of the French king; the guardian, protectress, and queen of France, who departed this life, that, like a devoted handmaiden, she might reverently meet our Lord Jesus Christ at his coming. Her death, a great loss and source of grief to the French, was prematurely brought on by manifold sorrows, amongst which were the death of her husband, King Louis, who was taken from her in the most agreeable time of her youth, leaving the French kingdom dependent on her, a matter of no slight solicitude; the sickly weakness of her son, his assumption of the cross, and his pilgrimage, from which he determined not to return; then his capture by the infidels, a circumstance to be lamented by all Christendom; also the disgraceful flight and subsequent death by drowning of Robert, count of Artois; again the incurable disease of Alphonso, count of Poitou; and lastly, the news which had been brought to her that her eldest son, the French king, who was fighting for God in the Holy Land, intended to remain there all his life and to die there, and thereby to obtain a heavenly kingdom in exchange for his earthly one. Thus, therefore, languished in desolation and prematurely died that most noble lady Blanche, the mother of the aforesaid princes, pledges of affection of which she had been bereaved. Seeing that death was near at hand, she left orders for her body to be buried at a nunnery at Pontoise, which she had founded and built in great magnificence; indeed, prior to her death she became a professed nun, and took the veil, over which was placed the crown, and she also wore the robes of a queen, and in this manner dressed she was buried becomingly. Thus, therefore, did the noble lady Blanche, a woman in sex, but a man in counsels, one worthy to be compared with Semiramis, bid farewell to the world, leaving the French kingdom comfortless and void of all consolation.

READING 7

Philip the Fair and Boniface VIII[14]

This emphatic statement of the papal monarchy doctrine is by no means the assertion of papal self-confidence that it might seem. It was issued in November 1302 by Pope Boniface VIII (1294–1303) as he was nearing the end of his stormy pontificate. King Edward I of England and King Philip IV (1285–1314) of France (called Philip the Fair) had been advancing the doctrine of royal authority against the claims of the international church. Boniface responded to Philip of France with *Unam Sanctam*—somewhat less than the assertion of papal self-confidence that it may appear, given the threat. Less than a year after its issue, Philip sent a band of French and Italian troops to confront Boniface at his residence at Anagni. Boniface died three weeks later, in a state of shock and humiliation.

A. UNAM SANCTAM, 1302

That there is one holy, Catholic and apostolic Church we are bound to believe and to hold, our faith urging us, and this we do firmly believe and simply confess; and that outside this Church there is no salvation or remission of sins, as her spouse proclaims in the Canticles, "One is my dove, my perfect one. She is the only one of her mother, the chosen of her that bore her" (Canticles 6:8); which represents one mystical body whose head is Christ, while the head of Christ is God. In this Church there is one Lord, one faith, one baptism. At the time of the Flood there was one ark, symbolizing the one Church. It was finished in one cubit and had one helmsman and captain, namely Noah, and we read that all things on earth outside of it were destroyed. This Church we venerate and

---

[14]From *The Crisis of Church and State, 1050–1300,* ed. Brian Tierney; Englewood Cliffs, N.J., Prentice Hall, 1964, pp. 188–189, 191.

this alone, the Lord saying through his prophet, "Deliver, O God, my soul from the sword, my only one from the power of the dog" (Psalm 21:21). He prayed for the soul, that is himself, the head, and at the same time for the body, which he called the one Church on account of the promised unity of faith, sacraments and charity of the Church. This is that seamless garment of the Lord which was not cut but fell by lot. Therefore there is one body and one head of this one and only Church, not two heads as though it were a monster, namely Christ and Christ's vicar, Peter and Peter's successor, for the Lord said to this Peter, "Feed my sheep" (John 21:17). He said "My sheep" in general, not these or those, whence he is understood to have committed them all to Peter. Hence, if the Greeks or any others say that they were not committed to Peter and his successors, they necessarily admit that they are not of Christ's flock, for the Lord says in John that there is one sheepfold and one shepherd.

We are taught by the words of the Gospel that in this Church and in her power there are two swords, a spiritual one and a temporal one. For when the apostles said "Here are two swords" (Luke 22:38), meaning in the Church since it was the apostles who spoke, the Lord did not reply that it was too many but enough. Certainly anyone who denies that the temporal sword is in the power of Peter has not paid heed to the words of the Lord when he said, "Put up thy sword into its sheath" (Matthew 26:52). Both then are in the power of the Church, the material sword and the spiritual. But the one is exercised for the Church, the other by the Church, the one by the hand of the priest, the other by the hand of kings and soldiers, though at the will and sufferance of the priest. One sword ought to be under the other and the temporal authority subject to the spiritual power. For, while the apostle says, "There is no power but from God and those that are ordained of God" (Romans 13:1), they would not be ordained unless one sword was under the other and, being inferior, was led by the other to the highest things. For, according to the blessed Dionysius, it is the law of divinity for the lowest to be led to the highest through intermediaries. In the order of the universe all things are not kept in order in the same fashion and immediately but the lowest are ordered by the intermediate and inferiors by superiors. But that the spiritual power excels any earthly one in dignity and nobility we ought the more openly to confess in proportion as spiritual things excel temporal ones. Moreover we clearly perceive this from the giving of tithes, from benediction and sanctification, from the acceptance of this power and from the very government of things. For, the truth bearing witness, the spiritual power has to institute the earthly power and to judge it if it has not been good. So is verified the prophecy of Jeremiah [1:10] concerning the Church and the power of the Church, "Lo, I have set thee this day over the nations and over kingdoms" etc.

Therefore, if the earthly power errs, it shall be judged by the spiritual power, if a lesser spiritual power errs it shall be judged by its superior, but if the supreme spiritual power errs it can be judged only by God not by man, as the apostle witnesses, "The spiritual man judgeth all things and he himself is judged of no man" (1 Corinthians 2:15). Although this authority was given to a man and is exercised by a man it is not human but rather divine, being given to Peter at God's mouth, and confirmed to him and to his successors in him, the rock whom the Lord acknowledged when he said to Peter himself "Whatsoever thou shalt bind" etc. (Matthew 16:19). Whoever therefore resists this power so ordained by God resists the ordinance of God unless, like the Manicheans, he imagines that there are two beginnings, which we judge to be false and heretical, as Moses witnesses, for not "in the beginnings" but "in the beginning" God created heaven and earth (Genesis 1:1). Therefore we declare, state, define and pronounce that it is altogether necessary to salvation for every human creature to be subject to the Roman Pontiff.

B.   THE INCIDENT AT ANAGNI, 1303

Behold, Reverend Father, at dawn of the vigil of the Nativity of the Blessed Mary just past, suddenly and unexpectedly there came upon Anagni a great force of armed men of the party of the King of France and of the two deposed Colonna cardinals. Arriving at the gates of Anagni and finding them open, they entered the town and at once made an assault upon the palace of the Pope and upon that of the Marquis, the Pope's nephew. . . .

After a time, however, the Marquis, nephew of the Pope, realizing that defense was no longer possible, surrendered to Sciarra and the captain, so that they spared his own life and those of his sons and companions. In this fashion were the Marquis and one of his sons taken and thrown into prison, while another son escaped by means of a hidden passage. When the Pope heard this reported, he himself wept bitterly, yet not even the Pope was in a position to hold out longer. Sciarra and his forces broke through the doors and windows of the papal palace at a number of points, and set fire to them at others, till at last the angered soldiery forced their way to the Pope. Many of them heaped insults upon his head and threatened him violently, but to them all the Pope answered not so much as a word. And when they pressed him as to whether he would resign the Papacy, firmly did he refuse—indeed he preferred to lose his head—as he said in his vernacular: "*E le col, e le cape!*" which means: "Here is my neck and here my head." Therewith he proclaimed in the presence of them all that as long as life was in him, he would not give up the Papacy. Sciarra, indeed, was quite ready to kill him, but he was held back by the others so that no bodily injury was done the Pope. Cardinal Peter of Spain was with the Pope all through the struggle, though the rest of his retinue had slipped away. Sciarra and the captain appointed guards to keep the Pope in custody after some of the papal doormen had fled and others had been slain. Thus [were] the Pope and his nephew taken in Anagni on the said vigil of the Blessed Mary at about the hour of vespers and it is believed that the Lord Pope put in a bad night.

The soldiers, on first breaking in, had pillaged the Pope, his chamber and his treasury of utensils and clothing, fixtures, gold and silver and everything found therein so that the Pope had been made as poor as Job upon receiving word of his misfortune. Moreover, the Pope witnessed all and saw how the wretches divided his garments and carted away his furniture, both large items and small, deciding who would take this and who that, and yet he said no more than: "The Lord gave and the Lord taketh away, etc." And anyone who was in a position to seize or to lay hold upon something, took and seized it and carried it off.

STUDY QUESTIONS

A What are the differences and similarities between the governance of England and France in this period?

B How would you characterize the tension between the kings of France and England on the one hand and their barons on the other?

C Which country has the stronger monarchy? Which country has the stronger government?

Reading 1: William the Conqueror Subdues Northern England

What role did castles play in William's subjection of England? Why does the author of this selection harbor such a low view of Norman women?

Reading 2: Four Writs of Henry II

How are these writs examples of some of the general legal and administrative trends in England at the time of Henry II? What role do the sheriffs and grand juries play in the administration of justice?

Reading 3: Magna Carta, 1215

What do the barons stand to gain from Magna Carta? The townspeople? Do you see any general principles that make the Magna Carta a cardinal document in legal history?

Reading 4: Statutes of Edward I

How can Edward's reign be seen as a conflict between statutory law versus customary law? What do the barons stand to lose from the Statute of Gloucester? What is John, earl of Warenne's theory of government?

Reading 5: Suger, Life of Louis VI

What aspects of the document are consonant with the Crusading mentality? What are the responsibilities of a king as perceived by Suger and Louis VI?

Reading 6: Documents Relating to Louis IX

How does Louis IX foster a cult of sacral kingship for the French monarchy? What were some of the difficulties Blanche faced in being a queen? What are the responsibilities of a king as perceived by Joinville and Louis IX? How would Louis IX respond to John, earl of Warenne (Reading 4B)?

Reading 7: Philip the Fair and Boniface VIII

To what degree does *Unam Sanctam* follow in the path of Gregory VII's *Dictatus Papae?* How might Boniface's humiliation at Anagni have led to his death a few weeks later?

MAJOR LOCATIONS MENTIONED IN PART THREE

THREE

THE LATE MIDDLE AGES

The late Middle Ages (c. 1300–1500) are difficult to characterize. The era was one of plague, depression, and strife, but it also witnessed the Italian Renaissance, the invention of printing, and the early voyages of discovery.

The Hundred Years War (1337–1453) brought death, starvation, and intermittent anarchy to the French countryside while driving the English monarchy to the brink of bankruptcy and forcing it to make significant concessions to Parliament. England suffered widespread disorder, a bloodcurdling peasants' revolt, the deposition and murder of kings, and a drawn-out civil war between rival aristocratic factions—the so-called Wars of the Roses (1455–1485). Spain, too, was afflicted by civil strife, as were Italy and central Europe. Yet by the close of the period, strong monarchies had reemerged in France, England, and Spain, and the Italian Renaissance had reached its height.

The late medieval Church was similarly troubled. The popes moved from faction-ridden Rome to Avignon in 1309 and remained there for more than a century. Between 1378 and 1415, the Church was torn by schism as two popes, and later three, contended for the spiritual supremacy of Christendom. The period ended with the papacy reunited and planted firmly back in Rome, but drained of much of its former prestige and international authority. The Protestant Reformation was just beyond the horizon.

The civil and economic unrest of the late Middle Ages was aggravated enormously by the onset of bubonic plague. Descending on Europe in 1348, the Black Death carried off perhaps a third of its population in the ensuing two years and returned periodically during the next three centuries. As a consequence of plague, warfare, and famine, Europe's population was lower in 1500 than in 1300, and most of its major cities had diminished accordingly. But in the last half of the fifteenth century, the population reversed its long downward trend and commerce began to revive. By 1500 there were clear signs that Europe had surmounted its late medieval crisis. Western civilization was moving into an era of renewed prosperity and global expansion.

CHAPTER 10

❀ CONSTITUTIONAL EUROPE

The Hundred Years War widened the gulf between the French and English systems of royal governance, propelling France toward the absolutism of early modern times while advancing the authority of Parliament in England. The war was far too expensive for either government to support with ordinary revenues. Whereas the French monarchy, under King Charles V, succeeded in establishing the right to tax its subjects relatively freely on the grounds of the military emergency, the English monarchy had to obtain Parliament's permission for extraordinary taxes. Therefore Parliament—more specifically the House of Commons—enjoyed considerable leverage; it insisted more and more that the monarchy grant its petitions in return for its own permission to levy new taxes. On rare occasions, it even exercised the right to impeach royal ministers (Reading 1). At the same time, a struggle among noble families to gain the benefits of political power undermined royal authority and stable government in England (Reading 2). Reading 3 describes a constitutional movement amidst the horrors of the Hundred Years War in fourteenth-century France—a movement led by the Paris merchant Étienne Marcel, who was subsequently assassinated. The recovery of French military fortunes in the next century is illustrated by Readings 4 and 5, on Joan of Arc and the military juggernaut of King Charles VII.

Sir John Fortescue, writing in the fifteenth century, distinguishes sharply and perhaps unfairly between the English and French regimes (Reading 6); his views should be compared with those of the French historian Philippe de Commynes, on monarchical authority in France (Reading 7).

The German monarchy (or Holy Roman Empire), battered by generations of struggle with the papacy and German princes, emerged from the Middle Ages in crippled condition (Reading 8). The Roman papacy was similarly weakened by its long exile in Avignon, its lapse into schism, its conflicts with Church councils, and its declining moral reputation (Readings 9–13).

READING 1

Documents Relating to Crown and Parliament in England[1]

These documents illustrate the changing relationship between crown and Parliament during the period of the Hundred Years War (1337–1453) and the split within Parliament between lords and commons. It was the commons (small-holding shire knights and representatives from towns) who wrung the most important privileges from the financially strapped monarchy. Step by step, the crown was surrendering its initiative as Parliament established control over direct taxation and used that power to compel the king to grant its petitions. On the principle of "redress before supply," Parliament was insisting that the king enact its petitions into law without alteration. Behind the mask of courtly and respectful language, one can discern some sharp-eyed negotiating over difficult constitutional issues.

A.   THE PARLIAMENT OF 1348

The knights of the shires and the others of the commons were told that they should withdraw together and take good counsel as to how our lord the king could be aided to his greatest advantage and to the least burdening of his people and at last gave their response:

Thus the said poor commons, to their own excessive hurt, grant to our lord the king three fifteenths[2] to be levied during three years, on condition that this aid shall be assigned and kept solely for the war of our lord the king and shall not be assigned to pay old debts; and also, no imposition, tax, nor loan be levied by the privy council without their grant and assent.

And afterwards the said commons were told that all individual persons who wished to present petitions in this parliament should do so, and the commons presented their petitions in the manner following:

Item. The commons pray the petitions presented in the last parliament shall be observed; and that by no bill presented in this parliament shall the responses already granted be changed: for the commons acknowledge no such bill as may be presented by any one to effect the contrary.

---

[1]From *English Historical Documents,* vol. IV, ed. A. R. Myers; New York, Oxford University Press, 1969, pp. 443, 446–447, 455, 460–462.

[2]A "fifteenth" was a tax of one-fifteenth of the value of all a person's property apart from real estate. Unlike modern taxes, which are levied on real estate or income, these assessments applied to the worth of an individual's movable goods.

Response: At an earlier time the king, by the advice of the prelates and lords of the land, made answer to the petitions of the commons regarding the law of the land, to the effect that neither the laws held in times past nor the process of the same law could be changed without making a new statute.

And there were two causes which specifically affected our lord the king: first, concerning the war which our lord the king had undertaken against his adversary of France, the question was what shall be done when the truce has ended? The other cause, concerning the peace of England, and how and in what manner it could best be kept. And the knights of the shire and the commons were told that they must treat together and what they felt they must show to the king and his council. These knights and commons discussed together on these matters for four days, and at last they answered:

Very dread lord, as for your war and the array of it, we are so ignorant and simple that we do not know, nor are we able, to counsel on these matters. Wherefore we pray your gracious lordship to have us excused from your order, and may it please you, by the advice of the great and wise men of your council to ordain on this point what shall seem best to you.

B.   THE "GOOD" PARLIAMENT OF 1376

Richard Lyons, merchant of London, was impeached and accused by the commons for many deceptions, extortions, and other crimes committed by him against our lord the king and against his people, both when he was in attendance on the household of the king and when he was collector of the king's customs, because he has put and caused to be put certain new imposition on wools and on merchandise without the assent of parliament; and he has levied and collected those impositions largely for his own use and the use of those who attend the king.

Thereupon the said Richard was ordered to prison during the king's pleasure, to be put to fine and ransom, according to the amount and heinousness of his offense, and that he lose his liberty [citizenship] in the city of London, and that he never hold office from the king, nor enter the council or the palace of the king.

C.   THE PARLIAMENT OF 1401

The commons showed to our lord the king that in several parliaments before this time their common petitions have not been answered before they made their grant of some aid or subsidy to our lord the king. And therefore they prayed our lord the king that for the great ease and comfort of the commons, our lord the king might be pleased to grant to the commons that they might have knowledge of the answers to their petitions before any such grant had thus been made.

D. THE PARLIAMENT OF 1407

The king our sovereign lord sitting in the council chamber, the lords spiritual and temporal summoned to this present parliament being with him, they discussed amongst themselves the estate of the realm, and the means necessary for its defense against its enemies, and they agreed that it would not be possible to resist their malice, unless our sovereign lord the king should be granted in this present parliament some notable aid and subsidy. And on this the lords were then asked the question, "What aid would suffice and be necessary in this case?" To which demand and question the lords answered severally that considering the needs of the king on the one hand, and the poverty of the people on the other, the least aid that would suffice would be to have one and a half tenths from the cities and boroughs and one and a half fifteenths from the other lay people, etc. On which, by the king's command, the commons were bidden to send before our lord the king and the lords a certain number of persons of their company to hear and report to their companions what our lord the king should have commanded them. When this was reported to the commons, they were much disturbed, saying and affirming that it was a great prejudice and derogation of their liberties. And when our lord the king heard that, he granted and declared with the advice and assent of the same lords in the following manner. That is to say, that in this present parliament and those to be held in the future, the lords may well discuss together with regard to the state and remedies—always provided that the lords for their part and the commons on their part shall not make any report to our lord the king about any grant made by the commons and assented to by the lords, until the lords and commons are of one assent and agreement in this matter; and then it shall be reported in manner and form as is customary, that is, by the mouth of the speaker of the commons for the time being, so that the lords and commons may have the thanks of our lord the king. Moreover our lord the king wishes, with the assent of the lords, that the proceedings in this present parliament set forth above shall not be turned to the prejudice or derogation of the liberty of the commons, but he wishes that he and all the other estates shall be as free as they were before.

E. THE PARLIAMENT OF 1414

Our sovereign lord, your humble and true lieges beseech unto your very righteousness that from this time forward, no law ever be made and engrossed as a law or statute, which should change the wording and the intention asked by the speaker[3] without the assent of the commons.

---

[3]Speaker of the House of Commons.

READING 2

Adam Usk, The Deposition of King Richard II, 1399[4]

It would be easy to imagine from reading just parliamentary records that England saw a smooth, almost decorous transition to representative government. But in the century and a half from 1327 to 1485, England saw five monarchs deposed, three of them murdered, one dead on the battlefield. English politics, no less than French, was a field of "mortal debate" for the great families.

Perhaps the most striking example is the deposition of Richard II. Richard had alienated the great barons of his realm; and when he struck out at Henry of Bolingbroke, the Duke of Lancaster, the barons struck back. Assembling a coalition, Henry trapped Richard, forced him to abdicate, and claimed the throne for himself. This event would reverberate for a century, as magnates struggled with the succession to Richard II.

Adam Usk was a cleric from western England who wrote a chronicle of these events. Though he disapproved of Richard II and ultimately joined Henry Bolingbroke, he also recognized the failings of Richard's opponents.

Two days before the end of July [Henry Bolingbroke] arrived at Bristol, and there he struck off the heads of Sir William le Scrope, the king's treasurer, and Sir John Bussy and Sir Henry Green, knights, the king's most evil councilors and the chief fosterers of his malice. There was I, the writer of this chronicle, present with my lord the archbishop of Canterbury; and I, through favor, made peace between the duke and the lordship of Usk, the place of my birth, which he had determined to harry, on account of the resistance of the lady of that place, the king's niece, there ordered; and I also got Sir Edward de Charlton, then husband of that lady, to be taken into the duke's following;[5] and I caused all the people of Usk, who for the said resistance had gathered at Montstarri, to their great joy to return to their own homes.

At length the duke came to Hereford with his host, on the second day of August, and lodged in the bishop's palace; and on the morrow he moved towards Chester, and passed the night in the priory at Leominster. The next night he spent at Ludlow, in the king's castle, not sparing the wine which was therein

---

[4]From *Chronicles of the Revolution, 1397–1400: The Reign of Richard II,* ed. and tr. Chris Given-Wilson; Manchester, England, Manchester University Press, 1993, pp. 157–161.

[5]Edward succeeded his brother John as Lord Charlton of Powys in 1401 and died in 1421; he had just married (in June 1399) Eleanor, daughter of Thomas Holand earl of Kent (d. 1397), Richard II's half-brother.

stored. At this place, I, who am now writing, obtained from the duke and from my lord of Canterbury the release of brother Thomas Prestbury, master in theology, a man of my day at Oxford and a monk of Shrewsbury, who was kept in prison by King Richard, for that he had righteously preached certain things against his follies; and I also got him promotion to the abbacy of his house.[6] Then, passing through Shrewsbury, the duke tarried there two days; where he made proclamation that the army should march on Chester, but should spare the people and the country, because by mediation they had submitted themselves to him. Wherefore many who coveted that land for plunder departed to their homes. But little good did the proclamation do for the country, as will be seen. The reasons why the duke decided to invade that country were: because, abetting the king, as has been said, it ceased not to molest the realm for the space of two whole years with murders, adulteries, thefts, pillage, and other unbearable wrongs; and because it had risen up against the said duke and against his coming, threatening to destroy him. Another cause was on account of the right of exemption of that country, wherein the inhabitants, however criminal elsewhere, and others entangled in debt or crime, were wont to be harbored, as in a nest of wickedness; so that the whole realm cried vengeance on them.

On the ninth day of August,[7] the duke with his host entered the county of Chester, and there, in the parish of Coddington and other neighboring parishes, taking up his camping ground and pitching his tents, nor sparing meadow nor cornfield, pillaging all the country round, and keeping strict watch against the wiles of the men of Chester, he passed the night. And I, the writer of this chronicle, spent a not uncheerful night in the tent of the lord of Powys. Many in neighboring places, drinking of the poisoned cups given to them by the people of Chester, perished. There also, from divers water-cisterns, which the men probed with spears, and from other hiding-places, vessels and much other goods were drawn forth and taken for plunder, I being present with the finders.

My lord of Canterbury and the earl of Northumberland went away to the king at the castle of Conway, to treat with him on the duke's behalf; and the king, on condition of saving his dignity, promised to surrender to the duke at the castle of Flint. And so, delivering up to them his two crowns, valued at one hundred thousand marks, with other countless treasure, he straightway set forth to Flint. There the duke coming to him with twenty thousand chosen men—the rest of his host being left behind to guard his quarters and the country and castle and city of Chester—sought the king within the castle, for he would not come forth. And he led him away prisoner to Chester castle, where he delivered him into safe keeping. Thus, too, he placed in custody certain lords, taken along with the king, to be kept till the parliament which was to begin on the morrow of Michaelmas-day.

[6]Thomas Prestbury had been arrested in April 1399. His election as abbot of Shrewsbury was confirmed on August 17, at Chester (CPR, 1396–9, 584, 692).
[7]Usk probably meant the eighth of August.

While the duke was then at Chester, three of the twenty-four aldermen of the city of London, on behalf of the same city, together with fifty other citizens, came to the duke, and recommended their city to him, under their common seal, renouncing their fealty to king Richard. And so the duke, having gloriously, within fifty days, conquered both king and kingdom, marched to London; and there he placed the captive king in the Tower, under fitting guard.

Next, the matter of setting aside King Richard, and of choosing Henry, duke of Lancaster, in his stead, and how it was to be done and for what reasons, was judicially committed to be debated on by certain doctors, bishops and others, of whom I, who am now noting down these things, was one. And it was found by us that perjuries, sacrileges, unnatural crimes, exactions from his subjects, re-duction of his people to slavery, cowardice and weakness of rule—with all of which crimes King Richard was known to be tainted—were reasons enough for setting him aside, and, although he was ready himself to yield up the crown, yet for better security was it determined, for the aforesaid reasons, that he should be deposed by the authority of the clergy and people; for which purpose they were summoned.

On St Matthew's day (September 21) I, the writer of this history, was in the Tower, wherein King Richard was a prisoner, and I was present when he dined, and I marked his mood and bearing, having been taken thither for that very pur-pose by Sir William Beauchamp. And there and then the king discoursed sor-rowfully in these words: 'My God!, a wonderful land is this, and a fickle; which hath exiled, slain, destroyed or ruined so many kings, rulers, and great men, and is ever tainted and toileth with strife and variance and envy;' and then he re-counted the histories and names of sufferers from the earliest habitation of the kingdom. Perceiving then the trouble of his mind, and how that none of his own men, nor such as were wont to serve him, but strangers who were but spies upon him, were appointed to his service, and musing on his ancient and wonted glory and on the fickle fortune of the world, I departed thence much moved at heart.

READING 3

Jean Froissart, The Rise and Fall of Étienne Marcel[8]

In 1356 the French suffered their second great military disaster of the Hundred Years War: they were routed at Poitiers by an English army led by King Edward III's eldest son, Edward the Black Prince, who captured the French king, John the Good, and held him for ransom. John's son and heir,

---

[8]From Froissart, *Chronicles,* tr. Geoffrey Brereton; Baltimore, Md., Penguin Books, 1968, pp. 146–150, 155–161.

Charles, duke of Normandy (the future King Charles V), tried to uphold the royal cause but could not rule as king while his father still lived. He was confronted by a bloody and brutal peasants' uprising known as the "Jacquerie revolt" (see Ch. 11, Reading 3) and by a uniquely assertive Estates General led by a Parisian cloth merchant named Étienne Marcel (c. 1317–1358), identified in this passage as "the Provost of merchants," whose effort at government through legislature cost him his life. The revolt of Marcel tainted the Estates General in France for more than a century. The author of this selection, Jean Froissart (1333–1400), was a scholar and cleric from Flanders, who traveled throughout Europe and served noble (and royal) families in France and England. Although very well-placed to observe these events, Froissart's sympathy for the crown and nobility colors his account.

If the English and their allies were jubilant at the capture of King John [the Good] at Poitiers, the kingdom of France was deeply disturbed. There was cause enough, for it brought loss and suffering to people of all condition, and the wiser heads predicted that greater evils were to come. Their sovereign was a prisoner and all the best of their knights were also in prison or dead.

In addition, those knights and squires who had returned from the battle were so blamed and detested by the commons that they were reluctant to go into the big towns.

So all the prelates of the church, bishops and abbots, all the nobility, lords and knights, the Provost of the merchants of Paris [Étienne Marcel] and the burgesses, and the councilors of the French towns, met together in Paris to consider how the realm should be governed until their king should be set free. They also wanted to find out what had happened to the vast sums which had been raised in the past through tithes, levies on capital, forced loans, coinings of new money, and all the other extortionate measures by which the population had been tormented and oppressed while the soldiers remained underpaid and the county inadequately protected. But of these matters no one was able to give an account.

It was therefore agreed that the prelates should elect twelve good men from among them, with powers, as representatives of the clergy, to devise suitable means of dealing with the situation described. The barons and knights also elected twelve of the wisest and shrewdest of their number to attend to the same matters, and the burgesses twelve in the same way. It was then decided by common consent that these thirty-six persons should meet frequently in Paris to discuss the affairs of the realm and put them in order. Questions of all kinds were to be referred to the Three Estates. Their acts and ordinances were to be binding on all the other prelates, nobles, and common people of the cities and towns.

Nevertheless, even at the beginning, several of those elected were viewed unfavorably by the Duke of Normandy and his council.[9]

As a first measure, the Three Estates stopped the coining of the money then being minted and took possession of the dies. Secondly, they required the Duke to arrest his father's Chancellor and the other financial officers and former councilors of the king, in order that they should render a true account of all the funds which had been levied and collected on their advice. When these high officials heard of this, they completely disappeared and were wise to do so.

Next, they appointed on their own authority officials with the duty of raising and collecting all the levies, taxes, tithes, loans, and other duties payable to the crown, and they had new coinage of fine gold minted.

At that time a knight called Sir Regnault de Cervoles, commonly known as the Archpriest, took command of a large company of men-at-arms assembled from many countries. These found that their pay had ceased with the capture of King John and could see no way of making a living in France. They therefore went towards Provence, where they took a number of fortified towns and castles by assault and plundered the whole country as far as Avignon. Pope Innocent VI and his cardinals who were at Avignon were in such fear of them that they hardly knew where to turn, and they kept their household servants armed day and night. After the Archpriest and his men had pillaged the whole region, the Pope and his college opened negotiations with him. He entered Avignon with most of his followers by friendly agreement, was received with as much respect as if he had been the king of France's son, and dined several times at the palace with the Pope and the cardinals. All his sins were remitted him and when he left he was given forty thousand crowns to distribute among his companions.

At that time also there arose another company of men-at-arms and irregulars from various countries, who subdued and plundered the whole region between the Seine and the Loire. As a result, no one dared to travel between Paris and Vendôme, or Paris or Orléans, or Paris and Montargis, and no one dared to remain there. These companies often carried their raids almost to Paris, or at other times towards Orléans or Chartres. They ranged the country in troops of twenty, thirty, or forty and they met no one capable of putting up a resistance to them.

These activities of what were known as the Free Companies [mercenaries] who attacked all travelers carrying valuables, began under the administration of the Three Estates. The nobles and prelates began to grow tired of the institution of the Estates and left the Provost of the Merchants and some of the burgesses of Paris to go their own way, finding that these were interfering more than they liked with the conduct of affairs.

It happened one day that the Provost of the Merchants assembled a great crowd of the common people of Paris who supported him, all wearing similar

---

[9]The Duke of Normandy was the dauphin Charles, son and heir of the captured King John the Good; on John's death he was crowned King Charles V (1364–1380).

caps by which they could recognize each other. He went to the palace surrounded by his men and entered the Duke of Normandy's room, where he asked him very sharply to shoulder responsibility for the affairs of the realm and give some thought to them, so that the kingdom—which would eventually be his—should be protected from the depredations of the Free Companies. The Duke replied that he would be quite ready to do so if he had the means at his disposal, but that it should be done by whoever collected the revenue and taxes belonging to the realm.

I do not know exactly how it happened, but such an angry argument arose that there, in the presence of the Duke of Normandy, three of the chief members of his council were killed, so close to him that his robe was splashed with blood and he himself was in great danger. But he was given one of the people's caps to put on his head, and was forced to pardon the murder of his three knights.

The Provost of the Merchants and his faction, knowing that they had incurred the resentment and hatred of their sovereign lord the Duke of Normandy, began to feel uneasy. Now it happened that inside Paris itself there had remained a large number of English and Navarrese mercenaries who had been retained by the Provost and the commons to help defend them against the Duke of Normandy. A disturbance arose between them and the Parisians, in which more than sixty of the soldiers were killed. The Provost of the Merchants was highly incensed by this and blamed the Parisians bitterly; but nevertheless, to appease the people, he took some hundred and fifty of the soldiers and imprisoned them in the Louvre, telling the citizens that he would punish them according to their crimes. This quieted the Parisians and after nightfall the Provost, who wished to propitiate the English mercenaries, released them from prison and sent them on their way.

When the English all assembled in Saint-Denis, they decided to avenge their comrades and the treatment inflicted on themselves. They sent a declaration of war to the Parisians and began to rove about outside the city killing and hacking to pieces any of the inhabitants who were bold enough to venture outside. The people of Paris fell into such distress and confusion that they no longer knew whom to trust. They began to murmur and be suspicious of everyone. The Duke of Normandy, for his part would not intervene as long as the Parisians were still ruled by the Provost of the Merchants. He sent them a public notification in writing that he would not make peace with them unless twelve of the citizens, to be chosen by himself, were surrendered to him at discretion. It is easy to understand why the Provost and others who knew they were inculpated were filled with alarm. They saw clearly enough, on considering the situation, that things could not continue as they were for long, for the people of Paris were beginning to cool in their enthusiasm for them and their party. They entered into secret negotiations with the English soldiers who were harrying Paris. A pact was made between the two parties, according to which the Provost and his supporters were to seize possession of the Porte Saint-Honoré and the Porte Saint-Antoine and to open those two gates at midnight to a combined force of English and Navarrese, who would come ready armed to ravage and destroy Paris.

On the very night when this was to happen, an inspiration from God awoke some of the citizens who had an understanding with the Duke of Normandy. These learnt that Paris was to be plundered and destroyed. They immediately armed themselves and all their friends and caused the news to be whispered about secretly, so as to gain more supporters.

Well-armed and numerous, they raised the banner of France to the cry of "Up with the king and the duke!" and were followed by the people. They went to the Porte Saint-Antoine where they found the Provost of the Merchants with the keys of the gate in his hands. Bitter accusations were hurled at the Provost and he was attacked and forced back. The people were in a tumult, clamoring and hooting. They shouted: "Death to the Provost and his friends! They have betrayed us! Kill them!"

In the midst of the commotion the Provost would gladly have escaped had he been able to, but was so close-pressed that he could not. Sir Jean de Chamy hit him on the head with an axe and stretched him on the ground. Then he was struck by others who did not leave off until he was dead, together with six others of his faction. A search was made through the streets and the city was put in a state of defense and strong guards posted over it for the remainder of the night.

As soon as the Provost and his supporters had been killed or caught, which took place of the evening of Tuesday, July 31, 1358, messengers were sent in haste with the news to the Duke of Normandy, who was at Meaux. He was naturally delighted and prepared to come to Paris. But before his arrival, the King of Navarre's Treasurer, Josseran de Mâcon, and Charles Toussac, an alderman of Paris, were executed as traitors in the Place de Greve. The bodies of the Provost and the others killed with him were dragged to the courtyard of St. Catherine's Church, in the Val des Ecoliers. Gashed and naked as they were, they were laid in front of the cross in the courtyard and left there for a long time, so that any who wished to see them could do so. Afterwards they were thrown into the Seine.

READING 4

Jean de Waurin, Joan of Arc[10]

This passage on Joan of Arc (c. 1412–1431), from the French historian Jean de Waurin's (d. 1474) contemporary chronicle, is less adulatory than most other accounts, and all the more interesting for that reason.

---

[10]From *English Historical Documents*, vol. IV, ed. A. R. Myers; New York, Oxford University Press, 1969, pp. 242–243.

While Orléans was besieged, there came to King Charles of France, at Chinon where he was then staying, a young girl who described herself as a maid of twenty years of age or thereabout, named Joan, who was clothed and habited in the guise of a man. This Joan had remained a long time at an inn and she was very bold in riding horses and leading them to drink and also in performing other feats and exercises which young girls are not accustomed to do; and she was sent to the king of France by a knight named Sir Robert de Baudricourt, captain of the palace of Vaucoulleurs appointed on behalf of King Charles. This Sir Robert gave her horses and five or six companions, and likewise instructed her, and taught her what she ought to say and do, and the way in which she could conduct herself, since she asserted that she was a maid inspired by divine providence, and sent to King Charles to restore him and bring him back into the possession of all his kingdom generally, from which he was, as she said, wrongfully driven away and put out. And the maid was, at her coming, in very poor estate; and she was about two months in the house of the king, whom she many times admonished by her speeches, as she had been instructed, to give her troops and aid, and she would repel and drive away his enemies, and exalt his name, enlarging his lordships, certifying that she had had a sufficient revelation concerning this. And she was then considered at court only as one deranged and deluded, because she boasted herself as able to achieve so great an enterprise, which seemed to the great princes a thing impossible, considering that all they together could not effect it. Nevertheless, after the maid had remained a good space at the king's court, she was brought forward and aided, and she raised a standard whereon she had painted the figure and representation of Our Lord Jesus Christ; indeed, all her words were full of the name of God. And she was many times examined by famous clerks and men of great authority in order to inquire and know more fully her intention, but she always held to her purpose, saying that if the king would believe her that she would restore him to his dominion. Maintaining this purpose she accomplished some operations successfully, whereby she acquired great renown, fame, and exaltation.

This maid went with the Duke of Alençon from Chinon to Poitiers, where he ordered that the marshal should take provisions and artillery and other necessary things to Orléans in force, whither the maid Joan wished to go; and she made request that they would give her a suit of armor to arm herself, which was delivered to her. Then, with her standard raised, she went to Blois where the muster was being made, and then to Orléans with the others; and she was always armed, in complete armor, and on this same journey many men-at-arms placed themselves under her.

When the maid had come into the city of Orléans, they gave her a good reception, and some were greatly rejoiced at seeing her in their company. And when the French troops who had brought the provisions into Orléans returned to the king, the maid remained there. And she was urged to go out to skirmish with the others by La Hire and some captains, but she made answer that she would not go unless the men-at-arms who had brought her were also with her: these were recalled from Blois and from the other places whither they had now withdrawn. And they returned to Orléans, where they were joyfully received by the maid. So she went out to them to welcome them, saying that she had well seen and considered the governance of the English, and that if they would believe in her she would make them all rich.

So she began that day to sally out of the town, and went with great alacrity to attack one of the English towers, which she took by force; and going on from that time she did some very marvelous things.

READING 5

Jean Chartier, Chronique du Roi Charles VII[11]

The Dauphin Charles, the future Charles VII (1422–1461), owed much to Joan of Arc for saving his Valois dynasty at the nadir of its fortunes and for urging his coronation at Reims Cathedral in 1422. But when Joan fell into the hands of the English, Charles made little effort to rescue her. Nevertheless, from Joan of Arc's time on, the tide turned decisively in favor of the French who, well before Charles VII's death in 1461, had driven the English from all of France except the port of Calais on the English Channel. Charles, in short, was the king who won the Hundred Years War, and this passage explains one part of how he did it. The author, Jean Chartier (d.1462), was a monk at St. Denis, connected to the French royal family through his father, William, a bishop of Paris, and his brother, Alain, secretary to Charles VII. His *Chronique de Charles VII,* from which this selection is taken, is a tribute to his patron and a vindication of the French side in the war.

Whoever might wish to make mention of all the valiant men and of their deeds which have been done during the recovery of Normandy would find it too long for recital or warning. But nevertheless one must make some mention and record of the matter for those who in time to come may wish to read or hear the method and means of the miraculous recovery of this duchy. First of all, the king of France imposed good order on the conduct of his men-at-arms. He caused all those men to be equipped with good and sure arms and weapons; and each had

[11]From *English Historical Documents,* vol. IV, ed. A. R. Myers; New York, Oxford University Press, 1969, pp. 262–263.

two mounted archers. And these men were paid every month, so that they did not dare nor venture during this war and conquest of Normandy to take any of the people prisoner for ransom, whether they were in obedience of the English or of their own side; nor did they seize any food without paying, except from the English or their adherents, in which case they could take it lawfully.

Just as important was the provision that the king had made in his artillery for warfare, and he had a number of bombards, great cannons, culverins, so that never in the memory of man did a Christian king have such numerous artillery, or so well furnished with powder, shot, and all things necessary to approach and take towns and castles, nor had more carriages to drag them nor gunners more experienced to handle them, which gunners were paid from day to day.

And it was a marvelous thing to see the bulwarks, ditches, moats, and mines before all the towns and castles that were besieged during the war; for there was not a town taken by composition [i.e., through engineering] which could not have been taken by assault, but the king, through this kindness, always wished to take them by composition, to avoid the shedding of human blood and the destruction of his own country.

READING 6

John Fortescue, On the English and French Monarchies[12]

Sir John Fortescue (c. 1394–c. 1476) was a distinguished English jurist who served as chief justice of the King's Bench. Shifting political configurations resulting from the Wars of the Roses drove him for a time into exile in France but did not diminish his admiration for the English system of government. In the following passage from The Governance of England (c. 1470), Fortescue contrasts French "royal lordship" with English "political and royal lordship." His bias toward the English system is evident.

There are two types of kingdoms, one of which is called a royal lordship, and the other is called a political and royal lordship.[13] They differ in that the first king may rule his people by such laws as he makes himself, and therefore he may set taxes and other impositions on them as he himself wishes, without their assent.

---

[12]From Sir John Fortescue, *The Governance of England,* ed. and tr. Charles Plummer; Oxford, England, The Clarendon Press, 1885, pp. 109–115; revised by J. W. Leedom.

[13]The Latin for these two types of government, a *dominium regale* and a *dominium politicum et regale,* was widely used in later discussions of the English government.

The second king may not rule his people by laws other than those they assent to, and therefore he may set no impositions upon them without their own assent.

It may perhaps be marveled at by some men why one realm is a royal lordship alone and the prince rules it by his law, called the royal law, and why another kingdom is a royal and political lordship and the prince rules it by a law called the royal and political law, since these two princes are of equal stature. This doubt may be answered in this manner: that the first constitution of these two realms upon the incorporation of them is the cause of this diversity. Now it seems to me it is shown openly enough why one king rules royally alone and the other politically and royally: for one kingdom began of and by the might of the prince, and the other began by the desire and institution of the people of the prince.

Now the French king reigns upon his people royally; yet neither St. Louis, once king there, nor any of his progenitors ever set taxes or other impositions upon the people of that land without the assent of the Three Estates, which, when they are assembled, are like the parliament in England.[14] And many of his successors kept this order until recently, when Englishmen made such war in France that the Three Estates dared not come together. And so because of that, and because of the great necessity which the French king had of good for the defence of that land, he took it upon himself to set taxes and other impositions upon the commons without the assent of the Three Estates; yet he would not and has not set such charges upon the nobles for fear of rebellion. And because the commons there, though they have complained, have not rebelled and are not ready to rebel, the French kings have every year since set such charges upon them, and augmented such charges, so that the commons are so impoverished and destroyed that they may hardly live. Truly they live in the most extreme poverty and misery, though they dwell in the most fertile land in the world. And because of this the French king does not have men of his own realm able to defend it, except for the nobles who bear no such impositions; rather, the king is forced to make his armies and retinues for the defence of his land up to foreigners, Scots, Spaniards, men of Germany, and of other nations, or else all his enemies might overrun him, for he has no defences of his own, except his castles and fortresses. Lo, this is the fruit of his royal law.

If the realm of England, which is an island, were ruled under such a law and such a prince, it would then be a prey to all other nations, and they would conquer, rob, or devour it, as was proved in the time of the Britons. But this land is ruled under a better law, and therefore the people of it are not in such penury, but rather they are wealthy and have all things necessary to the sustenance of nature. And so they are mighty, and able to resist the adversaries of this realm, and to beat other realms that do, or would do them wrong. Lo, this is the fruit of the royal and political law under which we live.

---

[14]The first Estates General, as the French parliament came to be known, did not actually meet until 1303.

READING 7

Philippe de Commynes, The French Monarchy[15]

Philippe de Commynes (1446–1511) was brought up in Burgundy, where he served as a councilor and diplomat; but sometime in the late 1460s he trasferred his allegiance to Louis XI, and he remained loyal to France until his death. His *Memoirs* are one of the most careful and judicious records of the age. Compare the opinions of Commynes and Fortescue (Reading 6) on the taxation power of the French crown.

Of all the kings in this world ours has least reason to say: "I have the privilege of levying on my subjects what I please." And those who ascribe these words to him to make him appear greater do him no honor; on the contrary, they cause him to be hated and feared by his neighbors, who would not want to live under his domination for anything in the world. But if our king, or those who want to exalt him or promote his reputation, were to say: "I have subjects who are so good and loyal that they never refuse me anything I request of them, and I am more feared and better obeyed by my subjects than any other prince in the world; my subjects endure all misfortunes and afflictions with more patience than any others, and bear less resentment for past sufferings," it seems to me that this would be very much to his credit, and I am sure that this is so. He should not say: "I take whatever I want and it is my prerogative, which I intend to keep." King Charles V [of France] never used such terms. As a matter of fact I have never heard any king say this, but I have heard it from their servants, who thought that they were doing their master a good turn. But, in my opinion, they misunderstood the interests of their lord, and they spoke this way in order to show humility before him and because they did not know what they were saying.

As an example of the goodness of the French, the first instance which comes to mind from our time is the convocation of the Three Estates in Tours [in 1484], after the decease of our good master, King Louis, may he rest in peace, which took place in 1483. It might have been thought at the time that such an assembly would be dangerous, and some persons of low estate and little virtue said then, and many times since, that it was a crime of lese majesty to consider having a meeting of the estates, and that it would only serve to diminish the authority of the king. But these are the very persons who commit the crime against God, the king, and the people. These words serve only those who are in positions of authority and esteem without having deserved it in any way, who are not

[15]From *The Memoirs of Philippe de Commynes,* ed. Samuel Kinser, tr. Isabelle Cazeaux; Columbia, S.C., University of South Carolina Press, 1969, pp. 359–361. Copyright University of South Carolina Press, 1969. Reprinted by permission.

qualified for their office, and who have never done anything except whisper in ears and talk about things of little value; these people are opposed to these great assemblies for fear that they may be recognized for what they are and that their practices may be condemned.

At the time everyone, whether of high, middle, or low rank, considered the kingdom to be very costly to maintain, for the people had endured and suffered for twenty years and more great and horrible taxes, and which amounted to some three million francs a year more than ever before. For Charles VII never levied more than 1,800,000 francs a year, and King Louis, his son, in the year of his death, raised 4,700,000 francs, not including funds for artillery and other supplies. And it was indeed pitiful to see and hear of the poverty of the people. But one good thing about our good master was that he did not hoard anything in the treasury; he collected everything and spent everything. He built large edifices to fortify and defend the towns and other places of the kingdom, and he did this to a much larger extent than all the kings who preceded him. He was very generous to the churches. In certain respects it would have been better if he had been less liberal, because he robbed the poor to give to those who had no need of it. In short, no one is perfect in this world.

And in this kingdom, which was so oppressed in many ways after the death of our king, was there any division against the king who now reigns? Did princes and their subjects rise up in arms against their young king? Did they wish to replace him with another? Did they wish to deprive him of his authority? Did they want to restrain him so that he would be unable to perform his role as a king and issue commands? Certainly not. Still, there were some people vainglorious enough to say that such things would have happened, had they not prevented it. People did the opposite of everything I said in my questions: for all of them came to him, whether they were princes, lords, or ordinary townsmen; all of them acknowledged him as their king and swore allegiance to him. The princes and the lords made their requests humbly, on their knees, handing in their demands in the form of petitions, and they established a council to which twelve of them were named. And then the king, who was only thirteen years old, gave orders, according to the advice of this council.

At the above-mentioned assembly of the Three Estates, certain requests and remonstrances were made with great humility for the good of the kingdom always remitting everything to the king's good pleasure and that of his council, and granting him whatever was asked of them, and whatever was shown by written documents to be necessary for the king's expenses, without saying anything. And the sum requested was 2,500,000 francs, which was enough, and all that heart could desire, and, if anything, it was too much rather than too little, unless something else should come up. And the estates begged that at the end of two years they should meet again, and in case the king did not have enough money, they would grant him as much as he pleased; and if he were engaged in war or if anyone were to offend him, they would put at his disposal their persons and their possessions without refusing him anything that he might need.

Is it with such subjects, who give so liberally to him, that the king should allege a privilege of being able to take at his pleasure? Would it not be fairer to God and to the world to raise money in this manner than with unordered will? For no prince can levy taxes otherwise than by authorization, as I said, unless he does it by tyranny and is excommunicated. But many are so stupid that they do not know what they can do or not in this respect.

READING 8

Charles IV, The Golden Bull, 1356[16]

The Golden Bull of 1356 is important less as an agent of constitutional change than as a recognition and regularization of political arrangements that had long been developing. The document must be read very carefully. Some of its phrases are empty verbiage, whereas its utter silence on the traditional papal role in disputed elections is most eloquent. The pope's exclusion from German politics should be understood in the light of Charles IV's prior concession to the papacy that he would exercise no authority in Italy without papal permission. In short, Germany and Italy were becoming disentangled at last.

Charles IV (1347–1378) pretends that the Golden Bull is a product of imperial initiative, but its provisions were actually hammered out in an assembly of German princes. The bull describes the emperor in grandiose terms as "ruler of the world," yet it is designed, point by point, to enhance the authority of the seven electoral princes and to assure the autonomy and indivisibility of their dominions at imperial expense. Charles was himself both emperor and, as hereditary king of Bohemia, an electoral prince. A careful reading will disclose the identities of the other six electors.

In the name of the holy and indivisible Trinity, amen. Charles the Fourth, by the favor of divine mercy emperor of the Romans, always augustus, and king of Bohemia, as a perpetual memorial does this. Every kingdom divided against itself shall be desolated, for its princes have become the companions of thieves.

[16]From *Select Historical Documents of the Middle Ages*, ed. E. F. Henderson; London, Charles Scribner's Sons, 1892, pp. 220–221; and *A Source Book for Mediaeval History*, ed. and tr. O. J. Thatcher and E. H. McNeal; New York, Charles Scribner's Sons, 1905, pp. 284–300.

Tell us, pride, how would you have reigned over Lucifer had you not had discord to aid you? Tell us, hateful Satan, how would you have cast Adam out of paradise if you had not divided him from his obedience? You have often spread discord among the seven electors of the holy empire, through whom the holy empire ought to be illuminated.

We, through the office by which we possess the imperial dignity, are doubly bound—both as emperor and by the electoral right that we enjoy—to put an end to future danger of discord among the electors themselves, to whose number we, as king of Bohemia, are known to belong. And so we have promulgated, decreed, and recommended for ratification these laws for the purpose of cherishing unity among the electors, and of bringing about a unanimous election, and of closing all avenues to that detestable discord and to the dangers that arise from it.

We decree and determine that, whenever the electoral princes are summoned, each one of them shall be bound to furnish on demand an escort and safe-conduct to his fellow electors or their representatives, within his own lands and as much farther as he can, for the journey to and from the city where the election is held. Any electoral prince who refuses to furnish escort and safe-conduct shall be liable to the penalties for perjury and to the loss of his electoral vote for that occasion. If there should arise any enmity or hostility between two electoral princes, it shall not be allowed to interfere with the safe-conduct which each is bound to furnish to the other.

It shall be the duty of the archbishop of Mainz to send notice of the approaching election to each of the electoral princes by his messenger, containing the following: first, the date on which the letter should reach the prince to whom it is directed; then the command to the electoral prince to come or to send his representatives to Frankfürt-am-Main, three months from that date. The form of the letter of notification and of the credentials of the representatives are appended to this document.

When news of the death of the king of the Romans has been received at Mainz, within one month from the date of receiving it the archbishop of Mainz shall send notice to all the electoral princes. But if the archbishop neglects or refuses to send such notices, the electoral princes are commanded to assemble on their own motion and without summons within three months from the death of the emperor, for the purpose of electing a king of the Romans and future emperor.

Mass shall be celebrated on the day after the arrival of the electors. The archbishop of Mainz administers this oath, which the other electors repeat:

I, archbishop of Mainz, archchancellor of the empire for Germany, electoral prince, swear on the holy gospels here before me, and by the faith which I owe to God and to the holy Roman empire, that with the aid of God, and according to my best knowledge and judgment, I will cast my vote for a person fitted to rule the Christian people. I will give my vote freely, uninfluenced by any agreement, price, bribe, promise, or anything of the sort, by whatever means it may be called. So help me God and all the saints."

After the electors have taken this oath, they shall proceed to the election, and shall not depart from Frankfürt until the majority have elected a king of the Romans and future emperor, to be ruler of the world and of the Christian people. If they have not come to a decision within thirty days from the day on which they took the above oath, after that they shall live on bread and water and shall not leave the city until the election has been decided.

Such an election shall be as valid as if all the princes had agreed unanimously and without difference upon a candidate. If any one of the princes has been hindered or delayed for a time, but arrives before the election is over, he shall be admitted and shall take part in the election at the stage that had been reached at the time of his arrival. According to the ancient and approved custom, the king of the Romans elect, immediately after his election and before he takes up any other business of the empire, shall confirm and approve by sealed letters for each and all of the electoral princes, ecclesiastical and secular, the privileges, charters, rights, liberties, concessions, ancient customs, and dignities, and whatever else the princes held and possessed from the empire at the time of the election; and he shall renew the confirmation and approval when he becomes emperor. The original confirmation shall be made by him as king, and the renewal as emperor. It is his duty to do this graciously and in good faith, and not to hinder the princes in the exercise of their rights.

In the case where three of the electors vote for a fourth electoral prince, his vote shall have the same value as that of the others to make a majority and decide the election.

It is known and recognized throughout the world that the king of Bohemia, the count palatine of the Rhine, the duke of Saxony, and the margrave of Brandenburg, by virtue of the principalities that they possess, have the right to vote in the election of the king of the Romans along with their co-electors, the ecclesiastical princes, and that they with the ecclesiastical princes are the true and legal electoral princes of the holy empire. In order to prevent disputes arising among the sons of these secular electoral princes, we have fixed the succession by the present law which shall be valid forever. On the death of one of the secular electoral princes his right, voice, and vote in the election shall descend to his firstborn son who is a layman; if the son has died before this, to the son's first-born son who is a layman. If the first-born son of the elector has died before this, without legitimate lay sons, by virtue of the present law the succession shall go to the elector's next oldest lay son and then to his heirs, and so on according to the law of primogeniture. In case the heir is under age the paternal uncle of the heir shall act as guardian and administrator until the heir comes of age, which shall be eighteen years.

When any electorate falls vacant for lack of heirs, the emperor or king of the Romans shall have the power to dispose of it, as if it reverted to the empire, saving the rights, privileges, and customs of the kingdom of Bohemia, according to which the inhabitants of that kingdom have the right to elect their king in case of a vacancy.

We also decree that no count, baron, noble, vassal, burgrave, knight, client, citizen, burgher, or other subject of the churches of Cologne, Mainz, or Trier, of whatever status, condition, or rank shall be cited, hailed, or summoned to any authority before any tribunal outside of the territories of these churches and their dependences, or before any judge, except the archbishops and their judges. We refuse to hear appeals based on the authority of others over the subjects of these princes.

We extend this right by the present law to the secular electoral princes, the count palatine of the Rhine, the duke of Saxony, and the margrave of Brandenburg, and to their heirs, successors, and subjects forever.

It is known that the right of voting for the king of the Romans and future emperor inheres in certain principalities, the possessors of which have also the other offices, rights, and dignities belonging to these principalities. We decree, therefore, by the present law that the electoral vote and other offices shall always be so united and conjoined that the possessor of one of these principalities shall possess and enjoy the electoral vote and all the offices, dignities, and appurtenances belonging to it, that he shall be regarded as an electoral prince, that he and no other shall be accepted by the other electoral princes and admitted to participation in the election and all other acts which regard the honor and advantage of the holy empire, and that no one of these rights shall ever be taken from him.

READING 9
Petrarch, The Papal Court at Avignon[17]

This somber portrait of the Avignon papacy, by the Italian humanist Francesco Petrarch (1304–1374), illustrates at once the papacy's diminishing reputation and Petrarch's addiction to rhetorical exaggeration. He was by no means the first critic to contrast papal wealth with apostolic poverty, nor were the Roman popes of the High Middle Ages immune from

---

[17]From *Readings in European History, vol. 1, ed.* James H. Robinson; Boston, Ginn & Company, 1904, pp. 502–503.

such criticism. But Petrarch's blade is particularly sharp and well polished, and his identification of fourteenth-century Avignon with ancient, hedonistic Babylon gained wide circulation.

Now I am living in France, in the Babylon of the West. The sun in its travels sees nothing more hideous than this place on the shores of the wild Rhone, which suggests the hellish streams of Cocytus and Acheron. Here reign the successors of the poor fishermen of Galilee; they have strangely forgotten their origin. I am astounded, as I recall their predecessors, to see these men loaded with gold and clad in purple, boasting of the spoils of princes and nations; to see luxurious palaces and heights crowned with fortifications, instead of a boat turned downwards for shelter.

Instead of holy solitude we find a criminal host and crowds of the most infamous satellites; instead of soberness, licentious banquets; instead of pious pilgrimages, unnatural and foul sloth; instead of the bare feet of the apostles, the snowy coursers of brigands fly past us, the horses decked in gold and fed on gold, soon to be shod with gold, if the Lord does not check this slavish luxury. In short, we seem to be among the kings of the Persians or Parthians, before whom we must fall down and worship, and who cannot be approached except presents be offered. O ye unkempt and emaciated old men, is it for this you labored? Is it for this that you have sown the field of the Lord and watered it with your holy blood? But let us leave the subject.

READING 10
William of Ockham, On Imperial and Papal Power[18]

The distinguished philosopher William of Ockham (c. 1290–1349), whom we have encountered earlier in his incarnation as a philosopher (see pp. 268–69), was no friend of the Avignon papacy. In this passage he contrasts the papacy as it should be with what, in his opinion, it had become.

---

[18]From Ewart Lewis, *Medieval Political Ideas, vol. 2;* New York, A. A. Knopf, 1954, pp. 613–615.

We may summarize what is involved in the sublimity of the pope's principate, because this consists of three things. First, that it is a principate in respect of spiritual things only, which are of greater dignity than secular things. Second, that it is a principate over free men, not over slaves, because no one is by divine law a slave of the pope. Third, that the pope can by divine law regularly or casually do all things that are necessary to the organization and government of the faithful, although his ordinary and regular power is limited by definite boundaries, which he is not regularly permitted to transgress. And what those boundaries are is clear from our argument, though it is not clear in which cases those things that are not regularly granted to him may be permitted him. Perhaps it is impossible to give a fixed general rule for these special cases; but in such cases the greatest caution must be used, according to the discretion and counsel of the wisest men, most sincerely zealous for justice, without any exception of persons, whether subjects or rulers, whether poor or rich, if they can be found. If, however, such men are not available, no action should be taken, lest the pope, because of the ignorance under which in fact he often labors, should dangerously transgress the ancient boundaries and make decisions which may be null and void by divine law itself.

We shall show how the church of Avignon, doing heavy and enormous injuries to all the faithful of Christ, is attempting to rule all Christians tyrannically, and how in order to do this more freely and without fear, but not without the mark of tyranny, it persecutes those who are so bold as to dispute about its power and about its good intention, so that in universities and other schools no doctor or lector dare to propose or accept for discussion and determination in any way any question that concerns the power of the pope, although to dispute about the power of the pope ought to be welcome and acceptable both to the pope and to all his subjects, that they may be subject only so far as is expedient, and no further. This knowledge is necessary to the pope also, lest he transgress the ancient boundaries set by his fathers. And therefore, if the pope strikes fear into those who dispute about his power, he deservedly opens himself to the suspicion that he does not intend to be restricted by the legitimate boundaries of his proper power but intends to rule his subjects tyrannically.

Moreover, it is not only right for learned men to inquire discreetly and with good intention what power the pope has, but it is also expedient and necessary for them to judge his deeds, if those deeds cannot possibly proceed from a good intention: that is, to decide that they are bad and reprehensible and at the proper place and time to assert this and intimate it to others; because everyone is permitted to judge concerning manifest things. Therefore, although when papal deeds could have been the result of good intentions they should have the benefit of the doubt, yet when they are such as could not have been done with good intentions, anyone is permitted to judge them; for such deeds of a pope are bound to be regarded as blameworthy.

READING 11

The Declaration of the Cardinals, On the Election of Urban VI, 1378[19]

Under strong international pressure, the Avignon pope Gregory XI moved the papal court back to Rome. Like many of his predecessors, he found the city difficult to govern, and he decided to return to Avignon. But Gregory died in 1378 before he could carry out his plan, and the resulting events, related here by the cardinals, gave rise to the great schism. Having declared their election of the Italian Urban VI (1378–1389) null and void, they elected another pope and returned with him to Avignon. Urban VI stayed on in Rome and appointed new cardinals.

The Declaration of the Cardinals thus pinpoints the origin of the schism, but it is not so much an objective account of events as a self-serving interpretation of them. Other sources make it clear that the cardinals elected Urban VI willingly, *before* being pressured by a mob of Romans who were unaware of the election. As archbishop of Bari, Urban had been an efficient but colorless ecclesiastical administrator. As pope, he surprised everyone by launching a campaign against clerical wealth and taking steps to reduce the cardinals' revenues. It was at that point that the cardinals repudiated Urban, fled Rome, and manufactured their cover story.

After the apostolic seat was made vacant by the death of our lord, pope Gregory XI, who died in March, we assembled in conclave for the election of a pope, as is the law and custom, in the papal palace, in which Gregory had died. . . . Officials of the city with a great multitude of the people, for the most part armed and called together for this purpose by the ringing of bells, surrounded the palace in a threatening manner and even entered it and almost filled it. To the terror caused by their presence they added threats that unless we should at once elect a Roman or an Italian they would kill us. They gave us no time to deliberate but compelled us unwillingly, through violence and fear, to elect an Italian without delay. In order to escape the danger which threatened us from such a mob, we elected Bartholomew, archbishop of Bari, thinking that he would have enough conscience not to accept the election, since everyone knew that it was made under such wicked threats. But he was unmindful of his own salvation and burning with ambition, and so, to the great scandal of the clergy and of the

[19]From *A Source Book for Mediaeval History,* ed. and tr. O. J. Thatcher and E. H. McNeal; New York, Charles Scribner's Sons, 1905, pp. 325–326.

Christian people, and contrary to the laws of the church, he accepted this election which was offered him, although not all the cardinals were present at the election, and it was extorted from us by the threats and demands of the officials and people of the city. And although such an election is null and void, and the danger from the people still threatened us, he was enthroned and crowned, and called himself pope and apostolic. But according to the holy fathers and to the law of the church, he should be called apostate, anathema, Antichrist, and the mocker and destroyer of Christianity.

READING 12

Catherine of Siena, Letter to Three Italian Cardinals[20]

Catherine of Siena (c. 1347–1380) was the youngest daughter of a dyer in Siena. Always devout, she joined the Dominican order around 1367 and dedicated herself to prayer and contemplation. Her mystical raptures engendered her reputation for sanctity, and she soon attracted a group of disciples from all countries, ages, and classes, whom she called her "family," but who were often known as the *Caterinati.*

Catherine was no lonely hermit content simply to lament the state of the world; she determined to change it. Though she never learned to read, she dictated a stream of letters to popes and cardinals about the state of the church and the world.

Catherine, who had prayed and harangued for a return of the papacy from Avignon, was appalled when she learned that the cardinals who had elected Urban VI (Reading 11) were defecting from him. This letter was sent to the three Italian cardinals who had elected Urban. Her hope of averting a schism was foiled, but Catherine remained tireless in her support of both Urban VI and of papal privilege.

In the name of Jesus Christ and of sweet Mary

I, Catherine, the slave and servant of the servants of Jesus Christ, write to you in His precious blood, in the desire of seeing you return to the true and most perfect light, of seeing you leave the great darkness and blindness into which you have fallen. Then you will be fathers to me; otherwise you will not be. So I call you fathers insofar as you depart from death and return to life (since for the mo-

[20]From, *Medieval Women Writers,* ed. Katharina M. Wilson; Athens, Ga., University of Georgia Press, 1984, pp. 259–265.

ment you have departed from the life of grace; you are members torn asunder from your head, from whom you received life). You will then be united in faith and obedience to the pope, Urban VI; it is in that obedience that they stand who have the light. With that light they know the truth and in knowing it they love it. What is not seen cannot be known and no man can love what he does not know. And one who does not love and fear his Creator loves himself with a sensual love and all that he loves, the delights, honors, and privileges of the world, he loves sensually. He has been created for love and cannot live without love. So he either loves God, or he loves himself and the world with a love that brings him death, since it fixes the eye of the intellect, darkened by his own love of self, upon these ephemeral objects that flit away like the wind. In this way he can know neither truth nor goodness. Falsehood is all he knows, since he has no light. For in truth if he had the light, he would know that from such love he derives nothing but pain and eternal death. This love makes him have a foretaste of hell in this life: the man who disordinately loves himself and the things of this world cannot endure himself.

What shows me that you are ingrates, boors, and hirelings? The persecution that you along with others have conducted and are still conducting against this Bride at the very time that you should have served as shields against the blows of heresy. In this matter you know full well that Urban VI is truly the pope, the supreme pontiff elected in an orderly election and without any fear, truly more by divine inspiration than by your human industry. Such was your message to us and that was the truth. Now you have turned your backs like wretched and cowardly knights. Your own shadow has made you afraid. You have left the truth that strengthened you and drawn near falsehood, which weakens both the soul and the body as it deprives you of grace, spiritual and temporal.

You said that you elected Pope Urban by reason of fear, something that is not so. Whoever says that (I speak to you now without reverence, since you have deprived yourselves of reverence) lies to his own damnation. You could say to me, "Why don't you believe me? We who elected him know the truth better than you." And I reply to you that you have yourselves shown me that you have departed from the truth in many ways and that I should not believe your contention that Pope Urban VI is not really the pope. If I turn my attention to the principle of your life, I do not find there so good and holy a life that you have in conscience withdrawn from falsehood. What shows me that your life is so poorly ordered? The poison of heresy. If I turn my attention to the election ordained by your mouths, then we have learned that you elected him canonically and not out of fear. What shows me that the election was a proper one in which you elected Lord Bartolommeo, the archbishop of Bari, as true pope, the present Urban VI? This truth was shown me in the solemnity of his coronation. That the solemnity was carried out in truth is shown by the reverence you paid to him and by the favors you asked of him, favors that you have enjoyed in all matters. This truth you cannot deny, unless you resort to lies.

Now they[21] have elected an antipope and you have done so along with them. Insofar as the act and the external appearances are concerned, such is your admitted conduct, since you say that you were present when the devils incarnate elected the devil. These are the wrongs you are committing now and have committed with regard to this devil, to call him pope (which he is not) and to do reverence to someone you should not. You have left the light and are going into the darkness; leaving the truth, you have associated with falsehood. On all sides I find nothing but falsehood. You should be executed and I truly announce your execution (and so discharge my conscience); it will fall upon you, unless you return to obedience in true humility.

Alas, no more of this, for the love of God! Seize the chance you have for flight. Humble yourselves beneath the powerful hand of God, in obedience to His vicar, while you still have the time. Once this time has passed, there is no further remedy. Admit your faults so that you may humble yourselves and acknowledge the infinite goodness of God, Who has not commanded the earth to swallow you or wild beasts to devour you. Rather He has granted you time to correct your soul. But if you do not acknowledge Him, what He has granted you as a grace will turn into a great judgment against you. But if you choose to return to the sheepfold and be nourished in truth at the breast of the Bride of Christ, you will be received with mercy by Christ in heaven and Christ on earth, despite the evil you have committed. I beseech you, delay no longer and do not fight against the goad of conscience that I know is constantly stinging you. Let not the confusion of your mind, of the evil you have committed, so overcome you that you abandon your salvation out of tedium and despair, as though there were no chance of finding a remedy. He does not want to act in this way. But, with lively faith, take a strong hold on hope in your Creator and with humility return to your yoke. The final offense of obstinacy and despair would be even worse and more displeasing to God and to the world. Therefore lift yourselves up with the light, since without the light you would walk in darkness, as you have walked until now.

But now let's speak naturally (there we are all equal in our affections), let's speak humanly: Christ on earth is an Italian and you are Italians. The only reason I see that you are not moved by patriotism as are those from across the Alps is your self-love. Throw it away at once and don't wait for any other time (time is not waiting for you); crush this desire beneath your feet, with a hatred of sin and a love of virtue.

Return, return. Do not wait for the rod of justice. I beg you, out of love for that precious blood that was shed with such fiery love for you, give refreshment to my soul that is seeking your salvation. I say nothing else to you. Remain in the holy and sweet love of God; bathe yourselves in the blood of the spotless Lamb, where you will lose all servile fear. With the light you will abide in holy fear. Jesus is sweet, Jesus is love.

---

[21]The French cardinals

READING 13
Decrees of the Conciliar Movement[22]

The great schism stimulated a movement by reform-minded churchmen to reorganize ecclesiastical governance on more or less the parliamentary model, with the papacy sharing its authority with Church councils. The following documents illustrate the rise and fall of the conciliar movement.

The Council of Pisa (decrees A and B) elected a "conciliar" pope but failed in its attempt to dethrone the popes of Rome and Avignon, both of whom asserted the traditional claim that the pope could be judged by no one. Against this claim, the churchmen at Pisa, and later at Constance (decrees C–E), affirmed the power of councils over popes and demanded that councils be convened on a regular basis. But the Council of Constance's success in healing the schism diminished the need of conciliar governance. Councils continued to meet regularly until the mid-fifteenth century, when the conciliar movement disintegrated under the pressure of papal opposition (decree F).

A. THE COUNCIL OF PISA, CONCILIAR JURISDICTION, 1409

This holy and general council, representing the universal church, decrees, and declares that the united college of cardinals was empowered to call the council, and that the power to call such a council belongs of right to the aforesaid holy college of cardinals, especially now when there is a detestable schism.

The council further declared that this holy council, representing the universal church, caused both claimants of the papal throne to be cited in the gates and doors of the churches of Pisa to come and hear the final decision [in the matter of the schism] pronounced, or to give a good and sufficient reason why such sentence should not be rendered.

B. THE COUNCIL OF PISA, OATH OF REFORM, 1409

We, each and all, bishops, priests, and deacons of the holy Roman Church, congregated in the city of Pisa for the purpose of ending the schism and of restoring the unity of the Church, on our word of honor promise God, the holy Roman Church, and this holy council now collected here for the aforesaid purpose, that, if any one of us is elected pope, he shall continue the present council and not dissolve it, nor, so far as is in his power, permit it to be dissolved until, through

[22]From *A Source Book for Mediaeval History,* ed. and tr. O. J. Thatcher and E. H. McNeal; New York, Charles Scribner's Sons, 1905, pp. 327–332.

it and with its advice, a proper, reasonable, and sufficient reformation of the universal church in its head and in its members shall have been accomplished.

C.   THE COUNCIL OF CONSTANCE, *HAEC SANCTA,*[23] 1415

This holy synod of Constance, being a general council, and legally assembled in the Holy Spirit for the praise of God and for ending the present schism, and for the union and reformation of the church of God in its head and in its members, in order more easily, more securely, more completely, and more fully to bring about the union and reformation of the church of God, ordains, declares and decrees as follows: And first it declares that this synod, legally assembled, is a general council, and represents the catholic church militant and has its authority directly from Christ; and everybody, of whatever rank or dignity, including also the pope, is bound to obey this council in those things which pertain to the faith, to the ending of this schism, and to a general reformation of the church in its head and members. Likewise it declares that if anyone, of whatever rank, condition, or dignity, including also the pope, shall refuse to obey the commands, statutes, ordinances, or orders of this holy council, or of any other holy council properly assembled, in regard to the ending of the schism and to the reformation of the church, he shall be subject to the proper punishment; and unless he repents, he shall be duly punished; and if necessary, recourse shall be had to other aids of justice.

D.   THE COUNCIL OF CONSTANCE, A PROGRAM OF REFORM, 1417

The holy council at Constance determined and decreed that before this holy council shall be dissolved, the future pope, by the grace of God soon to be elected, with the aid of this holy council, or of men appointed by each nation, shall reform the church in its head and in the Roman curia, in conformity to the right standard and good government of the church. And reforms shall be made in the following matters: 1. In the number, character, and nationality of the cardinals. 2. In papal reservations. 3. In annates, and in common services and little services.[24] 4. In the granting of benefices and expectancies. 5. In determining what cases may be tried in the papal court. 6. In appeals to the papal court. 7. In the offices of the *cancellaria,* and of the penitentiary. 8. In the exemptions and incorporations made during the schism. 9. In the matter of commends. 10. In the confirmation of elections. 11. In the disposition of the income of churches,

---

[23]*Haec sancta* is literally "This Council": the titles of conciliar decrees are taken from their opening words. Had we followed that custom, the present sourcebook would have been titled "Many Students."

[24]Annates, expectancies, and similar financial measures were payments made to the papacy by appointees to ecclesiastical offices.

monasteries, and benefices during the time when they are vacant. 12. That no ecclesiastical property be alienated. 13. It shall be determined for what causes and how a pope may be disciplined and deposed. 14. A plan shall be devised for putting an end to simony. 15. In the matter of dispensations. 16. In the provision for the pope and cardinals. 17. In indulgences. 18. In assessing tithes.

E. THE COUNCIL OF CONSTANCE, *FREQUENS,* 1417

A good way to till the field of the Lord is to hold general councils frequently, because by them the briers, thorns, and thistles of heresies, errors, and schisms are rooted out, abuses reformed, and the way of the Lord made more fruitful. But if general councils are not held, all these evils spread and flourish. We therefore decree by this perpetual edict that general councils shall be held as follows: The first one shall be held five years after the close of this council, the second one seven years after the close of the first, and forever thereafter one shall be held every ten years. One month before the close of each council the pope, with the approval and consent of the council, shall fix the place for holding the next council. If the pope fails to name the place the council must do so.

F. PIUS II, *EXECRABILIS,* 1460

The execrable and hitherto unknown abuse has grown up in our day, that certain persons, imbued with the spirit of rebellion, and not from a desire to secure a better judgment, but to escape the punishment of some offence which they have committed, presume to appeal from the pope to a future council, in spite of the fact that the pope is the vicar of Jesus Christ and to him, in the person of St. Peter, the following was said: "Feed my sheep" [John 21:16] and "Whatsoever thou shalt bind on earth shall be bound in heaven" [Matt. 16:18]. Wishing therefore to expel this pestiferous poison from the church of Christ and to care for the salvation of the flock entrusted to us, and to remove every cause of offence from the fold of our Saviour, with the advice and consent of our brothers, the cardinals of the holy Roman church, and of all the prelates, and of those who have been trained in the canon and civil law, who are at our court, and with our own sure knowledge, we condemn all such appeals and prohibit them as erroneous and detestable.

STUDY QUESTIONS

A What problems did governments face in the late Middle Ages?
B How did the governments discussed here—England, France, Germany, and the papacy—deal with these problems?
C Which governments emerged stronger? Which were weaker?

Reading 1: Documents Relating to Crown and Parliament in England

What rights did Parliament gain during this period? Which rights did the monarchy keep? (Pay particular attention to the Parliament of 1348: the Commons respond to a question posed by the king. The question isn't listed, but can you figure it out?)

Reading 2: Adam Usk, The Depostion of King Richard II, 1399

What reasons were given why Richard lost his throne? Who deposed him? How does Richard see the history of England? Is he right?

Reading 3: Jean Froissart, The Rise and Fall of Étienne Marcel

How did Étienne Marcel come to power? What problems did the government face? What caused his fall?

Reading 4: Jean de Waurin, Joan of Arc

Does Waurin believe that Joan was divinely inspired? How does he view her? Does his view differ from other ideas you may have heard about Joan?

Reading 5: Jean Chartier, Chronique du Roi Charles VII

What measures did Charles take to make sure the reconquered provinces would not be nostalgic for English rule? What sort of army does he rely on for his expedition?

Reading 6: John Fortescue, On the English and French Monarchies

What are the two kinds of lordships Fortescue describes? Which does he see as typical of England, and which of France?

Reading 7: Philippe de Commynes, The French Monarchy

How does Commynes describe the French monarchy? Would he agree with Fortescue? Commynes says the king's subjects are so good and loyal that they never refuse any request. Why not?

Reading 8: Charles IV, The Golden Bull, 1356

Who are the electoral princes of the empire? Who do they elect? The pope is not mentioned: why not? What measures are taken to prevent the pope from interfering in the selection of an emperor?

Reading 9: Petrarch, The Papal Court at Avignon

Much of this is pure hyperbole, but what genuine complaints lie beneath the rhetoric?

Reading 10: William of Ockham, On Imperial and Papal Power

What is Ockham's view of papal power? Over whom (and what) does the pope have authority? How does he believe the popes have misused this power?

Reading 11: The Declaration of the Cardinals, On the Election of Urban VI, 1378

What are the cardinals trying to justify? Does that make their testimony more or less reliable?

Reading 12: Catherine of Siena, Letter to Three Italian Cardinals

Catherine pulls no punches in her letter: what does she think of the election of Urban VI? What does she think of the schismatic cardinals? What parallels can you draw between Catherine and Joan of Arc?

Reading 13: Decrees of the Conciliar Movement

Can you trace the rise and fall of conciliarism in these decrees? What did these clerics believe were the main problems with the church? What was their solution? Why did conciliarism fail?

CHAPTER **11**

▓ AN AGE OF CONTRADICTIONS

Historians wrangle over the nature of the late Middle Ages: decline and despair, renaissance and renewal, tradition and continuity, disruption and transition have all been advanced as the keynote of the age. In fact, what makes the era so difficult to typify is that often two or three of these themes are evident in the same event: all are true to some extent, and no one is adequate.

The desperate and disruptive tendencies of the period are illustrated spectacularly by the Black Death (Reading 1). The elimination of perhaps one-third of the population resulted in a violent shift from land shortage to labor shortage, prompting property owners in both northern and southern Europe to seek legislation to freeze wages (Reading 2). These measures angered peasants and laborers and sometimes drove them into rebellion (Readings 3–5).

Similarly complex is the problem of reform and heresy (Readings 6–7). Neither was new in the period, and both had their origins centuries earlier; but the new critics often had roots in medieval universities, and their criticisms were both sharper and more thorough as a result—a trend that would lead, ultimately, to Martin Luther and the Reformation.

Yet it would be incorrect to characterize the era as wholly dismal or degenerate. Culture continued to flourish, poignantly captured by the remembrances of Doña Leonor López de Cordoba (Reading 8) and the feminist appeals of

Christine de Pisan (Reading 9). In fact, Christine is a good example of early Renaissance writers who, no less than Renaissance artists, disclose a characteristic blend of classicism, secularism, and Christianity. A Renaissance humanist such as Coluccio Salutati could write about Christian virtue and salvation (Reading 10), while a generation or two later the equally public Leon Battista Alberti (Reading 11) could gain fame as a designer of palaces and churches, both in the classical style, or his writings on architecture—also in the classical style.

Conversely, Florence, the nexus of Renaissance culture could, in the midst of the High Renaissance (1490s), fall under the spell of a fire-and-brimstone Dominican preacher, Savonarola, who believed he was receiving messages directly from God (document 12A)—and the Florentine people could afterwards condone his being burned at the stake (document 12B).

The frontiers of Europe, east and west, saw dramatic changes, beginning with the expansion of the Ottoman Turks in the southeast (Reading 13). The capture of Constantinople in 1453 was deeply shocking to western Europe, but for the Ottomans it was proof both of their power and their piety. A similar brew of religious—in this case Christian, rather than Islamic—and worldly motives underlay the earlier Iberian voyages of exploration (Reading 14), which also profited from major advances in geographical understanding (Reading 15).

The final document is an ode to one sort of personal freedom (Reading 16)—written originally in Spanish by a Portuguese poet, from a woman's point of view by a man, capturing a medieval theme in a modern idiom—that encapsulates this age of contradictions.

READING 1

Giovanni Boccaccio, The Black Death in Florence, 1348[1]

This eyewitness account is provided by the Florentine humanist Giovanni Boccaccio (1313–1375), one of the best minds and keenest observers of his time. Except for a touch of civic pride, Boccaccio writes with remarkable objectivity.

In the year of our Lord 1348, there happened at Florence, the finest city in all Italy, a most terrible plague, which, whether owing to the influence of the planets, or that it was sent from God as a just punishment for our sins, had broken out some years before in the Levant, and after passing from place to place and making incredible havoc all the way, had now reached the west. There, in spite of all the means that art and human foresight could suggest, such as keeping the city clear from filth, the exclusion of all suspected persons, and the publication of copious instructions for the preservation of health, and notwithstanding manifold humble supplications offered to God in processions and otherwise, it began to show itself in the spring of the aforesaid year, in a sad and wonderful manner. Unlike what had been seen in the east, where bleeding from the nose is the fatal prognostic, here there appeared certain tumors in the groin or under the arm-pits, some as big as a small apple, others as an egg; and afterwards purple spots in most parts of the body; in some cases large and but few in number, in others smaller and more numerous—both sorts the usual messengers of death. To the cure of this malady neither medical knowledge nor the power of drugs was of any effect; whether because the disease was in its own natural mortal, or that the physicians (the number of whom, taking quacks and women pretenders into the account, was grown very great) could form no just idea of the cause, nor consequently devise a true method of cure; whichever was the reason, few escaped; but nearly all died the third day from the first appearance of the symptoms, some sooner, some later, without any fever or other accessory symptoms. What gave the more virulence to this plague, was that, by being communicated from the sick to the hale, it spread daily, like fire when it comes in contact with large masses of combustibles. Nor was it caught only by conversing with or coming near the sick, but even by

[1]From *The First Century of Italian Humanism,* ed. Ferdinand Schevill; New York, F. S. Crofts & Co., 1928, pp. 32–34.

touching their clothes, or anything that they had before touched. It is wonderful, what I am going to mention; and had I not seen it with my own eyes, and were there not many witnesses to attest it besides myself, I should never venture to relate it, however worthy it were of belief. Such, I say, was the quality of the pestilential matter, as to pass not only from man to man, but, what is more strange, it has been often known, that anything belonging to the infected, if touched by any other creature, would certainly infect and even kill that creature in a short space of time. One instance of this kind I took particular notice of: the rags of a poor man just dead had been thrown into the street. Two hogs came up, and after rooting amongst the rags and shaking them about in their mouths, in less than an hour they both turned round and died on the spot.

These facts, and others of the like sort, occasioned various fears and devices amongst those who survived, all tending to the same uncharitable and cruel end; which was, to avoid the sick and every thing that had been near them, expecting by that means to save themselves. And some, holding it best to live temperately and to avoid excesses of all kinds, made parties and shut themselves up from the rest of the world; eating and drinking moderately of the best, and diverting themselves with music and such other entertainments as they might have within doors; never listening to anything from without to make them uneasy. Others maintained free living to be a better preservative, and would balk no passion or appetite they wished to gratify, drinking and reveling incessantly from tavern to tavern, or in private houses (which were frequently found deserted by the owners and therefore common to every one), yet strenuously avoiding, with all this brutal indulgence, to come near the infected.

And such, at that time, was the public distress that the laws, human and divine, were no more regarded; for the officers, to put them in force, being either dead, sick, or in want of persons to assist them, every one did just as he pleased. A third sort of people chose a method between these two: not confining themselves to rules of diet like the former, and yet avoiding the intemperance of the latter; but eating and drinking what their appetites required, they walked everywhere with perfumes and nosegays to smell to, as holding it best to corroborate the brain: for the whole atmosphere seemed to them tainted with the stench of dead bodies, arising partly from the distemper itself, and partly from the fermenting of the medicines within them. Others with less humanity, but perchance, as they supposed, with more security from danger, decided that the only remedy for the pestilence was to avoid it. Persuaded, therefore, of this and taking care for themselves only, men and women in great numbers left the city, their houses, relations, and effects, and fled into the country, as if the wrath of God had been constrained to visit those only within the walls of the city, or else concluding that none ought to stay in a place thus doomed to destruction.

READING 2

Wage and Price Laws After the Plague[2]

The plague described so vividly by Boccaccio savaged all Europe between 1347 and 1350, carrying off a great portion of the population. Labor was abruptly in short supply; land, relatively plentiful. As a consequence, the ruling class of virtually every European country, which lived primarily off agricultural profits, found its economic well-being severely jeopardized. The following measures, passed in the aftermath of the plague, showed the response in England and Italy; similar measures were taken in most other countries.

A.   THE CORN STATUTE OF FLORENCE, 1348

The peasants and tillers of the soil, all those who by indigence work and cultivate the land for a wage and by the day, may not ask, demand, or have a salary or wage higher than below mentioned: From the calends[3] of November to the calends of February each year, three sous and six deniers of small florins per day, or per task, providing themselves with all their expenses. From the calends of February to the calends of June, four sous of small florins per day or per task, providing themselves with all their expenses. From the calends of June to the calends of November they may not demand more than three sous of small florins per day or per task, under pain of one hundred sous each time for the contravener. And if the contravener cannot pay the fine he shall remain one month in the prison of the commune of Florence, and the punishment shall be executed thus. In this matter the oath of him who would have wished the work performed or he who would have paid the price shall be held.

B.   THE ORDINANCE OF LABORERS, 1349

The king to the sheriff of Kent, greeting. Because a great part of the people, and especially of workmen and servants, have lately died in the pestilence, many seeing the necessities of masters and great scarcity of servants, will not serve unless they may receive excessive wages, and others preferring to beg in idleness rather than by labor to get their living; we, considering the grievous incommodities which of the lack especially of plowmen and such laborers may hereafter

---

[2]From Georges Duby, *Rural Economy and Country Life in the Medieval West,* tr. Cynthia Postan; Columbia, University of South Carolina Press, 1968, p. 525; and *Translations and Reprints from the Original Sources of European History,* vol. 2; Philadelphia, University of Pennsylvania Press, 1902, pp. 3–5.

[3]The calends was the first day of the month.

come, have upon deliberation and treaty with the prelates and the nobles and learned men assisting us, with their unanimous counsel ordained:

That every man and woman of our realm of England, of what condition he be, free or bond, able in body, and within the age of sixty years, not living in merchandize, nor exercising any craft, nor having of his own whereof he may live, nor land of his own about whose tillage he may occupy himself, and not serving any other; if he be required to serve in suitable service, his estate considered, he shall be bound to serve him which shall so require him; and take only the wages, livery, meed, or salary which were accustomed to be given in the places where he oweth to serve, the twentieth year of our reign of England, or five or six other common years next before.[4] Provided always, that the lords be preferred before others in their bondmen or their land tenants, so in their service to be retained; so that, nevertheless, the said lords shall retain no more than be necessary for them. And if any such man or woman being so required to serve will not do the same, and that be proved by two true men before the sheriff, bailiff, lord, or constable of the town where the same shall happen to be done, he shall immediately be taken by them or any of them, and committed to the next gaol, there to remain under strait keeping, till he find surety to serve in the form aforesaid.

If any reaper, mower, other workman or servant, of what estate or condition he be, retained in any man's service, do depart from the said service without reasonable cause or license, before the term agreed, he shall have pain of imprisonment; and no one, under the same penalty, shall presume to receive or retain such a one in his service.

No one, moreover, shall pay or promise to pay to anyone more wages, liveries, meed, or salary than was accustomed, as is before said; nor shall anyone in any other manner demand or receive them, upon pain of doubling of that which shall have been so paid, promised, required or received, to him who thereof shall feel himself aggrieved; and if none such will sue, then the same shall be applied to any of the people that will sue; and such suit shall be in the court of the lord of the place where such case shall happen.

And if lords of towns or manors presume in any point to come against this present ordinance, either by them or by their servants, then suit shall be made against them in the form aforesaid, in the counties, wapentakes, and trithings, or such other courts of ours, for the penalty of treble that so paid or promised by them or their servants. And if any before this present ordinance hath covenanted with any so to serve for more wages, he shall not be bound, by reason of the said covenant, to pay more than at another time was wont to be paid to such a person; nor, under the same penalty, shall presume to pay more.

And because many strong beggars, as long as they may live by begging, do refuse to labor, giving themselves to idleness and vice, and sometimes to theft and other abominations; no one upon the said pain of imprisonment, shall, under

---

[4]That is, wages were to be fixed at pre-plague levels paid in 1347 or before.

the color of pity or alms, give anything to such, who are able to labor, or presume to favor them in their idleness, so that thereby they may be compelled to labor for their necessary living.

READING 3
Jean Froissart, The Jacquerie[5]

The attempts to freeze wages and prices at pre-plague levels were only one of a series of measures designed to turn political power into economic might. Viewed from the other end of the social scale—from the perspective of the peasant or laborer—such measures were hopelessly oppressive. The consequence was a series of popular revolts across Europe.

In France, economic hardship and noble incompetence in the Hundred Years War provoked a revolt of the peasants known as the "Jacquerie." French peasants—the Jacques and Jeannes of the countryside who give the revolt its name—expressed their anger in a bitter outburst of ferocity.

Certain people of the common villages, without any head or ruler, assembled together around Beauvais. In the beginning they were scarcely a hundred in number: they said how the noblemen of the realm of France, knights and squires, shamed the realm, and that it would be a great thing to destroy them all.

Thus they gathered together without any other counsel, and without any arms or armour, except with staves and knives, and so went to the house of a knight dwelling nearby. And they broke into his house and slew the knight, and the lady, and all his children, and burned his house. And then they went to another castle, and took the knight and bound him to a stake, and then violated his wife and his daughter before his eyes and then slew the lady, and his daughter, and all his other children, and then slew the knight. And so they did to many other castles and good houses; and they multiplied so that they were six thousand, and wherever they went they increased in number. So every gentleman fled from them, taking their wives and children with them, leaving their houses empty.

These mischievous people, thus assembled without leader or arms, robbed, burned and slew all gentlemen that they could lay hands on, and forced and ravished women and girls, and did such shameful deeds that no human creature ought to think on any of it: and whoever did the most mischief was most praised.

[5]Jean Froissart, *The Chronicles of Froissart,* tr. John Bourchier, Lord Berners, London, MacMillan and Co., 1895, pp. 136–137. Updated, with additional translation, by J. W. Leedom.

They slew a knight and afterwards put him on a spit and roasted him over a fire in the sight of his wife and his children; and after the lady had been forced and ravished with by ten or twelve of them, they made her eat of her husband and then killed her and all her children.

They made among them a king, one from Clermont in the Beauvaisis: they chose him that was the most uncouth of all, and they called him king Jacques Goodman,[6] and so thereby they were called companions of the Jacquerie.

They destroyed and burned in the country around Beauvais more than sixty good houses and strong castles, and destroyed more than a hundred castles and good houses of knights and squires in that country in the area around Laon and Soissons.

The better people of those afflicted regions sought help from their friends in Flanders, Brabant, Hainault and Hesbaye. So foreign gentlemen joined with those of the region, and attacked these people wherever they found them, and slew them in heaps, or hanged them upon trees. And the rest were rounded up, for they had all assembled together, and there were more than a hundred thousand of them. When they were asked why they did such evil deeds, they could not explain, only that they did what they saw others do, and that they thought they could destroy all the nobles and gentlemen of the world.

READING 4

Niccolo Machiavelli, The Ciompi[7]

Popular revolt was not just a rural phenomenon in the late Middle Ages: the city-republics of Italy and Spain and Germany were also torn by struggles that assumed the character of plain class hatred. One of the most notable of these was the revolt in Florence of the Ciompi, the wool-workers. From 1378 to 1382, the Ciompi directed successive waves of protest and rebellion against the government of Florence. The demands of the Ciompi initiated a period of more open government, although all their measures were eventually overturned.

The author of this selection, Niccolo Machiavelli, is best known as the writer of *The Prince,* a profoundly influential work of political theory. Like other medieval (and ancient) authors, the speeches Machiavelli included were designed to reflect what the writer believed to have been the viewpoint of the speaker, rather than an actual transcript.

[6]"Jacques Goodman" is not an actual person, but a personification of the peasant.
[7]Niccolo Machiavelli, *History of Florence,* ed. Charles W. Colby; New York, P. F. Collier & Son, 1901, pp. 141–153.

A disturbance arose, much more injurious to the republic than anything that had hitherto occurred. The greatest part of the fires and robberies which took place on the previous days were perpetrated by the very lowest of the people; and those who had been the most audacious, were afraid that when the greater differences were composed, they would be punished for the crimes they had committed; and that as usual, they would be abandoned by those who had instigated them to the commission of crime. To this may be added, the hatred of the lower orders toward the rich citizens and the principals of the Arts,[8] because they did not think themselves remunerated for their labor in a manner equal to their merits. For in the times of Charles I,[9] when the city was divided into Arts, a head or governor was appointed to each, and it was provided that the individuals of each art, should be judged in civic matters by their own superiors. When the companies of the Arts were first organized, many of those trades followed by the lowest of the people and the plebeians, were not incorporated, but were ranged under those Arts most nearly allied to them; and, hence, when they were not properly remunerated for their labor, or their masters oppressed them, they had no one of whom to seek redress, except the magistrate of the Art to which they were subject; and of him they did not think justice always attainable. Of the Arts, that which always had the greatest number of these subordinates, is the guild of woolworkers;[10] which being both then, and still, the most powerful body, and first in authority, supports the greater part of the plebeians and lowest of the people.

The lower classes, then, the subordinates not only of the Wool Guild, but also of the other Arts, were discontented, from the causes just mentioned. Meetings took place in different parts during night, to talk over the past, and to communicate the danger in which they were, when one of the most daring and experienced, in order to animate the rest, spoke thus:

"You see the whole city full of complaint and indignation against us; the citizens are closely united, and the Signors are constantly with the magistrates. You may be sure they are contriving something against us; they are arranging some new plan to subdue us. We must, therefore, I, think, in order to be pardoned for our old faults, commit new ones; redoubling the mischief, and multiplying fires and robberies; and in doing this, endeavor to have as many companions as we can; for when many are in fault, few are punished; small crimes are chastised, but great and serious ones rewarded. Our opponents are disunited and rich; their disunion will give us the victory, and their riches, when they have become ours, will support us. Be not deceived about the antiquity of blood by which they exalt themselves above us; for all men having had one common origin, are all equally ancient, and nature has made us all after one fashion. Strip us naked, and we shall all be found alike. Dress us in their clothing, and they in ours, we shall ap-

---

[8]The major guilds
[9]In 1264–1268
[10]The Wool Guild was called *i Ciompi,* for which the revolt is named.

pear noble, they ignoble—for poverty and riches make all the difference. We have no business to think about conscience; for when, like us, men have to fear hunger, and imprisonment, or death, the fear of hell neither can or ought to have any influence upon them. Therefore we must use force when the opportunity offers; and fortune cannot present us an opportunity more favorable than the present, when the citizens are still disunited, the Signoria paralyzed, and the magistrates terrified."

The tumult continued all day, and at night the rioters halted near the palace of Stefano, behind the Church of St. Barnabas. Their number exceeded six thousand, and before day-break they obtained by threats the ensigns of the trades, with which and the Gonfalon of justice, when morning came, they proceeded to the palace of the Provost, who refused to surrender it to them; they then took possession of it by force.

When the plebeians entered the palace, the standard of the Gonfalonier[11] of justice was in the hands of Michele de Lando, a wool-comber. This man, barefoot, with scarcely anything upon him, and the rabble at his heels, ascended the staircase, and, having entered the audience chamber of the Signoria, he stopped, and turning to the multitude said, "You see this palace is now yours, and the city is in your power; what do you think ought to be done?" To which they replied, they would have him for their Gonfalonier and lord; and that he should govern them and the city as be thought best. Michele accepted the command; and, as he was a cool and sagacious man, more favored by nature than by fortune, he resolved to compose the tumult, and restore peace to the city. To commence with justice the government he had acquired by favor, he commanded that no one should either burn or steal anything; while, to strike terror into all, he caused a gallows to be erected in the court of the palace. He began the reform of government by deposing the Syndics of the trades, and appointing new ones; he deprived the Signoria and the Colleagues of their magistracy, and burned the balloting purses containing the names of those eligible for office under the former government.

The Government, thus composed, restored peace to the city for the time; but though the republic was rescued from the power of the lowest plebeians, the inferior trades were still more influential than the nobles of the people, who, however, were obliged to submit for the gratification of the trades, of whose favor they wished to deprive the plebeians. This condition of things continued three years, during which many were exiled and put to death; for the government lived in constant apprehension, knowing that both within and without the city many were dissatisfied with them. Those within, either attempted or were suspected of attempting every day some new project against them; and those without, being under no restraint, were continually, by means of some prince or republic, spreading reports tending to increase the disaffection.

[11]The chief magistrate of the government.

READING 5

The English Peasants' Revolt, 1381[12]

This detailed description of the great Peasants' Revolt in England is drawn from the *Anonimalle Chronicle,* written in French by an unknown monk of St. Mary's, York. It is the most authoritative surviving history of the revolt and may well have drawn some of its information from a lost London chronicle. The writer was a contemporary, and, notwithstanding his obvious hostility toward the rebels, his account is generally trustworthy. A careful examination of the rebels' goals will suggest the reasons for his hostility.

In the year 1381, because the subsidies[13] were lightly granted at the parliament and because various lords and commons were advised that the subsidies were not duly or loyally levied, but commonly extracted from the poor and not from the rich, the king's council ordained certain commissions to make inquiry into each township how they were levied. One of these commissions was sent to Essex to a certain Thomas Brampton[14] who was regarded as a king or great magnate in that area because of the great estate that he kept. He had summoned before him a hundred of the neighboring townships, and wished to have from them a new subsidy. Then the men came together to the number of a hundred or more; on this Thomas ordered them put into prison; and the commons rose against him and would not be arrested, but tried to kill Thomas. And because of these doings Sir Robert Belknap, chief justice of the Common Pleas of our lord the king, was sent to the shire with a commission of inquiry and indictments against various persons. Therefore the commons rose against him and came before him and told him that he was a traitor to the king and the realm. [The peasants killed certain royal officials] as an example to others; for it was their purpose to slay all lawyers and all jurors and all the servants of the king they could find.

[The revolt spread in central and eastern England. Large masses of peasants and poor laborers converged on London, hoping for aid from the king.]

At the same time the commons[15] of Kent razed various places and tenements of the people who would not rise with them. They laid siege with energy to Rochester Castle, and the constable defended himself vigorously for half a day,

---

[12]From *The Great Revolt 1381,* C. W. C. Oman; Oxford, England, The Clarendon Press, 1906, pp. 186–205. Revised by J. W. Leedom.

[13]A newly enacted, unprecedented poll tax, i.e., a tax on all individuals. The idea was dropped after the revolt of 1381.

[14]A royal tax collector.

[15]The author uses the term "commons" [lowercase] to mean "common folk," not members of Parliament.

[18]Archbishop Simon Sudbury was also the king's chancellor.

but at last, for fear that he had of the multitude of men deaf to reason, he delivered up the castle to them. And there they made their chief a certain Wat Tyler of Maidstone to maintain them and be their counsellor. And on the next Monday they came to Canterbury [on June 10], and 4,000 of them entered into the church of St. Thomas and, kneeling down, they cried with one voice on the monks to elect a monk to be archbishop of Canterbury, "for he who is now archbishop is a traitor, and will be beheaded for his iniquity." And when they had done this, the commons went into the town to their fellows, and they summoned the mayor and the bailiffs to swear to be faithful and loyal to King Richard II[16] and to the true commons of England. And afterwards they took 500 men of the town with them to London.

At this time the commons had as their counselor a chaplain of evil disposition named Sir John Ball, who advised them to get rid of all the lords, and of the archbishops and bishops, and abbots, and priors, and most of the monks and canons, saying that their possessions should be distributed among the laity, for which statements he was esteemed among the commons as a prophet, and labored with them to strengthen them in their malice—and a fit reward he got, when he was hanged, drawn, and quartered, and beheaded as a traitor.

At this time the king was in a turret of the great Tower of London, and could see the manor of the Savoy[17] and the Hospital of Clerkenwell, and the house of Simon Hosteler near Newgate, all on fire at once. And next day, Friday, the commons of the countryside and the commons of London assembled in fearful strength, to the number of 100,000 or more. And some came to Tower Hill, and when the king knew that they were there, he sent them orders by messenger to join their friends at Mile End, saying that he would come to them very soon.

And at this time the king proclaimed to them that he would confirm and grant it that they should be free, and generally should have their will, and that they might go through all the realm and catch all the traitors and bring them to him in safety, and then he would deal with them as the law demanded. Under color of this grant Wat Tyler and some of the commons took their way to the tower, to seize the archbishop. There they cut off the heads of Master Simon Sudbury, the archbishop of Canterbury,[18] and of Sir Robert Hales, Prior of the Hospital of St. John's, treasurer of England, and of Sir William Appleton, a great lawyer and surgeon.

At this moment the mayor of London came up, and the king bade him go to the commons and make their chieftain come to him. And when he was summoned, he came to the king with great confidence, mounted on a little horse so the commons could see him. And he dismounted, holding in his hand a dagger

---

[16]This is the same Richard II (1377–99) whose deposition is described in Chapter 10, Reading 2 above.

[17]The London residence of the Duke of Lancaster, John the Gaunt; the present location of one of London's finest and most expensive hotels, the "Savoy."

[18]Archbishop Simon Sudbury was also the king's chancellor.

which he had taken from another man, and when he had dismounted he half bent his knee, and then took the king by the hand, saying to him, "Brother, be of good comfort and joyful, for you shall have, in the fortnight to come, praise from the commons even more than you have yet had, and we shall be good companions." And the king said, "Why will you not go back to your own country?" But the other answered with a great oath that neither he nor his fellows would depart until they had got their charter such as they wished to have it. And he [Wat Tyler] asked that from henceforth there should be no outlawry, and that no lord should have lordship save civilly, and that there should be equality among all people save only the king, and that the goods of the holy Church should not remain in the hands of the religious people, nor of parsons and vicars; but that the clergy already in possession should have a sufficient sustenance, and the rest of the goods should be divided among the people of the parish. And he demanded that there should be no more villeins in England, and no serfdom or villeinage, but that all men should be free and of one condition. To this the king gave an easy answer, and said that he should have all that he could fairly grant, reserving for himself only the regality of his crown; and then he bade him to go back to his home, without making further delay.

At this time a certain valet from Kent, who was in the king's retinue, asked that the said Wat might be pointed out to him; and when he saw him, he said aloud that he knew him for the greatest thief and robber in all Kent. And for these words Wat tried to strike him with his dagger; but because he strove to do so, the mayor of London, William Walworth, reasoned with the said Wat for his own violent behavior and spite, done in the king's presence, and arrested him. And at this Wat stabbed the mayor with his dagger in the stomach with great wrath; but, as it pleased God, the mayor was wearing armor and took no harm, but like a hardy and vigorous man drew his cutlass, and struck back at the said Wat and gave him a deep cut on the neck, and then a great cut on the head. And during this scuffle one of the king's household drew his sword, and ran Wat two or three times through the body, mortally wounding him.

And when the commons saw their chieftain, Wat Tyler, was dead in such a manner, they fell to the ground there among the wheat, like beaten men, imploring the king for mercy for their misdeeds. And the king granted them mercy, and most of them took to flight.

And afterwards the king sent out his messengers into diverse parts, to capture the malefactors and put them to death. And many were taken and hanged at London, and they set up many gallows around the city of London, and in other cities and boroughs of the south country. At last, as it pleased God, the king, seeing that too many of his liege subjects would be undone, and too much blood spilled, took pity in his heart, and granted them all pardon, on condition that they should never rise again, under pain of losing life or limb, and that each of them should buy his charter of pardon, and pay the king as fee for his seal [on the charter] twenty shillings, to make him rich. And so finished this wicked war.

The Lollard Conclusions, 1395[19]

Heresy had been a major problem for the church since the twelfth
century; and though the friars had made significant gains for orthodoxy,
the church was simply unable to eliminate heretical dissent. In part this
was because a more educated lay men and lay women began forming
their own opinions, in part because increasing ossification left the church
less flexible, and in part because the church itself, having instilled a
very high sense of moral purpose among the laity, became a victim of
the critics it had educated.

 Lollards—the name apparently is a slang term meaning "mumblers,"
from the prayers they recited—were a heretical sect in England who took
their lead from the Oxford philosopher John Wycliffe. At the end of the
fourteenth century, under the patronage of noble families, they became
quite prominent, but their influence faded when the staunchly traditional
Henry IV (1399–1413) became king. The following Lollard "conclusions,"
set forth in a document both presented to Parliament and nailed to the
door of Westminster Abbey, summarizes their views.

 1. That when the Church of England began to go mad after temporalities,
like its great step-mother the Roman Church, and churches were authorized by
appropriation in divers places, then faith, hope, and charity began to flee from
our Church, because pride, with its doleful progeny of moral sins, claimed this
under title of truth. This conclusion is general, and proved by experience, custom, and manner or fashion, as you shall afterwards hear.

 2. That our usual priesthood, which began in Rome and pretended to be of
power more lofty than the angels, is not that priesthood which Christ ordained
for His apostles. This conclusion is proved because the Roman priesthood is bestowed with signs, rites, and pontifical blessings, of small virtue, nowhere exemplified in Holy Scripture.

 3. That the law of continence enjoined on priests, which was first ordained
to the prejudice of women, brings sodomy into all the Holy church.

 4. That the pretended miracle of the sacrament of bread drives all men, but
a few, to idolatry, because they think that the Body of Christ, which is never
away from heaven, could by power of the priest's word be enclosed essentially
in a little bread which they show the people.

[19]From *Documents of the Christian Church,* ed. Henry Bettenson; Oxford, England, 1963,
pp. 175–179.

5. That exorcisms and blessings performed over wine, bread, water and oil, salt, wax, and incense, the stones of the altar, and church walls, over clothing, mitre, cross, and pilgrims' staves, are the genuine performance of necromancy rather than of sacred theology. This conclusion is proved as follows, because by such exorcisms creatures are honoured as being of higher virtue than they are in their own nature, and we do not see any change in any creature which is so exorcized, save by false faith which is the principal characteristic of the Devil's art.

6. That king and bishop in one person, prelate and judge in temporal causes, curate and officer in secular office, puts any kingdom beyond good rule. This conclusion is clearly proved because the temporal and spiritual are two halves of the entire Holy Church.

7. That special prayers for the souls of the dead offered in our Church, preferring one before another in name, are a false foundation of alms, and for that reason all houses of alms in England have been wrongly founded.

8. That pilgrimages, prayers, and offerings made to blind crosses or roods, and to deaf images of wood or stone, are pretty well akin to idolatry and far from alms. A corollary is that the service of the cross, performed twice in any year in our church, is full of idolatry, for if that should, so might the nails and lance be so highly honoured; then would the lips of Judas be relics indeed if any were able to possess them.

9. That auricular confession which is said to be so necessary to the salvation of a man, with its pretended power of absolution, exalts the arrogance of priests and gives them opportunity of other secret colloquies which we will not speak of; for both lords and ladies attest that, for fear of their confessors, they dare not speak the truth.

10. That manslaughter in war, or by pretended law of justice for a temporal cause, without spiritual revelation, is expressly contrary to the New Testament, which indeed is the law of grace and full of mercies. The corollary is that it is indeed robbery of poor folk when lords get indulgences from punishment and guilt for those who aid their army to kill a Christian people in distant lands for temporal gain, just as we too have seen soldiers who run into heathendom to get them a name for the slaughter of men; much more do they deserve ill thanks from the King of Peace, for by our humility and patience was the faith multiplied, and Christ Jesus hates and threatens men who fight and kill, when He says: 'He who smites with the sword shall perish by the sword!'

11. That the vow of continence made in our Church by women who are frail and imperfect in nature, is the cause of bringing in the gravest horrible sins possible to human nature, because, although the killing of abortive children before they are baptized and the destruction of nature by drugs are vile sins, yet connection with themselves or brute beasts or any creature not having life surpasses them in foulness to such an extent as that they should be punished with the pains

of hell. The corollary is that, widows and such as take the veil and the ring, being delicately fed, we could wish that they were given in marriage, because we cannot excuse them from secret sins.

12. That the abundance of unnecessary arts practiced in our realm nourishes much sin in waste, profusion, and disguise. The corollary is that since St. Paul says: 'having food and raiment, let us be therewith content,' it seems to us that goldsmiths and armourers, and all kinds of arts not necessary for a man, according to the apostle, should be destroyed for the increase of virtue.

This is our embassy, which Christ has bidden us fulfill, very necessary for this time for several reasons. And although these matters are briefly noted here they are however set forth at large in another book, and many others besides, at length in our own language, and we wish that these were accessible to all Christian people. We ask God then of His supreme goodness to reform our Church, as being entirely out of joint, to the perfectness of its first beginning.

READING 7

Charges of Heresy Against Jan Hus[20]

Jan Hus (1374–1415), a reformer from the University of Prague whose skepticism of the authority of the papacy and the Catholic clergy enraged them both, was invited to the Council of Constance (1415) (see p. 350) on the promise of an imperial safe conduct and was then burned at the stake. Hus was clearly indebted to Wycliffe; his own views, which influenced later generations of reformers, including Martin Luther, are recorded here.

There is only one holy universal Church, which is the totality of the predestined.

Priests living criminally in any manner whatever pollute the priestly power.

The papal dignity arose from Caesar and the papal preëminance and the institution emanated from the Caesar's power.

No one may reasonably assert without revelation about himself or another that he is the head of a particular holy church; nor the Roman pontiff that he is the head of the Roman church.

---

[20]From Matthew Spinka, *John Hus at the Council of Constance;* New York, Columbia University Press, 1965, pp. 260–265.

No one occupies the place of Christ or Peter unless he follows Him in morals; for in no other respect is it more appropriate to follow, nor has he otherwise received the procuratorial power from God; because for that vicarial office both the conformity of morals and of the instituting authority are required.

The pope is not the manifest or true successor of the prince of the apostles, Peter, if he lives in a manner contrary to Peter. And if he is avaricious, then he is the vicar of Judas Iscariot by living avariciously. For the same reason the cardinals are not the manifest and true successors of the college of Christ's other apostles unless they live after the manner of the apostles, observing the commands and counsels of the Lord Jesus Christ.

The priest of Christ living in accordance with His law, having knowledge of Scripture and a desire to edify the people, ought to preach, an alleged excommunication notwithstanding; and subsequently, that if the pope or another orders a priest so disposed not to preach, the inferior ought not to obey.

By ecclesiastical censures of excommunications, suspensions, interdicts, the clergy subject the lay people to themselves for their own exaltation and the increase of avarice, and by malice protect and prepare Antichrist's way.

If the pope is wicked then like the apostle Judas he is a devil, a thief, and son of perdition, and not the head of the holy Church militant; for he is not even its member, since the grace of predestination is the bond whereby the body of the Church and every member of it is linked indissolubly with the head.

The pope ought not to be called the most holy even according to office, for otherwise a king ought also be called the most holy according to office, and executioners and public criers ought to be called saints; indeed, even the devil should be called holy as being an official of God.

If the pope lives in a manner contrary to Christ, even if he had ascended by a rightful and legitimate election according to the established human constitution, he has nevertheless ascended otherwise than through Christ. For Judas Iscariot was elected to the episcopacy rightfully and legitimately by Jesus Christ who is God; nevertheless, he entered by another way into the sheepfold of the sheep.

The condemnation of the forty-five articles of Wycliffe decreed by the doctors is irrational and unjust, and the reason alleged for it is wrongly conceived.

There is not a spark of apparent evidence that there should be one head ruling the Church in spiritual matters that should always abide with the Church militant; that is evident, since it is known that the Church has been without a pope for a long time.

The apostles and the faithful priests of the Lord had firmly ruled the Church in things necessary to salvation before the papal office was instituted. They would do so if there were no pope—as is highly possible—until the Day of Judgment.

No one is secular lord, no one is prelate, no one is bishop while he is in mortal sin.

READING 8

Doña Leonor López de Cordoba, *Memories*[21]

Misfortunes fell not just on peasants and workers; no one was immune. Doña Leonor López (1362–1412), a member of one of the great noble families of Castile, wrote a history of her life and misfortunes, *Las Memorias* (c. 1390). Her experiences reflect the violence and ruthlessness of aristocratic conflict in the later Middle Ages. (Similar stories emerged from the Hundred Years War in late medieval France, the Wars of the Roses in late medieval England, and the incessant warfare among the city-states and principalities of contemporary Italy and Germany.) The murder of defenseless rivals has, of course, been a feature common to royal and aristocratic power struggles throughout history. But it was clearly more common in late medieval Christendom than in the preceding high medieval era, when aristocratic warfare was constrained by a chivalric code, a taboo against murdering high-born adversaries, and a preference for ransoming captives rather than killing them. Through all her calamities, Doña Leonor draws strength from her Christian Faith. But it is faith of a mystical kind in which priests and confessors are surprisingly inconspicuous.

Whoever reads this document know that I am Doña Leonor López de Cordoba, the daughter of my lord, Master Don Martin López de Cordoba, and Doña Sancha Carrillo, to whom God gave glory and paradise. I swear, by the meaning of the cross that I adore, that all that is written here is true, that I saw it, and it happened to me.

I am the daughter of the said master who was Lord of Calatrava in the time of King Pedro. The king did my father the honor of giving him the commission of Alcantara, which is in the city of Seville. The king then made him master of Alcantara and, in the end, of Calatrava. He rose to a very high estate, as can be discovered in the chronicles of Spain. And as I have said, I am the daughter of Doña Sancha Carrillo, niece and ward of King Alfonso of most illustrious memory, to whom God granted paradise, who was the father of King Pedro.

My mother died very early, and so my father married me at seven years old to Ruy Gutierrez de Henestrosa. He was the son of Juan Fernandez de Henestrosa, King Pedro's head valet, his chancellor of the royal seal, and head majordomo of Queen Blanca his wife; Juan Fernandez married Doña Maria de Haro, mistress of Haro and the Cameros. To my husband were left many of his father's

[21]From Elizabeth Alvilda Petroff, *Medieval Women's Visionary Literature;* Oxford, England, Oxford University Press, 1986, pp. 329–334; tr. Kathleen Lacey.

goods and several estates. He received three hundred mounted soldiers of his own, and forty strands of pearls as fat as chick-peas, and five hundred Moorish servants, and silver tableware worth two thousand marks. The jewels and gems of his house could not be written on two sheets of paper. All this came to him from his father and mother because they had no other son or heir.

That was how things stood when King Pedro was besieged at the castle of Montiel by his brother, King Enrique. King Enrique observed this, and because he could not enter Carmona by force of arms to satisfy himself about this deed, he ordered the constable of Castile to discuss terms with my father.

The terms that my father put forward were two. First, King Enrique's party was to free the princesses and their treasure to leave for England. The second condition was that my father, his children, his guard, and those in the town who had obeyed his orders would be pardoned by the king, and that they and their estates would be considered loyal. And so it was granted him, signed by the constable in the king's name. Having achieved this, my father surrendered the town to the constable in King Enrique's name, and he left there—with his children and the rest of the people—to kiss the king's hand. King Enrique ordered them to be arrested and put in the dungeon of Seville.

The king ordered my father to be beheaded in the Plaza de San Francisco in Seville, and his goods confiscated, as well as those of his son-in-law, guardsmen, and servants. The rest of us remained in prison for nine years, until King Enrique died. Our husbands each had seventy pounds of iron on their feet, and my brother, Don Lope López, had a chain between the irons in which there were seventy links. He was a boy of thirteen years, the most beautiful creature in the world.

A plague came into the prison, and so my brothers and all of my brothers-in-law and thirteen knights from my father's house all died. Sancho Mifiez de Villendra, my father's head valet, said to my brothers and sisters and me, "Children of my lord, pray to God that I live for your sakes, for if I do, you will never die poor." It was God's will that he died the third day without speaking. After they were dead they took them all out to the smith to have their chains taken off, like Moors.

No one from the house of my father, Master Don Martin López, remained in the dungeon except my husband and myself. At this time, the most high and illustrious King Enrique, of very sainted and illustrious memory, died; he ordered in his will that we were to be taken out of prison, and that all that was ours be returned. I stayed in the house of my lady aunt, Doña Maria Garcia Carrillo, and my husband went to demand his goods. Those who held them paid him little attention, because he had no rank or means to demand their return. You already know how rights depend on one's petition being granted. So my husband disappeared, and wandered through the world for seven years, a wretch, and never discovered relative nor friend who would do him a good turn or take pity on him. After I had spent seven years in the household of my aunt, Doña Maria

Garcia Carrillo, they told my husband, who was in Badajoz with his uncle Lope Fernandez de Padilla in the Portuguese War, that I was in good health and that my relatives had treated me very well. He mounted his mule, which was worth very little money, and the clothes he wore didn't amount to thirty maravedis, and he appeared at my aunt's door.

And after my husband arrived, as I said, I left the house of my lady aunt, which was in Cordoba next to San Ipólito, and my husband and I were received into some houses there, next to hers, and we came there with little rest.

For thirty days I prayed to the Virgin Saint Mary of Bethlehem. Each night on my knees I said three hundred Ave Marias, in order to reach the heart of my Lady aunt so she would consent to open a postern to her houses. Two days before my praying ended, I demanded of my lady aunt that she allow me to open that private entrance, so that we wouldn't walk through the street, past so many nobles that there were in Cordoba, to come eat at her table.

Another day, when only one day remained to complete my prayer, a Saturday, I dreamed I was passing through San Ipólito touching the alb. I saw in the wall of the courtyard an arch, very large and very tall. I entered through it and gathered flowers from the earth, and saw a very great heaven. At this I awoke, and I was hopeful that my Virgin St. Mary would give me a home.

At this time there was a robbery in the Jewish quarter, and I took in an orphan boy who was there. I had him baptized so that he would be instructed in the faith.

One day, coming with my lady aunt from mass at San Ipólito, I saw being distributed among the clerics of San Ipólito those grounds where I had dreamed there was the great arch. I implored my lady aunt, Doña Mencia Carrillo, to purchase that site for me, since I had been her companion for seventeen years, and she bought it for me. She gave these grounds to me with the condition—which she indicated—that I build a chapel (erected over the houses) for the soul of King Alfonso, who built that church in the name of St. Ipólito because he was born on that saint's day. Then, when I had done this favor, I raised my eyes to God and to the Virgin Mary, giving them thanks.

Now that possession of these grounds had been given to me, I opened a door on the very place where I had seen the arch which the Virgin Mary showed me. It grieved the abbots to hand over that site to me, for I was of a great lineage, and my children would be great. They were abbots, and had no need of great knights so near them. This I heard from a reliable voice, and I told them to hope in God that it would be so. I made myself so agreeable to them that I opened the door in the place that I wanted. God helped me by giving me that beginning of a house because of the charity I performed in raising the orphan in the faith of Jesus Christ. It was the Virgin St. Mary's will that with the help of my lady aunt, and by the labor of my hands, I built in that yard two mansions, and an orchard, and another two or three houses for servants.

In this period of time a very cruel plague came. My lady aunt did not want to leave the city; I requested of her the kindness to permit me to flee with my children so that they would not die. She was not pleased but she gave me leave. I left Cordoba and went to Santa Ella with my children. The orphan that I raised lived in Santa Ella, and he lodged me in his house. All of the neighbors of the town were delighted by my coming. They received me with warm welcome, for they had been servants of the lord my father, and so they gave me the best house there was in that place, which was that belonging to Fernando Alonso Media-barba. Being without suspicion, my lady aunt came there with her daughters, and I withdrew to a small room. Her daughters, my cousins, never got on well with me because of all the good their mother had done me. I suffered so much bitterness from them that it cannot be written.

The plague came there, so my lady left with her people for Aguilar, and she took me with her as one of her own daughters, for she loved me greatly and said great things of me. I had sent the orphan that I raised to Ezija. The night that we arrived in Aguilar, the boy came from Ezija with two small tumors in his throat and three carbuncles on his face, and with a high fever. In that house there were Don Alonso Fernandez, my cousin, and his wife and all of his household. Though all of the girls were my nieces and my friends, knowing that my servant came in such a condition, they came to me and said, "Your servant, Alonso, comes with the plague, and if Don Alonso Fernandez sees it he will be furious at his being here with such an illness."

And the pain that reached my heart anyone who hears this history can well understand. I became worldly wise and bitter. Thinking that through me such great sorrow had entered that house, I had Miguel de Santa Ella called to me. He had been a servant of the master, my lord and father, and I begged him to take that boy to his house. The wretched man was afraid, and he said, "Lady, how can I take him with the plague, which will kill me?" And I said to him, "Son, God would not want that." Shamed by me, he took the boy; and through my sins, thirteen persons who watched over him by night all died.

One night it was God's will that there was no one to watch over that sorrow-ful boy, for all who had until then watched over him had died. My son, who was called Juan Fernandez de Henestrosa like his grandfather, and who was twelve years and four months old, came to me and said, "Lady, is there no one to watch over Alonso tonight?" And I told him, "You watch over him, for the love of God." He replied to me, "Lady, now that the others have all died, do you want to kill me?" I said to him, "For my charity, God will take pity on me." And my son, so as not to disobey me, went to keep vigil. Through my sins, that night he was given the pestilence, and another day I buried him. The sick one lived after all the others had died.

Doña Teresa, the wife of my cousin Don Alonso Fernandez, became very angry because my son was dying in her house at that time. She ordered that he be removed from the house on account of his illness. I was so transfixed by grief that I could not speak for the shame that those words caused me. My poor son said, "Tell my lady Doña Teresa not to cast me away, for my soul will leave now for heaven." He died that night. He was buried in Santa Maria la Coronada, which is in the same town. Because Doña Teresa felt very hostile to me, and I did not know why, she ordered that he not be buried within the town. When they took him to be buried, I went with him. As I went through the streets with my son, people came out, making a great hue and cry, ashamed for me. They said, "Come out, lords, and see the most unfortunate, forsaken, and accursed woman in the world!"

READING 9

Christine de Pisan, *The Book of the City of Ladies*[22]

One of the most significant cultural trends of the late Middle Ages was the development of vernacular literature. Although Latin remained the language for virtually everything that we would today label "scholarship," all across Europe writers were discovering the expressive possibilities of "common" speech. Christine de Pisan (c. 1363–c. 1434), a native of Venice, spent much of her life in France. Her writings, all in French, made her one of the most productive and many-sided writers of late medieval Europe. In her lyric poetry, she expressed her abiding love for her dead husband, who left her a widow at twenty-five. Another of her poetic works, a verse history of humanity, runs from the Creation to Christine's own time. Her prose works include an autobiography; a famous defense of women against misogynistic tirades and caricatures, titled *The Letter to the God of Love;* a biography of King Charles V of France; a tribute to the victory of Joan of Arc; several works on current political affairs; a book of moral advice for women, titled *The Book of the City of Ladies;* and a book of similar advice for men. Having lived for a time at the French royal court, and having been something of a literary sensation, widely admired and praised as the equal of the Nine Muses, she spent her final years secluded in a convent living so inconspicuously that the exact year of her death is unknown.

May God be praised, for now our City is entirely finished and completed, where all of you who love glory, virtue, and praise may be lodged in great honor, ladies from the past as well as from the present and future, for it has been built and established for every honorable lady. And my most dear ladies, it is natural for the human heart to rejoice when it finds itself victorious in any enterprise and

[22]From Christine de Pisan, *The Book of the City of Ladies,* tr. Earl Jeffrey Richards; New York, Persea Books, 1982, pp. 254–257.

its enemies confounded. Therefore you are right, my ladies, to rejoice greatly in God and in honest morés upon seeing this new City completed, which can be not only the refuge for you all, that is, for virtuous women, but also the defense and guard against your enemies and assailants, if you guard it well. For you can see that the substance with which it is made is entirely of virtue, so resplendent that you may see yourselves mirrored in it, especially in the roofs built in the last part as well as in the other parts which concern you. And my dear ladies, do not misuse this new inheritance like the arrogant who turn proud when their prosperity grows and their wealth multiplies, but rather follow the example of your Queen, the sovereign Virgin, who, after the extraordinary honor of being chosen Mother of the Son of God was announced to her, humbled herself all the more by calling herself the handmaiden of God. Thus, my ladies, just as it is true that a creature's humility and kindness wax with the increase of its virtues, may this City be an occasion for you to conduct yourselves honestly and with integrity and to be all the more virtuous and humble.

And you ladies who are married, do not scorn being subject to your husbands, for sometimes it is not the best thing for a creature to be independent. This is attested by what the angel said to Ezra: Those, he said, who take advantage of their free will can fall into sin and despise our Lord and deceive the just, and for this they perish. Those women with peaceful, good, and discrete husbands who are devoted to them, praise God for this boon, which is not inconsiderable, for a greater boon in the world could not be given them. And they may be diligent in serving, loving, and cherishing their husbands in the loyalty of their heart, as they should, keeping their peace and praying to God to uphold and save them. And those women who have husbands neither completely good nor completely bad should still praise God for not having the worst and should strive to moderate their vices and pacify them, according to their conditions. And those women who have husbands who are cruel, mean, and savage should strive to endure them while trying to overcome their vices and lead them back, if they can, to a reasonable and seemly life. And if they are so obstinate that their wives are unable to do anything, at least they will acquire great merit for their souls through the virtue of patience. And everyone will bless them and support them.

So, my ladies, be humble and patient, and God's grace will grow in you, and praise will be given to you as well as the Kingdom of Heaven. For Saint Gregory has said that patience is the entrance to Paradise and the way of Jesus Christ. And may none of you be forced into holding frivolous opinions nor be hardened in them, lacking all basis in reason, nor be jealous or disturbed in mind, nor haughty in speech, nor outrageous in your acts, for these things disturb the mind and lead to madness. Such behavior is unbecoming and unfitting for women.

And you, virgin maidens, be pure, simple, and serene, without vagueness, for the snares of evil men are set for you. Keep your eyes lowered, with few words in your mouths, and act respectfully. Be armed with the strength of virtue against the tricks of the deceptive and avoid their company.

And widows, may there be integrity in your dress, conduct, and speech; piety in your deeds and way of life; prudence in your bearing; patience (so necessary!), strength, and resistance in tribulations and difficult affairs; humility in your heart, countenance, and speech; and charity in your works.

In brief, all women—whether noble, bourgeois, or lower-class—be well-informed in all things and cautious in defending your honor and chastity against your enemies! My ladies, see how these men accuse you of so many vices in everything. Make liars of them all by showing forth your virtue, and prove their attacks false by acting well, so that you can say with the Psalmist, "the vices of the evil will fall on their heads." Repel the deceptive flatterers who, using different charms, seek with various tricks to steal that which you must consummately guard, that is, your honor and the beauty of your praise. Oh my ladies, flee, flee the foolish love they urge on you! Flee it, for God's sake, flee! For no good can come to you from it. Rather, rest assured that however deceptive their lures, their end is always to your detriment. And do not believe the contrary, for it cannot be otherwise. Remember, dear ladies, how these men call you frail, unserious, and easily influenced but yet try hard, using all kinds of strange and deceptive tricks, to catch you, just as one traps for wild animals. Flee, flee, my ladies, and avoid their company—under these smiles are hidden deadly and painful poisons. And so may it please you, my most respected ladies, to cultivate virtue, to flee vice, to increase and multiply our City, and to rejoice and act well. And may I, your servant, commend myself to you, praying to God who by His grace has granted me to live in this world and to persevere in His holy service. May He in the end have mercy on my great sins and grant to me the joy which lasts forever, which I may, by His grace, afford to you. Amen.

READING 10

Coluccio Salutati, On the Active Life[23]

One element of late medieval culture was the attempt to live a more Christian life: that is part of the spirit of the Lollards and of Hus. From Italy came another approach. Coluccio Salutati (1331–1406) was a major Florentine humanist and civic official who in 1375 became chancellor of Florence. His writings stress the connection between humanistic scholarship and service to the city-state. In his letter to Pellegrino, Salutati

---

[23]From *Renaissance Italy: Was It the Birthplace of Modern Europe?* ed. Gene A. Brucker; New York, Holt, Rinehart, & Winston, Inc., 1958, pp. 35–36. Reprinted by permission of Gene A. Brucker and the publisher.

praises the active life over the contemplative life in the context of Christian piety and salvation. In another of his letters, however, he praises the monastic life, thus reflecting the medieval rhetorical tradition of celebrating the virtues of both action and contemplation. In some respects, Salutati is simply echoing St. Francis (see pp. 242–45), while in others, he is expressing the new civic humanism of the Renaissance.

Do not believe, my Pellegrino, that to flee from turmoil, to avoid the view of pleasant things, to enclose oneself in a cloister, or to isolate oneself in a hermitage, constitute the way of perfection. Within yourself is that which imprints upon your work the title of perfection, which receives those things which do not touch you, rather cannot touch you, if your mind and your spirit withdraws within itself, if it does not search outside of itself. If the spirit will not receive within itself these exterior objects—the square, the forum, the court, the most crowded place of the city—they will be for you a very remote retreat and a perfect solitude. If instead, either in the recollection of distant things or in the fascination of present ones, our spirit turns outwardly, I do not know what it profits to live a solitary life. For it is a characteristic of the spirit to think always of something, whether this be a thing comprehended by the senses, represented by the memory, constructed by the power of the intellect, or created by the feeling of desire. And tell me, Pellegrino, who do you believe was more beloved by God: Paul,[24] the inactive hermit, or the busy Abraham? Among the superior ones, there are more who dedicate themselves to the active life than occupy themselves solely with spiritual things, just as there are many more who save themselves in the active life than are chosen from the contemplative life.

You should not be pleased with your prayers; you should not believe that you have approached more closely to heaven; you should not condemn me for remaining in the secular world. Without doubt you, fleeing from the world, can fall from heaven to earth, while I, remaining in the world, can raise my heart to heaven. And if you provide for, serve, and think of your family, children, relatives, friends, you cannot fail to raise your heart to the heavens and please God. Perhaps, occupied in mundane things, you will please Him more, since you will not aspire for yourself alone to be in communion with God, but in conjunction with Him, who holds dear the things necessary for the family, pleasing to friends, salutary for the state, you will labor, to the extent that He gives you the opportunity.

---

[24]St. Paul the Hermit (d. c. 347), not Paul the Apostle.

And thus to conclude, while contemplation is better, more divine, and more sublime, still it must be united with action. Nor is it always necessary to remain fixed in that summit of speculation. And tell me, I pray you, what is examined in the Last Judgment, if not the works of mercy, even though neglected or incomplete? Whoever will have clothed the nude, fed the hungry, given drink to the thirsty, buried the dead, released the imprisoned, he will hear that most sweet appeal: "Come, blessed by My Father, enjoy the Kingdom prepared for you from the beginning of the world."

READING 11

Giorgio Vasari, Life of Leon Battista Alberti[25]

Both the author and the subject of this selection are significant. Leon Battista Alberti (1404–1472) of Florence was an architect, painter, musician, playwright, essayist, and athlete. He was one of the earliest writers to analyze perspective drawing, and his vastly influential *De re aedificatoria* emphasized the virtues of classical proportions in architecture. In many respects, Alberti is the "uomo universale," the "universal man" of the Renaissance.

The author, Giorgio Vasari (1511–1574), was a painter and architect in late Renaissance Italy, who founded one of the earliest known schools of art, the Accademia del Disegno, in 1563. His most famous and important work, however, is not his art, but rather his series of biographies of artists from Giotto to Michaelangelo, in which he develops his theme that "true" art, following the model of ancient masters, uncovers the essence of the subject.

The knowledge of letters and the study of the sciences are, without doubt, of the utmost value to all, and offer the most important advantages to every artist who takes pleasure therein; but most of all are they serviceable to sculptors, painters, and architects, for whom they prepare the path to various inventions in all the works executed by them; and, whatever may be the natural qualities of a man, his judgment can never be brought to perfection if he is deprived of the advantages resulting from the accompaniment of learning. Now that all this is true

[25]Giorgio Vasari, *Lives of Seventy of the Most Eminent Painters, Sculptors, and Architects,* vol. ii, tr. and ed. E. H. Blashfield, E. W. Blashfield, and A. A. Hopkins; New York, Charles Scribner's Sons, 1896, 1929, pp. 49–61.

is seen clearly in the instance of Leon Batista Alberti who, having given his attention to the study of Latin as well as to that of architecture, perspective, and painting, has left behind him books, written in such a manner that no artist of later times has been able to surpass him in his style and other qualities as an author, while there have been numbers, much more distinguished than himself, in the practice of art. Still, it is very generally supposed—such is the force of his writings, and so extensive has been their influence on the pens and words of the learned, his contemporaries and others—that he was, in fact, superior to all those who have surpassed him in their works. We are therefore not to be surprised if we find the renowned Leon Batista to be better known by his writings than by the works of his hand.

He gave his attention, not only to the acquisition of knowledge in the world of art generally, and to the examination of works of antiquity in their proportions, but also, and much more fully, to writing on these subjects, to which he was by nature more inclined than to the practice of art. Leon Batista was well versed in arithmetic, and a very good geometrician; he wrote ten books respecting architecture in the Latin tongue. He likewise wrote three books on painting, and composed a dissertation on tractile forces, containing rules for measuring heights. Leon Batista was moreover the author of the *Libri della vita civile,*[26] with some other works of an erotic character, in prose and verse: he was the first who attempted to apply Latin measures to Italian verse.

In the year 1457, when the very useful method of printing books was invented by Giovanni Gutenberg, a German, Leon Batista discovered something similar the method of representing landscapes, and diminishing figures by means of an instrument, namely, by which small things could in like manner be presented in a larger form, and so enlarged at pleasure: all very extraordinary things, useful to art, and certainly very fine.

It happened about this time, that Giovanni di Paolo Rucellai resolved to adorn the principal façade of Santa Maria Novella, entirely with marble, at his own cost; whereupon he consulted with Leon Batista, who was his intimate friend, and having received from him not advice only, but a design for the work also, he determined that it should by all means be put into execution, that so he might leave a memorial of himself. Rucellai, therefore, caused the work to be at once commenced, and in the year 1477, it was finished, to the great satisfaction of all the city; the whole work being much admired, but more particularly the door, for which it is obvious that Leon Batista took more than common pains.

It is said that the same architect produced the design for the palace and gardens, erected by the Rucellai family in the Via della Scala, an edifice con-

---

[26]The book circulated under several different names, and is now recognized as Alberti's *Del governo della famiglia,* that is, *On Governing the Family.* Alberti's book on family life is a gold mine for social historians of late medieval Italy.

structed with much judgment, and which is therefore exceedingly commodious.[27] For the same family of Rucellai, and in a similar manner, Leon Batista erected a chapel in the church of San Braneazio, which rests on large architraves, supported on the side where the wall of the church opens into the chapel by two columns and two pilasters. This is a very difficult mode of proceeding, but gives great security, and is accordingly among the best works produced by this architect. In the centre of this chapel is an oblong tomb in marble of an oval form, and similar, according to an inscription engraved on the tomb itself, to the sepulchre of Christ at Jerusalem.

About the same time, Ludovico Gonzaga, Marquis of Mantua, having determined to construct the apse, or tribune, and the principal chapel in the Nunziata, the church of the Servites in Florence, after the design and model of Leon Batista, caused a small square chapel, very old, and painted in the ancient manner, which was at the upper end of that church, to be demolished, and in its place made the tribune above-mentioned. It has the fanciful and difficult form of a circular temple surrounded by nine chapels, all surmounted by a round arch, and each having the shape of a niche. It is true that the plan is by no means easy of accomplishment, but there is a want of grace both in the whole and in the details, insomuch that it could not possibly have a good effect. And that this is true in respect of the larger parts may be shown by the great arch which forms the entrance to the tribune; for this, which is very beautiful on the outer side, appears on the inner, where it must of necessity turn with the turn of the chapel, which is round, to be falling backwards, and is extremely ungraceful. Leon Batista would, perhaps, not have fallen into this error, if to the knowledge he possessed, and to his theories, he had added the practice and experience acquired by actual working; another would have taken pains to avoid this difficulty, and sought rather to secure grace and beauty to his edifice.

In painting, Leon Batista did not perform any great work, or execute pictures of much beauty; those remaining to us from his hand—and they are but very few—do not display a high degree of perfection, seeing that he was more earnestly devoted to study than to design. Yet he knew perfectly well how to give expression to his thoughts with the pencil, as may be seen in certain drawings by his hand in our book.

Leon Batista Alberti was a man of refined habits and praiseworthy life, a friend of distinguished men, liberal and courteous to all. He lived honourably and like a gentleman, as he was, all the course of his life, and finally, having attained to a tolerably mature age, he departed, content and tranquil, to a better life, leaving behind him a most honourable name.

[27]The famous Palazzo Rucellai, a landmark in Florence.

READING 12
Savonarola in Florence[28]

The difficulty in characterizing the late Middle Ages is evident, perhaps
most strikingly, in the history of Florence. It was a wealthy commercial
city, devastated by the plague; a cultural powerhouse that squandered its
energies in petty, indecisive wars; a champion of The city that boasted the
likes of Salutati and Alberti also supported Girolamo Savonarola
(1452–1498), a spellbinding Dominican preacher who settled in Florence
in 1490, when the Renaissance was at its height. Savonarola became prior
of the Dominican house of San Marco in Florence in 1491, and in
subsequent years his preaching captivated the Florentine populace. He
won further acclaim by persuading an invading French army to spare
Florence, and in 1496 he persuaded the Florentine people to engage in
"the burning of the Vanities," in which they cast into a bonfire their
cosmetics, fake hair, and pornographic books. But he fell afoul of the
Borgia pope, Alexander VI (whom he insulted publicly and frequently); and
Alexander, referring to Savonarola as a "meddlesome friar," arranged to
have him tried for heresy. The Florentines, frightened by the papal action—
and perhaps growing tired of Savonarola—raised no serious objections to
his being burned at the stake. Both Savonarola's successes and failures
shed light on the scope and meaning of the Renaissance.

A.   GIROLAMO SAVONAROLA, *COMPENDIUM REVELATIONUM,* 1497

Almighty God, seeing that the sins of Italy continue to multiply, especially those
of her princes, both ecclesiastical and secular, and unable to bear them any
longer, decided to cleanse his church with a mighty scourge. He wanted this
scourge to be foretold in Italy for the welfare of his chosen people, so that, fore-
warned, they might prepare. Since Florence lies in the center of Italy as the heart
of a man, God deigned to choose her for the task of making the proclamation.
And so, choosing me, useless and unworthy among all his servants, he arranged
for me to come to Florence on the orders of my superiors in the year of our lord
1489. And in the same year I began publicly to expound the Book of the Apocalypse in our church of San Marco. I continually set forth three things: first, that
the renovation of the Church would come about in these times; second, that all
of Italy would be mightily scourged before God brought about this renovation;
third, that these two things would come about soon. I labored to prove these

[28]From Donald Weinstein, *Savonarola and Florence;* Princeton, N.J., Princeton University
Press, 1970, pp. 68–71; and Francesco Guicciardini, *The History of Florence,* tr. D. Weinstein;
Princeton, N.J., Princeton University Press, 1972, pp. 356–358.

three conclusions by rational arguments, by figures from scriptures, and by other analogies and parables that can only be derived from scriptures. Later I began to reveal that I knew these events by a different light than that of the understanding of scripture alone. At last I began to disclose the matter more openly, admitting that my words were divinely inspired. One of the things I repeated often was: "Thus says the Lord God, 'The sword of the Lord shall be over the earth swiftly and soon!'" And another was: "Let the just rejoice and exult, prepare your minds against temptation by reading, meditation and prayer, and free yourselves from a second death." These words were not from the holy scriptures, as some thought, but newly come forth from heaven at just that time.

Then, as the king of the French was approaching and a revolution in the Florentine state was imminent [in 1494], although God's sword had appeared to me, as well as the great spilling of blood in this city, nevertheless, I began fervently to hope that this prophecy was not without some conditions, that if the people were repentant the most indulgent God might abate at least a part of his judgment. Thus, on 1 November and on the two days following, I spared neither voice nor lungs and, as everyone knows, I cried out so loudly from the pulpit as almost to wear myself out, "O Italy, these adversities have come to you because of your sins; O Florence these adversities have come to you because of your sins; O clergy, this tempest has arisen on your account. O nobles, O wise men, O humble folk, the mighty hand of God is upon you; neither power nor wisdom nor light can withstand it. The Lord is awaiting you, that he might show his pity on you. Convert, therefore, to the Lord with all your heart, because he is kind and compassionate. If you do not, he will avert his eyes from you forever."

B.   FRANCESCO GUICCIARDINI, SAVONAROLA AND FLORENCE, 1561

The pope[29] had accused Savonarola of slanderously preaching against the comportment of the clergy and the papal court, of stirring up discord in Florence, and of disseminating doctrine that was not entirely orthodox. For these reasons, the Dominican had been several times summoned to Rome, but he had refused to appear, alleging various excuses. Finally, the pope separated him from the fellowship of the church. As a result of this excommunication he abstained from preaching for several months, and had he abstained longer he would have obtained absolution without any difficulty. For the pope personally took little account of Savonarola, and was moved to proceed against him more as a result of the suggestions and persuasion of the monk's adversaries.

But it seemed to Savonarola that his reputation was declining as a result of his silence, or that, at any rate, the object of his endeavors was impeded by it, since his purpose was mainly served by his vehemence in preaching. And so,

[29]Pope Alexander VI, in 1497

scorning the pope's commandments, he publicly affirmed that the excommunication that had been promulgated against him was unjust and invalid, contrary to
the will of God and harmful to the public weal.

His preaching stirred up great dissensions. For on the one hand his adversaries, whose authority among the people grew greater every day, detested such
disobedience and reproved him because his foolhardiness might result in changing the pope's mind [about an alliance with Florence]. On the other hand, his partisans defended him, alleging that divine works should not be interfered with because of simple concern over human consequences, nor should popes be
permitted under such justifications to commence meddling in the affairs of the republic. Finally this quarrel became so heated that one of the Dominican monks
who was a disciple of Savonarola and one of the Franciscans agreed upon a trial
by fire in the presence of the entire populace, so that the Dominican being either
spared or burned would make it clear to everybody whether Savonarola was a
prophet or a fraud. For he had earlier preached that as a sign of the truth of his
predictions he would obtain, when there was need for it, the grace from God to
pass through the fire without harm. But now he was angry that the decision to
carry on the experiment had been made without his knowledge, so he cleverly
tried to prevent it; but since the matter had already gone so far on its own mo-
mentum it was necessary finally to proceed further. So on the chosen day, the two
friars, accompanied by all the brothers of their order, came to the piazza which is
in front of the public palace; but there the Franciscan learned that Savonarola had
ordered his friar to bear the Host in hand when he entered into the flames. At this
the Franciscans began to protest, alleging that their opponents were seeking to
place the authority of the Christian faith in danger, since if the Host should be
burned, the faith of the ignorant would decline considerably. And since
Savonarola, who was present, insisted on this order, it was impossible for the experiment to proceed. Savonarola lost so much prestige by this that on the next day
his adversaries seized arms and stormed the monastery of San Marco where he
was living and led him, with two of his friars, to the public prison.

Savonarola was then examined under torture (although not very dolorous)
and later the deposition of these examinations was published. According to this
trial record (which cleared him of all the calumnies imputed to him, such as covetousness or having held secret dealings with princes) the things which he had
prophesized were declared to have been predicted, not on the basis of divine revelation, but as his own opinion based on deep study of the scriptures; nor had he
been moved by any malign intention or cupidity to acquire ecclesiastical emi-
nence, but rather he had greatly desired that his work should result in the convocation of a council which would reform the corrupt manners of the clergy and
bring back the Church of God to a state as similar as possible to what it had been
at the time of the Apostles.

On the basis of this deposition, confirmed by Savonarola, but in such concise
terms that his words could be given various interpretations, he and the two other

friars were, by sentence of the General of the Dominican Order and by Bishop Romolino, stripped of their holy orders and left to the jurisdiction of the secular court, by whom they were hanged and burned. To this spectacle of degradation and torture there thronged no less a multitude of men than those who, on the day appointed for the experiment of entering into the fire, had rushed to the same place in expectation of the miracle which he had promised. Savonarola's death did not extinguish the diversity of judgments and emotions of the citizens, because many still reputed him to be an imposter, and many believed that the confession which had been published had been falsely fabricated or else that his delicate physical state had been much more influenced by the pain of the torture than by truth.

READING 13

The Capture of Constantinople, 1453[30]

The fortunes of the eastern Roman empire declined precipitously after the Fourth Crusade. Though the empire lived on and from time to time managed a revival of both its power and cultural influence, it never fully recovered. By 1453 all that remained was the city of Constantinople, surrounded by the new power in the eastern Mediterranean, the Ottoman Turks. Initially, the Turks could only reduce the city to the status of a dependency; they didn't capture it until the Sultan Mehmed II (1451–1481) determined to put all the resources of his empire into the effort.

WHAT SULTAN MEHMED KHAN GAZIL DID WHEN HE HAD RETURNED FROM KARAMAN

He wanted to cross to Rumeli[31] at Gallipoli, but they said to him, "O mighty Sultan! Infidel ships have come and have closed the straits at Gallipoli!"

So they took the Sultan and led him to Kojaeli. They made camp at Akcahisar, on the shore of the Bosphorus above Istanbul.[32]

There, where his father had crossed, he crossed to Rumeli and made camp opposite Akcahisar.

---

[30]From *Islam, from the Prophet Muhammad to the Capture of Constantinople*, vol. 1, ed. Bernard Lewis; New York, Harper & Row Publisher, 1974, pp. 144–148.
[31]"Rumeli" refers to the land of the Romans.
[32]"Istanbul" may be a slang term meaning "the city." It was still known as Constantinople at this time.

He said to Halil Pasha, "Lala[33] here I need a fortress!" In short, he gave orders at once and had the fortress built, and it was completed.

Then he dispatched Akcayluoglu Mehmed Bey, saying, "Make haste and besiege Istanbul."

Mehmed Bey came, cleared the people from the city gates, and drove away the sheep and goats from the adjoining villages. The Emperor was told, "The Turk has struck us to the heart and pulled our house down on our heads."

The Emperor said, "Neighborliness between them and us is like the neighborliness of the falcon and the crow."

Then he said, "If there is any way of saving ourselves from this Turk, we must appeal again to our friend Halil Pasha. Now we must send Halil Pasha some little fish."

He filled the bellies of these fish with florins and sent them to Halil Pasha. The Emperor had a vizier whose name was Master Luke.[34] He said, "Ha! Halil Pasha will swallow the fish and it won't do you any good. He is no longer concerned about helping you. Look to your own resources."

They brought Halil the fish. He ate the fish and put the contents in his money chest. Then he acted for the infidels. He went to the Sultan and spoke many words to him about the infidels.

The Sultan said, "Ha Lala, let the summer come and then we shall see. What God commands, that we shall do."

They had been busy for some time with preparations for the conquest of the city. When all was ready and summer came, Sultan Mehmed said, "We shall spend this summer in Istanbul."

They came and made camp around the walls of Istanbul. From the land side and with ships on the sea they enclosed the city all around. There were 400 ships on the sea, and 70 ships sailed over Galata across the dry land. The warriors stood ready and unfurled their flags. At the foot of the walls they went into the sea and made a bridge over the water. They attacked.

The fighting went on, day and night, for fifty days. On the fifty-first day the Sultan ordered free plunder. They attacked. On the fifty-first day, a Tuesday, the citadel was captured. There was good booty and plunder. Gold and silver and jewels and fine stuffs were brought and stacked in the camp market. They began to sell them. They made the people of the city slaves and killed their Emperor, and the gazis embraced their pretty girls. On Wednesday they arrested Halil Pasha and his sons and his officers and put them in prison. Theirs is a long story, but I have cut it short, because all this is well known, concerning what they did to Halil Pasha.

---

[33]Tutor or guardian, a form of address used by princes to their tutors and ministers.
[34]The Byzantine *Megadux* Lucas Notaras.

In short, on the first Friday after the conquest, they recited the communal prayer in Santa Sofia, and the Islamic invocation was read in the name of Sultan Mehmed Khan Gazi, the son of Sultan Murad Khan Gazi, the son of Sultan Mehmed Khan Gazi, the son of Sultan Bayezid Khan, the son of Murad Hünkar Gazi, the son of Orkhan Gazi Khan, the son of Osman Gazi Khan, the son of Ertugrul Gazi Khan, the son of Sultan Sülemanshah Gazi Khan of the house of Gökalp, the son of Oguz Khan. I have set forth their family tree in the first chapter.

This victory was achieved by Sultan Mehmed Khan in the year 857 of the Hijra [1453].

READING 14

Gomes Azurara, The Motives of Prince Henry the Navigator[35]

Gomes Eannes de Azurara (d. 1474) was advanced to the offices of chief archivist and royal chronicler of the kingdom of Portugal a year after he wrote this account. He is our best authority for the early Portuguese voyages down the west coast of Africa sponsored by Prince Henry the Navigator (1394–1460), whom Azurara calls "the Lord Infant" or "the Prince." Prince Henry played a part in the Portuguese capture of the North African port of Ceuta in 1415. Afterward, from his court at Sagres in Portugal, he collected geographical and navigational data from the expeditions that he sent westward to the Atlantic islands and southward down the African coast. Azurara, writing as a court historian, is obviously providing an unflawed portrait.

We imagine that we know a matter when we are acquainted with the doer of it and the end for which he did it. And since in former chapters we have set forth the Lord Infant as the chief actor in these things, giving as clear an understanding of him as we could, it is meet that in this present chapter we should know his purpose in doing them. And you should note well that the noble spirit of this Prince, by a sort of natural constraint, was ever urging him both to begin and to carry out very great deeds. For which reason, after the taking of Ceuta he always

[35]From *The Chronicle of the Discovery and Conquest of Guinea,* vol. 1, tr. C. R. Beazley and E. Prestage; London, Hakluyt Society Publications, 1899, pp. 27–30.

kept ships well armed against the Infidel, both for war, and because he had also a wish to know the land that lay beyond the isles of Canary and Cape Bojador [Morocco], since before his own time, neither by writings, nor by the memory of man, was known with any certainty the nature of the land beyond that Cape. Some said indeed that Saint Brandan had passed that way; and there was another tale of two galleys rounding the Cape, which never returned. But this doth not appear at all likely to be true, for it is not to be presumed that if the said galleys went there, some other ships would not have endeavored to learn what voyage they had made. And because the said Lord Infant wished to know the truth of this—since it seemed to him that if he or some other lord did not endeavor to gain that knowledge, no mariners or merchants would ever dare to attempt it— (for it is clear that none of them ever trouble themselves to sail to a place where there is not a sure and certain hope of profit)—and seeing also that no other prince took any pains in this matter, he sent out his own ships against those parts, to have manifest certainty of them all. And to this he was stirred up by his zeal for the service of God and of the King Edward his Lord and brother, who then reigned. And this was the first reason of his action.

The second reason was that if there chanced to be in those lands some population of Christians, or some havens, into which it would be possible to sail without peril, many kinds of merchandise might be brought to this realm, which would find a ready market, and reasonably so, because no other people of these parts traded with them, nor yet people of any other that were known; and also the products of this realm might be taken there, which traffic would bring great profit to our countrymen.

The third reason was that, as it was said that the power of the Moors in that land of Africa was very much greater than was commonly supposed, and that there were no Christians among them, nor any other race of men; and because every wise man is obliged by natural prudence to wish for a knowledge of the power of his enemy; therefore the said Lord Infant exerted himself to cause this to be fully discovered, and to make it known determinately how far the power of those infidels extended.

The fourth reason was because during the one and thirty years that he had warred against the Moors, he had never found a Christian king, nor a lord outside this land, who for the love of our Lord Jesus Christ would aid him in the said war. Therefore he sought to know if there were in those parts any Christian princes, in whom the charity and the love of Christ was so ingrained that they would aid him against those enemies of the faith.

The fifth reason was his great desire to make increase in the faith of our Lord Jesus Christ and to bring to Him all the souls that should be saved, understanding that all the mystery of the Incarnation, Death, and Passion of our Lord Jesus Christ was for this sole end—namely the salvation of lost souls—whom the said Lord Infant by his travail and spending would fain bring into the true path. For he perceived that no better offering could be made unto the Lord than this; for if God promised to return one hundred goods for one, we may justly believe that for such great benefits, that is to say for so many souls as were saved by the efforts of this Lord, he will have so many hundreds of guerdons in the kingdom of God, by which his spirit may be glorified after this life in the celestial realm. For I that wrote this history saw so many men and women of those parts turned to the holy faith, that even if the Infant had been a heathen, their prayers would have been enough to have obtained his salvation. And not only did I see the first captives, but their children and grandchildren as true Christians as if the Divine grace breathed in them and imparted to them a clear knowledge of itself.

But over and above these five reasons I have a sixth that would seem to be the root from which all the others proceeded: and this is the inclination of the heavenly wheels. For, as I wrote not many days ago in a letter I sent to the Lord King, that although it be written that the wise men shall be Lord of the stars, and that the courses of the planets (according to the true estimate of the holy doctors) cannot cause the good man to stumble; yet it is manifest that they are bodies ordained in the secret counsels of our Lord God and run by a fixed measure, appointed to different ends, which are revealed to men by his grace, through whose influence bodies of the lower order are inclined to certain passions. And if it be a fact, speaking as a Catholic, that the contrary predestinations of the wheels of heaven can be avoided by natural judgment with the aid of a certain divine grace, much more does it stand to reason that those who are predestined to good fortune, by the help of this same grace, will not only follow their course but even add a greater increase to themselves.

READING 15

Paolo de Toscanelli, Sailing West to Go East[36]

Paolo del Pozzo Toscanelli (1397–1482), a great geographer and mapmaker of the fifteenth century, makes it clear in this intriguing passage—written in 1474, some years before Columbus's first voyage—that Columbus was by no means the first European to believe that one might encounter Asiatic lands by sailing westward across the Atlantic. Toscanelli, prefiguring Columbus in other ways, shows how Italians were establishing contacts with Iberia in order to exploit seagoing explorations.

[36]From *A Source Book in Geography,* ed. George Kish; Cambridge, Mass., Harvard University Press, 1978, pp. 306–307.

To Ferdinand Martins, Canon of Lisbon, Paolo the physician gives greeting.

It was pleasing to me to have intelligence concerning your health, and concerning your favour and familiar friendship with that most generous and magnificent prince, your king. Whereas I have spoken with you elsewhere concerning a shorter way of going by sea to the lands of spices, than that which you are making by Guinea; the most serene King now wishes that I should give some explanation thereof, or rather that I should so set it before the eyes of all, that even those who are but moderately learned might perceive that way and understand it.

But though I know that this could be shown by the spherical form, which is that of the world; nevertheless I have determined to show it in the way in which charts of navigation show it, and this both that it may be more readily understood, and that the work may be easier.

Wherefore I send to His Majesty a chart,[37] made by my hands, wherein your shores are shown, and the islands from which you may begin to make a voyage continually westwards, and the places whereunto you ought to come, and how much you ought to decline from the pole or from the equinoctal line, and through how much space, i.e., through how many miles, you ought to arrive at the places most fertile in all spices and gems. And do not wonder if I call those places where the spices are western, whereas they are commonly called east: because to those that sail by navigation those places are ever found in the west, though if we go by land they will always be found in the east.

It is said only merchants stay in these islands; for here there is so great an abundance of men sailing with merchandise, that in all the rest of the world they are not as they are in a most noble port called Zaiton, for they say that every year a hundred large ships of pepper are brought into that port, without counting other ships bearing other spices. That country is very populous, and very rich, with a multitude of provinces and kingdoms and cities without number, under one prince who is called the Great Kan [sic], which name in Latin means *rex regum* (king of kings), whose seat and residence are chiefly in the province of Katay.[38] His ancestors desired to have fellowship with the Christians. For it is now two hundred years since they sent to the Pope and asked for several men learned in the faith, in order that they might be enlightened. But those who were sent went back, being hindered on their journey. In the time of Eugenius,[39] also, one came to Eugenius and spoke of their great goodwill towards Christians. And I held speech with him for a long time on many things, on the greatness of the royal buildings, and on the greatness of the rivers of wondrous breadth and length, and on the multitude of cities on the banks of the rivers; and how on one river there are established about two hundred cities, and marble bridges of great breadth and length adorned with columns on every side. This country is worthy of being sought by the Latins, not only because from thence may be obtained

---

[37]Now lost
[38]Cathay, or China.
[39]Eugenius IV (1431–1447).

vast grains of gold and silver and gems of every kind, and of spices that are never brought to us; but also because of the wise men, learned philosophers and astrologers, by whose genius and arts that mighty and magnificent province is governed and wars are also waged. These things I write to give some little satisfaction to your demand, in so far as the shortness of the time allowed, and my occupations suffered; being ready to satisfy your Royal Majesty in the future as much further as may be desired. Given at Florence, 25th June 1474.

READING 16

Gil Vicente, *Dicen Que Me Casa Yo*[40]

We conclude with an ode from Portuguese poet Gil Vicente. About Vicente (c. 1470–1536) very little is known until the production of his first play in Lisbon in 1502. For the next thirty-five years he was the court playwright of Portugal, though he wrote plays and poems in Portuguese, Spanish, and fragments of half a dozen other languages. *Dicen que me casa yo* is charming in its language (Spanish), its rhymes, its clever adoption of a female voice, and is an especially nice example of a popular theme in late medieval and Renaissance ballads.

They say I should go get a man—
But I'll avoid it, if I can
I'd rather live by my caprice
In these mountains; then I can cease
    To worry about married war and peace.
They say I should go get a man—
But I'll avoid it, if I can.

Mother, I won't be a wife
And live a plain, dull, simple life
And squander gifts with which I'm rife
    That were given by God's gracious plan
They say I should go get a man—
But I'll avoid it, if I can.

He's not been born, this alleged man
Who is destined yet to take my hand

---

[40]Gil Vicente, *Obvas Completas,* vol I, ed. Marques Bvaga; Lisbon, Livraria sá da Costa, 1958, pp. 57–58. Tr. J. W. Leedom.

And now because—when the world I scan—
  I know my charm's true talisman,
They say I should go get a man—
But I'll avoid it, if I can.

STUDY QUESTIONS

A Was this really, as the chapter title states, an age of contradictions?
B What evidence do you find for decline? For renewal? For a renaissance?
C How has religion changed in this period? Is this age more or less religious than those that had preceded it?

Reading 1: Giovanni Boccaccio, The Black Death in Florence, 1348

What was the disease like? How did people respond to it? What steps did they take to avoid the plague?

Reading 2: Wage and Price Laws After the Plague

Why were these regulations passed? Who did they help? Why do they help explain the popular revolts in this era?

Reading 3: Jean Froissart, The Jacquerie

What did the peasants want? At this time, France and Flanders were often hostile to one another; yet "the better people of those afflicted regions" banded together to fight the peasants. Why?

Reading 4: Niccolo Machiavelli, The Ciompi

What is the cause of this revolt? What do you think of the speech at the center of this report? What does Machiavelli think of it?

Reading 5: The English Peasants' Revolt, 1381

What caused the revolt? Why did "their fellows" in the towns join them? What did they want? Why?

Reading 6: The Lollard Conclusions, 1395

The Lollards developed their own theory of church history. What is it? What reforms do they propose? How do their views compare to those of Jan Hus (Reading 7)?

Reading 7: Charges of Heresy Against Jan Hus

What are the main elements of Hus's beliefs? Why are these threatening to the church? In what ways are his views similar to the Lollards' (Reading 6)? What does this tell you about religious sentiment in the era?

Reading 8: Doña Leonor López de Cordoba, *Memories*

What misfortunes befell Doña Leonor and her family? Where does she find solace? What does this tell you about religious sentiment in the era?

Reading 9: Christine de Pisan, *The Book of the City of Ladies*

What categories of women does Christine de Pisan single out? How are they treated differently? What advice applies to all of them? Is class or gender the greater divide in her views?

Reading 10: Coluccio Salutati, On the Active Life

In what ways is Salutati expressing a new ideal? Could this have been written by a monk? A friar?

Reading 11: Giorgio Vasari, Life of Leon Battista Alberti

To what is Alberti's lasting fame attributed? What are his main virtues? Does Alberti seem to be a "Renaissance man"? Why?

Reading 12: Savonarola in Florence

Does Savonarola seem to be a "Renaissance man"? How is he similar to Joan of Arc or Catherine of Siena (Chapter 10, Readings 4 and 12)? What explains his popularity? Why did he fall?

Reading 13: The Capture of Constantinople, 1453

What preparations did Mehmed make for taking Istanbul? Why was this such a prize?

Reading 14: Gomes Azurara, The Motives of Prince Henry the Navigator

What are the reasons Azurara gives for Henry's voyages? How do these compare to the motives of the crusaders (Chapter 5, Reading 4)? Is it possible to separate Henry's ideas into secular and spiritual?

Reading 15: Paolo de Toscanelli, Sailing West to Go East

What is Toscanelli's argument? What motives does he offer for making such a journey? How do his views compare with those of Henry the Navigator?

Reading 16: Gil Vicente, *Dicen Que Me Casa Yo*

What does Vicente present as the drawbacks to married life? What are the benefits of living alone? Given that the author is a man, can this poem be considered a genuine feminist sentiment?

WEB RESOURCES ⌨

ARGOS (Limited area search of the Ancient & Medieval Internet) http://argos. evansville.edu/

The Bibliothèque Nationale de France presents *The Age of King Charles V (1338–1380)* (1,000 Illuminations from the Department of Manuscripts): http://www.bnf.fr/enluminures/aaccueil.shtm

Cantus, database for Ecclesiatical Latin Chant: http://publish.uwo.ca/~cantus/

Christian Classics Ethereal Library (includes writings by church fathers and a Classics Library as well as a Study Bible and Encyclopedia of Christianity): http://www.ccel.org/

Cyberpsalter, home page for Psalter studies (gathers and links resources for the study of medieval psalter manuscripts. Psalter studies encompass the contents, codicology, functions, and audiences of these widely used medieval books. The Pierpont Morgan Library has recently granted Cyberpsalter permission to reproduce all of the full-page illustrations of the manuscript M.43, the Huntingfield Psalter, as well as its calendar pages and selected initials): http://www.cyberpsalter.org/index.html

Digital Scriptorium: A Prototype Image Database & Visual Union Catalog of Medieval and Renaissance Manuscripts (Bancroft Library of the University of California, Berkeley, and Columbia University's Rare Book and Manuscript Library): http://sunsite.berkeley.edu/Scriptorium/

Douay-Rheims Bible (English translation of Latin Vulgate), First Published by the English College at Douay, A.D. 1609: http://www.cybercomm.net/~dcon/drbible.html

Ecole Initiative (hypertext encyclopedia of early church history to the Reformation; image gallery of saints and biblical figures [though many are contemporary icons]; an extensive collection of primary texts, though this seems to have not been updated recently since the New Advent and Ethereal Library links are no longer current or working; a collections of articles; a glossary; and a searchable chronology): http://www2.evansville.edu/ecoleweb/

Exploring Ancient World Cultures Internet Index (tracks a variety of resources relevant to ancient and medieval times; divided into five sub-indices: a chronology, an essay index, an image index, an Internet site index and a primary text index; the chronology goes through 1509 C.E.): http://eawc.evansville.edu/eawcindex.htm

Internet Medieval Sourcebook (links to numerous primary and secondary sources, as well as sections on hagiography, medieval music and movies, and a collection of public-domain images): http://www.fordham.edu/halsall/sbook.html

Katty B's Free Medieval ClipArt (definitely not academic and not all images are medieval, but if you are putting together a web site, there might be something of use to be found here): http://members.nbci.com/katslair/freebies/freebies.htm

The Labyrinth (free, organized access to electronic resources in medieval studies through a World Wide Web server at Georgetown University. The Labyrinth's easy-to-use menus and links provide connections to databases, services, texts, and images on other servers around the world): http://www.georgetown.edu/labyrinth/labyrinth-home.html

Matrix (collection of resources for the study of women's religious communities A.D. 500–1500 maintained by Yale University; has a Monasticon, biographies, extensive bibliography, image library, glossary, selected secondary articles, and a chartulary of primary texts): http://matrix.bc.edu/MatrixWebData/matrix.html

MedArt (a fairly large collection of images from France and England, well documented, with a third General section under construction): http://info.pitt.edu/~medart/

The Medieval Bookstore (links to Amazon.com, but provides an easier method for locating books of interest): http://tuscanytrading.com/books/index.htm

Medieval History at About.com (directory put together by experts, subdivided into specific categories): http://historymedren.about.com/homework/historymedren/

The Medieval Review (online journal of reviews of scholarly texts, formerly Bryn Mawr Medieval Review): http://www.hti.umich.edu/t/tmr/

MEDIEV-L (unmoderated discussion list serv for medievalists, focusing on history from roughly 300 to 1500 A.D.; archives): http://historymedren.about.com/gi/dynamic/offsite.htm?site=http%3A%2F%2Fkuhttp.cc.ukans.edu%2F%7Emedieval%2F are accessible by date or by thread. Send a message with no subject to listproc@raven.cc.ukans.edu and put "sub mediev-I Your Name" in the message body. mailto:listproc@raven.cc.ukans.edu

NetSERF: The Internet Connection for Medieval Resources (well-organized directory of almost 1,500 links): http://www.netserf.org/

ORB, the Online Reference Book for Medieval Studies (an encyclopedia, library of full-length textbooks, reference shelf of primary and secondary texts, teaching resources, general interest sites, and external links): http://orb.rhodes.edu/

Scholasticism by Joseph Rickaby; New York, Dodge Publishing Company, 1908 (e-text): http://www.knuten.liu.se/~bjoch509/works/aquinas/scholasticism/scholas1.htm

Thesaurus Musciarum Latinarum (evolving database of the entire corpus of Latin music theory written during the Middle Ages, at the University of Indiana; browsable, searchable, and downloadable): http://www.music.indiana.edu/tml/start.html

Writings of the Church Fathers (at New Advent with links to Aquinas's Summa Theologia and the Catholic Encyclopedia): http://www.newadvent.org/fathers/

WWW Medieval Resources (links to texts, databases, libraries, and historical sites, especially useful is the list of and information about discussion lists): http://ebbs.english.vt.edu/medieval/medieval.ebbs.html

ACKNOWLEDGMENTS

TEXT CREDITS

1:2 Reprinted from J. Stevenson, ed., A NEW EUSEBIUS: DOCUMENTS ILLUSTRATIVE OF THE HISTORY OF THE CHURCH TO A.D. 337. Copyright © 1957 Society for Promoting Christian Knowledge. Reprinted with permission.

1:4 Pharr, C., THE THEODOSIAN CODE AND NOVELS AND THE SIRMONDIAN CONSTITUTIONS. Copyright © 1952 by Princeton University Press. Reprinted by permission of Princeton University Press.

1:8 Pharr, C., THE THEODOSIAN CODE AND NOVELS AND THE SIRMONDIAN CONSTITUTIONS. Copyright © 1952 by Princeton University Press. Reprinted by permission of Princeton University Press.

1:10 From John Moorhead, tr., VICTOR OF VITA, A HISTORY OF THE VANDAL PERSECUTION. Reprinted by permission of Liverpool University Press.

1:11 Reprinted by permission of the publishers and the Trustees of the Loeb Classical Library from SIDONIUS LETTERS: VOL. II, Loeb Classical Library Volume L 420, translated by W.B. Anderson, pp. 239, 241, 253, 255, 275, Cambridge, Mass.: Harvard University.

2:1 From THREE BYZANTINE SAINTS, ed. and tr. E. Dawes and N.H. Baynes; Crestwood, N.Y., St. Vladimi'rs Seminary Press. Copyright © 1948. Reprinted with permission.

2:4 From D.J. Geanakopolos, BYZANTIUM, CHURCH SOCIETY, & CIVILIZATION AS SEEN THROUGH CONTEMPORARY EYES; Chicago, University of Chicago Press, 1984, pp. 245–247. Reprinted with permission.

2:6 From Pope Gelasius's letter to Emperor Anastasius, in THE CRISIS OF CHURCH AND STATE, 1050–1300, ed. Brian Tierney; Englewood Cliffs, N.J., Prentice-Hall, Inc., 1964, pp. 13–14. Reprinted by permission.

2:10 From Eddius, "The Life of St. Wilfrid of Hexham," in LIVES OF THE SAINTS, tr. J.F. Webb; London, Penguin Books. Copyright © 1965, pp. 141–143. Reprinted with permission.

2:13 From Ibn Ishaq, "Life of the Prophet," in THE LIFE OF MOHAMMAD, A TRANSLATION OF ISHAQ'S SIRA RASUL ALLAH, ed. and tr. A. Guillaume; Karachi, Oxford University Press, 1955. Reprinted by permission of Oxford University Press.

2:14 From Andrew Palmer, THE SEVENTH CENTURY IN WEST-SYRIAN CHRONICLES. Copyright © 1993. Reprinted with permission of Liverpool University Press.

3:1 From THE CRISIS OF CHURCH AND STATE, ed. Brian Tierney; Englewood Cliffs, N.J., Prentice-Hall, Inc., 1964, pp. 19–20. Reprinted with permission.

3:2 Reprinted from THE LETTERS OF ST. BONIFACE, tr. E. Emerton. Copyright © 1940 Columbia University Press. Used with permission.

3:5 From THE MEDIEVAL WORLD, 300–1300, 2nd ed., ed. Norman Cantor; New York, Macmillan Publishing Co., Inc., 1968, pp. 132-139. Reprinted with permission.

3:9 From THE REIGN OF CHARLEMAGNE, ed. H.R. Lyon and J. Percifal; London, Edward Arnold, Ltd., 1975, pp. 74–79. Reprinted by permission of Edward Arnold, Ltd.

3:11A From ENGLISH HISTORICAL DOCUMENTS, c. 500–1042, ed. and tr. Dorothy Whitelock; Oxford, Oxford University Press, © 1968, pg. 768. Reprinted with permission.

3:11B Stewart C. Easton and Helene Wieruszowski, THE ERA OF CHARLEMAGNE, New York, Van Nostrand Company, Inc., 1961, pp. 174–176.

3:12 From PERIPHYSEON (THE DIVISION OF NATURE), by John Scotus Erigena, translated by I.P. Sheldon-Williams, revised by John O'Meara. Copyright © 1987.

3:13 Reprinted from HANDBOOK FOR WILLIAM: A CAROLINGIAN WOMAN'S COUNSEL FOR HER SON by Dhuoda, translated by Carol Neel, by permission of the University of Nebraska Press. Copyright © 1991 by the University of Nebraska Press.

4:1 From CAROLINGIAN CHRONICLES, ed. and tr. Bernhard W. Schloz; Ann Arbor, University of Michigan Press. Copyright © 1970. Reprinted by permission of the University of Michigan Press.

4:3E From Georges Duby, RURAL ECONOMY AND COUNTRY LIFE IN THE MEDIEVAL WEST, Columbia, University of South Carolina Press, 1976, pp. 204–205.

4:5 From THE TENTH CENTURY, ed. R.S. Lopez; New York, Holt, Rinehart & Winston, 1959, pp. 14–15; by permission.

4:8 From THE PLAYS OF ROSWITHA, tr. Christopher St. John; New York, Cooper Square Publishers, Inc., 1966, pp. 71–91.

4:11 From THE GRAENLENDIGA SAGA, in THE VINLAND SAGAS: THE NORSE DISCOVERY OF AMERICA, ed. and tr. Magnus Magnusson and Hermann Palsson; London, Penguin Classics, pp. 54–58. Copyright Magnus Magnusson and Hermann Palsson, 1965. Reprinted by permission of Penguin Books, Ltd.

5:1 From ENGLISH HISTORICAL DOCUMENTS, VOLUME II, 1042–1189, ed. D.C. Douglas and G.W. Greenaway; Oxford, Oxford University Press, © 1953, pp. 970–971. Reprinted with permission.

5:2 Pages 161, 174–176 from SELF AND SOCIETY IN MEDIEVAL FRANCE: THE MEMOIRS OF ABBOTT GUIBERT OF NOGENT by

John F. Benton. Copyright © 1970 by John F. Benton. Reprinted by
permission of HarperCollins Publishers, Inc.

5:3 From FEUDAL SOCIETY IN MEDIEVAL FRANCE, translated and edited
by Theodore Evergates. Copyright © 1993 University of Pennsylvania Press.
Reprinted with permission of the publisher.

5:4A From FOURTEEN BYZANTINE RULERS by Michael Psellus, translated
by E.R.A. Sewter (Penguin Classics, 1966). Copyright © 1966 E.R.A.
Sewter. Reprinted by permission of Penguin Books, Ltd.

5:4C From THE ALEXIAD OF ANNA COMNENA, translated by E.R.A.
Sewter (Penguin Classics, 1969). Copyright © 1969 E.R.A. Sewter.
Reprinted by permission of Penguin Books, Ltd.

5:4D From THE FIRST CRUSADE, edited by Edward Peters. Copyright
© 1971 University of Pennsylvania Press. Reprinted with permission of the
publisher.

5:5 From THE RECORDS OF MEDIEVAL EUROPE by Carolly Erickson,
copyright © 1971 by Carolly Erickson. Used by permission of Doubleday, a
division of Random House, Inc.

7:2 From THE LETTERS OF HILDEGARD OF BINGEN, VOL. I, edited by
Joseph L. Baird & Radd K. Ehrman, translated by Joseph L. Baird & Radd K.
Ehrman, copyright © 1994 by Oxford University Press, Inc. Used by
permission of Oxford University Press, Inc.

7:4 From EARLY DOMINICANS, SELECTED WRITINGS, ed. Simon
Tugwell. Copyright © 1982. Reprinted by permission of the Paulist Press.

7:5 From W Wakefield and A.P. Evans, ed., HERESIES OF THE HIGH
MIDDLE AGES. Copyright © 1969 Columbia University Press. Reprinted
with permission.

7:6 From THE BIRTH OF POPULAR HERESY, (Documents of Medieval
History Series), ed. and tr. R.I. Moore; London, Edward Arnold, Ltd., 1975,
pp. 144–145. Reprinted by permission.

7:7 From DISCIPLINARY DECREES OF THE GENERAL COUNCILS, ed.
and tr. H.J. Schroeder; St. Louis, B. Herder Book Co., 1937, pp. 242–244.

7:9 From THE FAITH AND PRACTICE OF Al-GHAZALI, by
W.M. Montgomery Watt; Chicago, Kazi Publications, © 1982, pp. 19–26.

7:10 From Peter Abelard, SIC ET NON (YES AND NO), 1138, ed. and tr. Brian
Tierney, SOURCES OF MEDIEVAL HISTORY, 4th edition; New York,
Alfred A. Knopf, 1983, pp. 172–175.

7:11 From Thomas Aquinas, SUMMA TEOLOGIAE, ed. Thomas Gilby.
Copyright © 1969. Reprinted by permission of Cambridge University Press.

7:12 From Arthur Hyman and James H. Walsh, PHILOSOPHY IN THE
MIDDLE AGES; Indianapolis, Hackett Publishing Company, 1973,
pp. 542–549.

7:13 From Anne Fremantle, THE AGE OF BELIEF; New York, Signet Books,
1954, pp. 208–209.

8:2 From Otto of Freising, THE DEEDS OF FREDERICK BARBAROSSA,
tr. C.C. Mierow. Copyright © 1966, pp. 181–184. Reprinted with permission.

8:5 From Dante Alighieri, ON WORLD-GOVERNMENT, or DE
MONARCHIA, tr. H.W. Schneider; New York, The Liberal Arts Press, 1950,
pp. 42–45.

9:3 From ENGLISH HISTORICAL DOCUMENTS, vol. 3, 1189–1327, ed. and
tr. Harry Rothwell; London, Eyre & Spottiswoode, 1975, pp. 316–324.
Reprinted by permission.

9:4B From THE CHRONICLE OF WALTER OF GUISBOROUGH, Camden
Society, vol. 89, 3rd series, ed. Harry Rothwell; London, 1957, pg. 216;
tr. David S. Spear.

9:4A From SOURCES OF ENGLISH CONSTITUTIONAL HISTORY, ed. and
tr. Carl Stephenson and Frederick G. Marcham. Copyright © 1972. Reprinted
by permission.

9:4C From SOURCES OF ENGLISH CONSTITUTIONAL HISTORY, ed. and
tr. Carl Stephenson and Frederick G. Marcham. Copyright © 1972. Reprinted
by permission.

9:7 From THE CRISIS OF CHURCH AND STATE, 1050–1300, ed. Brian
Tierney; Englewood Cliffs, N.J., Prentice-Hall, Inc., 1964, pp. 188–189, 191.

10:1 From ENGLISH HISTORICAL DOCUMENTS, vol. IV, ed. A.R. Myers; New York, Oxford University Press, 1969, pp. 443, 446–447, 455, 460–462.

10:2 Reprinted by permission of the author.

10:3 From CHRONICLES by Jean Froissart, translated by Geoffrey Brereton (Penguin Classics, 1968). Copyright © 1968 Geoffrey Brereton. Reprinted by permission of Penguin Books, Ltd.

10:4 From ENGLISH HISTORICAL DOCUMENTS, vol. IV, ed. A.R. Myers; New York, Oxford University Press, 1969, pp. 242–243.

10:5 From ENGLISH HISTORICAL DOCUMENTS, vol. IV, ed. A.R. Myers; New York, Oxford University Press, 1969, pp. 262–263.

10:7 From THE MEMOIRS OF PHILIPPE DE COMMYNES, ed. Samuel Kinser, tr. Isabelle Cazeaux; Columbia, S.C., University of South Carolina Press, 1969, pp. 359–361. Copyright University of South Carolina Press. Reprinted by permission.

10:10 From MEDIEVAL POLITICAL IDEAS by Ewart Lewis, copyright © 1954 by Alfred A. Knopf, Inc. Used by permission of Alfred A. Knopf, a division of Random House, Inc.

10:12 From MEDIEVAL WOMEN WRITERS, ed. Katharina M. Wilson. Reprinted by permission of the University of Georgia Press.

11:1 From THE FIRST CENTURY OF ITALIAN HUMANISM, ed. Ferdinand Schevill; New York, F.S. Crofts & Co., 1928, pp. 32–34.

11:2A From Georges Duby, RURAL ECONOMY AND COUNTRY LIFE IN THE MEDIEVAL WEST, Columbia, University of South Carolina Press, 1976, pg. 525.

11:6 Selection © Oxford University Press, 1963. Reprinted from DOCUMENTS OF THE CHRISTIAN CHURCH, edited by Henry Bettenson (2nd edition, 1963), by permission of Oxford University Press.

11:7 From Matthew Spinka, JOHN HUS AT THE COUNCIL OF CONTANCE. Copyright © 1965 Columbia University Press. Reprinted with permission.

11:8 "The Memories of Dona Leonor Lopez de Corododa," translated by
Kathleen Lacey, copyright © 1985 by Kathleen Lacey, from MEDIEVAL
WOMEN'S VISIONARY LITERATURE, edited by Elizabeth Petroff. Used
by permission of Oxford University Press, Inc.

11:9 THE BOOK OF THE CITY OF LADIES by Christine de Pizan, translated
by Earl Jeffrey Richards. Copyright © 1982, 1998 by Persea Books, Inc.
Reprinted by permission of Persea Books Inc. (New York).

11:10 From RENAISSANCE ITALY: WAS IT THE BIRTHPLACE OF
MODERN EUROPE? ed. Gene A. Brucker; New York, Holt, Rinehart &
Winston, Inc., © 1958, pp. 35–36. Reprinted by permission.

11:12A Weinstein, Donald, SAVONAROLA AND FLORENCE. Copyright
© 1971 by Princeton University Press. Reprinted by permission of Princeton
University Press.

11:12B Francesco Guicciardini, THE HISTORY OF FLORENCE,
tr. D. Weinstein. Copyright © 1972 by Princeton University Press.
Reprinted by permission of Princeton University Press.

11:13 From THE CAPTURE OF CONSTANTINOPLE, Vol. I, ed. Bernard
Lewis; New York, Harper & Row, © 1974, pp. 144–148.

11:15 From A SOURCE BOOK IN GEOGRAPHY, ed. George Kish;
Cambridge, Mass., Harvard University Press, 1978, pp. 306–307. Reprinted
with permission.

PHOTO CREDITS

6-1   Alinari/Art Resource, NY.

6-2   From Edward James, The Franks (Oxford: Basil Blackwell, 1988), p. 60.

6-3   From R. Bruce-Mitford, *The Sutton Hoo Ship-Burial,* Volume I (British
Museum Publications; London. 1975), p. 138. Copyright: British Museum.

6-4   Foto Marburg/Art Resource, NY.

6-5   Foto Marburg/Art Resource, NY.

6-6   Foto Marburg/Art Resource, NY.

6-7   Foto Marburg/Art Resource, NY.

6-8   Cambridge University Collection of Air Photographs: copyright reserved.

6-9   Giraudon/Art Resource, NY.

6-10   Giraudon/Art Resource, NY.

6-11   Giraudon/Art Resource, NY.

6-12   Foto Marburg/Art Resource, NY.

6-13   Giraudon/Art Resource, NY.

6-14   Foto Marburg/Art Resource, NY.

6-15   Foto Marburg/Art Resource, NY.

6-16   From Geoffrey Hindley, Castles of Europe (Paul Hamln, Middlesex, 1968), p. 148.

6-17   From F. Bordeje's *Castles Itinerary in Spain;* photo from Alberto A. Weissmuller, *Castles from the Heart of Spain* (Clarkson Potter, Inc.: NY, 1967), p. 61.

6-18   Alinari/Art Resource, NY.

6-19   Foto Marburg/Art Resource, NY.

6-20   The Pierpont Morgan Library/Art Resource, NY.

6-21   Reunion des Musees Nationaux/Art Resource, NY.